D1741518

SHAPING THE SINGLE EUROPEAN MARKET IN THE FIELD OF FOREIGN DIRECT INVESTMENT

The Treaty of Lisbon (2009) has brought foreign direct investment (FDI) within the scope of the European Union's common commercial policy (CCP). In light of this development, this book analyses the internal and external dimension of EU law and policy in the field of FDI. It takes four perspectives: (i) the operation of the internal market mechanism to direct investment; (ii) the implications of the Lisbon amendments to the CCP under Article 207 TFEU for the Union's competence and practice in the field of FDI; (iii) the interaction between EU law and Member States' bilateral investment treaties (BITs) with third countries; (iv) the interplay between EU law and BITs that are currently in force between two Member States (intra-EU BITs).

The book focuses on the extent to which the European Union operates as a Single Market for EU and non-EU investors. In doing so, it analyses the EU and international regulatory framework on the admission, treatment and protection of FDI within, to and from the Single European Market. It uses close jurisprudential analysis and examines the context, purpose and evolution of EU legal integration in the field of FDI. It thereby traces the principles underlying the European international economic order in the field of FDI.

Volume 44 in the series Modern Studies in European Law

Shaping the Single European Market in the Field of Foreign Direct Investment

Philip Strik

·HART·
PUBLISHING
OXFORD AND PORTLAND, OREGON
2016

Published in the United Kingdom by Hart Publishing Ltd
16C Worcester Place, Oxford, OX1 2JW
Telephone: +44 (0)1865 517530
Fax: +44 (0)1865 510710
E-mail: mail@hartpub.co.uk
Website: http://www.hartpub.co.uk

Published in North America (US and Canada) by
Hart Publishing
c/o International Specialized Book Services
920 NE 58th Avenue, Suite 300
Portland, OR 97213-3786
USA
Tel: +1 503 287 3093 or toll-free: (1) 800 944 6190
Fax: +1 503 280 8832
E-mail: orders@isbs.com
Website: http://www.isbs.com

First published in hardback 2014
Paperback edition, 2016

Hart Publishing is an imprint of Bloomsbury Publishing plc.

British Library Cataloguing in Publication Data
Data Available

ISBN: HB: 978-1-84946-542-7
PB: 978-1-50990-704-5

Typeset by Hope Services, Abingdon
Printed and bound in Great Britain by
Lightning Source UK Ltd

Acknowledgments

This study is based on my PhD dissertation, which I have defended successfully at the University of Cambridge in November 2011. It has been updated in view of the many developments in the field and takes account of the state of the law up to 31 August 2013.

I would like to thank Professor Sir Alan Dashwood QC, who supervised me during the first half of my doctoral research and then continued to be a great source of advice and insight, both academically and personally. He introduced me to a whole different level of working in the field of EU law. He also made my time in Cambridge special by wisely suggesting to me to join Sidney Sussex College and by inviting me repeatedly to Glebe Farm. Professor Catherine Barnard took me over in my second year and supervised me with a great deal of care, support and energy. This study would never have taken its present shape without her exceptional commitment, insightful feedback and continuous encouragement. I feel extremely privileged to have worked with her. I am also very thankful to the Gates Cambridge Trust for the generous financial support for my time in Cambridge and various research trips.

The following persons have kindly shared their observations with me in the course of my research: Gabriela Alexandru, Tomas Baert, Selma Blank, Frits Bolkestein, Jean-François Brakeland, Colin Brown, Marta Busz, Angelos Dimopoulos, Antonio Fernández-Martos, Joni Heliskoski, Christophe Hillion, Jan-Peter Hix, Franck Hoffmeister, Wolfgang Igler, Carlos Jimeno Verdejo, Alexandra Koutoglidou, Pieter-Jan Kuijper, Ken Lennan, Nikos Lavranos, Bernd Martenczuk, Petr Ondrusek, Klaus Ossmann, Leopoldo Rubinacci, Manfred Schekulin, Ramon Torrent, Pauline Weinzierl and Myrto Zambarta. I would like to thank them for their time and insight.

I would like to thank all my colleagues in the EU law team in the Directorate for Legal Affairs at the Ministry of Foreign Affairs of the Netherlands, in particular: Mielle Bulterman, Tom de Gans, Ivo van der Steen, Jurian Langer, Marianne Gijzen and Joost Hoogveld. Special thanks are also due to 'BBBZ9'. Needless to say, all the views expressed in this book are strictly personal and do not necessarily reflect the position of the Kingdom of the Netherlands.

I wish to thank my father, mother and sister for their enormous support. They have always been there for me along the way and in every possible way. I dedicate this study to my late grandfather, FL Jochems (*opa Loek*), who cared so much about my whereabouts in life and then passed away shortly before the reaching of this important milestone.

Contents

Table of Cases

European Court of Human Rights

EFTA Court

Other Jurisdictions

Netherlands Hoge Raad

Table of Legislation

EU secondary legislation

National legislation

Abbreviations

ACT	advance corporation tax
AG	Advocate General
BIT	bilateral investment treaty
BLEU	Belgo-Luxembourg Economic Union
CCP	common commercial policy
CETA	Comprehensive Economic and Trade Agreement
CJEU	Court of Justice of the European Union
DCFTA	Deep and Comprehensive Free Trade Agreement
DTC	Double Taxation Convention
EA	Europe Agreement
ECHR	European Convention on Human Rights
ECT	Energy Charter Treaty
ECtHR	European Court of Human Rights
EEA	European Economic Area
EEC	European Economic Community
EIA	Economic Integration Agreement
EMA	Euro-Mediterranean Agreement
EMU	Economic and Monetary Union
EP	European Parliament
EPA	Economic Partnership Agreement
FDI	foreign direct investment
FET	fair and equitable treatment
FTA	Free Trade Agreement
GATS	General Agreement on Trade in Services
GATT	General Agreement on Tariffs and Trade
ICC	International Chamber of Commerce
IGC	intergovernmental conference
IMF	International Monetary Fund
LCIA	London Court of International Arbitration
MAI	Multilateral Agreement on Investment
MFN	most favoured nation
MoU	Memorandum of Understanding
NAFTA	North-Atlantic Free Trade Agreement
NT	national treatment
OECD	Organisation on Economic Cooperation and Development
PCA	Partnership and Cooperation Agreement
QMV	qualified majority voting

REIO	regional economic integration organisation
SAA	Stabilisation and Association Agreement
SEA	Single European Act
SCC	Stockholm Chamber of Commerce
SWF	sovereign wealth fund
TEU	Treaty on the European Union
TFEU	Treaty on the Functioning of the European Union
TRIMs	Trade-related Investment Measures
TRIPS	Trade-related Aspects of Intellectual Property Rights
TTIP	Transatlantic Trade and Investment Partnership
UNCLOS	United Nations Convention on the Laws of the Sea
UNCTAD	United Nations Committee on Trade and Development
VCLT	Vienna Convention on the Law of Treaties
WTO	World Trade Organization

1

Introduction: EU Legal Integration in the Field of Foreign Direct Investment

Si le marché commun ne peut être que régional . . . ce n'est pas à dire pour autant qu'il s'oppose au reste du monde ou disloque la division internationale du travail. Il donne au contraire à ces économies réunies la force nécessaire pour réduire la protection de la zone à laquelle il s'étend . . . et établir avec d'autres pays qui ne croiraient pas pouvoir s'y joindre, des relations cependant plus étroites que celles qu'ils entretenaient auparavant avec chacun de ces Etats séparés.[1]

T HIS STUDY INVESTIGATES the EU legal organisation in the field of foreign direct investment[2] (FDI). It looks at four aspects of EU legal integration in the field of FDI. First, it probes the operation of the internal market mechanism in relation to direct investment (chapter 2). Secondly, it assesses the implications of the Lisbon reform of the common commercial policy (CCP) for the Union's competence and practice in the field of FDI (chapter 3). Thirdly, it analyses the interplay between EU law and Member State bilateral investment treaties (BITs) with third countries (chapter 4). Fourthly, it looks at the interaction between EU law and BITs that are currently in force between two Member States (chapter 5). These various aspects of EU legal integration in the field of FDI are approached from the perspective to what extent the Single European Market is – and is increasingly – a *single* market in the field of FDI.

This introductory chapter elaborates in more detail on the scope and structure of this study. Before doing so, it first underlines the significance of FDI in the process of European integration. The EU regulatory context with regard to both the liberalisation and protection of FDI is then introduced. The chapter subsequently investigates the various definitions of FDI that can be found in different types of

---

[1] Spaak Report, *Rapport des Chefs de Délégations aux Ministres des Affaires Etrangères, Secretariat of the International Conference* (Brussels, 21 April 1956) 14–15. Translation: 'If the common market can only be regional . . . this does not mean that it is set against the rest of the world or dislocates the international division of labour. On the contrary, it gives these reunited economies the necessary strength to reduce the protection of the area that it comprises . . . and to establish with other countries that did not think they could join, closer relations than they maintained before with each of those individual States.'

[2] Foreign direct investment, as opposed to foreign portfolio investment, reflects a lasting interest by a resident entity in one economy in an enterprise resident in another economy with the aim of exercising influence. For more elaborate analysis, see section IV and accompanying notes.

international instruments that deal with FDI in view of their specialised purpose, before giving a short overview of some of the achievements in international rule-making in the field of FDI in which the Union and the Member States have been involved.

I. SETTING THE SCENE: EUROPEAN INTEGRATION AND FDI

On 1 December 2009, the Treaty of Lisbon[3] entered into force. Whereas the Constitutional Treaty[4] was eventually not ratified, the amendment of the EU Treaties and their renaming into the current Treaty on the European Union (TEU[5]) and the Treaty on the Functioning of the European Union (TFEU[6]) pursuant to the Treaty of Lisbon is the latest landmark in the evolution of the Union's[7] constitutional architecture. The point of departure of this study is one of the important changes in EU primary law as a result of the entry into force of the Treaty of Lisbon, which is that FDI has been brought under the scope of the (now) TFEU provisions on the common commercial policy (CCP). While the Treaty of Nice[8] had already extended the scope of the CCP so as to include trade in services and the commercial aspects of intellectual property, the Lisbon reform of the CCP seems to complete the scope of Union competences insofar as concerns its external economic relations. It directly reflects the increased importance of FDI in a globalised economy and its concomitant prominence on the agenda of international economic relations.

In view of the Union's post-Lisbon FDI competence, the European Commission published a Communication on 7 July 2010 in which it outlined the main orientations for a comprehensive EU international investment policy.[9] The Commission formulates 'openness to investment' through the progressive abolition of restrictions as a 'touchstone' of a common international investment policy.[10] In addition, the development of a common international investment policy is presented as an important complement to Europe's internal agenda for competitiveness and jobs.

---

[3] Treaty of Lisbon amending the Treaty on European Union and the Treaty establishing the European Community [2007] OJ C306/1.

[4] Treaty establishing a Constitution for Europe [2004] OJ C310/1.

[5] Consolidated version of the Treaty on the European Union [2010] OJ C83/13.

[6] Consolidated version of the Treaty on the Functioning of the European Union [2010] OJ C83/47. The Treaty on the European Community (EC) was renamed the TFEU.

[7] Pursuant to the adoption of the Treaty of Lisbon, the Union has succeeded and replaced the Community (Article 1 TEU). This study refers to the 'Community' as the relevant legal entity insofar as concerns the pre-Lisbon era, except when a degree of continuity between the Community and the Union is implied in a specific context.

[8] Treaty of Nice amending the Treaty on European Union, the Treaties establishing the European Communities and certain related acts [2001] OJ C80/1.

[9] Communication from the Commission to the Council, the European Parliament, the European Economic and Social Committee and the Committee of the Regions, 'Towards a comprehensive European international investment policy', COM(2010)343 final, 7 July 2010, Brussels.

[10] Ibid 4.

The Lisbon Strategy,[11] which was renewed in 2005 so as to focus the Union's activities on achieving economic growth and more jobs, had already been supplemented by the 2006 Communication on Global Europe.[12] In that Communication, the Commission outlined, inter alia, a strategy for creating business opportunities for European companies in a globalising economy by the opening of third-country markets. Similarly, the proposed common international investment policy is explicitly linked to the successor of the Lisbon strategy: the Europe 2020 strategy.[13] Against the backdrop of the financial and economic crisis, this proposal outlines a strategy to achieve high levels of employment, productivity and social cohesion in the Union. The common international investment policy is supposed to contribute to these objectives by stimulating non-EU investment in the Single Market and by creating opportunities for EU companies to invest in third countries.

These ambitious proposals reflect the importance of FDI for the economy of the Single Market. Over the years, the Member States have openly embraced economic globalisation. Direct investment has been welcomed as a source of employment and as a catalyst of technological progress. In addition, EU companies have been eager to invest outside the Single Market. The Union has in the meantime become one of the most important sources and recipients of world FDI flows. Before the financial and economic crisis, it can be observed that the Union's share of world FDI outflows in 2006, excluding intra-EU direct investment, was no less than 34 per cent.[14] In the same year, the Union received 20 per cent of world FDI flows and it thereby surpassed the United States as largest recipient of FDI. At the same time, the largest share of extra-EU FDI flows was from and to the United States. In 2006, 48.1 per cent of EU inward FDI inflows originated from the United States, while 27.7 per cent of EU outward FDI flowed to the United States.[15] Furthermore, in 2006, 35 per cent of total EU FDI stock in third countries was in the United States, while 46.4 per cent of non-EU stock in the Single Market was held by US investors.[16]

As a result of the financial and economic crisis, global FDI flows fell by 39 per cent in 2009.[17] EU FDI flows were also severely affected. EU FDI in third countries

---

[11] Communication from President Barroso in agreement with Vice-President Verheugen to the Spring European Council, 'Working together for growth and jobs: a new start for the Lisbon Strategy', COM(2005)24 final, 2 February 2005, Brussels; Communication from the Commission to the European Council, 'A citizen's agenda: delivering results for Europe', COM(2006)211 final, 10 May 2006, Brussels.

[12] Communication from the Commission to the Council, the European Parliament, the European Economic and Social Committee and the Committee of the Regions, 'Global Europe: competing in the world, a contribution to the EU's growth and jobs strategy', COM(2006)567 final, 4 October 2006, Brussels.

[13] Commission Communication, 'Europe 2020: a strategy for smart, sustainable and inclusive growth', COM(2010)2020, 3 March 2010, Brussels.

[14] Eurostat, *European Union Foreign Direct Investment Yearbook 2008* (2008) 14 (covering data from 2001–2006).

[15] Ibid 15.

[16] Ibid 29 and 44.

[17] OECD, WTO and UNCTAD, *Report on G20 Trade and Investment Measures, September 2009 to February 2010* (8 March 2010) 17.

fell by 30 per cent in 2008 and by 28 per cent in 2009.[18] FDI flows into the Single Market dropped by 60 per cent in 2008, while recovering by 26 per cent in 2009.[19] During 2008 to 2010, EU FDI flows overall remained severely affected by the global financial and economic crisis. In this period, EU FDI flows to emerging economies, such as China, were generally affected less than flows to economic partners such as the United States. In 2009, EU FDI stock in the United States accounted for 31 per cent and in Switzerland for 14 per cent of EU FDI stock in third countries, while EU FDI stock in emerging countries such as China and India continued to grow. In 2011, both FDI outflows and inflows from and into the Single Market increased, even though they remained considerably below the peak directly before the economic and financial crisis. Nevertheless, the Union is at present amongst the most important players in world FDI flows. In view of the importance of FDI for the economy of the Single Market, it is important to observe that the Union's post-Lisbon FDI competence could enable the Union to defend European interests in the world economy in a more effective way.

While direct investment from and into the Single Market is a constituent element of the Union's external economic relations, intra-EU direct investment still holds a much larger share of total EU FDI flows than extra-EU direct investment. For instance, intra-EU direct investment in the period 2004–2006 accounted for 76 per cent of total EU FDI flows.[20] Also here, the financial and economic crisis left its mark by leading to a decrease of intra-EU direct investment by 42 per cent in 2008.[21] It is clear, however, that intra-EU direct investment is part of the hard core of Single Market integration. To this effect, the internal market freedom of establishment and free movement of capital have from the early years of European integration served to eliminate restrictions on direct investment between the Member States. In addition, the adoption of secondary legislation in numerous fields has served to improve the conditions for competition between companies within the Single Market. The shaping of the external dimension of the Single Market in the field of direct investment in fact lags behind the more elaborate EU legal framework for the liberalisation of direct investment within the Single Market. While third-country direct investment has become subject to EU secondary legislation, the absence of the explicit FDI competence of the (then) European Community has worked against the development of a more comprehensive external FDI regime. The question also arises how and to what extent the admission and treatment of non-EU controlled companies in the Single Market is governed by the freedom of establishment and the free movement of capital.

The recent extension of the (now) TFEU provisions on the CCP to FDI also underscores the important point that the shaping of the external dimension of the Single Market in the field of direct investment lags behind that in other areas of

[18] Eurostat, *Europe in Figures: Eurostat Yearbook 2012* (2012) 93, available at http://epp.eurostat.ec.europa.eu/cache/ITY_OFFPUB/KS-CD-12-001/EN/KS-CD-12-001-EN.PDF.

[19] Ibid.

[20] Eurostat, *Yearbook 2008* (above n 14) 11.

[21] Eurostat news release, 68/2009, 14 May 2009.

external economic relations. While the Community's founding treaty provided the legal basis for the creation of the customs union, which was to facilitate the functioning of the common market, provisions with regard to the external dimension of this market as regards issues of deeper integration, such as services and FDI, were conspicuously absent. The Union has meanwhile become one of the major protagonists in trade negotiations in the context of the World Trade Organization (WTO), and the Treaty of Nice extended the scope of the CCP to trade in services and the commercial aspects of intellectual property. Insofar as concerns FDI, the Community, together with the Member States, has concluded a significant number of agreements containing investment-related provisions with third countries, which focus mainly on the liberalisation of direct investment. However, the Union's external practice in the field of FDI has continuously been identified by the Commission as an area requiring a more comprehensive effort.[22] It has taken more than 50 years after the entry into force of the Treaty of Rome for the Union's external competence under the provisions on the CCP to have been extended to FDI.

Important impediments to the shaping of the Single European Market in the field of FDI remain, however. To some extent, the Member States have different interests that can be reflected in different priorities, such as in relation to their national industries. At the same time, the Member States find themselves in competition in order to attract FDI. They do so, inter alia, by means of specific characteristics of their tax climates and through economic diplomacy. It can be observed that, before the economic and financial crisis, the main recipients of extra-EU FDI from 2001–2006 were the United Kingdom (19 per cent of total extra-EU FDI inflows), the Netherlands (8.5 per cent) and France (7.9 per cent).[23] The Member States also have different outward investment patterns, both to other Member States and to third countries.[24] For example, France, Germany and the Netherlands were reportedly the main investors within the Single Market in 2008.[25] At the same time, no less than 26 per cent of total EU FDI outflows was accounted for by the United Kingdom.[26] Companies from different Member States compete on the international plane. For a long time, some Member States have also maintained privileged economic relations with third countries, as reflected in their own networks of bilateral investment treaties (BITs).

A common international investment policy will contribute to the Union speaking with one voice in external relations in the field of FDI. It will also enable a level playing field to be created for both extra-EU FDI flows into the Union and EU FDI flows into third countries. While there is agreement between the Commission, the Council and the European Parliament on the need for an ambitious policy on

---

[22] Communication from the Commission to the Council, 'Need for Community action to encourage European investment in developing countries and guidelines for such action', COM(78)23 final, 30 January 1978, Brussels, 5; Commission Communication COM(2006)567 (above n 12) 6–7; Commission Communication COM(2010)343 (above n 9) 4.

[23] Eurostat, *Yearbook 2008* (above n 14) 45.

[24] See, eg P Nunnenkamp, 'European FDI Strategies in Mercosur Countries' (2001) 3 *JWI* 457.

[25] Eurostat news release, 68/2009 (above n 21).

[26] Ibid 25.

both the liberalisation and protection of investment, the development and implementation of the common international investment policy is likely to be a challenging process.[27] Negotiations in the field of investment with a number of third countries, such as Canada, the United States, Singapore and India, are currently taking place. The Union is also in the process of putting in place the institutional machinery for the Union and the Member States to participate in investor-state dispute settlement under Union investment agreements. To this effect, the Commission has made a proposal regarding the modalities for allocating responsibility between the Union and the Member States for breaches of a Union investment agreement, as well as for the conduct of disputes.[28] Meanwhile, Regulation 1219/2012[29] establishing transitional arrangements for Member State BITs with third countries has been adopted in order to address the status of existing Member State investment agreements with third countries from the perspective of the Union's post-Lisbon FDI competence and their replacement by Union investment agreements.

II. EUROPEAN FDI POLICIES AND THE LIBERALISATION OF FDI

There is a trend of increased openness to FDI in the Single Market, which is reflected in the main orientations of the common international investment policy. At the same time, the issue of protectionism has remained alive in the Union. As in all periods of economic downturn, the financial and economic crisis increased the risk of individual Member State action with a view to restricting, or at least controlling, capital flows. The rise in unemployment constitutes one of the pressures for protectionism in this context in view of the possible further negative effect on employment of corporate take-overs and the subsequent relocation of activities.[30] Although there has seemingly been no major impact of the financial and economic crisis on FDI policies, the United Nations Committee on Trade and Development (UNCTAD) has observed that protectionism could result from the creation of obstacles to outward investment so as to prevent capital outflows or the favouring of domestic, over foreign, investment.[31] UNCTAD has also noted the risk of 'covert' protectionism, such as restricting inward investment by unjustifiably invoking national security exceptions and by favouring products with

---

[27] See Council of the European Union, *Conclusions on a Comprehensive European International Investment Policy* (Luxembourg, 25 October 2010); European Parliament resolution of 6 April 2011 on the future European international investment policy.

[28] Proposal for a Regulation of the European Parliament and of the Council establishing a framework for managing financial responsibility linked to investor-state dispute settlement tribunals established by international agreements to which the European Union is a party, COM(2012)335 final, 21 June 2012, Brussels.

[29] Regulation 1219/2012 of the European Parliament and of the Council of 12 December 2012 establishing transitional arrangements for bilateral investment agreements between Member States and third countries [2012] OJ L351/40.

[30] *Report prepared by the OECD, the WTO and UNCTAD on G20 Trade and Investment Measures from September to February 2010* (8 March 2010) 6.

[31] UNCTAD, *World Investment Report* (2009) 31.

high domestic content in government procurement. Economic recovery could also trigger economic nationalism in the longer term. In particular, the gradual outflow of public funds from flagship industries could be coupled with an attempt to protect national champions from foreign take-overs.

The Union and the Member States had already started to re-evaluate some of the benefits of FDI before the financial and economic crisis.[32] This is evidenced by concerns in the Union about investment by sovereign wealth funds (SWFs).[33] These state-owned investment vehicles are funded from accumulated foreign-exchange reserves in their sponsor countries (eg China, Abu Dhabi, Kuwait, Russia and Norway) and manage a diversified portfolio of domestic and international financial assets. They have become a source of investment of systemic importance, stirring worries not only about the risk that these investments may interfere with the normal functioning of market economies, but also that these holdings could be used as instruments by non-EU governments to gain strategic control over certain industries, rather than merely reflecting financial considerations.[34] In this context, the Commission has stated that the Union remains committed to openness to investment and free movement of capital in an increasingly globalised international financial system.[35] However, the Commission has also expressed that it may want to formulate a common response to challenges posed by SWFs, possibly even by restricting such investment.[36] In 2011, a proposal was reportedly floated by Commissioners Tajani and Barnier to introduce a Union screening mechanism on grounds of national security by a centralised vetting committee for non-EU FDI flows into the Single Market, similar to the screening mechanisms of the United States, Canada, Australia, Japan and China.[37] The proposal appears not to have acquired sufficient traction.

Openness to FDI is seen as implying risks in a number of specific sectors. First, the Commission has stated the need to avoid the sale of European defence- and security-related industries and the reduction of these industries 'to the status of sub-supplier'.[38] It has been observed that there is no mechanism at a Union level

---

[32] See, eg 'Do not panic over foreign wealth', *Financial Times*, 29 April 2008; 'Left in the cold: foreign bidders find themselves out of favour', *Financial Times*, 25 April 2008.

[33] See Communication from the Commission to the European Parliament, the Council, the European Economic and Social Committee and the Committee of the Regions, 'A common European approach to Sovereign Wealth Funds', COM(2008)115 final, 26 February 2008, Brussels.

[34] Ibid 4.

[35] See, eg Commission Communication COM(2006)567 (above n 12); Communication from the Commission to the European Parliament, the Council, the European Economic and Social Committee and the Committee of the Regions, 'The European interest: succeeding in the age of globalisation', COM(2007)581 final, 3 November 2007, Brussels.

[36] Commission Communication COM(2008)115 (above n 33) 5. For analysis, see B de Meester, 'Europees- en internationaalrechtelijke aspecten van Sovereign Wealth Funds' (2008) 6 *Sociaal-Economische Wetgeving* 214.

[37] 'Analysis: rising foreign investment fuels EU vetting debate', Reuters, 8 March 2011, available at http://uk.reuters.com/article/2011/03/08/uk-eu-industry-investment-idUKTRE7272C720110308.

[38] Communication from the Commission to the Council, the European Parliament, the European Economic and Social Committee and the Committee of the Regions on European defence: industrial and market issues, COM(2003)113, 11 March 2003, Brussels.

under which the acquisition of participation by third-country investors in the European defence and security industries can be restricted, controlled or monitored.[39] In the light of reported attempts by companies from third countries to increase their influence over strategic European businesses in these sectors,[40] it has been suggested that direct investment from third countries in European defence and security-related industries should be monitored and that national control schemes that exist in some Member States, but which continue to fragment the Single Market, should be harmonised.[41]

Secondly, the perception of risks associated with third-country direct investment is reflected in the context of recently adopted EU secondary legislation in the energy sector.[42] On 19 September 2007, the Commission proposed the third energy package as part of the reorganisation of the European internal gas and electricity markets in accordance with the strategy of unbundling transmission networks from activities of production and supply. This strategy obliges vertically integrated undertakings to transfer the ownership of transmission systems to another legal person. The two Directives contain provisions with the effect that transmission systems or transmission system operators must not be controlled by investors from third countries in case this puts at risk the security of energy supply for the Member States and the Union.[43] Some commentators had already reported with regard to the 2007 proposal that it came at a time when relations between the Union and Russia in the energy sector were tense, with a number of disruptions of oil and gas supply to the Union since 2005 and the restructuring of the Russian energy market in favour of state-owned undertakings.[44] In addition, the renationalisation of Yukos, as well as Royal Dutch Shell and BP having had to withdraw their interests in lucrative projects, were seen as having propelled the Union to embark upon a policy of reciprocity in relation to the admission of FDI in the energy sector.

A number of Member States have, moreover, adopted legislation in recent years that is potentially more restrictive of foreign investment. In 2005, France revised its authorisation procedure for foreign investment in specific sectors with implications for public policy, public security or national defence.[45] In 2009, Germany adopted a new foreign investment code, under which the German fed-

---

[39]   K von Wagau and B Rapp-Jung, 'The Case for a European System Monitoring Foreign Investment in Defence and Security' (2008) 1 *CML Rev* 47.

[40]   See, eg 'EADS bid to restrict foreign ownership', *Financial Times*, 7 March 2008.

[41]   Wagau and Rapp-Jung, 'The Case for a European System' (above n 39) 47.

[42]   See, eg 'Germany opposes tighter investment rules', *Financial Times*, 6 October 2008; 'EU reaches deal on foreign energy investors', *Financial Times*, 10 October 2008.

[43]   Directive 2009/72 of the European Parliament and of the Council of 13 July 2009 concerning the common rules for the internal market in electricity, Art 11 [2009] OJ L211/55; Directive 2009/73 of the European Parliament and of the Council of 13 July 2009 concerning common rules for the internal market in natural gas, Art 11 [2009] OJ L211/94.

[44]   See, eg V van Hoorn, '"Unbundling", "Reciprocity" and the European Internal Energy Market: WTO Consistency and Broader Implications for Europe' (2009) 1 *European Energy and Environmental Law Review* 51.

[45]   Code monétaire et financier législatif, art R153-1 and 2, as established by Décret no 2005-1739 of 30 December 2005; last modified by Décret no 2012-691 of 7 May 2012.

eral government can block third-country direct investment in Germany if such investment would threaten German public security and public order.[46] Public opposition to inflows of FDI has, moreover, become more prominent in the United Kingdom.[47] Following the take-over of the British confectionery company Cadbury by the American company Kraft Foods, the possibility for the government to block foreign investment became the subject of public debate in the run-up to the general election in May 2010. Stirring hostility to inward FDI was not only the cultural sensitivity over a much-valued household name, but also the fear that Britain would lose jobs and expertise due to the closure of factories. While British firms were falling prey to hostile take-overs, it was alleged that their foreign counterparts were often protected from that type of acquisition.

The imposition of restrictions on foreign ownership, obligatory screening and approval procedures, stipulations that foreign investors must show economic benefits, as well as constraints on foreign personnel, are familiar ways of controlling inward FDI. Importantly, however, irrespective of the perceived risks associated with FDI, the desire to monitor, control and even potentially to block unwanted foreign investors by a Member State could not only give rise to incompatibilities with the law of the internal market in the field of direct investment, but it is also likely to clash with the objective of openness to third-country direct investment that the Commission has set for the common international investment policy. The process of EU legal integration in the field of FDI thus needs to be appreciated particularly in the light of a gradual opening up to direct investment and the remaining possibilities for restrictions, not only within the Single Market but also in relations of the Union and the Member States with third countries.

III. EUROPEAN INTEGRATION AND INVESTMENT PROTECTION

The development and implementation of a common international investment policy pursuant to the Union's post-Lisbon FDI competence also automatically opens up another important dimension of EU legal integration in this field. While the issue of investment *liberalisation* in relation to both the internal and the external dimension of the Single Market is in part subject to the Union *acquis*, the issue of investment *protection* is so far largely dealt with by Member State bilateral investment treaties (BITs). Rather than pooling sovereignty in this field, the Member States have from the early years of European integration separately concluded BITs with third countries. This practice initially served mainly the promotion of European outward investment through its protection. The total number of extra-EU BITs (currently amounting to more than 1,000 treaties) has become a constituent element in shaping the external dimension of the Single Market in the field of FDI. While Union external agreements in this field have so far focused on

---

[46] Dreizehntes Gesetz zur Änderung des Aussenwirtschaftsgesetzes und der Aussenwirtschaftsverordnung, BGBI, 2009 I, 770.

[47] See, eg 'Small island for sale', *Economist*, 27 March 2010.

issues of market access and treatment, Member State BITs focus predominantly on the protection of established investments against interferences with property rights, such as discrimination, unfair and inequitable treatment and expropriation without appropriate compensation, in conjunction with access to investor-state arbitration. These two parallel patterns of external action of the Union and the Member States in the field of FDI have long been complementary.

While the practice of the conclusion of BITs by the Member States has developed independently from Union initiatives in the same field, existing Member State BITs cannot be seen in isolation from EU law. First, Member State investment agreements raise questions of compatibility with EU law. This is evidenced by the recent 'BITs' judgments,[48] in which the EU Court ruled that the transfer clauses in pre-accession BITs of Austria, Sweden and Finland, which guarantee the free movement of capital to and from these countries, are incompatible with the (now) TFEU provisions under which the Council can take restrictive measures as regards capital transfers to and from third countries (Articles 64(2), 66 and 75/215 TFEU).[49] The capital transfer clauses in the agreements at issue in these cases, as well as those in many other Member State BITs with third countries, now need to be renegotiated in view of the EU law obligations of the Member States.

Secondly, the Commission has proposed that the investment-related provisions in Union external agreements be broadened to the issue of investment protection. With a view to the inclusion of investor-state dispute settlement provisions in Union external agreements, the Commission has issued a proposal for a Regulation on financial responsibility.[50] This instrument will provide the modalities for allocating responsibility for breaches of a Union investment agreement between the Union and the Member States, for the conduct of disputes under these agreements, as well as for the issue of payments. This important step in the development of the Union's international investment policy can only be evaluated in light of the Member States' existing practice of concluding BITs with third countries.

Thirdly, in view of the Union's post-Lisbon FDI competence and the development of the common international investment policy, Regulation 1219/2012[51] establishing transitional arrangements for Member State BITs with third countries has been adopted, which addresses the status of existing Member State investment agreements with third countries. For existing Member State BITs with third countries, Regulation 1219/2012 establishes a requirement of notification and a replacement mechanism. In addition, Regulation 1219/2012 contains an authorisation mechanism for the amendment of existing bilateral investment treaties and for the conclusion of new bilateral investment treaties. As a result, the

---

[48] C-205/06 *Commission v Austria* [2009] ECR I-1301; C-249/06 *Commission v Sweden* [2009] ECR I-1335; C-118/07 *Commission v Finland* [2009] ECR I-10889.
[49] See text at chapter 4, II.A and accompanying notes.
[50] Proposal for a Regulation COM(2012)335 (above n 28).
[51] Regulation 1219/2012 (above n 29).

Member States' external BIT practice is now part of the overarching framework of the Union's common international investment policy.

All Member State BITs were originally concluded with third countries. Nevertheless, some of the Member States, which have acceded to the Union more recently, have imported such investment agreements into the Union as international legal commitments between two Member States. Following the accession of Bulgaria, Romania and Croatia, there are about 200 BITs in force between Member States.[52] These intra-EU BITs cannot be seen in isolation from EU law either. The added value of intra-EU BITs for investors in the Single Market is disputed by the Commission in view of the investment protection rights enshrined in the EU legal order.[53] In addition, these agreements raise questions of compatibility with EU law. Since under intra-EU BITs investment protection rights are granted to investors from one Member State, but not from others, these agreements have been argued to be incompatible with the EU principle of equal treatment.[54] Arbitral tribunals have already dealt with the question what implications accession to the Union of these formerly third countries has had for the validity of the investment agreements concerned, as well as with questions of compatibility between EU law and the investment treatment standards enshrined in intra-EU BITs.[55]

Arbitral tribunals have recently also taken a more explicit stance on the way in which EU law may feature as applicable law in investor-state arbitration under intra-EU BITs.[56] While arbitral tribunals have so far not been very assertive in interpreting the rights held by investors under EU law, the question arises whether EU law permits disputes involving issues of EU law between an investor from one Member State, on the one hand, and another Member State, on the other, to be decided not in one of the courts of the Member States or in Luxembourg, but by an arbitral tribunal under an intra-EU BIT. At the same time, it seems difficult to square these concerns with regard to the interplay between investor-state arbitration under intra-EU BITs and EU law with the fact that the Union is itself, together with the Member States, a contracting party to the Energy Charter Treaty (ECT). The ECT also provides for the possibility of investor-state arbitration, so that investors from one EU Member State can bring a claim directly against another EU Member State.[57] The Commission has recommended that they be terminated

---

[52] Annex to the *2008 Annual EFC Report to the Commission and the Council on the Movement of Capital and Freedom of Payments*, no 17363/08 (Brussels, 17 December 2008) para 16.

[53] See Note by the European Commission, DG Markt, of November 2006 on free movement of capital, quoted in *Eastern Sugar BV v Czech Republic*, Partial Award of 27 March 2007, SCC no 088/2004, para 126, available at http://italaw.com/sites/default/files/case-documents/ita0259_0.pdf.

[54] See text at chapter 5, IV and accompanying notes.

[55] See *Eastern Sugar BV v Czech Republic* (above n 53); *Saluka Investments BV v Czech Republic*, Partial Award of 17 March 2006, available at http://italaw.com/sites/default/files/case-documents/ita0740.pdf.

[56] *Eureko v Slovak Republic*, Permanent Court of Arbitration Case no 2008-13, Award on Jurisdiction, Arbitrability and Suspension of 26 October 2010.

[57] See *Electrabel SA v Hungary*, ICSID Case no ARB/07/19, Award of 30 November 2012.

and could in future take steps to challenge the existence of these agreements.[58] Some Member States have in fact already started to terminate their intra-EU BITs.[59] A study of EU legal integration in the field of FDI therefore raises important questions with regard to the future of these agreements.

The Lisbon reform of the (now) TFEU provisions on the CCP potentially has a significant impact on the progressive shaping of the external dimension of the Single European Market in the field of FDI. It also automatically opens up a number of other issues with regard to the EU legal organisation in the field of FDI, such as the operation of the internal market mechanism in relation to direct investment and the interplay between EU law and Member State investment agreements. These elements of Single Market integration in the field of FDI are the subject of this study. As will be shown, even if FDI is part of the hard core of Single Market integration and the Union is the most advanced regional economic integration organisation, the precise contours of a number of facets of EU legal integration in the field of direct investment are still in the process of being worked out. Before outlining in more detail the scope and structure of this study, the next two sections address the various definitions of FDI to be found in international instruments that regulate different aspects of FDI, as well as the limited achievements so far in multilateral rule-making in the field of FDI by both the Union and the Member States.

IV. DEFINITIONS OF FDI IN DIFFERENT TYPES OF INTERNATIONAL INSTRUMENTS

Even though the term 'investment' is now widely used in the body of international rules that regulates this phenomenon, it originates from the discipline of economics.[60] The economic literature distinguishes foreign direct investment from foreign portfolio investment. Whereas the purpose of foreign portfolio investment is merely to obtain a financial return, FDI is usually part of an international corporate strategy to establish a permanent position in another economy.[61] FDI has been defined in the economic literature as 'the transfer of capital by a company in one country to another country to create or take over an establishment there which it wants to control'.[62] FDI is thus a category of international investment that involves a situation in which the foreign investor owns an amount of shares or voting power

---

[58] November 2006 note by DG Internal Market and Services to the Economic and Financial Committee, quoted in *Eastern Sugar v Czech Republic*, Partial Award of 27 March 2007, SCC no 088/2004, para 126, available at http://italaw.com/sites/default/files/case-documents/ita0259_0.pdf.

[59] 2(13) *IAReporter*, 6 August 2009.

[60] P Juillard, 'Freedom of Establishment, Freedom of Capital and Freedom of Investment' (2001) 2 *ICSID Review* 322, 326.

[61] R Gilpin, *Global Political Economy, Understanding the International Economic Order* (Princeton, NJ, Princeton University Press, 2001) 278.

[62] W Molle, *The Economics of European Integration: Theory, Practice, Policy*, 5th edn (Aldershot, Ashgate, 2006) 125.

that allows him to participate effectively in the management of the enterprise or its control. Subsumed under the concept of FDI are subsidiaries, in which the foreign investor owns between 50 to 100 per cent of the share capital. Holdings in which the foreign investor owns less than 50 per cent of the share capital can also qualify as FDI, provided that the investors is able to participate in the management of the enterprise. Moreover, branches, which are unincorporated in the host economy, can be included.[63] By contrast, portfolio investors do not participate in the management of the enterprise or its control, even if the relationship with a firm can be long-term. The exclusive rationale behind portfolio investment is the value of the capital and the return that is generated.

Direct investors can be individuals and groups of individuals, as well as incorporated and unincorporated entities.[64] Even governments and government agencies can be direct investors. However, FDI is usually an important element of the production and trading strategies of multinational firms so as to enhance their international competitiveness. It is possible to distinguish between at least two important reasons why a firm goes multinational by creating or taking over a commercial presence in another country.[65] First, specific parts of the production chain can be relocated to low-cost destinations so as to acquire low-cost inputs and thus decrease production costs. This type of strategy generally increases intra-industry trade and thus creates trade. Secondly, part of the production chain can be replicated in another country so as to better serve a local market. This strategy can be incentivised by the possibility to avoid tariffs and can involve a duplication of the production process by establishing additional plants. It thereby for the most part substitutes for trade.

Important inter-linkages therefore exist between issues of trade and FDI. Some aspects of treatment of FDI moreover relate to classic issues of commercial policy, such as the access of a foreign investor to import and export licences. At the same time, it is clear that the regulation of FDI does not necessarily pursue trade objectives, such as the fostering of sales. Regulatory approaches to FDI can even conflict with trade objectives. For instance, changes in investment conditions, such as pursuant to a restriction of export quotas, can discourage foreign investment and violate investment protection standards, but can at the same time be perceived to serve a country's trade interests. By consequence, international rule-making with

---

[63] See also Communication from the European Community and its Member States to the WTO Working Group on the Relationship between Trade and Investment, WT/WGTI/W/115, 16 April 2002, para 17, which refers to 'all incorporated (subsidiary and associates) or unincorporated (branches) enterprises in which a direct investor owns 10 per cent or more of the ordinary shares or voting power or the equivalent'. It is furthermore submitted that, '[s]hould a direct investor control the company with less than 10 per cent of the ordinary shares[,] the following criteria could be taken into account to determine whether a direct investment relationship exists: (a) representation in the Board of Directors; (b) participation in policy-making processes; (c) inter-company transactions; (d) the interchange of managerial personnel; (e) provision of technical information; (f) provision of long-term loans at lower than existing market rates'.

[64] IMF, *Balance of Payment Manual* (1993) 87, available at www.imf.org/external/pubs/ft/bopman/bopman.pdf.

[65] Molle, *Economics of European Integration* (above n 62) 125.

regard to the admission, treatment and protection of FDI, whilst interacting with trade issues, constitutes an independent area of international economic relations, which is not automatically part of a country's trade policy.

For the purpose of international rule-making in the field of FDI, a distinction can be drawn between three regulatory issues which, even if they are not mutually exclusive, can be roughly equated with the various stages of a direct investment.[66] First, there is the issue of the admission of FDI.[67] This refers to the stage at which the host state decides whether a direct investor is allowed to invest and which (if any) restrictions or conditions an investor faces. This pre-entry phase is arguably more adequately referred to as the admission of FDI than as market access, since the latter is a trade concept that is linked to a product entering a market. Secondly, there is the issue of movements of capital in relation to FDI. A direct investment is often accompanied by a transfer of capital, although it can also happen that an investor raises funds in the host economy. Thirdly, there is the issue of investment treatment. This is more adequately referred to as post-establishment treatment, since it concerns the specific way in which commercial presences, such as a subsidiary or a branch, are allowed to operate after their establishment. An important aspect of investment treatment in international rule-making in the field of FDI is the issue of investment protection, such as by means of adequate compensation in the case of expropriation. In view of the different regulatory issues associated with FDI, it constitutes a multifaceted economic phenomenon, which does not only involve a transfer of capital, but also raises issues with regard to the conditions under which an investor is allowed to invest and the legal framework that an enterprise is subjected to in a foreign economy. The different regulatory issues associated with FDI are reflected in the various international instruments that deal with FDI, which in turn contain different definitions of investment in function of their regulatory purpose.

It is only from the 1960s that the term 'investment' and, concomitantly, that of 'direct investment' have found their way into international economic law.[68] At the same time, there is no single accepted legal definition of FDI. International instruments define FDI differently, which in part reflects the different regulatory issues that such instruments deal with.[69] First, there are international instruments that contain a so-called enterprise-based definition of direct investment. Crucial for this type of definition of direct investment, which focuses on the establishment or acquisition of a business enterprise, is the element of control of a direct investor

---

[66] For analysis, see R Torrent, 'Derecho comunitario e inversiones extranjeras directas: Libre circulación de los capitales vs. regulación no discriminatoria del establecimiento. De la *golden share* a los nuevos *open skies*' (2007) *Revista Española de Derecho Europeo* 283.

[67] See T Pollan, *Legal Framework for the Admission of FDI* (Utrecht, Eleven International Publishing, 2006).

[68] Juillard, 'Freedom of Establishment' (above n 60).

[69] See Communication from the European Community and its Member States to the WTO Working Group on the Relationship between Trade and Investment, WT/WGTI/W/115, 16 April 2002, paras 3–5. For analysis of the different rationales of different kinds of investment instruments, see UNCTAD, *Scope and Definition*, UNCTAD/ITE/IIT/11 (vol II) (Geneva, 1999).

over the enterprise. An example is the General Agreement on Trade and Services (GATS), Article XXVIII(m) of which refers to a 'juridical person of another Member' as meaning:

a juridical person which ... (ii) in the case of the supply of a service through commercial presence, [is] *owned or controlled* by: 1. natural persons of that Member; or 2. juridical persons of that other Member. (emphasis added)

Similarly, for the purpose of determining the types of measures that come within the substantive scope of the TFEU freedom of establishment within the Union, the Court of Justice of the European Union (CJEU) has emphasised the element of control in referring to:

national provisions which apply to holdings by nationals of the Member State concerned in the capital of a company established in another Member State, giving them *definite influence* on the company's decisions and *allowing them to determine* its activities. (emphasis added)[70]

The issues of the admission and treatment of FDI hold a central place in international instruments that contain an enterprise-based definition of FDI.

Secondly, a transaction-based definition of direct investment is contained in international instruments that primarily serve the liberalisation of various types of capital movements, amongst which are those in relation to direct investment. The definition of 'direct investment' used by the International Monetary Fund (IMF), for example, is that of an investment:

[which reflects] the objective of obtaining a lasting interest by a resident entity in one economy (direct investor) in an enterprise resident in another economy (direct investment enterprise).[71]

Crucial in this definition is the existence of a lasting interest, which implies two criteria.[72] First, there should be a long-term relationship between the direct investor and the enterprise. Secondly, there should be a certain degree of influence, without this necessarily amounting to control, by the investor on the management of the enterprise. Along these lines, the 2003 Code on the Liberalisation of Capital Movements of the Organisation on Economic Cooperation and Development (OECD) defines 'direct investment' as an:

investment for the purpose of establishing lasting economic relations with an undertaking such as, in particular, investments which give the possibility of exercising an effective influence on the management thereof.[73]

---

[70] C-524/04 *Thin Cap Group Litigation* [2007] ECR I-2107, para 27.
[71] IMF, *Balance of Payment Manual* (above n 64) 86.
[72] Ibid.
[73] OECD, *Code of Liberalisation of Capital Movements* (2003) 30 (Annex 1, IA). This includes 'the creation or extension of a wholly-owned enterprise, subsidiary or branch, and acquisition of full ownership of an existing enterprise; participation in a new or existing enterprise; and a loan of five years or longer' (Annex 1, IB).

In addition to singling out the establishment of lasting economic links with an enterprise, this definition identifies the requirement of the possibility to exercise 'effective influence' on the management of an enterprise in order to qualify as direct investment. An example in EU law of an instrument that contains a transaction-based definition of direct investment is Directive 361/88, which referred to:

> [i]nvestments of all kinds by natural persons or commercial, industrial or financial undertakings, and which serve to establish or to maintain lasting and direct links between the person providing the capital and the entrepreneur to whom or the undertaking to which the capital is made available in order to carry on an economic activity.[74]

This instrument served the aim of the progressive liberalisation of capital movements within the Single Market.

Thirdly, international instruments that primarily serve the purpose of investment protection contain a so-called asset-based definition of investment, which usually covers both direct and portfolio investment. The definition of 'investment' in Member State BITs typically refers to 'any kind of assets' with regard to five non-exclusive categories: (i) movable and immovable property and any other property rights such as mortgages, liens or pledges; (ii) shares in and stock and debentures of a company and any other form of participation in a company; (iii) claims to money or to any performance under contract having a financial value; (iv) intellectual property rights, technical processes, trademarks, goodwill and know-how; (v) business concessions conferred by law or under contract, including concessions to search for, cultivate, extract or exploit natural resources.[75] The Energy Charter Treaty (ECT), which is specifically geared towards trade and investment in the energy sector, is partly modelled on provisions in BITs and contains a similarly wide definition of the types of assets that are protected under the agreement.[76] It refers to investment as meaning 'every kind of asset, owned or controlled directly or indirectly by an Investor'.[77] International agreements that contain an asset-based definition of investment usually cover aspects of the post-

---

[74] Council Directive 88/361 of 24 June 1988 for the implementation of Article 67 of the Treaty, Annex [1988] OJ L178/5. For analysis, see text at chapter 2, I.A and accompanying notes.

[75] See United Kingdom-Ukraine BIT, Art 1(a).

[76] On the ECT in relation to the EU Treaties, see HJ Schroth, 'The Energy Charter Treaty (ECT) in the Context of the Treaties of the European Union' in T Wälde (ed), *The Energy Charter: An East-West Gateway for Investment & Trade* (London, Kluwer Law International, 1996) 240–48; E Paasivirta, 'The European Union and the Energy Sector: The Case of the Energy Charter Treaty' in M Koskenniemi (ed), *International Law Aspects of the European Union* (The Hague, Kluwer Law International, 1998) 197–214.

[77] Article 1(6) ECT. It is stated to include: '(a) tangible and intangible, and movable and immovable, property, and any property rights such as leases, mortgages, liens, and pledges; (b) a company or business enterprise, or shares, stock, or other forms of equity participation in a company or business enterprise, and bonds and other debt of a company or business enterprise; (c) claims to money and claims to performance pursuant to contract having an economic value and associated with an [i]nvestment; (d) [i]ntellectual [p]roperty; (e) [r]eturns; (f) any right conferred by law or contract or by virtue of any licences and permits granted pursuant to law to undertake any [e]conomic [a]ctivity in the [e]nergy [s]ector'.

establishment treatment of FDI (in particular its protection) and capital transfers in relation to such investments, such as the return of profits.

V. INTERNATIONAL RULE-MAKING IN THE FIELD OF FDI

The liberalisation of FDI touches on important *domestic* regulatory issues. Some of the possible advantages for host countries associated with FDI are that it can represent a source of employment, usually involves a transfer of skills and technology, and that FDI is taxable in many ways.[78] There is thus an international trend towards the liberalisation of FDI, in which different countries compete for FDI. Yet, states may also perceive a need to restrict FDI. Among the various factors shaping the policies behind the admission of FDI are a number of historical, economic and cultural considerations.[79] States have historically-fed positive or negative attitudes towards foreign investment. For instance, the liberalisation of capital movements has raised concerns about the loss of economic sovereignty, since it can give rise to controlling stakes in national industries by large multinational corporations over which domestic authorities, it is sometimes feared, have little power.[80] The admission of FDI can, moreover, involve economic considerations, such as in relation to a state's competition policy or financial and monetary policy, but also cultural ones, such as in the audio-visual services sector. The treatment of FDI can give rise to issues of investor behaviour, such as with regard to the protection of the environment and social policy.[81] Important questions of political economy therefore arise in the context of the regulation of FDI, which are not necessarily restricted to strategically important or culturally sensitive sectors.[82] The regulation of FDI raises many complex issues that feature high on political agendas.

This, in turn, has made it difficult to agree on *international* rules in the field of FDI.[83] It has been observed that, until the late 1970s, the international regulation of FDI mainly focused on the issue of investment protection.[84] In the aftermath of

---

[78] See S Young and N Hood, 'Inward Investment Policy in the European Community in the 1990s' (1993) 2 *Transnational Corporations* 35.

[79] Pollan, *Legal Framework* (above n 67) 3 ff.

[80] SJ Kobrin, 'Sovereignty@Bay: Globalization, Multinational Enterprise, and the International Political System' in AM Rugman and TL Brewer (eds), *The Oxford Handbook of International Business* (Oxford, Oxford University Press, 2001) 181–205.

[81] For views of the Community and the Member States on how to tackle investors' behaviour in host countries, see Communication from the European Union and its Member States to the WTO Working Group on the Relationship between Trade and Investment, WT/WGTI/W/81, 20 September 1999.

[82] See NM Jensen, *Nation-States and the Multinational Corporation: A Political Economy of Foreign Direct Investment* (Princeton, NJ, Princeton University Press, 2006); KJ Vandevelde, 'The Political Economy of a Bilateral Investment Treaty' (1998) 4 *AJIL* 621.

[83] See S Ostry, *A New Regime for Foreign Direct Investment*, Occasional Paper 53 (Washington, DC, Group of Thirty, 1997); TL Brewer and S Young, *The Multilateral Investment System and Multinational Enterprises* (Oxford, Oxford University Press, 1998).

[84] P Juillard, *L'évolution des sources du droit des investissements* (Collected Courses of the Hague Academy of International Law, 1994) 9, 22 ff.

decolonisation, newly independent states were suspicious of foreign investment, which they perceived as a form of foreign domination, and demanded economic self-determination, including the right to nationalise foreign property. The main fear of these countries was that the same repression which they were exposed to during colonial times would now be extended by foreign control of their industries.[85] Yet, developing countries have increasingly appreciated some of the positive impacts associated with FDI, such as inflows of capital, job creation and the transfer of technology. Therefore, the regulatory focus in more recent international instruments seems to have shifted somewhat from the issue of investment protection to the issue of investment liberalisation.[86] Notwithstanding the difficulties associated with agreeing on international rules in the field of FDI, a number of important multilateral instruments have been concluded by the Union and the Member States in the context of the OECD and the WTO, which deal with issues of FDI.

The OECD Codes on the Liberalisation of Capital Movements and the Liberalisation of Current Invisible Operations were adopted in 1961. They provide legally binding rules on the progressive, non-discriminatory liberalisation of capital movements in relation to FDI and include a right of establishment for non-resident investors among a number of developed countries. Under these instruments, the contracting states are gradually – and unilaterally – supposed to reduce barriers to foreign investment on the basis of a system of peer review, rather than to embark upon reciprocity-based liberalisation. Article 1(a) of the Capital Movements Code stipulates that members need to 'progressively abolish ... restrictions on movement of capital to the extent necessary for effective economic cooperation' and 'treat all non-resident owned assets in the same way irrespective of the date of their formation', as well as 'permit the liquidation of all non-resident owned assets and the transfer of such assets or of their liquid proceeds'. The Current Invisible Operations Code deals with service businesses and financial transactions. Article 1 requires contracting states to eliminate all restrictions on operations such as trade, insurance, tourism and professional services. While these codes are binding on the contracting states, they lack an enforcement mechanism.

The Multilateral Agreement on Investment (MAI) was supposed to establish more systematic and uniform rules in the field of investment between the contracting parties of the OECD. However, the negotiations in the context of the OECD collapsed in October 1998 when France withdrew from the negotiations.[87]

---

[85] M Sornarajah, *The International Law on Foreign Investment*, 3rd edn (Cambridge, Cambridge University Press, 2010) 24–30.

[86] Juillard, *L'évolution des sources* (above n 84).

[87] For analysis of some of the political, legal and economic issues pertaining to the MAI, as well as the reasons for its failure, see J Karl, 'Das Multilaterale Investitionsabkommen (MAI)' (1998) 6 *Recht der internationalen Wirtschaft* 432; P Juillard, 'MAI: A European View' (1998) 3 *Cornell International Law Journal* 477; N Schrijver, 'A Multilateral Investment Agreement from a North-South Perspective' in E Nieuwenhuys and MMTA Brus (eds), *Multilateral Regulation of Investment* (The Hague, Kluwer Law International, 2001) 17–33.

Pursuant to the Draft Consolidated Text, national treatment (NT) and most favoured nation (MFN) treatment were to be accorded to 'the establishment, acquisition, expansion, operation, management, maintenance, use, enjoyment, and sale or other disposition of investments'.[88] It also provided for minimum standards of investment protection and contained investor-state dispute settlement provisions. Unlike other OECD-based rules, this instrument was thus supposed to deal not only with the issue of investment liberalisation, but also with that of investment protection.

Following the non-ratification of the Havana Charter by the United States in the late 1940s, which would have created the International Trade Organisation, issues of investment were long ignored in the context of the General Agreement on Tariffs and Trade (GATT). The Uruguay Round (1986–1994) placed issues of FDI (albeit rather unostentatiously) back on the agenda of multilateral trade negotiations. As a result, a number of agreements that are administered by the WTO address issues of FDI.[89] The GATS contains commitments on the admission and treatment of commercial presences in the field of services on the basis of special schedules of commitments and thus serves the liberalisation of FDI in the services sector.[90] Directly relevant for direct investment is also the Agreement on Trade-related Investment Measures (TRIMs), which deals with investment measures that have a restrictive and distorting effect on trade in goods, such as local origin requirements and trade-balancing requirements. In addition, aspects of investment protection are dealt with under the Agreement on Trade-related Aspects of Intellectual Property Rights (TRIPS), which contains standards of protection pertaining to intangible assets such as copyrights and trademarks. In the context of the WTO, it later proved impossible to move forward on the so-called Singapore issues, one of which is trade and investment, at the 2003 Cancun Ministerial Council. FDI has consequently been taken off the Doha Development Agenda of negotiations.

Since international rule-making in the field of FDI is mostly reciprocity-based and, in view of the wide range of regulatory issues that it touches on, fairly slow, there exists only a fragmented multilateral legal framework. As a result of the rather limited achievement on the liberalisation (let alone the protection) of FDI in multilateral settings such as the OECD and the WTO, the more successful track for international rule-making in the field of FDI has been the bilateral one. Provisions on the admission and treatment of FDI can be found in existing Union

---

[88] Multilateral Agreement on Investment, Draft Consolidated Text, DAFFE/MAI(98)7/REV1, 22 April 1998, Art III, 1-2, 13.

[89] P Sauvé, 'A First Look at Investment in the Final Act of the Uruguay Round' (1994) 5 *Journal of World Trade* 5. See also Working Party of the Trade Committee, *The Investment Architecture of the WTO*, TD/TC/WP(2002)41/FINAL, 14 April 2003.

[90] This is the so-called third mode of supply of services under the GATS, where a service is provided by means of the establishment of a subsidiary or a branch. By contrast, under the first mode of supply of services, only the service crosses the border, such as with the operation of telecentres. Under the second mode, the consumer travels abroad, such as in the case of tourism. Under the fourth mode, there is a temporary presence of natural persons supplying a service, such as when consultants attend a business meeting.

external agreements and the Member States are contracting parties to a large number of BITs. These will be further investigated in this study. Also, the regional track has increasingly been considered as an important setting for international rule-making in the field of FDI. For instance, Chapter 11 of the North-Atlantic Free Trade Agreement (NAFTA) contains elaborate commitments on the liberalisation and protection of FDI, which are partly modelled on those in BITs, including investor-state dispute settlement provisions. The ECT is also a regional investment instrument. Yet, arguably the most important regional setting for international rule-making in the field of FDI is the European Union, which forms the subject of this study.

VI. SCOPE AND STRUCTURE OF THIS STUDY

This study investigates the legal organisation of FDI in the oldest and most advanced regional economic integration organisation in the world: the European Union. Much existing research into Single Market integration, insofar as concerns both the internal market and the CCP, has a trade-related focus.[91] At the same time, the importance of FDI for the economy of the Single Market is manifest since the 1980s and it has become one of the focal areas in international economic law. The increased importance of FDI in international economic relations is reflected in the Union's post-Lisbon external FDI competence and the development of the common international investment policy. It has also precipitated an increase in scholarly interest in Single Market integration in the field of FDI.[92] This study aims to contribute to this recent scholarship by closely analysing a number of aspects of EU legal integration in the field of FDI. The main focus is to

[91] See, eg P Eeckhout, *The European Internal Market and International Trade: A Legal Analysis* (Oxford, Clarendon Press, 1994); M Maresceau, *The European Community's Commercial Policy after 1992: The Legal Dimension* (Dordrecht, Martinus Nijhoff, 1993); SV Konstantinidis, *The Legal Regulation of the European Community's External Relations after the Completion of the Internal Market* (Boston (MA), Dartmouth Publishing, 1996); P Demaret (ed), *Relations extérieures de la Communauté européenne et marché intérieur: aspects juridiques et fonctionnels* (Brussels, Story-Scientia, 1988).

[92] Among recent studies of various aspects of the EU legal organisation in the field of FDI are: M Bungenberg, A Reinisch and C Tietje (eds), *EU and Investment Agreements: Open Questions and Remaining Challenges* (Nomos, Baden-Baden, 2013); A Dimopoulos, *EU Foreign Investment Law* (Oxford, Oxford University Press, 2012); F Benyon, *Direct Investment, National Champions and the EU Treaty Freedoms* (Oxford, Hart Publishing, 2010); C Kessedjian and C Leben (eds), *Le droit européen et l'investissement* (Paris, Éditions Panthéon-Assas, 2009); S Hindelang, *The Free Movement of Capital and Foreign Direct Investment: The Scope of Protection under EU Law* (Oxford, Oxford University Press, 2009); T Eilmansberger, 'Bilateral Investment Treaties and EU Law' (2009) 2 *CML Rev* 383; A Emch, 'News from Luxembourg: Is the New EU Investment Law Taking Shape?' (2008) 6 *Journal of World Investment and Trade* 497; A Dimopoulos, 'The Common Commercial Policy after Lisbon: Establishing Parallelism between Internal and External Economic Relations?' (2008) *CYELP* 101; A Radu, 'Foreign Investors in the EU: Which "Best Treatment"? Interactions between Bilateral Investment Treaties and EU Law' (2008) 2 *European Law Journal* 237; J Ceyssens, 'Towards a Common Foreign Investment Policy? Foreign Investment in the European Constitution' (2005) 3 *Legal Issues of European Integration* 259; W Shan, 'Towards a Common European Community Policy on Investment Issues' (2001) 3 *Journal of World Investment and Trade* 604; R Torrent, *Derecho y Práctica de las Relaciones Exteriores en la Unión Europea* (Barcelona, Cedecs, 1998) 81–114.

probe to what extent the European Union actually is – and is increasingly – a single market for both EU and non-EU direct investors.

The point of departure of this study is the Union's post-Lisbon FDI competence and the challenge of developing and implementing a common international investment policy more than 50 years after the entry into force of the Treaty of Rome. The common international investment policy is likely to have far-reaching implications for the Union's treaty-making practice by including both the liberalisation and protection of FDI. The further development of the external dimension of the Single Market in the field of FDI could increase the extent to which the Single Market constitutes a truly 'single' market for third-country investors. At the same time, the common international investment policy interacts with the internal legal organisation in the field of direct investment within the Single Market, because it raises the question in what circumstances EU and non-EU investors can successfully invoke the TFEU freedom of establishment and free movement of capital. The automatic granting of rights of secondary mobility to third-country direct investors within the Single Market under the freedom of establishment can be contrasted with the absence of a comprehensive Union regime with regard to the admission and treatment of third-country direct investment in the Single Market. This study therefore analyses the operation of the internal market mechanism in relation to direct investment (chapter 2), before turning to an examination of the implications of the Lisbon reform of the CCP for the Union's competence and practice in the field of FDI (chapter 3).

Further EU legal integration in the field of FDI pursuant to the Union's post-Lisbon FDI competence raises questions with regard to its possible consequences for the continued existence and application of Member State BITs. In view of the Union's post-Lisbon FDI competence, Regulation 1219/2012 establishes a requirement of notification and a replacement mechanism for existing Member State BITs with third countries, and an authorisation mechanism for the amendment of existing BITs and the conclusion of new BITs. A close legal analysis of these transitional arrangements necessitates an assessment of the way in which Member State BITs with third countries interact with EU law, as well as an analysis of the EU legal framework that governs this interaction. Since the continued existence and application of intra-EU BITs also raise the issue of their compatibility with EU law, the EU legal framework that governs the various facets of the interaction between EU law and these intra-EU agreements will subsequently be closely analysed. This study first probes the interplay between EU law and Member State BITs with third countries (chapter 4), before delving into the interaction between EU law and intra-EU BITs (chapter 5). Chapter 6 brings together the various interrelated strands of analysis of the different chapters of this study and concludes.

For the purpose of this study, a selection from the many legal issues pertaining to the progressive shaping of the Single Market in the field of FDI necessarily had to be made. The issues which have been selected bring to light to what extent the Single European Market increasingly manifests itself as a *single* market in the field of FDI. This study uses close jurisprudential analysis and examines thoroughly the context, purpose and evolution of various aspects of EU legal integration in the field of FDI. It thereby traces the principles underlying the European international economic order in the field of FDI. Insofar as concerns terminology, FDI in principle refers to any direct investment with a cross-border dimension. This study sticks as much as possible to the terminology of the TFEU, where FDI exclusively refers to a transaction occurring between a Member State and a third country.[93] Since 'direct investment' can refer both to transactions with an intra-EU and with an extra-EU dimension, this study specifies whether one, the other or both are at issue in a specific context.

---

[93] See also Hindelang, *Capital and Foreign Direct Investment* (above n 92) 74–78.

2

The Operation of the Internal Market Mechanism in Relation to Direct Investment

Because Europe is demonstrating a newfound vitality, because envious eyes are being cast on a market of 320 million people with high standards of living, there are those who have no compunction about accusing us of digging moats and building drawbridges. Let us not be taken in by this. Our accusers are those who would like to see an open Europe with no common policy, no reactions, no political will. Our accusers are those who, within their own walls, enact protectionist trade laws or devise ways of slowing down the first tentative moves towards market liberalization. We would say this to them: *the single market will be open, but it will not be given away.* (emphasis added)[1]

T
HIS CHAPTER LOOKS at the application of the internal market mechanism to direct investment. Even if there is no TFEU freedom that is exclusively devoted to direct investment, direct investors hold important rights to invest under the TFEU provisions on freedom of establishment and free movement of capital. In addition, while the internal market mechanism deals mainly with intra-EU direct investment, a particularly contentious issue is its bearing on direct investment to and from third countries. The chapter first explores the underlying integrative strategy of these two TFEU freedoms as regards direct investment, as well as the fact that Article 63 TFEU can be invoked by third-country investors whereas Articles 49/54 TFEU are inward-looking. It subsequently turns to the interpretative problems arising from the area of overlap in the application of these two TFEU provisions to direct investment, which is particularly important in a third-country context. The chapter then looks in detail at the post-establishment treatment of third-country direct investment in the Single Market.

With reference to the political and economic context of international rule-making in the field of FDI that has been laid down in the previous chapter, this chapter shows that the internal market mechanism does not operate with the

---

[1] Jacques Delors, speech before the European Parliament in Strasbourg, 17 January 1989, available at www.cvce.eu/content/publication/2003/8/22/b9c06b95-db97-4774-a700-e8aea5172233/publishable_en.pdf.

effect that the Union and the Member States have unilaterally given third-country direct investors the right to invest in the Single Market insofar as such investment primarily constitutes establishment. As regards the post-establishment treatment of third-country direct investment in the Single Market, it is argued that a distinction needs to be drawn between the post-establishment treatment of third-country direct investment in the internal economy of a Member State and the rights of intra-EU mobility for non-EU direct investors. The internal market mechanism operates differently with respect to these two aspects of the post-establishment treatment of third-country direct investment as a result of the inward-looking nature of the freedom of establishment. The automatic granting of rights of secondary mobility to third-country direct investors will be contrasted with the absence of a comprehensive Union regime with regard to the admission and treatment of third-country direct investment in the Single Market.

I. INTERNAL MARKET INTEGRATION IN THE FIELD OF DIRECT INVESTMENT

This section looks at the constitutive features of EU legal integration so far as concerns direct investment within the Single Market. It first clarifies the terminology and analyses the integrative strategy of the Single Market in the field of direct investment. It then investigates why the free movement of capital was extended to capital transfers to and from third countries in view of the fact that the other TFEU freedoms apply only to intra-EU situations.

A. Terminology and Integrative Strategy

Article 3(3) TEU states that the Union shall establish an 'internal market'. Article 26(2) TFEU provides that the internal market 'shall comprise an area without internal frontiers in which the free movement of goods, persons, services and capital is ensured in accordance with the provisions of the Treaties'. The Single European Act (SEA) set the Union an objective to complete European market integration by 31 December 1992 as part of the so-called Single Market programme. While the CJEU had already been using the term 'Single Market' since the early 1960s,[2] the terms 'internal market' and 'Single Market' have mostly been used interchangeably.[3] In the typology outlined by Belassa, the four freedoms of the Single European Market constitute a so-called 'common market'.[4] While a 'free trade area' and a 'customs union' are forms of regional economic integration that focus exclusively on the free movement of products, which can be traded, it is

---

[2] See 32/65 *Italy v Council and Commission* [1966] ECR 389, 405; 15/81 *Gaston Schul* [1982] ECR 1409, para 33.

[3] CS Barnard, *The Substantive Law of the EU, The Four Freedoms*, 3rd edn (Oxford, Oxford University Press, 2010) 12; K Mortelmans, 'The Common Market, the Internal Market and the Single Market: What's in a Market?' (1998) 1 *CML Rev* 101.

[4] See B Balassa, *The Theory of Economic Integration* (London, Allen and Unwin, 1962).

a distinctive feature of a common market that it allows for the free movement of production factors, such as labour, capital and enterprise.[5] The abolition of restrictions on direct investment is therefore an important feature of Single Market integration. Yet, there is no TFEU freedom that is exclusively devoted to direct investment.

With regard to the operation of the internal market mechanism in relation to direct investment, the European Commission has stated on the basis of the Court's case law that:

> the acquisition of controlling stakes in a domestic company by an EU investor, in addition to being a form of capital movement, is also covered under the scope of the right of establishment.[6]

Indeed, both Article 49 TFEU on freedom of establishment and Article 63 TFEU on free movement of capital are relevant for an analysis of the legal organisation of direct investment in the Single Market. It is settled case law that national provisions which apply to holdings by nationals of the Member State concerned in the capital of a company established in another Member State, giving them definite influence on the company's decisions and allowing them to determine its activities, come within the substantive scope of the TFEU provisions on freedom of establishment.[7] Furthermore, direct investment often involves a movement of capital in the sense of Article 63 TFEU. The close link between freedom of establishment and free movement of capital was first recognised by the CJEU in *Casati*, when it observed that the:

> freedom to move certain types of capital is, in practice, a precondition for the effective exercise of other freedoms guaranteed by the Treaty, in particular the right of establishment.[8]

In view of the possibilities for interaction between freedom of establishment and free movement of capital so far as concerns direct investment, the predominant purpose and underlying integrative principles of these two TFEU freedoms will be discussed in turn.

The freedom of establishment includes the right to take up and pursue activities as self-employed persons and to set up and manage undertakings under the conditions laid down for its own nationals by the law of the Member State of establishment.[9] It allows an EU investor to participate, on a stable and continuous basis, in the economic life of a Member State other than his state of origin and to profit therefrom, thus contributing to the 'economic and social interpenetration'

---

[5] W Molle, *The Economics of European Integration: Theory, Practice, Policy*, 5th edn (Aldershot, Ashgate, 2006) 11; D Swann, *The Economics of Europe, From Common Market to European Union*, 9th edn (London, Penguin, 2000) 171, who refers to enterprise in addition to labour and capital.

[6] Communication of the Commission, 'Certain legal aspects concerning intra-EU investment' [1997] OJ C220/15, para 4.

[7] C-196/04 *Cadbury Schweppes* [2006] ECR I-7995, para 31.

[8] 203/80 *Casati* [1981] ECR 2595, para 8.

[9] C-251/98 *Baars* [2000] ECR I-2787, para 27.

in the Union.[10] The exercise of the freedom of establishment involves the genuine and actual pursuit of an economic activity in the host Member State.[11] While Article 49 TFEU secures the freedom of establishment for nationals of a Member State on the territory of another Member State, Article 54 TFEU extends the freedom of establishment to legal persons. An EU investor thus exercises his rights under the TFEU freedom of establishment where a shareholding constitutes a lasting link with a company in the host economy and allows the investor not only to participate, but also to have a definite influence on the management of a company.[12] The freedom of establishment, moreover, applies both to the establishment of new undertakings and to the acquisition of shares in pre-existing undertakings.[13]

The freedom of establishment covers both the admission and post-establishment treatment of direct investment. So far as concerns the underlying integrative strategy of this TFEU freedom, Article 49 TFEU gives effect to the principle of non-discrimination enshrined in Article 18 TFEU by laying down an obligation of national treatment.[14] In addition, the freedom of establishment extends to instances of both direct and indirect discrimination.[15] Directly discriminatory national measures can be saved under Article 52(1) TFEU only on grounds of public policy, public security or public health. The criteria to be fulfilled by indirectly discriminatory measures are that they must be applied in a non-discriminatory way, be justified by imperative requirements, be suitable for securing the objective that they pursue and they must not go beyond what is necessary in order to attain that objective.[16] Furthermore, the rights enshrined in Articles 49/54 TFEU do not merely involve an obligation on the host Member State to treat foreign nationals and companies in the same way as nationals of that Member State. Articles 49/54 TFEU also prohibits the Member State of origin from hindering the establishment in another Member State of one of its nationals or of a company incorporated under its legislation, as well as the establishment in another Member State of nationals of Member States residing on its territory.[17]

---

[10]   C-55/94 *Gebhard* [1995] ECR I-4165, para 25.

[11]   But see C-167/01 *Inspire Art* [2003] ECR I-10155, para 95, where the Court confirmed that a company which is formed in one Member State solely for the purpose of establishing in a second Member State, where its entire business is to be conducted, is capable of invoking the freedom of establishment.

[12]   C-524/04 *Thin Cap Group Litigation* [2007] ECR I-2107, para 27.

[13]   C-411/03 *SEVIC Systems AG* [2005] ECR I-10805, para 19.

[14]   C-1/93 *Halliburton Services* [1994] ECR I-1137, para 12.

[15]   C-330/91 *Commerzbank* [1993] ECR I-4017, para 14: 'the rules regarding equality of treatment forbid not only overt discrimination by reason of nationality or, in the case of a company, its seat, but all covert forms of discrimination which, by the application of other criteria of differentiation, lead in fact to the same result'. For a critical analysis of the Court's restriction- or obstacle-based approach, see CS Barnard, 'Restricting Restrictions: Lessons for the EU from the US?' (2009) 3 *CLJ* 575. See also E Spaventa, 'From Gebhard to Carpenter: Towards a (Non-)Economic European Constitution' (2004) 3 *CML Rev* 743.

[16]   C-55/94 *Gebhard* [1995] ECR I-4165, para 37.

[17]   C-446/03 *Marks & Spencer* [2005] ECR I-10837, para 31.

Direct investment is also addressed in EU law under the free movement of capital. Whereas capital mobility was long subsidiary to the other Treaty freedoms in the earlier stages of Single Market integration,[18] Article 63(1) TFEU now provides that:

> Within the framework of the provisions set out in this Chapter, all restrictions on the movement of capital between Member States and between Member States and third countries shall be prohibited.[19]

In the words of Flynn, capital movements cover 'those resources used for, or capable of, investment intended to generate revenue'.[20] As such, the free movement of capital covers financial assets, such as cash, bonds and shares. The freeing up of capital transactions essentially meant that the Member States were obliged to make foreign currency available to enable these transactions to take place.[21] A principal problem was the imposition of exchange controls by Member States with the aim of safeguarding their balance of payments and to ensure domestic monetary autonomy.[22] However, the substantive scope of the TFEU provisions on free movement of capital has been interpreted widely so as to cover factors potentially affecting the optimum allocation of capital, such as tax measures.[23] Similar to the freedom of establishment, free movement of capital has been found to catch indistinctly applicable rules that are nonetheless discriminatory, unless they can be justified.[24]

The notion of capital movements relates to a wider range of economic activities than only direct investment. This can readily be observed from the nomenclature

---

[18] Before the Treaty of Maastricht, the Treaty provisions on movement of capital (Art 67(1) EEC Treaty) only laid down the obligation for capital movements to be liberalised 'to the extent necessary to ensure the proper functioning of the common market' and were not directly effective. See Case 203/80 *Casati* [1981] ECR 2595, para 10.

[19] The Court ruled that free movement of capital is directly effective in Joined Cases C-163/94, C-165/94 and C-250/94 *Sanz de Lera* [1995] ECR I-4830, para 41. The freedom of payments, which is enshrined in Art 63(2) TFEU, will not be considered, since remunerations do not constitute an investment. For the distinction between capital and payments, see Joined Cases 286/82 and 26/83 *Luisi and Carbone* [1984] ECR 377, para 21.

[20] L Flynn, 'Coming of Age: The Free Movement of Capital Case Law 1993–2002' (2002) 4 *CML Rev* 773, 776.

[21] Swann, *Economics of Europe* (above n 5) 184 ff.

[22] Under Art 1(1) of the First Directive for the implementation of Article 67 EEC [1960] OJ 43/921, the Member States had to 'grant all *foreign exchange authorisations* required for the conclusion or performance of transactions or for transfers between residents of Member States in respect of . . . capital movements' such as direct investment (emphasis added). For a similar focus on the removal of exchange controls, see EEC Commission, *The Development of a European Capital Market, Report of a Group of Experts Appointed by the EEC Commission* (1966) 85–88 (Segré Report); White Paper from the Commission to the European Council on Completing the Internal Market, COM(85)310 final, 14 June 1985, Brussels, 32–34.

[23] S Kingston, 'A Light in the Darkness: Recent Developments in the ECJ's Direct Tax Jurisprudence' (2007) 5 *CML Rev* 1321.

[24] C-463/00 *Commission v Spain* [2003] ECR I-4581, para 56. For analysis, see A Emch, 'News from Luxembourg: Is the New EU Investment Law Taking Shape?' (2008) 6 *Journal of World Investment and Trade* 497, 508 ff.

enshrined in the first Annex to Directive 361/88,[25] in which 13 different types of capital movement are classified in relation to the economic nature of the assets and liabilities they concern. Direct investment constitutes the first heading in this non-exhaustive list of capital movements. The CJEU has held that capital movements include, inter alia, the granting of credit on a commercial basis,[26] the reselling of shares,[27] inheritances,[28] investments in real estate[29] and immovable property,[30] as well as direct and portfolio investments.[31] While Article 63 TFEU prohibits restrictions on capital movements, Article 64(2) TFEU provides the Council with a legislative competence to:

> adopt measures on the movement of capital to or from third countries involving direct investment – including investment in real estate – establishment, the provision of financial services or the admission of securities to capital markets.

Moreover, Article 64(3) TFEU provides that

> Notwithstanding paragraph 2, only the Council, acting in accordance with a special legislative procedure, may unanimously and after consulting the European Parliament, adopt measures which constitute a step backwards in Union law as regards the liberalisation of the movement of capital to or from third countries.

The Court has confirmed that the reference to direct investment in Article 64 TFEU does not in any way impinge on the substantive scope of Article 63 TFEU.[32] In other words, the latter provision is directly effective in relation to the economic activities that are explicitly mentioned in Article 64 TFEU.

Because EU primary law does not define the concept of 'direct investment', reference is often made to Directive 88/361.[33] The first Annex of this Directive breaks down the concept of direct investment into four categories:

> (1) [e]stablishment and extension of branches or new undertakings belonging solely to the person providing the capital, and the acquisition in full of existing undertakings; (2) [p]articipation in new or existing undertakings with a view to establishing or maintaining lasting economic links; (3) [l]ong-term loans with a view to establishing or maintaining lasting economic links; (4) [r]einvestment of profits with a view to maintaining lasting economic links.

---

[25] Council Directive 88/361 of 24 June 1988 for the implementation of Article 67 of the Treaty [1988] OJ L178/5.

[26] C-452/04 *Fidium Finanz* [2006] ECR I-9521.

[27] C-265/04 *Bouanich v Skatteverket* [2006] ECR I-923.

[28] C-513/03 *Van Hilten-van der Heijden* [2006] ECR I-1957.

[29] C-386/04 *Centro di Musicologia* [2006] ECR I-8293.

[30] C-451/05 *Elisa* [2007] ECR I-8251.

[31] Joined Cases C-282/04 and 283/04 *Commission v Netherlands* [2006] ECR I-9141.

[32] C-101/05 *A v Skatteverket* [2007] ECR I-11531, para 26. With reference to (now) Article 64(1) TFEU, see below n 52.

[33] C-446/04 *FII Group Litigation* [2006] ECR I-11753, para 179: 'the nomenclature of capital movements annexed [to Directive 88/361 has] indicative value, for the purposes of defining the term "movement of capital" . . . subject to the qualification, contained in the introduction to the nomenclature, that the list set out therein is not exhaustive'.

The emphasis on the establishment of lasting economic links accords with the transaction-based definition of FDI in other international instruments that liberalise cross-border capital movements. It is, moreover, absent in the definition of various types of portfolio investment in the same instrument, such as operations in securities on the capital market with purely financial aims. The focus on lasting links is also evidenced by an explanatory note in the same Annex, which defines 'direct investment' as:

> Investments of all kinds by natural persons or commercial, industrial or financial undertakings, and which serve to establish or to maintain lasting and direct links between the person providing the capital and the entrepreneur to whom or the undertaking to which the capital is made available in order to carry on an economic activity. This concept should therefore be understood in its widest sense.

In view of the fact that Article 63 TFEU deals with the freedom of capital movements, the concept of direct investment in this definition presupposes a transfer of capital.[34] That a movement of capital cannot be entirely equated with the concept of direct investment is reflected in the fact that Article 64 TFEU refers to movements of capital 'involving direct investment'. In other words, the wording of the TFEU provisions on free movement of capital seems to suggest that they deal with capital transfers only *in relation to* direct investment and not with the entire transaction of direct investment.[35]

Because direct investment often involves a movement of capital, it has a prominent place in Directive 88/361. However, since the regulatory issues involved with a transfer of capital may differ depending on the economic activity that is involved, it is important to bear in mind the economic context of any movement of capital. That such a movement of capital is always linked to a specific economic activity or underlying transaction is underscored by the fact that Article 64 TFEU does not only refer to capital movements in relation to 'direct investment', but also in relation to 'establishment'. The reference to both 'direct investment' and 'establishment' in the TFEU provisions on free movement of capital suggests that 'direct investment' is not necessarily the same economic activity as the concept of 'establishment' in the light of Article 49 TFEU. Indeed, where a self-employed person establishes itself in another Member State, without there being an investment giving rise to a lasting interest, this does not constitute direct investment.[36] Furthermore, this double reference implies that the exercise

---

[34] Economists consider direct investment to be a specific kind, or subcategory, of capital transfers. See Molle, *Economics of European Integration* (above n 5) 126.

[35] The same picture is borne out by other language versions of the Treaty. The Dutch version speaks of capital movements 'in verband met directe investeringen'; the French version of 'movement de capitaux à destination ou en provenance de pays tiers, lorsqu'ils impliquent des investissements directs'; the Italian version refers to capital movements 'in relazione a investimenti diretti'; the German version to capital movements 'im Zusammenhang mit Direktinvestitionen'; and the Spanish version to capital movements 'que supongan inversiones directas'. But see C-174/04 *Commission v Italy* [2005] ECR I-4933, para 28.

[36] S Hindelang, *The Free Movement of Capital and Foreign Direct Investment: The Scope of Protection under EU Law* (Oxford, Oxford University Press, 2009) 86.

of freedom of establishment rights does not necessarily preclude that same activity from simultaneously involving a capital movement in relation to direct investment for the purpose of Article 63(1) TFEU. Establishment, in the form of direct investment or not, can involve a transfer of capital. However, the multifaceted economic activity of direct investment (or establishment) arguably cannot be entirely equated with such a transfer of capital.

The issue of the admission and treatment of direct investment has thus been subsumed under the TFEU provisions on establishment and capital movements. Their regulatory purposes are similarly inspired by the general principles underpinning the common market, such as the principle of non-discrimination on grounds of nationality, which requires out-of-state natural and legal persons, as well as capital, to enjoy the same treatment as their in-state equivalents. Since the enjoyment of national treatment can also be a burden for a foreign economic operator in respect of domestic economic operators, the TFEU freedoms have also been ruled to catch indistinctly applicable national rules that nevertheless hinder market access, unless they can be justified. Nevertheless, there seems to be a different regulatory emphasis between freedom of establishment and free movement of capital insofar as the free movement of capital focuses predominantly on issues of market access, while the concept of establishment deals with the admission and to a larger degree with the post-establishment treatment of direct investment.[37] This is evidenced by the much larger amount of secondary legislation with a sectoral approach in the field of establishment, which provides for harmonisation and mutual recognition rules.

B. External Dimension of Articles 49/54 and 63 TFEU

The TFEU freedoms focus on economic integration within the Single Market. Articles 49/54 TFEU is purely inward-looking, so that third-country investors seeking access to the Single Market cannot invoke the freedom of establishment. This was confirmed by the CJEU in *Opinion 1/94*, where it ruled that:

> the sole objective of [the chapter on freedom of establishment] is to secure the right of establishment . . . for nationals of Member States.[38]

The TFEU provisions on freedom of establishment, moreover, do not extend to situations that involve the establishment in a third country of a Member State national or of a company incorporated under the legislation of a Member State.[39] Neither does the freedom to provide services apply to third-country economic

---

[37] R Torrent, 'Derecho comunitario e inversiones extranjeras directas: Libre circulación de los capitales vs. regulación no discriminatoria del establecimiento. De la *golden share* a los nuevos *open skies*' (2007) *Revista Española de Derecho Europeo* 283.

[38] *Opinion 1/94* [1994] ECR I-5267, para 81.

[39] C-157/05 *Holböck* [2007] ECR I-4051, para 28.

operators.[40] The same applies to the free movement of goods[41] and the free movement of workers.[42] By contrast, it follows from the wording of Article 63 TFEU that the free movement of capital applies not only to intra-EU capital movements, but also to capital transfers from and into the Single Market.[43]

The free movement of capital as laid down in the Treaty of Rome was initially limited to the extent necessary to ensure the proper functioning of the common market.[44] Member States thus did not aspire to complete free movement of capital as an object in itself. It has been suggested that the Member States did not want to give up the right to restrict capital flows, because they needed that instrument for the effective control of internal macro-economic and monetary developments.[45] There was the fear that capital outflows would depreciate the currency and drive up the rate of inflation, which would require monetary measures and fiscal contraction to offset it.[46] Since the free movement of capital was initially not directly effective,[47] it was to be achieved exclusively through the adoption of secondary legislation.[48] There have been continuous efforts to progressively liberalise capital movements within the Single Market, but up to 1987 this did not result in instruments reaching beyond the stipulations of the Treaty. Not until the Treaty of Maastricht was the free movement of capital incorporated into the (then) EC Treaty as a fully-fledged fundamental freedom (the fourth freedom[49]).

(Then) Article 73b EC also explicitly extended the free movement of capital to third countries. Germany and the Netherlands were the main proponents of an extension of capital liberalisation to third countries, while France had proposed not including the free movement of capital vis-à-vis third countries in the Maastricht amendments.[50] The hesitation of some Member States to extend capital mobility to third countries was mainly grounded in concerns over the possibility of extracting similar concessions from third countries, the link between full capital mobility and the freedom to establish in the Union, as well as the possibility for

---

[40] C-452/04 *Fidium Finanz* [2006] ECR I-9521, para 25.

[41] See 51/75 *EMI Records* [1976] ECR 811, para 17: 'the Provisions of the Treaty on commercial policy do not . . . lay down any obligation on the part of the Member States to extend to trade with third countries the binding principles concerning the free movement of goods between Member States'.

[42] Article 45(1) TFEU: 'Freedom of movement for workers shall be secured within the Union'.

[43] This notwithstanding, Art 64(2) TFEU stipulates that the European Parliament and the Council '[endeavour] to achieve the objective of free movement of capital between Member States and third countries to the greatest extent possible' in adopting measures on the movement of capital to and from third countries involving, inter alia, direct investment.

[44] See text to n 18.

[45] Molle, *Economics of European Integration* (above n 5) 122.

[46] D Mayes and J Kilponen, 'Factor Mobility' in AM El-Agraa, *The European Union, Economics and Policies*, 8th edn (Cambridge, Cambridge University Press, 2007) 144.

[47] See 203/80 *Casati* [1981] ECR 2595.

[48] For a historical overview of secondary legislation in the field of capital movements, see JA Usher, 'The Evolution of the Free Movement of Capital' (2007–2008) 5 *Fordham International Law Journal* 1533, 1535 ff; J Snell, 'Free Movement of Capital: Evolution as a Non-Linear Process' in P Craig and G de Búrca (eds), *The Evolution of EU Law*, 2nd edn (Oxford, Oxford University Press, 2010) 547.

[49] C-463/00 *Commission v Spain* [2003] ECR I-4581, para 68.

[50] AFP Bakker, *The Full Liberalization of Capital Movements in Europe: The Monetary Committee and Financial Integration 1958–1994* (Dordrecht, Kluwer, 1995) 230–31.

positive discrimination in favour of European companies.[51] Bakker observes that these concerns prompted the Member States to allow the continuation of existing restrictions vis-à-vis third countries.[52]

Different explanations have been advanced as to why the scope of application of Article 73b EC was extended to capital movement to and from third countries.[53] At an international level the collapse of the Bretton Woods system of fixed exchange rates in 1971 propelled the lifting of monetary restrictions hindering the free international flow of capital. International financial deregulation had put new competitive pressures on national financial systems because it increased the possibilities for companies to tap into pools of capital outside their home markets. Furthermore, capital movements had already been substantially liberalised between the Member States and third countries in accordance with the OECD Code of Liberalisation of Capital Movements. Since many Member States had already liberalised extra-EU capital transfers, capital inflows and outflows could not effectively be prevented in any case. One explanation therefore focuses on the sense among the Member States that capital movements with third countries had already been liberalised to a significant extent, although this does not necessarily explain why the extension of free movement of capital to third countries had to be incorporated in EU primary law.[54]

The entry into force of Articles 73a–h EC (later 56–60 EC) on 1 January 1994 coincided with the commencement of the second stage of Economic and Monetary Union (EMU), the third stage of which was the adoption in 1999 of the euro as the common currency of 11 of the then 15 Member States. While free movement of capital is a precondition of a monetary union,[55] it is also beyond doubt that the extension of the free movement of capital to third countries is related to the establishment of EMU.[56] The objective of extending free movement of capital to third countries is linked to the need to assure the international money market as regards the availability of the euro and thus to support the credibility of the euro as an

---

[51] Ibid 233.

[52] Ibid. The standstill provision enshrined in (now) Article 64(1) TFEU provides that '[t]he provisions of [now] Article 63 shall be without prejudice to the application to third countries of any restrictions which exist on 31 December 1993 under national or Union law adopted in respect of the movement of capital to or from third countries involving direct investment, including in real estate, establishment, the provision of financial services or the admission of securities to capital markets. In respect of restrictions existing under national law in Bulgaria, Estonia and Hungary, the relevant date shall be 31 December 1999.'

[53] Most extensively, see R Abdelal, *Capital Rules: The Construction of Global Finance* (Cambridge, MA, Harvard University Press, 2007) 54–85.

[54] DS Smit, 'Capital Movements and Third Countries: The Significance of the Standstill-Clause ex-Article 57(1) of the EC Treaty in the Field of Direct Taxation' (2006) 4 *EC Tax Review* 203, 204.

[55] *Report to the Council and the Commission on the Realization by Stages of Economic and Monetary Union in the Community* (Werner Report), Supplement to Bulletin II–1970 of the European Communities, 10: 'A monetary union implies inside its boundaries the total and irreversible convertibility of currencies, the elimination of margins of fluctuation in exchange rates, the irrevocable fixing of parity rates and the complete liberalisation of movements of capital'.

[56] Snell, 'Free Movement of Capital' (above n 48) 551.

international reserve currency.[57] A macro-economic incentive for extending free movement of capital to third countries is that this prevents Member States from influencing the exchange rate of the single currency by restricting transfers of capital to and from third countries.

Notwithstanding what might have been the incentive for extending (then) Article 73b EC to capital transfers to and from third countries, the CJEU has divorced its interpretation of the free movement of capital with third countries from this specific political and economic background. This is evidenced by *A v Skatteverket*,[58] which dealt with the differential taxation of inbound dividends from shares owned by A, a Swedish national, in company X, which had its registered office in Switzerland. Swedish law provided for a tax exemption on dividends received from companies established in a European Economic Area (EEA) state, but not on dividends received from companies established elsewhere. A argued that this discouraged investment in these companies. In respect of the argument that the free movement of capital in relation to third-country investments had to be interpreted in the light of the specific rationale for extending the Treaty provisions on free movement of capital to third countries, the Court held that:

> even if the liberalisation of the movement of capital with third countries may pursue objectives other than that of establishing the internal market, such as, in particular, that of ensuring the credibility of the single Community currency on world financial markets and maintaining financial centres with a world-wide dimension . . ., it is clear that, when the principle of free movement of capital was extended, pursuant to [then] Article 56(1) EC, to movement of capital between third countries and the Member States, the latter chose to enshrine that principle in that article in the same terms for movements of capital taking place within the Community and those relating to relations with third countries.[59]

In other words, the free movement of capital to and from third countries could not be interpreted more restrictively in view of the fact that the rationale for extending Article 63(1) TFEU to extra-EU capital movements differed from the objective of the liberalisation of intra-EU capital movements. Since extra-EU capital movements are placed within Article 63(1) TFEU, and insofar as the Swedish law discouraged EU investment outside the EEA, the measure was caught by Article 63(1) TFEU.

While the Court in *A v Skatteverket* divorced its interpretation of the free movement of capital with third countries from the specific political and economic background of its extension to third-country situations, it did recognise that a distinction can be drawn in respect of possible justifications for restrictions to intra-EU and extra-EU capital movements.[60] In particular, the Court noted that

---

[57] Usher, 'The Evolution of the Free Movement of Capital' (above n 48) 1543; K Ståhl, 'Free Movement of Capital between Member States and Third Countries' (2004) 2 *EC Tax Review* 47, 52.
[58] C-101/05 *A v Skatteverket* [2007] ECR I-11531.
[59] Ibid para 31.
[60] Ibid para 37.

the legal context for capital transfers to and from third countries is different from that within the Single Market.[61] In the first place, there are various derogations to be applied to such movements that may not be applied to intra-EU capital movements.[62] In addition, the Court indicated both that a wider array of public interests may be accepted in an extra-EU context and that the proportionality principle may be interpreted differently in third-country situations.[63] As a result, the Court took the view that:

> the taxation by a Member State of economic activities having cross-border aspects which take place within the Community is not always comparable to that of economic activities involving relations between Member States and third countries.[64]

In view of the third-country situation concerned, the Court considered that it could not be verified whether the tax exemption at issue would be given for the correct amount of shares and ruled that the Swedish measure was, for that reason, justified on grounds of securing the effectiveness of fiscal supervision.[65]

Some of the intervening Member States had argued in *A v Skatteverket* that compliance with the prohibition laid down in Article 63(1) TFEU would lead to the unilateral liberalisation of capital movements on the part of the Union without the assurance of equivalent liberalisation on the part of the third countries concerned.[66] The Union would thus lose an important bargaining chip and no longer be able to negotiate liberalisation of capital movements with those countries, since Article 63 TFEU would have already automatically and unilaterally opened up the Single Market.[67] They also observed that the provisions on free movement of capital in association agreements with third countries often had a more limited scope than that of Article 63 TFEU.[68] If that provision was applied in

[61] Ibid para 32.

[62] The Court pointed to Art 59 EC (now Art 66 TFEU: '[w]here, in exceptional circumstances, movements of capital to or from third countries cause, or threaten to cause, serious difficulties for the operation of economic and monetary union, the Council, on a proposal from the Commission and after consulting the European Central Bank, may take safeguard measures with regard to third countries for a period not exceeding six months if such measures are strictly necessary'); and Art 60 EC (now Art 75 TFEU :'[w]here necessary to achieve the objectives set out in Article 67, as regards preventing and combating terrorism and related activities, the European Parliament and the Council, acting by means of regulations in accordance with the ordinary legislative procedure, shall define a framework for administrative measures with regard to capital movements and payments, such as the freezing of funds, financial assets or economic gains belonging to, or owned or held by, natural or legal persons, groups or non-State entities'; see also Art 215(1) TFEU: '[w]here a decision, adopted in accordance with Chapter 2 of Title V of the Treaty on European Union, provides for the interruption or reduction, in part or completely, of economic and financial relations with one or more third countries, the Council, acting by a qualified majority on a joint proposal from the High Representative of the Union for Foreign Affairs and Security Policy and the Commission, shall adopt the necessary measures'). Unlike Art 75 TFEU, ex Art 60 EC referred exclusively to movements of capital to and from third countries. For a more elaborate discussion of these derogations in the context of the 'BITs' judgments, see chapter 3.

[63] See also F Benyon, *Direct Investment, National Champions and the EU Treaty Freedoms* (Oxford, Hart Publishing, 2010) 84.

[64] C-101/05 *A v Skatteverket* [2007] ECR I-11531, para 37.

[65] Ibid para 63.

[66] Ibid para 29.

[67] Ibid para 30.

[68] See chapter 3.

the same way in third-country situations as it was applied in an intra-EU context, those provisions would in their view be meaningless.[69] In relation to these arguments, the Court held that the loss of negotiating power and reciprocity was not a decisive consideration in determining whether a tax measure restricted capital movements to or from third countries in relation to Article 63(1) TFEU.

The potentially far-reaching effect of Article 63 TFEU on tax measures in relation to capital movements to and from third countries has prompted the Member States to include the new Article 65(4) as part of the TFEU provisions on free movement of capital. It provides that:

> In the absence of measures pursuant to Article 64(3) [allowing the Council to restrict the free movement of capital to and from third countries], the Commission or, in the absence of a Commission decision within three months from the request of the Member State concerned, the Council, may adopt a decision stating that restrictive tax measures adopted by a Member State concerning one or more third countries are to be considered compatible with the treaties in so far as they are justified by one of the objectives of the Union and compatible with the proper functioning of the internal market. The Council shall act unanimously on application by a Member State.

It seems that the politically sensitive nature of the application of the TFEU provisions on free movement of capital to tax measures in relation to capital transfers to and from third countries has propelled the Member States to reinstate a certain hierarchy between free movement of capital in intra-EU and third-country situations.[70] In principle, this would seem logical because the purpose of the extension of free movement of capital to third countries does not seem to have been to address every factor potentially affecting the optimal allocation of capital in extra-EU situations. In addition, it may be hard to identify any specific objective in respect of the internal market as regards the type of tax measures at issue in *A v Skatteverket*. In particular, it would seem difficult to argue that a tax measure that potentially restricts the free movement of capital with third countries for that reason also impedes the functioning of the internal market. Article 65(4) TFEU moreover implies that the Council can now decide by unanimity on the compatibility with the Treaties of national measures instead of the CJEU, which is an indication of the politically sensitive nature of the application of the free movement of capital to national measures in third-country situations.

To conclude this section, both the freedom of establishment and the free movement of capital are relevant to direct investment. While the freedom of establishment does not apply to third-country situations, the free movement of capital can be invoked by third-country investors when seeking access to the Single Market. Even if the incentive for extending Article 63 TFEU to third-country situations was not the same as that for intra-EU capital liberalisation, the Court has observed that the free movement of capital to and from third countries is in principle enshrined in EU primary law in the same terms as intra-EU capital mobility. As a result, the same

---

[69] C-101/05 *A v Skatteverket* [2007] ECR I-11531, para 30.
[70] Snell, 'Free Movement of Capital' (n 48) 573.

type of measures are covered by Article 63 TFEU in relation to intra-EU capital movements and to extra-EU capital movements. At the same time, since the legal context of extra-EU capital movements may differ from that of intra-EU capital movements, the Court has indicated that a particular restriction on capital transfers to or from a third country may be justified where it could not be in an intra-EU context.

II. ADMISSION OF THIRD-COUNTRY DIRECT INVESTMENT INTO THE SINGLE MARKET AND ISSUES OF DEMARCATION BETWEEN ARTICLES 49/54 AND 63 TFEU

Given that Article 63 TFEU applies to third-country direct investment and Articles 49/54 TFEU do not, the importance of demarcating between the freedom of establishment and the free movement of capital is readily apparent. In particular, a wide interpretation of the scope of application of Article 63 TFEU so as not merely to cover capital transfers in relation to direct investment, but to include the entire transaction of direct investment, including aspects more properly considered as constituting establishment, is tantamount to granting to third-country investors rights under the TFEU provisions on free movement of capital that they were purposely denied under the TFEU provisions on freedom of establishment.

This section analyses different ways in which this area of overlap can be dealt with on the level of the application of Articles 49/54 and 63 TFEU, which is particularly relevant in third-country situations. The section first argues that a protection-based approach to direct investment, premised upon the parallel application of Articles 49/54 and 63 TFEU, constitutes an unsatisfactory way of dealing with this area of overlap. The section then discusses the exclusive application of either the TFEU provisions on freedom of establishment or those on free movement of capital as part of the 'centre of gravity' test, which has recently been applied by the CJEU.

A. A Protection-based Approach in the Application of Articles 49/54 and 63 TFEU?

Two views have emerged in the literature on how to deal with the area of substantive overlap between Articles 49/54 and 63 TFEU in relation to direct investment.[71] While on one view a national measure that constitutes an obstacle to direct investment should be subjected to scrutiny (so far as possible) in the light of one TFEU freedom or of the other, on the other view such measures should be assessed in the light of both the freedom of establishment and free movement of capital. The

---

[71] Hindelang, *Capital and Foreign Direct Investment* (above n 36) 81 ff; H Fleischer 'Case C-367/98 *Commission v Portugal*, Case C-483/99 *Commission v France* and Case C-503/99 *Commission v Belgium*' in (2003) 2 *CML Rev* 493, 498 (note).

approach that favours the parallel application of Articles 49/54 and Article 63 TFEU to direct investment tends to support the view that direct investment with a third-country dimension automatically falls within the scope of Article 63 TFEU because Article 49 TFEU does not apply to third-country investments, since otherwise these investments would not receive protection.[72] This protection-based approach, which favours considering the comprehensive phenomenon of direct investment under the TFEU provisions on free movement of capital, rests (at least in part) on the assumption that the freedom of establishment and free movement of capital are not distinguishable in their scope of application in relation to direct investment.[73] As a result, the exclusive application of Article 49 TFEU to majority holdings cannot be justified, since direct investment as a sub-category of capital movements is protected by Article 63 TFEU.

Those arguing in favour of the parallel application of Articles 49/54 and 63 TFEU to direct investment find support in case law dealing with intra-EU situations. In a number of cases, the CJEU pointed at the potential overlap in the scope of application of the freedom of establishment and free movement of capital but did not determine whether the application of either of those TFEU freedoms could supersede the application of the other. An example is the case of *Baars*,[74] which concerned the differential taxation of holdings of natural persons in undertakings depending on the domicile of the natural person in issue. In relation to a 100 per cent holding of Mr Baars, who was resident in the Netherlands, in a company incorporated in and with a seat in Ireland, the Court took the view that a:

> 100% holding in the capital of a company having its seat in another Member State undoubtedly brings such a taxpayer within the scope of application of the Treaty provisions on the right of establishment.[75]

After having established an impermissible restriction of the freedom of establishment, the Court found that there was simply 'no need' to consider the application of the free movement of capital.[76] The scrutiny of national measures in the light of these two TFEU freedoms, without distinguishing between their respective scope of application, has been referred to as a matter of 'procedural economy'.[77] That is to say, even if this approach may have resulted in the incorrect legal classification of some of the disputes in issue, this was of no further consequence, since they dealt with purely intra-EU situations and a similar test of compatibility is applied under Articles 49/54 and 63 TFEU.

Those favouring the parallel application of the freedom of establishment and the free movement of capital to direct investment, moreover, find support in the

---

[72] S Hindelang, 'The EC Treaty's Freedom of Capital Movement as an Instrument of International Investment Law?' in A Reinisch and C Knahr (eds), *International Investment Law in Context* (Utrecht, Eleven International Publishing, 2008) 54.

[73] Ibid 59.

[74] C-251/98 *Baars* [2000] ECR I-2787.

[75] Ibid para 21.

[76] Ibid para 42.

[77] Opinion of AG Kokott of 14 July 2005 in C-265/04 *Bouanich v Skatteverket* [2006] ECR I-923.

fact that the Court has often adopted a wide interpretation of the substantive scope of application of the free movement of capital. This is evidenced by the 'Golden Shares' cases,[78] which concern the compatibility with EU law of national systems which grant the executive certain prerogatives to intervene in the share structure and in the management of privatised undertakings in strategically important sectors of the economy. These special powers can take various forms, such as of procedures for administrative authorisations, shares to which privileges are attached and the appointment of members of company bodies. The Commission has challenged these 'golden shares' for imposing restrictions on private shareholdings and on effective participation in the management and control of privatised companies.[79] So far as concerns the question of the applicable freedom, Advocate General (AG) Colomer has consistently taken the view that the 'Golden Shares' cases should be dealt with exclusively under the provisions on freedom of establishment. In his view:

> In each case, what the defendant Member State is seeking to control, using powers of intervention as regards share structure, transfer of assets or certain management decisions, is the formation of the privatised company's corporate will (either by intervening in the composition of the membership or by influencing specific management decisions), an aspect which has little to do with the free movement of capital referred to in [then] Article 56 EC.[80]

The Court, by contrast, has focused its scrutiny of the measures on their compatibility with Article 63 TFEU. After an infringement of the free movement of capital had been established, it took the view that there was '*no need* for a separate examination of the measures at issue in the light of the Treaty rules concerning freedom of establishment' (emphasis added).[81]

The more recent *Volkswagen*[82] case similarly shows the wide interpretation by the CJEU of the substantive scope of application of the free movement of capital in relation to national measures that pose an obstacle to direct investment, as well as the lack of an attempt by the Court to determine whether the German measure at issue was more appropriately tested against the free movement of capital or against the freedom of establishment. The case concerned the compatibility with the EC Treaty of a series of privileges granted to the German State and a region,

---

[78]   The first series of 'Golden Shares' cases were C-367/98 *Commission v Portugal* [2002] ECR I-4731, C-483/99 *Commission v France* [2002] ECR I-4781 and C-367/98 *Commission v Belgium* [2002] ECR I-4809.

[79]   As regards the first series of 'Golden Shares' cases, a distinction can be drawn between the French and Portuguese legislation, which laid down the requirement of prior approval for the acquisition of substantial shareholdings and has thus been qualified as laying down *access* restrictions, and the Belgian rules, which constituted *management* restrictions. See Fleischer (above n 71) 495.

[80]   Opinion of AG Colomer of 6 February 2003 in Joined Cases C-463/00 *Commission v Kingdom of Spain* [2003] ECR I-4581 and C-98/01 *Commission v United Kingdom* [2003] ECR I-4641, para 36. See also Opinion of AG Colomer of 2 July 2001 in Joined Cases C-367/98 *Commission v Portugal* [2002] ECR I-4731, C-483/99 *Commission v France* [2002] ECR I-4781 and C-503/99 *Commission v Belgium* [2002] ECR I-4809, para 21.

[81]   C-483/99 *Commission v France* [2002] ECR I-4781, para 36.

[82]   C-112/05 *Commission v Germany* [2007] ECR I-8995.

the Land of Lower Saxony. The so-called Volkswagen Law limited the voting rights of every shareholder to a maximum of 20 per cent of Volkswagen's share capital. At the same time, a majority of over 80 per cent of shares represented was required for resolutions of the general assembly, in contrast to the general company law, which required only a majority of 75 per cent. In addition, the Federal State and the Land of Lower Saxony could each appoint two representatives to Volkswagen's supervisory board irrespective of the level of their shareholdings. In this case, the Commission did not advance any specific line of argument in support of any restriction on the freedom of establishment.[83] Even if the Court observed that the disputed provisions of the Volkswagen Law addressed, at least in part, the situation of a possible take-over of Volkswagen by a shareholder seeking to exercise a controlling influence over the undertaking, the Court dismissed the action insofar as it was based on a breach of Articles 49/54 TFEU and continued its assessment exclusively in the light of Article 63 TFEU.[84] This type of analysis implies not only that the Volkswagen Law could be tested against the free movement of capital irrespective of whether the potential restriction concerned a shareholding that conferred decisive influence, but also that there was no need to demarcate between the scope of application of the freedom of establishment and the free movement of capital.

The non-exclusive application of Articles 49/54 and 63 TFEU to direct investment has, moreover, found sway in rulings of both the German Bundesfinanzhof[85] and the United Kingdom High Court.[86] For example, the Bundesfinanzhof was seized with an action in relation to the taxation by Germany of dividends from majority shareholdings in the United States and Taiwan. The Bundesfinanzhof took the view that the fact that the share holdings in the United States and Taiwanese companies conferred direct influence did not preclude the situation from falling under the scope of application of both the freedom of establishment and the free movement of capital.[87] It considered that the free movement of capital was affected as much as the freedom of establishment, as a result of which the national measure was struck down in the third-country situations in question.[88] In this case, the Bundesfinanzhof did not distinguish between Articles 49/54 and 63 TFEU on the level of their scope of application, apparently because the national tax legislation in question was applicable independently of the size of the holding.

A more explicit protection-based approach in the parallel application of Articles 49/54 and 63 TFEU in third-country situations can be found in the *FII Group Litigation* case, in which Henderson J of the UK High Court concurred with the claimant's view that Article 63 TFEU could be relied upon even where

---

[83]   Ibid paras 14–16.
[84]   Ibid para 16.
[85]   IR 7/08, 26 November 2008.
[86]   *Test Claimants in the FII Group Litigation v Commissioners for HM Revenue and Customs* [2008] EWHC 2893 (Ch), 27 November 2008.
[87]   IR 7/08, 26 November 2008, para 3(aa).
[88]   Ibid para 3(bb).

the companies concerned were in a relationship conferring control, provided that the national legislation in question was not intended to apply exclusively to companies in such a relationship.[89] Henderson J also took the view that the exclusive application of Articles 49/54 TFEU to a situation involving a majority holding in the case of *Burda*[90] could not be transposed to a third-country context because that case concerned an intra-EU investment.[91] In other words, Henderson J suggested that different internal market freedoms may be applicable to the same types of holdings in relation to the same type of measures and other factual circumstances in the context of intra-EU situations, on the one hand, and extra-EU situations, on the other, since Articles 49/54 TFEU do not apply to third-country situations.

A protection-based approach has also been advanced in the Netherlands by AG Wattel, who defended the view that Article 63 TFEU may apply to majority holdings in view of the fact that Articles 49/54 TFEU are not applicable to third-country situations.[92] He took the view that, since Articles 49/54 and 63 TFEU cannot concurrently apply to situations with a third-country dimension, because Articles 49/54 TFEU are inward-looking, it would only be relevant to distinguish between the substantive scope of application of these two freedoms in an intra-EU context, where both freedoms actually find application.[93] Moreover, he observed that the application of Article 63 TFEU to minority holdings, but not to majority holdings, would have the important consequence that unjustified obstacles to majority holdings by third-country investors would not be caught by the internal market freedoms, but those in relation to minority holdings would be.[94] Furthermore, he considered that the free movement of capital could have a different substantive scope of application in third-country situations from that in intra-EU situations.[95] AG Wattel also challenged the view that Article 63 TFEU would be meaningless with respect to majority holdings, for which he found support in the fact that Article 64 TFEU makes allowance for restrictions on capital movement from and into the Single Market in relation to 'establishment'.[96]

---

[89] *Test Claimants in the FII Group Litigation* (above n 86) paras 74–84. See also the appeal in the Court of Appeal [2010] EWCA Civ 103, 23 February 2010, para 69.

[90] C-284/06 *Burda* [2008] ECR I-4571.

[91] *Test Claimants in the FII Group Litigation* (above n 86) para 84.

[92] Opinion of AG Wattel of 28 November 2006 in Hoge Raad Case 43339. The position of Advocate General in the Netherlands is comparable to that of Advocates General at the CJEU.

[93] Ibid para 4.2.

[94] Ibid. AG Wattel here seems to echo AG Alber in C-251/98 *Baars* [2000] ECR I-2787, para 50: 'Contrary to the position in regard to the right of establishment, the size of the shareholding acquired is immaterial [in regard to the free movement of capital]. The provisions in question afford protection even when all a company's shares are held or acquired, since otherwise the protection enjoyed by an investor would be inversely proportional to the size of his shareholding. However, if the holding in a company reaches a size which enables the investor to exercise a decisive influence over the undertaking's decision-making, the right of establishment will supplement free movement of capital. Such an investment . . . would be protected by the EC Treaty under two separate heads.'

[95] Ibid.

[96] Opinion of AG Wattel (above n 92) para 4.6. The Hoge Raad ruled along the lines of the 'centre of gravity' approach in its judgment of 26 September 2008 in Case 43339, para 3.2.4.

The parallel application of Articles 49/54 and 63 TFEU to direct investment as part of a protection-based approach is not convincing. The argument for the application of Article 63 TFEU to majority holdings on the ground that direct investment is protected by Article 63 TFEU as a subcategory of capital movements overlooks the fact that this provision by its wording only applies to capital transfers in relation to direct investment (as well as establishment) and therefore does not seem to catch any type of restriction to the multifaceted phenomenon of direct investment.[97] In addition, from the fact that the freedom of establishment does not apply to third-country situations, it seems hard to deduce that majority holdings would necessarily need to be considered under Article 63 TFEU instead. Importantly, this argument mixes up considerations based on the territorial and on the substantive scope of application of the freedom of establishment and free movement of capital. The CJEU has never suggested that the free movement of capital would have a different substantive scope of application in an intra-EU and an extra-EU context. On the contrary, the Court in *A v Skatteverket* took the view that the substantive scope of application of Article 63 TFEU is the same with regard to intra-EU and extra-EU capital transfers, although there can be differences on the level of the justification of restrictions on capital movements in third-country situations.[98]

The need to distinguish between the scope of application of Articles 49/54 and 63 TFEU finds support in the reciprocal reservations in the TFEU provisions themselves. While Article 49(2) TFEU provides that the freedom of establishment is 'subject to the provisions of the Chapter relating to capital', Article 65(2) TFEU stipulates that:

> [t]he provisions of this chapter shall be without prejudice to the applicability of restrictions on the right of establishment which are compatible with the Treaties.

Even if the expression 'subject to the provisions of the Chapter relating to capital' enshrined in Article 49(2) TFEU seems to have lost much of its relevance,[99] Article 65(2) TFEU is relevant in the post-Maastricht era. Since Article 63 TFEU is now directly effective and, contrary to Articles 49/54 TFEU, extends to third-country situations, it would seem to follow from Article 65(2) TFEU that a third-country economic operator may not circumvent permissible restrictions on the freedom of establishment by invoking Article 63 TFEU where the freedom of establishment is primarily affected.[100] In other words, these mutual cross-reservations would seem to serve the purpose that, as Member States are under different kinds of obligations under both TFEU provisions, the room for manoeuvre under

---

[97] See, eg: Hindelang, *Capital and Foreign Direct Investment* (above n 36) 110.

[98] C-101/05 *A v Skatteverket* [2007] ECR I-11531, para 31.

[99] As has already been pointed out, in the pre-Maastricht era, the Treaty provisions on free movement of capital were much less potent than the Treaty provisions on freedom of establishment. It was thus important that the substantive scope of (now) Art 49/54 TFEU was not over-stretched so as to catch measures that primarily affect the free movement of capital.

[100] Opinion of AG Bot of 11 November 2007 in C-101/05 *Skatteverket v A* [2007] ECR I-11531, para 96; Opinion of AG Kokott of 14 July 2005 in C-265/04 *Bouanich v Skatteverket* [2006] ECR I-923, n 58.

one freedom is not necessarily affected by the other in areas of substantive overlap.[101]

Even if both Articles 49/54 TFEU and Article 63 TFEU are relevant to direct investment, a distinction should therefore be drawn in the application of the freedom of establishment and free movement of capital in view of the fact that these provisions seem to have a different bearing on different aspects of the multifaceted phenomenon of direct investment. The parallel application of Articles 49/54 and 63 TFEU to FDI could have the result that measures, which would be permissible under the TFEU provisions on establishment, would be struck down under Article 63 even though the freedom of establishment aspect prevails over the free movement of capital aspect.

B. 'Centre of Gravity' Approach in the Application of Articles 49/54 and 63 TFEU

Given the different territorial scope of Articles 49/54 and 63 TFEU, the CJEU has been more careful in its analysis of which TFEU freedom to apply in recent years. The essential characteristic of this recent case law is that the Court recognises that the freedom of establishment aspect of a national measure may supersede the free movement of capital aspect in the field of direct investment, and vice versa.[102] In doing so, the Court has started to depart from a wide interpretation of the substantive scope of application of the TFEU provisions on capital movements in relation to direct investment. At the same time, the Court has recognised that the free movement of capital aspect of a national measure may prevail in a situation that involves a controlling holding that would otherwise fall under the substantive scope of application of the freedom of establishment.

Fidium Finanz[103] initiated the pattern of case law in which the Court more clearly distinguished between the internal market freedoms in their application to third-country situations. The Court was asked to rule on the compatibility with (now) Articles 56 and 63 TFEU of German legislation, which denied companies incorporated under Swiss law and having their registered office and central administration in Switzerland the right to grant credit, on a commercial basis, to customers established in Germany on the ground that these companies did not have the authorisation required by German law to provide financial services in Germany.

---

[101] AG Kokott in *Bouanich* took the cross-reservations to mean that neither one nor the other freedom is ousted in cases of substantive overlap, but they could be applied alongside each other (para 71). A better approach seems to be the one by AG Alber in his Opinion of 14 October 1999 in C-251/98 *Baars* [2000] ECR I-2787. He understands the cross-reservations to indicate that there is an area of substantive overlap between these two Treaty freedoms while underscoring the need to limit their parallel application in certain cases. His approach to the cross-reservations is that they evidence that an infringement of one freedom is not *per se* an infringement of the other (paras 24–25). Alternatively, it can be submitted that the substantive compatibility of national measures with the freedom which is primarily affected creates the presumption of legality in the light of the other freedom.

[102] This type of 'centre of gravity' analysis had already been applied, for example, in the context of distinguishing between ex Arts 43/48 and 49 EC. See C-55/94 *Gebhard* [1995] ECR I-4165, paras 25–28.

[103] C-452/04 *Fidium Finanz* [2006] ECR I-9521.

One of the issues was whether the granting of credit in these circumstances primarily constituted the provision of a service or a movement of capital. The Grand Chamber held that:

> where a national measure relates to the freedom to provide services and the free movement of capital at the same time, it is necessary to consider to what extent the exercise of those fundamental liberties is affected and whether, in the circumstances of the main proceedings, one of those *prevails over* the other. (emphasis added)[104]

The Court considered that the purpose of the German rules was mainly to supervise the provision of financial services.[105] Importantly, although the measures also reduced cross-border financial traffic relating to those services, the Court held that this was merely 'an *unavoidable consequence* of the restriction on the freedom to provide services' (emphasis added).[106] In those circumstances, the Court did not apply those two freedoms in tandem. Since considerations relating to the freedom to provide services prevailed over the free movement of capital aspect of the potential restriction, the Court applied the freedom to provide services even if this meant that the company in question could therefore not derive rights from the internal market freedoms in the third-country situation in question.

This type of 'centre of gravity' approach in the application of the internal market freedoms in third-country situations has been confirmed by the CJEU for Articles 49/54 and 63 TFEU with respect to direct investment in *Thin Cap*.[107] This case concerned the British legislation on thin capitalisation[108] that provides for the re-characterisation of interest payments on intra-group loans as a distribution of profit, which increases the tax liability of the borrowing company. The national tax legislation applied only to situations in which the lending company had a controlling holding in the borrowing company, or where the lending company was itself controlled by a company that had a controlling holding in the borrowing company. As with the situation in *Fidium Finanz*, the Grand Chamber considered that:

> If . . . it were to be accepted that that legislation has restrictive effects on . . . the free movement of capital, such effects must be seen as an *unavoidable consequence* of any restriction on freedom of establishment and do not justify an independent examination of that legislation in the light of [Article] 56 EC. (emphasis added)[109]

The questions referred to the Court were thus to be answered exclusively in the light of Article 49 TFEU. The measure could not, however, be tested against Articles 49/54 TFEU, since it affected the freedom of establishment of the lending

---

[104] Ibid para 34.
[105] Ibid para 45.
[106] Ibid para 48.
[107] C-524/04 *Thin Cap Group Litigation* [2007] ECR I-2107.
[108] Thin capitalisation refers to the situation where a company's debt outweighs its equity as a proportion of total capital. Debt finance in intra-group situations can be advantageous when national tax systems grant interest deductions on intra-group loans. National legislation on thin capitalisation, such as in the case of *Thin Cap*, limits the amount that can be claimed as an interest deduction on such loans.
[109] *Thin Cap Group Litigation* (above n 107) para 34.

company, which as an American company was not connected to the legal order of any of the Member States.[110] This, in turn, did not, however, justify a separate examination of the measure in the light of Article 63 TFEU. In other words, an obstacle to direct investment with a third-country dimension may predominantly fall within the substantive scope of Articles 49/54 TFEU, even if the free movement of capital is also restricted.

It is not only in third-country situations that the Court has become more careful in distinguishing between Articles 49/54 and 63 TFEU in their application to controlling shareholdings. A new approach in the application of Articles 49/54 and 63 TFEU in the context of the 'Golden Shares' jurisprudence found sway in *Commission v Italy*.[111] In this case, the Third Chamber drew a distinction between national measures enabling the Italian authorities merely to obstruct the acquisition of shareholdings, and measures giving the Italian authorities a right to veto certain company decisions. The Court took the view that both Articles 49/54 and 63 TFEU could potentially apply to the former situation, depending on whether other shareholders have the power to determine in a definite manner the activities of the company.[112] By contrast, only Articles 49/54 TFEU apply to the latter type of situation, since that measure affects only those shareholders capable of exerting a definitive influence on the management of the company.[113] Although the case did not involve a third-country situation, AG Colomer had pointed to the importance of demarcating between the scope of application of the TFEU provisions on freedom of establishment and those on free movement of capital in relation to direct investment in view of possible future claims by third-country investors.[114]

Given that the CJEU has become more careful in distinguishing between the scope of application of Articles 49/54 and 63 TFEU in relation to direct investment, the question arises how to conceptualise more concretely the distinction between the freedom of establishment and free movement of capital in their application to controlling shareholdings. One way to do so has been articulated by AG Alber in *Baars*. He argued that:

> the border between the simple investment of capital shares in an undertaking established in another Member State, and actual establishment in that Member State, should be set at a point where a shareholder ceases to confine himself to the mere provision of capital in support of a particular business activity carried on by another person, and begins to become involved himself in conducting the business. Such involvement requires the shareholder to go beyond simply exercising voting rights, and to participate in a way which will enable him to exercise real influence over the company's business decisions.[115]

---

[110] Ibid para 98.
[111] C-326/07 *Commission v Italy* [2009] ECR I-2291. See M O'Brien 'C-326/07 *Commission v Italy*' in (2010) 1 *CML Rev* 245 (note).
[112] Ibid para 38.
[113] Ibid para 39.
[114] See the Epilogue in the Opinion of AG Colomer of 6 November 2008 in C-326/07 *Commission v Italy* [2009] ECR I-2291, paras 89–92.
[115] Opinion of AG Alber of 14 October 1999 in C-251/98 *Baars* [2000] ECR I-2787, para 33.

Similarly, AG Colomer has consistently said that the concept of establishment is related to the 'formation of the corporate will' by the shareholder, whereas the movement of capital merely refers to transfers of assets.[116] The Court has laid down the criterion of definite and decisive influence for the purpose of determining whether a shareholding involves the exercise of Articles 49/54 TFEU rights instead of Article 63 TFEU rights.[117] In this respect, AG Geelhoed has observed in the first *FII Group Litigation* case that the threshold of 'definite influence' serves the purpose of demarcating the scope of application of Articles 49/54 TFEU from that of Article 63 TFEU, while the lower threshold of 'effective participation' is used for demarcating between direct and portfolio investment in relation to the Council's legislative competence under (now) Article 64(2) and (3) TFEU.[118] Upon this view, the distinction between freedom of establishment and free movement of capital on the basis of the criterion of definite and decisive influence is not the same as the distinction between direct and portfolio investment as made in Directive 88/361.[119]

So far as concerns the precise threshold for meeting the criterion of definite and decisive influence, the Court has considered it to have been met in the context of shareholdings of 100 per cent (*Baars*, *FII Group Litigation I*), 75 per cent (*Thin Cap*), 66.66 per cent (*Holböck*) and 50 per cent (*Cadbury Schweppes*). It follows from a ruling of the Third Chamber that it is also conceivable that shareholdings of 5 per cent gives rise to a position of definite and decisive influence when a company has a large number of small shareholders.[120] At the same time, in the first *FII Group Litigation* case a shareholding of 10 per cent was not sufficient to qualify as conferring definite and decisive influence.[121] In other words, the size of the shareholding is not all-important. There may still be definite and decisive influence in case of a minority holding depending on the size of the other shareholdings. By contrast, the lower threshold for a shareholding to fall under the scope of applica-

---

[116] Opinion of AG Colomer of 6 February 2003 in Joined Cases C-463/00 *Commission v Kingdom of Spain* [2003] ECR I-4581 and C-98/01 *United Kingdom of Great Britain and Northern Ireland* [2003] ECR I-4641, para 36.

[117] C-524/04 *Thin Cap Group Litigation* [2007] ECR I-2107, para 27: 'definite influence'. But see Opinion of AG Geelhoed of 6 April 2006 in C-446/04 *FII Group Litigation* [2006] ECR I-11753, para 32: 'decisive influence'. But see also C-284/06 *Burda* [2008] ECR I-4571, para 70: 'In principle, a holding of that size in Burda's capital by RCS gives the latter the right to exercise *definite and decisive* influence over its subsidiary's activities within the meaning of the case-law cited in the previous paragraph of the present judgment' (emphasis added).

[118] Opinion of AG Geelhoed of 6 April 2006 in C-446/04 *FII Group Litigation* [2006] ECR I-11753, para 119: '[i]t is for the national court to decide whether, in a given case, the investment that a UK company holds in a company resident in a third country serves to establish or maintain "lasting and direct links" with the latter company, allowing the UK company to "participate effectively in the management of the company or in its control". I would observe, however, that this is clearly a lower threshold than the "decisive influence" test to which I referred in the context of distinguishing between the scope of application of [ex] Articles 43 and 56 [EC]'. But see Hindelang, *Capital and Foreign Direct Investment* (above n 36) 85 ff.

[119] This seems to be implied in the Opinion of AG Alber in *Baars* (above n 115).

[120] C-326/07 *Commission v Italy* [2009] ECR I-2291, para 38.

[121] See also Joined Cases C-436/08 and C-437/08 *Haribo* [2011] ECR I-305, para 36.

tion of Article 63 TFEU would seem to be underscored by *Commission v Italy*,[122] in which the First Chamber considered that a shareholding of 2 per cent falls under the substantive scope of (now) Article 63 TFEU.

Given the fact that the CJEU has recognised that the freedom of establishment aspect of a restriction by a national measure may supersede the free movement of capital aspect, as well as vice versa, it is important to examine the way in which this 'centre of gravity' test has been applied by the Court. The case law shows that both the purpose of the legislation and the nature of the shareholding are import-ant factors in determining whether a national measure primarily affects the free-dom of establishment or the free movement of capital. For example, in *Thin Cap*, since the national measure addressed only majority holdings, the Grand Chamber considered the alleged restriction exclusively in the light of Articles 49/54 TFEU. In the first *FII Group Litigation* case, the Grand Chamber held that a measure, which applied indistinctly to majority and minority shareholdings, could fall within the scope of both Articles 49/54 and 63 TFEU.[123] Since the nature of the holding of some of the parties to the dispute had not been put before the Court, the national measure was tested against both the freedom of establishment and the free movement of capital.[124]

In *Scheunemann*, which concerned taxation of an acquisition of a shareholding in a capital company established in a third country through inheritance, the Second Chamber recalled that national provisions, which apply to shareholdings acquired solely with the intention of making a financial investment, with no intention of influencing the management and control of the undertaking, must be examined exclusively in the light of the free movement of capital.[125] The Court then observed that the German legislation specified a shareholding so high that the shareholder in the capital company is able to influence its management and control, and imposed conditions designed to ensure that the shareholder does not intervene solely with the intention of making a financial investment.[126] Restrictive effects on the free movement of capital would therefore be an unavoidable conse-quence of a restriction on the freedom of establishment and the national mea-sures at issue thus affected primarily the freedom of establishment.[127] In addition, the testator had a 100 per cent holding in the capital of the company concerned, so that it was able to exert definite influence over its decisions and to determine its activities. As a result, there was 'no need' to examine the national measure at issue in light of the free movement of capital.[128] Moreover, since the capital company was established in a third country, Article 49 TFEU did not apply to the situation at hand.

---

[122] C-174/04 *Commission v Italy* [2005] ECR I-4933.
[123] C-446/04 *FII Group Litigation* [2006] ECR I-11753, para 36.
[124] Ibid para 38.
[125] C-31/11 *Marianne Scheunemann v Finanzamt Bremerhaven* (nyr, 2012), para 23.
[126] Ibid para 29.
[127] Ibid para 30
[128] Ibid paras 31–32.

This type of 'centre of gravity' approach does not mean that any type of measure in relation to a shareholding that confers definite and decisive influence and control is scrutinised in the light of Articles 49/54 TFEU. That position would render nugatory the references to capital movements involving establishment and direct investment in the TFEU provisions on free movement of capital. The case of *Glaxo*,[129] which arose in the context of the restructuring of the Glaxo Wellcome group, shows that the free movement of capital aspect can prevail over the freedom of establishment aspect in respect of a controlling shareholding. Even if the case dealt with an intra-group situation involving a controlling holding, AG Bot referred to a number of characteristics of the situation that militated in favour of the exclusive application of Article 63 TFEU.[130] The national legislation in question, which applied indistinctly to majority and minority holdings, addressed a certain practice that was not intended to obtain a controlling shareholding in the undertaking making the distribution. That practice was, moreover, part of a series of capital movements that did not transform or otherwise affect the decision-making mechanism within the group of companies in issue. The legislation was intended to combat practices which sought to obtain an undue tax advantage. The First Chamber also considered that the free movement of capital aspect of the situation in *Glaxo* prevailed over the freedom of establishment aspect.[131] It pointed, in particular, to the purpose of the legislation in issue, which was to prevent non-resident shareholders from obtaining an undue tax advantage, rather than addressing a practice that had the objective of exercising the freedom of establishment or that resulted from exercising that freedom. The mere fact that the case involved a controlling shareholding, moreover, did not justify an independent examination of that legislation in the light of Article 49 TFEU.

The Grand Chamber judgment in *FII Group Litigation II*[132] provides further guidance for situations in which the centre of gravity test is applied, with the effect that third-country situations involving controlling shareholdings are examined in the light of Article 63 TFEU, rather than Articles 49/54 TFEU. *FII Group Litigation II* served to clarify a number of aspects of the judgment in *FII Group Litigation I* on the same subject matter. By its fourth question, the referring court asked whether a company that is resident in a Member State and has a shareholding in a company resident in a third country giving it definite influence over the decisions of the latter company and enabling it to determine its activities may rely upon Article 63 TFEU in order to challenge a Member State measure that does not apply exclusively to situations in which the parent company exercises decisive influence over the company resident in a third country.[133] The Court recalled that the purpose of the legislation must be taken into account for the determination of whether national legislation regarding tax treatment of dividends falls under the

---

[129] C-182/08 *Glaxo* [2009] ECR I-8591.

[130] Opinion of AG Bot of 9 July 2009 in C-182/08 *Glaxo* [2009] ECR I-8591, para 88.

[131] C-182/08 *Glaxo* [2009] ECR I-8591, para 50.

[132] C-35/11 *Test Claimants in the FII Group Litigation v Commissioners of Inland Revenue* (nyr, 2012).

[133] Ibid para 88.

scope of Articles 49/54 TFEU or Article 63 TFEU.[134] National legislation that only applies to shareholdings which enable the shareholder to confer decisive influence on a company's decisions falls within the scope of Article 49 TFEU, while national provisions that apply to shareholdings acquired solely with the intention of making a financial investment without any intention to influence the management and control of the undertaking must be examined exclusively in the light of Article 63 TFEU.[135] When a measure applies indistinctly to shareholdings that confer decisive influence and shareholdings not conferring such influence, the facts of the case must be taken into account in order to determine whether the situation falls primarily within the scope of one or the other internal market freedom.[136]

Importantly, however, the Court ruled that, as regards the UK legislation on tax treatment of dividends from third countries at issue in the proceedings, it was in fact sufficient to look at the purpose of the legislation – rather than also at the facts of the case, ie the type of shareholding at issue – in order to determine whether the measure falls within the scope of Article 63 TFEU, even if the measure applied indistinctly to controlling holdings and holdings not conferring such influence.[137] The Court took the view that a company resident in a Member State may rely on Article 63 TFEU in order to call into question the legality of national legislation relating to the tax treatment of dividends from a third country, which does not apply exclusively to situations in which the parent company exercises decisive influence over the company paying the dividends.[138] The Court recognised that it is important to ensure that the interpretation of Article 63 TFEU as regards relations with third countries does not enable economic operators who do not fall within the limits of the territorial scope of freedom of establishment to profit from that freedom.[139] Since the measure at issue only concerned tax treatment of dividends, the Court took the view that the national legislation at issue does not relate to the conditions for access of a company from that Member State to the market in a third country or of a company from a third country to the market in that Member State. The Court also pointed out that this interpretation is consistent with Article 64(1) TFEU, which refers to capital movements involving establishment or direct investment.[140]

In other words, the Court took the view in *FII Group Litigation II* that the free movement of capital aspect prevails over the freedom of establishment aspect in situations where national legislation concerns tax treatment of dividends from third countries, where the legislation at issue applies indistinctly to holdings conferring definite and decisive influence and holdings not conferring such influence, even if the situation at hand concerns a controlling shareholding. It follows from the purpose of national legislation, which concerns tax treatment of dividends in

[134] Ibid para 90.
[135] Ibid paras 91–92.
[136] Ibid para 94.
[137] Ibid para 96.
[138] Ibid para 99.
[139] Ibid para 100.
[140] Ibid paras 101–2.

third-country situations and which does not apply exclusively to holdings conferring decisive influence, that it is not necessary to look at the size of the shareholding in order to determine whether the situation falls within the scope of the free movement of capital or of the freedom of establishment. Importantly, the Court recognised that Article 63 TFEU should not grant rights to economic operators in third-country situations that they were purposely denied as a result of the more limited territorial scope of application of Articles 49/54 TFEU. At the same time, the Court rightly pointed to the fact that Article 64(1) TFEU refers to capital movements 'in relation to establishment and direct investment' and thereby recognised that a measure may primarily concern capital transfers in relation to establishment, rather than the conditions for establishment themselves.

Two aspects of the judgment in *FII Group Litigation II* remain unclear, however. First, the Court suggests that the centre of gravity approach in the application of Articles 49/54 and 63 TFEU in third-country situations may differ from that in intra-EU situations. The Court took the view that in intra-EU situations it may be necessary to take into account the facts of a case when a national measure applies indistinctly to shareholdings that confer decisive influence and those that do not, whereas in a third-country situation it may be sufficient to look only at the purpose of the national legislation.[141] In this regard, AG Jääskinen more explicitly advanced the view that in third-country situations 'criteria for the applicability of [the freedom of establishment and free movement of capital] [do] not need to be established, or indeed cannot be established, as only the rules concerning free movement of capital can apply'.[142] While not going so far as to follow this line of reasoning, the Court arguably does similarly mix up considerations based on the substantive and the territorial scope of application of the freedom of establishment and the free movement of capital. The Court seemingly introduces a distinction in the criteria for the application of Articles 49/54 and 63 TFEU to intra-EU and third-country situations, without however providing further explanation of the merits of such an approach.[143]

---

[141] Ibid paras 93–96.

[142] Opinion of AG Jääskinen of 19 July 2012 in C-35/11 *Test Claimants in the FII Group Litigation v Commissioners of Inland Revenue* (nyr, 2012), para 115.

[143] But see C-284/06 *Burda* [2008] ECR I-4571 (Fourth Chamber), para 72, in which the Court tested a national measure on the taxation of dividends, which applied indistinctly to majority and minority holdings, against the freedom of establishment, since the dispute before the referring Court related exclusively to a shareholding conferring definite influence over the decisions of the company distributing the dividends. See also C-303/07 *Aberdeen Property Fininvest Alpha Oy* [2009] ECR I-5145 (First Chamber), paras 30–36, in which the Court, in relation to a national measure that applied indistinctly to majority and minority holdings, ruled that the referred question should be answered with respect to Arts 49/54 TFEU alone, since the company receiving the dividends in question held 100 per cent of the shares in the distributing company. And see C-157/05 *Winfried L Holböck v Finanzamt Salzburg-Land* [2007] ECR I-4051 (Fourth Chamber), para 31, in which the Court, with regard to national legislation on the taxation of dividends that applied irrespective of the extent of the holding which the shareholder had in the company making the distribution, did not determine whether Mr Holböck (an Austrian national who held two-thirds of the share capital of a Swiss company) was justified in invoking Art 63 TFEU, but merely held that, '"even if" Mr Holböck was entitled to do so, the national legislation in issue would be covered by the stand-still clause'. The legislation in question had already been ruled to be incompatible with the free movement of capital in an intra-EU context in C-315/02 *Lenz* [2004] ECR I-7063.

Secondly, it remains unclear whether the centre of gravity approach in the application of Articles 49/54 and 63 TFEU to direct investment in third-country situations warrants a similarly exclusive focus on the purpose of the national legislation at issue outside the specific context of tax treatment of dividends. The Court arguably does not give clear further guidance on the limits of testing indistinctly applicable national measures in the light of Article 63 TFEU in addition to the criterion that a measure should not affect the conditions of market access for economic operators. It can be submitted that the specific purpose of the legislation at issue in *FII Group Litigation II* should arguably weigh more prominently than the event that the constellation of facts at issue concerns a third-country situation in the application of the centre of gravity test to Articles 49/54 and 63 TFEU with regard to direct investment in third-country situations.

To sum up the analysis of this section, direct investment constitutes an area of substantive overlap between the freedom of establishment and the free movement of capital. Articles 49/54 TFEU do not apply to third-country situations, while Article 63 TFEU does. The Court has recognised the need to distinguish between the substantive scope of application of these two TFEU freedoms so as not to grant rights to third-country investors that they are denied under the freedom of establishment. The Court's more recent case law follows a centre of gravity approach, under which the aspect of a situation that is primarily affected by the alleged restriction should be looked at. Therefore, the guiding principle is that national measures are not struck down under the free movement of capital when they are primarily restrictions on the freedom of establishment, even if they also affect transfers of capital in relation to direct investment, as well as vice versa. For this, the Court looks first at the purpose of the national measures and then (but not always in third-country situations, at least so far as concern tax treatment of dividends) at the type of shareholding of the investor. Where a national measure only has restrictive effects on shareholdings that do not confer decisive influence, Article 63 TFEU is necessarily primarily affected, because such a shareholding could not constitute establishment. By contrast, in the case of a controlling shareholding, whether to apply Article 63 TFEU depends on the purpose of the national measure in issue. Recent case law shows that Article 63 TFEU can be primarily affected in a third-country situation where an indistinctly applicable national measure has a restrictive effect on a controlling holding.

III. POST-ESTABLISHMENT TREATMENT OF THIRD-COUNTRY DIRECT INVESTMENT IN THE SINGLE MARKET

Notwithstanding the difficulties of interpretation arising from the substantive overlap of the freedom of establishment and the free movement of capital in their application to direct investment, the admission of third-country direct investment into the Single Market is governed only to a limited extent by the internal market mechanism as a result of the inward-looking nature of Articles 49/54

TFEU. The different territorial scope of application of Articles 49/54 and 63 TFEU moreover has important consequences for the post-establishment treatment of third-country direct investment in the Single Market. This section addresses the question in what circumstances the TFEU freedoms can effectively be invoked by direct investors, which have already established as legal persons in the Single Market, but where the relevant share capital is controlled from outside the Single Market.

After noting the lack of a comprehensive Union regime for the admission and treatment of third-country direct investment in the Single Market, the section first argues that a distinction is to be drawn between the post-establishment treatment of third-country direct investment in the internal economy of a Member State and the issue of rights of intra-EU mobility for third-country direct investors. The section then explores the scope for inconsistencies between EU primary law and relevant Union and Member State practice as regards the post-establishment treatment of third-country direct investment in respect of Article 54 TFEU.

A. Rights of Intra-EU Mobility for Third-Country Direct Investors as Distinguished from their Participation in the Internal Economy of One of the Member States

Article 28 TFEU provides that there shall be a common customs tariff in relations with third countries. Following the conclusion of the Treaty of Rome, there was a progressive move towards a single external tariff, which was established in 1968, as well as towards the harmonisation of non-tariff barriers. As a result, uniform conditions for the importation of goods have been established for every Member State. Moreover, Article 29 TFEU[144] provides that, once non-EU goods have legally entered the Single Market, they are in 'free circulation', so that they can benefit from the same rights as goods originating in the Union. In other words, rights of intra-EU mobility are granted to goods which have lawfully entered the Single Market. By contrast, there is no equivalent Union regime for the admission and treatment of third-country direct investment. While Article 207(1) TFEU now seemingly lays down a requirement for future Union measures shaping the external dimension of the Single Market in the field of FDI to be premised upon 'uniform principles', there has never been an equally comprehensive effort to create a level playing field for FDI flows into the Single Market.

---

[144] 'Products coming from a third country shall be considered to be in free circulation in a Member State if the import formalities have been complied with and any customs duties or charges having equivalent effect which are payable have been levied in that Member State, and if they have not benefited from a total or partial drawback of such duties or charges.'

This does not mean, however, that there is a legislative vacuum with regard to direct investment from third countries. So far as Union autonomous measures are concerned, the CJEU held in *Opinion 1/94* that, although the sole objective expressly mentioned in the TFEU provisions on freedom of establishment is the attainment of that freedom for nationals of the Member States, this does not prohibit the Union institutions:

> from using the powers conferred on them in that field in order to specify the treatment which is to be accorded to nationals of non-member countries.[145]

Consequently, EU secondary legislation may stipulate the conditions for the admission and treatment to be accorded to non-EU direct investment in specific sectors. For instance, the Court in *Opinion 1/94* referred to a number of Directives in the financial services sector, under which financial institutions, having received authorisation to supply certain financial services in one Member State, may pursue such activities in other Member States.[146] Secondary legislation can, moreover, contain restrictions on inbound FDI into the Single Market. For example, the Gas[147] and Electricity[148] Directives provide for the possibility of restricting direct investment from third countries. Similarly, Union external agreements often contain provisions on the admission and treatment of third-country direct investment, which will be investigated in more detail in the next chapter. Although such measures are building blocks for a Union external FDI regime, they do not create uniform conditions for the admission and the treatment to be accorded to third-country direct investment in the Single Market.

Third-country direct investment in the Single Market is, moreover, subject to the laws of the Member States. In essence, as a result of the different territorial scope of application of Articles 49 and 63 TFEU, Member States can impose restrictions and specific requirements on third-country direct investment, provided that these do not primarily affect and unduly restrict the rights that investors hold under the free movement of capital. In addition, Member State legislation may not be incompatible with EU secondary legislation and external agreements. An example of such Member State legislation is the foreign investment code of Germany, under which the German federal government can block third-country direct investment in Germany if such investment would threaten German public policy or public order.[149] Similarly, France has recently revised its

---

[145] *Opinion 1/94* [1994] ECR I-5267, para 90.

[146] Second Council Directive 89/646 of 15 December 1989 on the coordination of laws, regulations and administrative provisions relating to the taking up and pursuit of the business of credit institutions [1989] OJ L386/1; Second Council Directive 90/619 of 8 November 1990 on the coordination of laws, regulations and administrative provisions relating direct life assurance [1990] OJ L330/50.

[147] Directive 2009/73 of the European Parliament and of the Council of 13 July 2009 concerning common rules for the internal market in natural gas, Art 11 [2009] OJ L211/94.

[148] Directive 2009/72 of the European Parliament and of the Council of 13 July 2009 concerning common rules for the internal market in electricity, Art 11 [2009] OJ L211/55.

[149] Dreizehntes Gesetz zur Änderung des Aussenwirtschaftsgesetzes und der Aussenwirtschafts-verordnung, BGBl, 2009 I, 770. For critical analysis, see T Müller-Ibold, 'Foreign Investment in Germany: Restrictions Based on Public Security Concerns and Their Compatibility with EU Law' in

authorisation procedure for foreign investment with implications for public policy, public security or national defence.[150] Both national instruments contain provisions that apply specifically to FDI flowing into the Single Market. Member States have also maintained different exceptions to the free admission of FDI in the services sector in the specific schedules of commitments under the General Agreement on Trade in Services (GATS).[151] These types of national measures are further evidence of the lack of uniform conditions for the admission and treatment of FDI flowing into different Member States from outside the Single Market.

In addition to the absence of a comprehensive Union regime for the admission and treatment of third-country direct investment, there are limits to the way in which the internal market mechanism pertains to the post-establishment treatment of FDI in the Single Market as a result of the inward-looking nature of the freedom of establishment. Importantly, the freedom of establishment does not apply to the initial post-establishment treatment of third-country direct investors in the Single Market. So far as the application of the freedom of establishment is concerned, the initial post-establishment treatment of third-country direct investment therefore concerns the participation of a third-country investor in the internal economy of a Member State. Such investment may be subject to specific EU secondary legislation. Yet it is only when secondary rights of mobility within the Single Market are subsequently invoked that the freedom of establishment comes into play.

The limited bearing of the internal market mechanism on the initial post-establishment treatment of third-country direct investment is illustrated by *Thin Cap*,[152] which dealt with UK tax legislation on the re-characterisation of interest payments as a redistribution of profits in the context of intra-group loans. Some of the test cases involved a parent company, resident in a third country, controlling an EU-resident subsidiary, either directly or indirectly through another EU-resident subsidiary. In all cases the United Kingdom-resident company receiving the loan was controlled through a shareholding of 75 per cent by a non-resident company. After taking the view that the freedom of establishment aspect of the case prevailed over the free movement of capital aspect in respect of the tax legislation at issue with regard to intra-group loans, the CJEU took the view that Article 49 TFEU has no bearing on the application of national legislation:

C Herrmann and JP Terhechte (eds), *European Yearbook of International Economic Law* (Heidelberg, Springer, 2010); C Tietje, *Beschränkungen ausländischer Unternemensbeteiligungen zum Schutz vor "Staatsfonds" – Rechtliche Grenzen eines neuen Investitionsprotektionismus*, Policy Papers on Transnational Economic Law (Transnational Economic Law Research Center, 2007), available at www2.jura.uni-halle.de/telc/PolicyPaper26.pdf.

[150] Code monétaire et financier législatif, art R153-1 and 2, as established by Décret no 2005-1739 of 30 December 2005; last modified by Décret no 2012-691 of 7 May 2012.

[151] See the various limitations on market access for commercial presences in the schedules of commitments to the GATS (available at http://tsdb.wto.org/default.aspx). For example, Portugal has maintained the following limitation in the field of telecommunications services: 'The direct or indirect participation of natural persons, who are non-nationals of EC Member States or non-EC companies or firms in the capital of carriers of complementary telecommunications services, whose exploitation involves the use of complementary telecommunications infrastructures, cannot exceed 25 per cent'.

[152] C-524/04 *Thin Cap Group Litigation* [2007] ECR I-2107.

to a situation in which a resident company is granted a loan by a company which is resident in another Member State and which does not itself have a controlling shareholding in the borrowing company and where each of those companies is directly or indirectly controlled by a common parent company which is resident, for its part, in a non-member country.[153]

In other words, the common parent company could not benefit from the freedom of establishment, because it was resident in a third country and therefore not connected to the legal order of any of the Member States. At the same time, even though the loan was structured through a subsidiary of the parent company in a Member State, this intermediate lending company had not exercised any freedom of establishment rights, because it did not have a controlling holding in the borrowing company. In view of the inward-looking nature of the TFEU freedom of establishment, the initial post-establishment treatment of third-country direct investment (in this case of the intermediate lending company) thus concerns the participation of third-country direct investors (in this case of the common parent company) in the internal economy of a Member State. The internal market mechanism has no bearing on such a third-country situation, unless the treatment at issue primarily falls within the scope of application of the free movement of capital.[154]

In addition, the judgment in *Thin Cap* shows that an intra-EU capital movement (in this case an intra-group loan) can, depending on the economic context in which it takes place, primarily be considered as being part of the economic activity of establishment. The Court recognised the importance of the fact that the third-country parent company could decisively influence the funding decisions of both the intermediate lending company and the borrowing company.[155] In other words, what was important was not the origin of the loan capital, but the nationality of the natural or legal person controlling the loan capital. Even an intra-EU capital flow can thus primarily concern the post-establishment treatment of third-country direct investment in the internal economy of a Member State and fall outside the scope of application of both Articles 49/54 and 63 TFEU. It follows that the internal market mechanism can operate differently with respect to capital flows within the Single Market in a situation where the capital is directly or indirectly controlled from outside the Single Market.

The lack of a comprehensive Union regime for the admission and treatment of third-country direct investment and the inward-looking nature of the freedom of establishment, moreover, raise the issue of secondary rights of mobility for third-country investors under the internal market mechanism. In the field of trade in goods, the operation of the principle of free circulation under Article 29 TFEU is facilitated by the fact that the Union has a common policy in respect of the

---

[153] Ibid para 98.
[154] The Court drew the same distinction between the treatment of third-country direct investment in the internal economy of a Member State, on the one hand, and the issue of rights of intra-EU mobility, on the other hand, in *Opinion 2/92* [1995] ECR I-521, paras 7–8. The Court specified that the participation of foreign-controlled undertakings in intra-EU trade is covered by the internal market rules.
[155] *Thin Cap Group Litigation* (above n 152), para 99.

importation of third-country goods. The common customs tariff prevents non-EU goods from entering the Single Market via the Member State with the lowest tariffs for them to be sold in other Member States that have higher tariffs vis-à-vis imports from third countries by benefitting from the free movement of goods. The close link between the principle of free circulation for goods originating in third countries and the existence of a uniform admission regime as regard the external dimension of the Single Market as a result of the establishment of the common commercial policy was recognised by the CJEU in *Donckerwolcke*.[156] In this case, the Court held that:

> The assimilation to products originating within the Member States of goods in 'free circulation' may only take full effect if these goods are subject to the same conditions of importation both with regard to customs and commercial considerations, irrespective of the state in which they were put in free circulation.[157]

In the view of the Court, a uniform admission regime did not merely facilitate the working of rights of intra-EU mobility for goods originating in third countries, but it followed from the 'system of the Treaty' that such secondary rights of mobility were in fact conditional upon the establishment of a common commercial policy.[158]

Following this logic, in the early years of the common market, Member States were still allowed to restrict intra-Community trade in products originating in third countries for which there was not yet a uniform Community import regime. For a long time, restrictions on the intra-Community mobility of goods originating from third countries could be imposed by the Member States under (then) Article 115 EC on the condition that they notified such measures to the other Member States and the Commission. The Commission retained the right to require the amendment or abolition of such measures. Restrictions could be imposed where there was a lack of uniform conditions of importation, both as a result of national measures of commercial policy and sub-quota in Community measures, as well as in the case of economic difficulties in one or more Member States. These were much used in relation to sensitive products, such as motor vehicles, textiles, clothing and bananas, even beyond the transition period for the establishment of the common commercial policy.[159] Subsequent Council regulations that sought to establish uniform conditions of importation still contained a safeguard mechanism for the Commission to take appropriate measures, as well as a provision leaving scope for the adoption of national policies.[160]

It can be observed that uniformity is a less critical imperative in the field of establishment than in the field of trade in goods and that uniformity is therefore a

---

[156] 41/76 *Donckerwolcke* [1976] ECR 1921.

[157] Ibid para 25.

[158] Ibid para 24.

[159] For analysis, see ELM Völker (ed), *Protectionism and the European Community*, 1st edn (Deventer, Kluwer Law and Taxation, 1983).

[160] See, eg Council Regulation 3285/94 of 22 December 1994 on the common rules for imports, Arts 18 and 24 [1994] OJ L349/53.

less prominent feature of the Union's legislative approach in respect of establish-ment.[161] Nevertheless, it has been suggested that there is a close similarity between the principle of free circulation in the field of trade in goods and the issue of secondary rights of mobility enjoyed by third-country direct investors.[162] Despite the lack of a comprehensive Union regime for the admission and treatment of third-country direct investment, it can indeed be observed that both the Court and AG Geelhoed in *Thin Cap* assumed that the intermediate lending company, estab-lished in one of the Member States (Ireland), could have invoked Articles 49/54 TFEU if the intermediate lending company had had a controlling holding in the borrowing company.[163] In other words, the national measure could have affected the freedom of establishment of the intermediate lending company, had the direct investment been structured differently. It follows that companies in the Single Market, which are controlled by third-country investors, can invoke the freedom of establishment so far as concerns their establishment in another Member State.[164] Upon this logic, a company, even if it is controlled by a third-country parent com-pany, effectively ceases to be a 'foreign' company and assumes the corporate nationality of the host Member State of initial establishment so that it can invoke the freedom of establishment for the purpose of investing in a second Member State.

At the same time, the concern has been expressed that third-country direct investors could thus circumvent certain restrictions of a Member State vis-à-vis third-country direct investment by first establishing as a legal person in a Member State with a liberal admissions policy and subsequently invoking Articles 49/54 TFEU in order to establish in another Member State.[165] In addition, as a result of the secondary rights of mobility enjoyed by non-EU-controlled companies in the Single Market, the preferential treatment of EU companies by the Union legisla-tor in principle seems to be prohibited so far as their rights of intra-EU mobility are concerned.[166] That this type of concern is real is evidenced by the German and French investment codes, mentioned above, which both provide for a definition of corporate investors on the basis of control, in fact distinguishing between EU

---

[161] M Cremona, 'The External Dimension of the Single Market: Building (on) the Foundations' in CS Barnard and J Scott (eds), *The Law of the Single European Market: Unpacking the Premises* (Oxford, Hart Publishing, 2002) 374.

[162] J Karl, 'The Competence for Foreign Direct Investment, New Powers for the European Union?' (2004) 3 *Journal of World Investment and Trade* 413, 414.

[163] C-524/04 *Thin Cap Group Litigation* [2007] ECR I-2107, para 99. Opinion of AG Geelhoed of 29 June 2006 in ibid para 97.

[164] J Ceyssens, 'Towards a Common Foreign Investment Policy? Foreign Investment in the European Constitution' (2005) 3 *Legal Issues of European Integration* 259, 261. But see R Torrent, *Derecho y Práctica de las Relaciones Exteriores en la Unión Europea* (Barcelona, Cedecs, 1998) 96 ff; R Torrent, 'The Contradictory Overlapping of National, EU, Bilateral, and the Multilateral Rules on Foreign Direct Investment: Who is Guilty of Such a Mess' (2011) 5 *Fordham International Law Journal* 1377, 1394 ff.

[165] Y Loussouarn, 'Le droit d'établissement des sociétés' (1990) 2 *Revue trimestrielle de droit européen* 229, who speaks of 'conséquences néfastes d'un tel laxisme' (236) and of 'libéralisme excessif' (238).

[166] For a discussion in the context of the Community's reciprocity policy in the late 1980s and early 1990s in the field of financial services, see P Eeckhout, *The European Internal Market and International Trade: A Legal Analysis* (Oxford, Clarendon Press, 1994) 62 ff.

and third-country natural or legal persons.[167] Provisions to this effect can, moreover, be found in Union secondary legislation.[168] Such Union and Member State legal instruments pierce the corporate veil and look at the natural or legal person by which a certain legal entity is controlled for the purpose of determining the legal nexus between a corporate investor and the legal order of a Member State.[169] The question that arises is whether and in what circumstances that type of provision is consistent with Articles 49/54 TFEU. The remainder of this section explores the relevant case law and practice so far as it concerns the rights of intra-EU mobility enjoyed in the Single Market by corporate entities, which are controlled by third-country natural or legal persons.

B. Scope for Inconsistencies between Articles 49/54 TFEU and Relevant Union and Member State Treatment

Article 49 TFEU can be invoked only by nationals of one of the Member States. The CJEU has repeatedly held that it is for each Member State, having regard to EU law, to lay down the conditions for the acquisition and loss of nationality.[170] Yet, even if third-country nationals cannot invoke Article 49 TFEU, secondary rights of mobility can be granted to them under Union secondary legislation.[171] For example, Directive 2003/109 provides for a number of specific grounds upon which third-country nationals who are long-term residents in one Member State may reside in a second Member State.[172] In addition, more far-reaching (but still fairly limited) rights of intra-EU mobility are granted under EU secondary legislation as part of a policy of attracting third-country nationals for the purpose of highly qualified employment.[173] Such EU secondary legislation in the field of free movement of persons evidences a similar logic for the granting of secondary rights of mobility as in the field of trade in goods. In principle, the granting of secondary rights of mobility for third-country nationals is facilitated by uniform conditions for their admission so far as concerns the external dimension of the Single Market. Where such uniform conditions of admission are absent, the Member States are

---

[167] Dreizehntes Gesetz (above n 149) 770; Code monétaire et financier législatif, art R153-1. On the French code, see also Commission press release, 12 October 2006, IP/06/1353.

[168] See text at III.B and accompanying notes.

[169] For a similar type of analysis in an international legal context, see P Acconci, 'Determining the Internationally Relevant Link between a State and a Corporate Investor: Recent Trends concerning the Application of the "Genuine Link" Test' (2004) 1 *Journal of World Investment and Trade* 139.

[170] C-135/08 *Rottmann* [2010] ECR I-1449, para 39.

[171] P Oliver, 'Non-Community Nationals and the Treaty of Rome' (1985) *Yearbook on European Law* 57; M Hedemann-Robinson, 'Third-Country Nationals, European Union Citizenship, and Free Movement of Persons: A Time for Bridges rather than Divisions' (1996) *Yearbook on European Law* 321.

[172] Council Directive 2003/109 of 25 November 2003 concerning the status of third-country nationals who are long-term residents, Art 14(2) [2004] OJ L16/44.

[173] Council Directive 2009/50 of 25 May 2009 on the conditions of entry and residence of third-country nationals for the purposes of highly qualified employment, Art 18 [2009] OJ L155/17.

at liberty to restrict the intra-EU mobility of third-country natural persons unless such rights are granted under EU secondary legislation.

So far as legal persons are concerned, Article 54 TFEU extends the freedom of establishment to:

> companies or firms formed in accordance with the law of a Member State and having their registered office, central administration or principal place of business within the Union.[174]

These criteria serve as connecting factors with the legal system of a Member State, as does nationality in the case of natural persons.[175] On the face of it, Article 54 TFEU merely stipulates the criteria of incorporation and seat as determining when a legal entity comes within the personal scope of application of the freedom of establishment. In this respect, it is interesting to observe that the French and the Italian delegations proposed adding a third paragraph to (now) Article 54 TFEU in the run-up to the conclusion of the Treaty of Rome, pursuant to which companies, even if they are established within the Single Market under the laws of one of the Member States, would not be able to invoke the freedom of establishment if they were controlled by third-country natural or legal persons.[176] However, this proposal was rejected.[177]

In view of the criteria enshrined in Article 54 TFEU, the Court observed in *Daily Mail*[178] that companies are creatures of national law and exist only by virtue of the national legislation that determines their incorporation and functioning.[179] Similarly, in *Cartesio*,[180] the Court noted that, since there is no uniform EU law definition of the companies that may benefit from the TFEU freedom of establishment on the basis of a single connecting factor, the question whether Articles 49/54 TFEU apply to a company that seeks to benefit from the rights enshrined in that provision is a preliminary matter that can be resolved only by the applicable

---

[174] It is specified that "'[c]ompanies or firms" means companies or firms constituted under civil or commercial law, including cooperative societies, and other legal persons governed by public or private law, save those which are non-profit-making'.

[175] For analysis of the Court's case law in relation to corporate mobility in the Union, see CHJI Panayi, 'Corporate Mobility in Private International Law and European Community Law: Debunking Some Myths' (2009) *Yearbook on European Law* 123.

[176] Proposal by the French delegation of 17 January 1957: 'Toutefois, un Etat membre peut demander à la Commission que soient exclues du bénéfice desdits articles les sociétés au sens de l'alinéa précédent qui, bien qu'établies sur le territoire d'un des Etats membres et constituées conformément aux lois de cet état, sont soumises à une influence prépondérante exercée par des ressortissants d'un Etat tiers ou des capitaux étrangers à la Communauté' (Doc MAE 47/57). ['However, a Member State may request the Commission that companies, as referred to in the previous paragraph, be excluded from the benefit of those provisions when they are controlled by third country nationals or capital from outside the Community, even if they are established on the territory of one of the Member States and constituted in conformity with its legislation' trans]. On 8 January 1957, a similar proposal had been made by both the French and the Italian delegation (Doc MAE 157/57).

[177] Proposal of 4 February 1957, Doc MAE 363/57. For analysis, see Y Scholten, 'Company Law in Europe' (1966–67) *CML Rev* 377.

[178] 81/87 *Daily Mail* [1998] ECR 5483.

[179] Ibid para 19.

[180] C-210/06 *Cartesio* [2008] ECR I-9641.

national law.[181] While some Member States only require the registered office to be in their territory (the 'incorporation' theory), other Member States also require the *siège réel* (that is, the central administration of a company) to be situated in their territory (the 'real seat' theory). Article 54 TFEU lays down criteria for determining corporate nationality which are acceptable to the holders of both theories and places on the same footing, as connecting factors, the registered office, central administration and principal place of business of a company.[182]

The reference in Article 54 TFEU to companies 'formed in accordance with the law of a Member State' is therefore not to be interpreted as a concession to the incorporation theory,[183] but is merely intended to ensure that only companies that have a legal presence within the Single Market, as opposed to third-country economic operators, could benefit from the freedom of establishment within the Single Market. From the explicit criteria enshrined in Article 54 TFEU it seems to follow that, even if the central administration of an incorporated entity is outside the Single Market, such a company can invoke the freedom of establishment in Member States that operate the incorporation theory. On the other hand, branches of companies whose head office is outside the Union (known as 'direct branches') will not be able to do so, since a branch is a place of business but is not incorporated.[184] In addition, the Court has confirmed that Article 54 TFEU simply defines the class of persons to whom the right of establishment applies, so that it does not give rise to substantive rights different from those secured by Article 49 TFEU.[185]

The issue of whether Article 54 TFEU allows Member States to discriminate between companies on the basis of the nationality of their shareholders arose in *Factortame II*,[186] which dealt with the 'nationality' of ships, as opposed to the nationality of natural and legal persons. The United Kingdom had amended its legislation on the registration of fishing vessels in order to put a stop to the practice known as 'quota hopping', whereby fishing quotas were allegedly 'plundered' by vessels flying the British flag but lacking any genuine link with the United Kingdom.[187] A fishing vessel was only eligible to be registered in the new register if (a) the vessel was British-owned; (b) the vessels were managed, and its operations were directed and controlled, from within the United Kingdom; and (c) any charterer, manager or

---

[181] Ibid para 109.

[182] Ibid para 106.

[183] But see H Groeben, J von der Thiessing and CD Ehlermann, *Kommentar zum EWG-Vertrag*, 4th edn (Baden-Baden, Nomos, 1991) 1023, 1026.

[184] Cremona, 'External Dimension' (above n 161) 370 ff. For a definition of a 'branch' in EU law, see 33/78 *Somafer* [1978] ECR 2183, para 12: 'the concept of branch, agency or other establishment implies a place of business which has the appearance of permanency, such as the extension of a parent body, has a management and is materially equipped to negotiate business with third parties so that the latter, although knowing that there will if necessary be a legal link with the parent body, the head office of which is abroad, do not have to deal directly with such parent body but may transact business at the place of business constituting the extension'.

[185] C-70/95 *Sodemare* [1997] ECR I-3395, para 25.

[186] C-221/89 *Factortame II* [1991] ECR I-3905.

[187] Ibid para 4.

operator of the vessel was a qualified person or company.[188] The Court took the view that the competence to determine the conditions for the registration of vessels is vested in the Member States.[189] However, a Member State has to comply with the prohibition of discrimination against nationals of other Member States in exercising that power.[190] The Court held that:

> a condition of the type at issue in the main proceedings which stipulates that where a vessel is owned or chartered by natural persons they must be of a particular nationality and where it is owned or chartered by a company the shareholders and directors must be of that nationality is contrary to Article [49 TFEU].[191]

A company that is controlled by nationals of another Member State could thus not be precluded from owning or chartering a vessel in the United Kingdom, since such a restriction constitutes a violation of the principle of non-discrimination enshrined in Articles 49/54 TFEU.[192] At the same time, *Factortame II* does not explicitly take into consideration the issue of discrimination against companies that are controlled by third-country natural or legal persons, which the Court did not need to on the facts of the case.[193]

From the formalistic criteria enshrined in Article 54 TFEU it would seem that the nationality of the host Member State could be more easily obtained by legal persons than by natural persons. While it is clear that a non-profit company is excluded from invoking Article 54 TFEU,[194] even a mailbox-company seems to be included in the personal scope of application of the freedom of establishment. The 1962 General Programme for the elimination of restrictions on the freedom of establishment laid down the condition that a legal person must be involved on a stable and continuous basis in the economic life of a Member State in order to be able to invoke the freedom of establishment.[195] However, this requirement of

---

[188] Ibid para 6.

[189] Ibid para 13.

[190] Ibid para 14.

[191] Ibid para 30. To this the Court added in para 31 that '[s]uch a condition is also contrary to [Article 55 TFEU] of the Treaty, under which Member States must accord nationals of the other Member States the same treatment as their own nationals as regards participation in the capital of companies or firms within the meaning of Article [54 TFEU]'.

[192] For critical analysis, see C Noirfalisse, 'The Community System of Fisheries Management and the *Factortame* Case' (1992) *Yearbook on European Law* 324, who argues that the Court effectively put the cart before the horse by allowing a national of a Member State to invoke the freedom of establishment to obtain the nationality of the host Member State where it wants to establish (347). This argument, however, hinges on the possibility to equate the registration of ships with the granting of nationality to natural and legal persons.

[193] In the view of Cremona, *Factortame II* does not apply to third-country nationals, so that Member States can attach nationality conditions to the formation of companies. However, once a third-country subsidiary is formed, it will receive Union treatment. See Cremona, 'External Dimension' (above n 161) 370.

[194] 182/83 *Fearon* [1984] ECR 3677, para 8.

[195] The 1962 Programme général pour la suppression des restrictions à la liberté d'établissement stipulates with regard to the beneficiaries of freedom of establishment: 'des sociétés . . . à condition que, dans le cas où elles n'ont que leur siège statutaire à l'intérieur de la Communauté ou dans un pays ou territoire d'outre-mer, leur activité présente un lien effectif et continu avec l'économie d'un Etat membre ou d'un pays ou territoire d'outre-mer, étant exclu que ce lien puisse dépendre de la nationalité,

economic activity has not been confirmed by the CJEU, at least not for EU direct investors. In *Centros*,[196] the Court was asked to rule on whether a Member State (Denmark) could refuse the registration of a branch of a company which has its registered office in another Member State (the United Kingdom) where that company does not carry on any business in that Member State, and when the purpose of the branch is to enable the company concerned to carry on its entire business in the Member State in which that branch is to be set up so as to circumvent a more restrictive company law in that Member State.[197] The Court held that:

> the fact that a national of a Member State who wishes to set up a company chooses to form it in the Member State whose rules of company law seem to him the least restrictive and to set up branches in other Member States cannot, in itself, constitute an abuse of the right of establishment.[198]

In the view of the Court, a requirement for the registered office to carry out business in the United Kingdom in order for it to be able to invoke the freedom of establishment and set up a branch in Denmark constitutes an obstacle to the exercise of the freedom of establishment, which could not be justified with reference to an abuse of rights.[199]

The requirement in the 1962 General Programme of being engaged in stable and continuous economic activity in a Member State in order for a direct investor to be able to invoke the freedom of establishment has thus been denied for EU direct investors. A requirement of substantive business activity for companies which are controlled by third-country natural or legal persons, but not for EU companies, would in itself amount to discriminatory post-establishment treatment of third-country direct investors. At the same time, in view of the inward-looking nature of the freedom of establishment, it cannot be excluded that such a requirement could be justified in the context of circumventing constructions by third-country direct investors where this would not be the case as regards EU companies.[200]

notamment des associés ou des membres des organes de gestion ou de surveillance ou des personnes détenant le capital social' [1962] OJ 36. ['companies on condition that, if they only have their statutory seat within the Community or in an overseas country or territory, their activity constitutes an effective and continuous link with the economy of a Member State or of an overseas country or territory, it being excluded that this link could depend on nationality, in particular of the partners or members of management or supervising bodies or of persons holding the share capital' trans]. The Programme has been ruled to '[provide] useful guidance for the implementation of the relevant provisions of the Treaty'. See 79/85 *Segers* [1986] ECR 2375, para 15.

[196] C-212/97 *Centros* [1999] ECR I-1459.
[197] Ibid para 14.
[198] Ibid para 27.
[199] See also C-167/01 *Inspire Art* [2003] ECR I-10155, para 95, where the Court took the view that '[t]he reasons for which a company chooses to be formed in a particular Member State are, save in the case of fraud, irrelevant with regard to the application of the rules on freedom of establishment'.
[200] So far as the post-establishment treatment of commercial presences in the services sector is concerned, see also Art V(6) GATS: '[a] service supplier of any other Member that is a juridical person constituted under the laws of a party to a [regional economic integration agreement] shall be entitled to treatment granted under such agreement, provided that it engages in *substantive business operations* in the territory of the parties to such agreements' (emphasis added).

An examination of Article 54 TFEU and the relevant case law therefore indicates that the formalistic criteria of incorporation and of seat are guiding for the purpose of determining whether a company in the Single Market, which is controlled by third-country natural or legal persons, can invoke the TFEU freedom of establishment. As a result, rights of intra-EU mobility are in principle granted to legal persons in the Single Market which are controlled by third-country direct investors. The same picture does not emerge, however, from an examination of Union secondary legislation as regards the post-establishment treatment of third-country direct investment, such as in the field of air transport and energy. Rather, a number of instruments can be identified that define the nationality of a corporate entity on the basis of ownership and control, so that the specified treatment in those instruments does not apply to companies in the Single Market that are directly or indirectly controlled by third-country nationals.[201]

For instance, in the field of air transport, Regulation 1008/2008 provides common rules for the operation of air services in the Union.[202] Article 4(f) stipulates that an undertaking shall be granted an operating licence by the competent licensing authority of a Member State provided that:

> Member States and/or nationals of Member States own more than 50% of the undertaking and effectively control it, whether directly or indirectly through one or more intermediate undertakings, except as provided for in an agreement with a third country to which the [Union] is a part.[203]

Moreover, Article 2(9) specifies that:

> 'effective control' means a relationship constituted by rights, contracts or any other means which, either separately or jointly and having regard to the considerations of fact or law involved, confer the possibility of directly or indirectly exercising a decisive influence on an undertaking, in particular by: (a) the right to use all or part of the assets of an undertaking; (b) rights or contracts which confer a decisive influence on the composition, voting or decisions of the bodies of an undertaking or otherwise confer a decisive influence on the running of the business of the undertaking.

In other words, a company which is incorporated in one of the Member States does not qualify for an operating licence where it is controlled by third-country natural or legal persons, even if this is through one or more intermediate holding companies in the Single Market.

Similar types of provisions can be found in EU secondary legislation in the energy sector. Directive 2009/72 provides for common rules for the internal market in the field of electricity.[204] Under Article 11(1), where certification is requested

---

[201] See also Torrent, 'The Contradictory Overlapping of National, EU, Bilateral, and the Multilateral Rules' (above n 164) 1378 ff.

[202] Regulation 1008/2008 of the European Parliament and of the Council of 24 September 2008 on common rules for the operation of air services in the Community [2008] OJ L293/3.

[203] Article 2(3) stipulates that 'undertaking' means 'any natural or legal person, whether profit-making or not, or any official body whether having its own legal personality or not'.

[204] Directive 2009/72, Art 11.

by a transmission system owner or a transmission system operator which is controlled by a person or persons from a third country or third countries, or when there are circumstances that would result in a person or persons from a third country or third countries acquiring control of a transmission system or transmission system operator, the regulatory authorities in question must notify the Commission. In addition, Article 11(3)(b) stipulates that the regulatory authority shall refuse the certification if it has not been demonstrated that this will not put at risk the security of energy supply of the Member State and the Community. In other words, regulatory authorities may be under an obligation to refuse certification where an incorporated entity in one of the Member States is owned or controlled by non-EU nationals.[205] Notwithstanding the fact that rights of intra-EU mobility are in principle granted to companies in the Single Market which are controlled by third-country direct investors, these are examples of secondary legislation that operates differently in relation to companies which have been constituted in accordance with the laws of a Member State but which are directly or indirectly controlled by non-EU natural or legal persons.

The issue of discriminatory treatment of non-EU companies in the Single Market also came up in the context of accession to the Union of eight Central and Eastern European countries. A non-binding Memorandum of Understanding (MoU) on the interplay with EU law of pre-existing BITs with the United States was concluded on 22 September 2003 between the Commission, the Central and Eastern European countries concerned and the United States.[206] The MoU draws a distinction between Union and Member State exceptions to national treatment of non-EU companies. It states that Article 54 TFEU does not distinguish between companies according to the nationality of their owners, so that restrictions by a Member State on the exercise of the right of establishment by companies satisfying the criteria of that provision, but controlled by an American natural or legal person, can be challenged in the national courts.[207] The MoU added, however, that:

> Article [54 TFEU] does not prevent the [Union] legislator to provide for different treatment of third country companies and firms according to their ownership in the pursuit of a common policy or when adopting measures under specific treaty provisions (e.g., Article [64(2) TFEU]).[208]

Moreover, and in contrast, Article 54 TFEU would not allow the Union legislator to authorise individual Member States to adopt measures which are not consistent with that provision. The MoU thus advances an interpretation of the operation of the internal market mechanism in relation to FDI, pursuant to which legal persons that are incorporated in one of the Member States, but which are controlled by

---

[205] See also Directive 2009/73, Art 11.
[206] Understanding concerning Certain US Bilateral Investment Treaties, signed by the United States, European Commission, and candidate countries for accession to the European Union, 22 September 2003, available at www.state.gov/s/l/2003/44366.htm.
[207] Ibid annex G, paras 2–3.
[208] Ibid annex G, para 4.

American natural or legal persons, are in principle granted Union treatment. Yet, while the Union can subject non-EU companies to differential treatment so far as concerns their intra-EU mobility, the Member States cannot do so.

There seems to be a prima facie inconsistency between the rights of secondary mobility of corporate entities that are controlled by third-country natural or legal persons, on the basis of an interpretation of the formalistic criteria of incorporation and seat enshrined in Article 54 TFEU and the relevant case law, on the one hand, and a restriction of such rights of intra-EU mobility under EU secondary legislation, on the other hand. At the same time, in view of the application of the formalistic criteria enshrined in Article 54 TFEU, it is arguable that such restrictions on the intra-EU mobility of non-EU controlled companies could in some instances be easier to justify than in relation to EU companies under Article 52(1) TFEU, such as on grounds of public policy or public security.[209] A parallel could here perhaps be drawn with the case of *A v Skatteverket*, where the Court ruled that restrictions on extra-EU capital transfers may be easier to justify than restrictions on intra-EU capital transfers. It seems possible to argue, at least in principle, that the same type of reasoning could be applied to restrictions on the secondary rights of mobility of third-country direct investors, as opposed to those of EU direct investors, because the former are effectively part of a third-country situation. For instance, it has been observed that the restrictions on third-country direct investment in the context of the energy Directives make sure that third-country energy providers are not treated *more* favourably than investors within the Union who are, inter alia, subject to the TFEU rules on competition.[210]

There seems to be more difficulty with the interpretation of Article 54 TFEU in the MoU, pursuant to which a distinction ought to be drawn between the differential treatment of third-country direct investors by the Union and by the Member State. If the EU legislator were to prescribe the differential post-establishment treatment of non-EU undertakings in situations where it would be incompatible with Article 54 TFEU for the Member States to do so, there is the risk that the Union legislator would infringe EU primary law in the adoption and implementation of EU secondary legislation.[211] On the other hand, there is now potentially more scope for the justification of such differential treatment by the Union, as opposed to by the Member States, in view of the Union's exclusive competence under Article 207 TFEU to conduct a common policy in the field of FDI on the basis of uniform principles.[212] This requires an integrated approach to the post-establishment treatment of third-country direct investment.

---

[209] See, by analogy, the case law on requirements of public security and overriding reasons of public interest as justification for restrictions on the free movement of capital: C-171/08 *Commission v Portugal* [2010] ECR I-6817, para 69; C-274/06 *Commission v Spain* [2008] ECR I-26, paras 35–39.

[210] Benyon, *Direct Investment* (above n 63) 97.

[211] See, by analogy, in the context of free movement of goods, 15/83 *Denkavit* [1984] ECR 2171, para 15.

[212] This aspect of the Union's newly acquired exclusive external FDI competence will be further considered in chapter 3.

This section has shown that the automatic granting of rights of secondary mobility to third-country direct investors contrasts with the absence of a Union external FDI regime. The automatic granting of rights of intra-EU mobility to companies, which are controlled by third-country natural or legal persons, increases the interdependence between the Member States so far as concerns the external dimension of the Single Market in the field of direct investment. Where the Union or an individual Member State wants to restrict or impose specific requirements on third-country direct investment, such restrictions could in some circumstances be effectively imposed only if the internal market mechanism does not preclude the differential treatment of legal persons that are formed in accordance with the laws of one of the Member States, but which are directly or indirectly controlled by third-country natural or legal persons. For that reason, in respect of particularly sensitive sectors, Member State foreign investment codes, as well as Union secondary legislation and external practice, provide for the possibility of limiting the secondary rights of mobility for companies, which are directly or indirectly controlled by third-country natural or legal persons. Although potentially giving rise to inconsistencies with the formalistic criteria of incorporation and seat under Article 54 TFEU, this type of restriction may be easier to justify than in respect of EU companies and perhaps more so for the EU legislator than for a Member State.

IV. CONCLUSION

Direct investment constitutes an area of substantive overlap between the freedom of establishment and the free movement of capital. While Article 63 TFEU applies to third-country situations, Articles 49/54 TFEU are inward-looking. The precise scope and nature of the rights that direct investors hold under the internal market mechanism with regard to the admission and treatment of their investments are still in the process of being crystallised. The CJEU has in recent case law adopted a 'centre of gravity' approach to the operation of the internal market mechanism to direct investment, so that direct investment falls within the scope of application of Articles 49/54 TFEU, rather than Article 63 TFEU, insofar as a national measure primarily affects conditions of establishment. As a result, the Union and the Member States have not unilaterally given third-country direct investors the right to invest in the Single Market insofar as specific transactions primarily constitute establishment. At the same time, recent case law shows that Article 63 TFEU can be primarily affected in the case of national measures having a restrictive effect on a controlling shareholding.

Furthermore, it has been demonstrated that a distinction is to be drawn between the post-establishment treatment of third-country direct investment in the internal economy of a Member State and the issue of rights of intra-EU mobility for third-country direct investors. This is a consequence of the inward-looking nature of the internal market mechanism in respect of establishment. An application of the formalistic criteria of incorporation and seat enshrined in Article 54 TFEU contrasts with the absence of a comprehensive Union regime with regard to the admission and treatment of FDI flowing into the Single Market. At the same time, both Member State and relevant Union practice shows that legal persons, which prima facie meet the requirements of Article 54 TFEU, have nevertheless not been granted secondary rights of mobility where they are directly or indirectly controlled by third-country natural or legal persons. Such restrictions to or additional requirements for third-country direct investors could in practice be easier to justify than in the case of EU investors. Against this backdrop, the Union's post-Lisbon FDI competence may contribute to the shaping of a more comprehensive Union external FDI regime. This is the subject of the next chapter.

3

The Lisbon Reform of the Common Commercial Policy: Implications for Union Competence and Practice in the Field of FDI

In the long run, a comprehensive investment policy will keep Europe as the world's number one player in the field of foreign direct investment, ensure the best deal for all European businesses, invigorate growth and create jobs at this crucial time.[1]

T HE LISBON REFORM of the TFEU provisions on the common commercial policy (CCP) has resulted in an explicit Union external FDI competence. Prior to the Treaty of Lisbon, a significant number of Union external agreements already contained investment-related provisions, which predominantly dealt with the liberalisation of FDI. Following an important communication[2] issued on 7 July 2010, the European Commission has integrated the issue of investment liberalisation and that of investment protection, which was hitherto left to the Member States, as part of a common Union international investment policy for the post-Lisbon era. The Commission takes the view that comprehensive investment provisions ought not only to find their way into Union external agreements covering a broader range of matters, but should also be the subject of stand-alone Union investment agreements. Against that backdrop, this chapter assesses the implications of the Lisbon reform of the CCP for the Union's competence and practice in the field of FDI.

The first section deals with the extent to which the post-Lisbon TFEU provisions on the CCP have changed the scope and nature of the Union's external competence in the field of FDI, and it deals with the limits of this competence. The second section explores the implications of the inclusion of a reference to 'foreign direct investment' (FDI) in the TFEU provisions on the CCP for the Union's treaty-making practice. The third section investigates the interplay between the Union's emerging post-Lisbon external practice in the field of FDI

---

[1] European Commissioner for Trade, Karel De Gucht, Press statement, IP/10/907, 7 July 2010.
[2] Communication from the Commission to the Council, the European Parliament, the European Economic and Social Committee and the Committee of the Regions, 'Towards a comprehensive European international investment policy', COM(2010)343 final, 7 July 2010, Brussels.

and the Union's internal legal organisation in that field in relation to both the primary and secondary rights of mobility of third-country direct investors in the Single Market. The chapter shows that the Union's treaty-making practice could, as a result of the common international investment policy, move beyond the scope of the subject matter of the existing intra-EU regime in the field of direct investment. So far as concerns the post-establishment treatment of FDI in the Single Market, the chapter shows that the further development of the external dimension of the Single Market in the field of FDI may increase the extent to which the Single Market constitutes a truly 'single' market for third-country investors.

I. UNION EXTERNAL COMPETENCE IN THE FIELD OF FDI BEFORE AND AFTER LISBON

This section assesses the implications of the Lisbon reform of the CCP for the scope and nature of the Union's external competence in the field of FDI. The section first analyses the evolution of Community external competence under the EC Treaty provisions on the CCP in the pre-Lisbon era. It then discusses possible alternative legal bases which empowered the Community to assume investment-related commitments with third countries. The section subsequently examines the scope and nature of the Union's post-Lisbon FDI competence, as well as its limits. It is argued that the Lisbon reform of the CCP enables the Union to assume international commitments as regards both the liberalisation and protection of FDI, thus enabling the CCP to further develop into a more autonomous policy area with respect to the internal legal organisation in the field of direct investment. The section also discusses a number of apparent limits to the Union's post-Lisbon FDI competence.

A. Limited Community Competence in the Field of FDI under the Pre-Lisbon Provisions on the CCP

The story of the early years of the CCP and, particularly, of the Court's rulings on the nature and scope of Community competence in that field is well known. The provisions of the Treaty on the European Economic Community (EEC) on the CCP essentially empowered the Community to take responsibility for the external dimension of the customs union following the abolition of internal tariffs and customs duties.[3] To this end, the provisions on the CCP conferred competence in the field of trade and provided a procedural framework, as well as a number of

---

[3] The predominant focus of the CCP was laid down in Art 110 EEC, which provided that '[b]y establishing a customs union between themselves the Member States aim to contribute, in conformity with the common interest, to the harmonious development of world trade, the progressive abolition of restrictions on international exchanges and the lowering of customs barriers'.

transitional provisions.[4] The Court initially took a wide approach to both the nature and the scope of Community competence in the field of commercial policy. In *Opinion 1/75*,[5] it ruled that the Member States could not invoke a concurrent power in relation to the granting of export credits.[6] Unilateral Member State action would not only lead to disparities in the conditions for granting export credits, but would also distort the institutional framework, call into question the mutual trust within the Community and prevent the latter from fulfilling its task in the defence of the common interest.[7] In *Opinion 1/78*,[8] the Court interpreted the scope of Community competence in the field of commercial policy broadly and thereby laid the ground for future disputes on the limits of this exclusive competence.[9] In the view of the Court, a restrictive interpretation of the scope of the CCP to the traditional aspects of external trade, instead of linking it to the evolutionary nature of the international regulation of trade, would result in the CCP becoming nugatory in the course of time.[10] It would moreover risk causing disturbances in intra-Community trade by reason of the disparities which would then exist in certain sectors of economic relations with third countries.

As a result of the gradual expansion of the international trade agenda in the context of the Uruguay Round (1986–94), where agreement was reached on the conclusion of the Marrakesh Agreement establishing the World Trade Organization, the question arose whether the Community's exclusive external competence under the provisions on the CCP extended to trade-related areas such as services and intellectual property. Issues of investment had been discussed during the Uruguay Round, even though the development of comprehensive rules on the liberalisation and protection of investment was not formally part of the negotiations. For present purposes, the most important investment-related agreement in the context of the WTO is the General Agreement on Trade in Services (GATS).[11] As was explained in chapter 1, that agreement deals, inter alia, with services that are supplied by means of a commercial presence, which is essentially FDI in the tertiary sector of production.

The question of whether the Community was exclusively competent, inter alia, under Article 113 of the EC Treaty to conclude the WTO Agreement was put before the CJEU in *Opinion 1/94*.[12] This ruling, at least to some, heralded the end

---

[4] Articles 111–16 EEC. For a discussion of the transitional provisions in the field of commercial policy, see the text at chapter 4, III and accompanying notes.
   [5] *Opinion 1/75* [1975] ECR 1355.
   [6] Ibid 1364.
   [7] Ibid 1364.
   [8] *Opinion 1/78* [1979] ECR 2871.
   [9] Ibid para 45: 'Article [133] empowers the Community to formulate a commercial "policy", based on "uniform principles" thus showing that the question of external trade must be governed from a wide point of view and not only having regard to the administration of precise systems such as customs and quantitative restrictions'.
   [10] Ibid.
   [11] The WTO package also included the TRIPS Agreement and an Agreement on TRIMs. See text at chapter 1, V.
   [12] *Opinion 1/94* [1994] ECR I-5267.

of an era of expansive rulings as regards the external competence of the Community, even if it mainly confirmed the techniques for attribution and the grounds for exclusivity of Community competence found in the classic authorities.[13] In relation to the GATS,[14] the Court took the view that the first mode of supply of services, which is rendered by a supplier established in one country to a consumer residing in another, without any of them crossing any border, was 'not unlike trade in goods' and thus fell within the scope of the pre-Nice EC Treaty provisions on the CCP.[15] The same, however, could not be said about the other three modes of supply of services.[16] By examining whether the concept of trade in services was sufficiently analogous to that of trade in goods, the Court emphasised that the pre-Nice EC Treaty provisions on the CCP dealt essentially with issues of trade. The Court came to the conclusion that trade in services, including FDI in the services sector, is for the most part substantially different to trade in goods. Indeed, unlike goods, a service provided by a third-country natural or legal person cannot so easily be channelled to a Member State through another Member State.[17] This is because it is difficult for a service to be traded on its own, after it has been produced, and become the object of further transactions.[18] There is thus less of a need to prevent trade diversion by means of a uniform external policy in the field of services, which had been recognised by the Court as a ground for exclusivity under the provisions on the CCP in *Opinion 1/75*. In the view of the Court, however, trade in services other than by means of the first mode of supply fell entirely outside of the scope of the pre-Nice EC Treaty provisions on the CCP.[19]

Soon after, the CJEU issued its ruling in *Opinion 2/92*,[20] in which the Court determined whether the Community was exclusively competent under (then) Article 113 EC to participate in the Third Revised Decision of the OECD on national treatment. That Decision deals with the conditions for the operation of undertakings that are owned or controlled by nationals of other OECD member countries, such as subsidiaries or branches. The Decision leaves unaffected the

---

[13] See AA Dashwood and J Heliskoski, 'The Classic Authorities Revisited' in AA Dashwood and C Hillion (eds), *The General Law of EC External Relations* (London, Sweet and Maxwell, 2000) 3. But see JHJ Bourgeois, 'The EC in the WTO and Advisory Opinion 1/94: An Echternach Procession' (1995) 3 *CML Rev* 763; T Tridimas and P Eeckhout, 'The External Competence of the Community and the Case-Law of the Court of Justice: Principle versus Pragmatism' (1994) *Yearbook on European Law* 143.

[14] It was not disputed during the proceedings that the Community was exclusively competent to conclude the agreement on TRIMs. The exclusivity of Community competence in relation to TRIPS was disputed, but will not be discussed.

[15] *Opinion 1/94* [1994] ECR I-5267, para 44.

[16] Ibid paras 45–47.

[17] Ibid.

[18] CWA Timmermans, 'Common Commercial Policy (Article 113 EEC) and International Trade in Services' in F Capotorti, CD Ehlermann et al (eds), *Du droit international au droit d'intégration: Liber Amicorum Pierre Pescatore* (Baden-Baden, Nomos, 1987) 679.

[19] The Court also pointed out that transport services continued to be governed by the provisions on the common transport policy in (now) Title VI TFEU, rather than by the provisions on the CCP. See *Opinion 1/94* [1994] ECR I-5267, paras 48–53.

[20] *Opinion 2/92* [1995] ECR I-521.

right of OECD member countries to regulate the entry or conditions of establish-ment of foreign undertakings. It establishes a procedure for the notification and examination of measures constituting exceptions to national treatment. The Court was thus asked to rule on the Community's competence to enter into com-mitments with third countries on the issue of the post-establishment treatment of FDI. In line with its ruling in *Opinion 1/94*, the Court took the view that the con-ditions for the participation of foreign-controlled undertakings in trade between the Member States and third countries are the subject of the CCP.[21]

However, the Court made clear that the same did not apply to the conditions for the participation of foreign-controlled undertakings in trade *between the Member States*, which are covered by the internal market rules.[22] In other words, the issue of secondary rights of mobility of third-country direct investors as regards trade between the Member States fell outside the scope of the CCP. The Court moreover observed that the Decision related mainly to the participation of foreign-controlled undertakings 'in the internal economic life of the Member States'; in other words, to the initial post-establishment treatment of third-coun-try direct investment.[23] It can be inferred that this issue did not fall under the EC Treaty provisions on the CCP either, which related exclusively to issues of trade and not to the issue of establishment.[24] As a result, the Third Revised Decision on national treatment relates only partially to trade with third countries, so that Article 113 EC did not confer exclusive competence on the Community to par-ticipate in the entire scope of the subject matter of the Third Decision.

It was thus clear that the scope of the pre-Nice EC Treaty provisions on the CCP did not extend to issues of FDI, except so far as the limited issue of the involvement of foreign-controlled undertakings in trade in goods with third countries was concerned. Pursuant to the Nice reform of the CCP, the scope of the CCP was extended to the negotiation and conclusion of agreements in the fields of trade in services and the commercial aspects of intellectual property.[25] The Court has confirmed in *Opinion 1/08*[26] that, while the cross-frontier supply of services continued to be covered by (then) Article 133(1) EC, Article 133(5) EC extended the Community's external competence to all three other modes of sup-ply of services.[27] In doing so, the Court rejected the submission of Spain that only the first and second modes of the supply of services within the meaning of Article

---

[21] Ibid para 24.
[22] Ibid para 25.
[23] Ibid para 24.
[24] Ibid para 24. For analysis, see the text at chapter 2, III.A and accompanying notes.
[25] The newly added Art 133(5)(1) EC provided that '[p]aragraphs 1 to 4 shall also apply to the nego-tiation and conclusion of agreements in the fields of trade in services and the commercial aspects of intellectual property, in so far as those agreements are not covered by the said paragraphs and without prejudice to paragraph 6'. For analysis, see M Cremona, 'The External Dimension of the Single Market: Building (on) the Foundations' in CS Barnard and J Scott (eds), *The Law of the Single European Market: Unpacking the Premises* (Oxford, Hart Publishing, 2002) 376; J Heliskoski, 'The Nice Reform of Article 133 EC on the Common Commercial Policy' (2001) 1 *Journal of International Commercial Law* 1, 6.
[26] *Opinion 1/08* [2009] ECR I-11129.
[27] Ibid para 118.

I(2) GATS would be covered by these provisions.[28] Spain had supported its argument by pointing out that only the first and second modes correspond to the concept of freedom to provide services within the meaning of the law of the internal market.[29] The Court held that there was nothing to permit the inference that Article 133(5) EC only extended the Community's competence in the field of trade in services to the second mode of supply.[30] Rather, the Court took the view that the concept of 'trade in services' under the GATS assumes particular importance in the sphere of external action in that context.[31]

While the Nice reform of the CCP thus extended the Community's competence to FDI in the services sector, it also contained a number of provisions that reserved the possibility for the Member States to act in that field. In the first place, Article 133(5)(4) EC provided that Article 133(5) EC did not affect the right of the Member States to maintain and conclude agreements in the fields covered by that provision. As a result of Article 133(5)(4) EC, competence under the third mode of GATS was therefore arguably shared, so that it could be exercised by the Community, by the Member States, or jointly.[32] Article 133(6)(1) EC provided that an agreement could not be concluded by the Council if it included provisions which would go beyond the Community's internal powers.[33] Moreover, Article 133(6)(2) EC institutionalised shared competence for the conclusion of agreements relating to cultural and audio-visual services, educational services, and social and human health services.[34] By *requiring the joint participation* of the Community and the Member States,[35] that provision:

> [allowed] the interest of the Community in establishing a comprehensive, coherent and efficient external commercial policy to be pursued whilst at the same time allowing the special interests which the Member States might wish to defend in the sensitive areas identified by that provision to be taken into account.[36]

---

[28] Ibid para 120.
[29] Ibid para 67.
[30] Ibid para 120.
[31] Ibid para 121.
[32] C Herrmann, 'Common Commercial Policy after Nice: Sisyphus Would Have Done a Better Job' (2002) 1 *CML Rev* 7, 19. But see M Krajewski, 'External Trade Law and Constitutional Treaty: Towards a Federal and More Democratic Common Commercial Policy?' (2005) 1 *CML Rev* 91, 96, who argues that the Member States could not conclude an agreement jointly with the Community under this provision.
[33] For more analysis of this provision, see the text at I.C and accompanying notes.
[34] In relation to this provision, the Court moreover rejected the predominant purpose approach of the Commission and the European Parliament, under which Art 133(6)(2) EC would only cover agreements that concern 'exclusively or predominantly trade in services' in the sectors referred to in that provision. The Court took the view that, upon that interpretation, the areas of sensitive services specified in Art 133(6)(2) would fall within or outside of the shared competence of the Community and its Member States depending solely on whether a specific agreement deals only with trade in such sensitive services or whether it deals at the same time with trade in other types of services. See *Opinion 1/08* [2009] ECR I-11129, para 140.
[35] Ibid para 134.
[36] Ibid para 136.

It was pointed out earlier that the Court ruled in *Opinion 1/75* that the special interests of the Member States in pursuing a commercial policy could not be accommodated while pursuing the Community interest in respect of the granting of export credits. In the view of the Court, the expansion of the international trade agenda had thus prompted the inclusion of trade-related issues as part of the scope of the CCP in fields where the Member States hold special interests that do not necessarily run counter to the Community interest.[37]

The Community's external competence under the post-Nice EC Treaty provisions on the CCP covered FDI in the services sector. The issue of establishment of non-EU direct investors in the Single Market in the services sector, but not in others, was thus covered by the Community's competence under the post-Nice EC Treaty provisions on the CCP. Intra-EU trade in services, even by foreign-controlled companies, arguably continued to be predominantly an internal market issue, however. Moreover, Article 133 EC contained important exceptions to exclusivity in the field of trade in services. In view of the limited scope and shared nature of Community competences in the field of FDI under the CCP before Lisbon, the question arises whether investment-related commitments in relations with third countries could be assumed by the Community under alternative legal bases.

B. Alternative Legal Bases for Assuming Commitments with Third Countries in the Field of FDI

It was argued by the Commission in *Opinion 1/94*, but rejected by the CJEU, that the Community holds exclusive external competence in the field of FDI in the services sector under (now) Article 50(1) TFEU on freedom of establishment. This argument could have been advanced in a similar fashion in relation to FDI in other sectors of production. The Commission argued that such exclusive external competence could flow implicitly from the Community's internal powers, from the existence of legislative acts giving effect to that internal competence, or from the need for the Community to participate in the GATS for the attainment of an internal objective.[38] The Court not only rejected the assertion that exclusive external competence can come into being by virtue merely of the existence of an internal power upon a principle of parallel powers, but also confirmed that, even if such internal powers have been exercised, the Member States only lose their right to assume obligations with third countries as and when there are common rules that could be affected by those obligations.[39]

---

[37] Ibid para 163. In view of ex Art 133(6)(3) EC, the Court also confirmed that transport services continued to fall outside the scope of the CCP (para 173).

[38] *Opinion 1/94* [1994] ECR I-5267, para 72. See the current Art 3(2) TFEU: 'The Union shall also have exclusive competence for the conclusion of an international agreement when its conclusion is provided for in a legislative act of the Union or is necessary to enable the Union to exercise its internal competence, or in so far as its conclusion may affect common rules or alter their scope.'

[39] Ibid paras 74–77, with reference to 22/70 *Commission v Council (AETR)* [1971] ECR 263, paras 17–18.

In addition, the Court observed that the chapter on freedom of establishment contains no provision on the problem of the first establishment of nationals of non-member countries, so that no exclusive competence in that field could be inferred from those provisions.[40] As was discussed in chapter 2, the freedom of establishment does not extend to the issue of the initial post-establishment treatment of foreign-controlled undertakings in the internal economy of the host Member State.[41] The Court has also confirmed that the freedom of establishment does not extend to situations which involve the establishment in a third country of a Member State national or of a company incorporated under the legislation of a Member State.[42] While Community secondary legislation may specify the treatment to be accorded to third-country direct investment in the Single Market, in the view of the Court this was not sufficient to trigger an exclusive external competence in the entire field covered by the GATS under the EC Treaty provisions on freedom of establishment or Community secondary legislation in the field of trade in services.

The Court did not accept the argument that without participation of the Community in the GATS the coherence of the internal market would be impaired. The Court held that freedom of establishment for nationals of the Member States is not 'inextricably linked' to the treatment to be afforded to nationals of third countries in the Community or to nationals of Member States of the Community in third countries.[43] While the Court held that the Community does not hold an exclusive external competence under the EC Treaty provisions on freedom of establishment so far as FDI in the services sector is concerned, it also did not explicitly confirm a non-exclusive implied power in this field. Yet, this does not warrant the conclusion that the Community was not empowered under the EC Treaty provisions on freedom of establishment to assume commitments with third countries in this field, since a successful argument could possibly have been made for implied non-exclusive competence upon the application of the so-called 'complementarity principle'.[44] In this respect, it can be observed that the WTO Agreement, so far as matters within Community competence were concerned, was concluded, inter alia, on the basis of the EC Treaty provisions on freedom of

---

[40] *Opinion 1/94* [1994] ECR I-5267, para 81.

[41] This follows from C-524/04 *Thin Cap Group Litigation* [2007] ECR I-2107, para 98.

[42] C-157/05 *Holböck* [2007] ECR I-4051, para 28.

[43] *Opinion 1/94* [1994] ECR I-5267, para 86. The Court thereby distinguished the issues arising in the context of the conclusion of the GATS from the constellation of facts in *Opinion 1/76* [1977] ECR 741.

[44] See Dashwood and Heliskoski, 'The Classic Authorities Revisited' (above n 13) 11 ff. This more generous facilitation test for the attribution of implied non-exclusive Union competence seems to be reflected in Art 216(1) TFEU: 'The Union may conclude an agreement with one or more third countries or international organisations where . . . the conclusion of an agreement is necessary in order to achieve, within the framework of the Union's policies, one of the objectives referred to in the Treaties'. While Article 216(1) TFEU does refer to the 'necessity' of concluding a Union agreement, the legal parameters differ from those under the stricter necessity test for the attribution of *exclusive* Union competence in Art 3(2) TFEU: 'The Union shall also have exclusive competence for the conclusion of an international agreement when its conclusion . . . is necessary to enable the Union to exercise its internal competence'.

establishment.[45] Moreover, the Court confirmed in *Opinion 1/94* that external competence under the GATS does arise, and becomes exclusive, after the adoption of secondary legislation dealing with that issue in the spheres covered by such legislation.[46] In *Opinion 1/94*, however, the Court observed that this was not the case in all services sectors at that point in time.[47]

The (now) TFEU provisions on free movement of capital by their wording apply to capital transfers to and from third countries. Pursuant to Article 63(1) TFEU, all restrictions on the movement of capital between Member States and between non-Member States are prohibited.[48] Article 64(2) and (3) TFEU,[49] moreover, enable the Council to adopt measures on capital movements to or from third countries involving, inter alia, direct investment. It has been argued by some that the Union and the Member States share external competence in the field of FDI under these provisions.[50] Notwithstanding the complex issues of demarcation between the TFEU provisions on freedom of establishment and on free movement of capital, it was argued in chapter 2 that the TFEU provisions on capital movements do not deal with the comprehensive phenomenon of direct investment. Measures affecting holdings by non-EU investors in EU companies, which confer control over a company's decisions and allow the investor to determine its activities, fall in the realm of the TFEU provisions on establishment, unless a measure primarily affects transfers of capital in relation to FDI. The scope of Union competence under the TFEU provisions on free movement of capital in relation to FDI is thus fairly limited. Additionally, insofar as these provisions enable the Union to assume international commitments with the effect of liberalising capital transfers,

---

[45] See Council Decision 94/800 of 22 December 1994 concerning the conclusion on behalf of the European Community, as regards matters within its competence, of the agreements reached in the Uruguay Round multilateral negotiations (1986–1994) [1994] OJ L336/1, which refers, inter alia, to (then) Arts 54 and 57 EC. In this respect, it can be submitted that treatment of FDI in the services sector under the GATS also involves intra-EU rights of mobility in the sense of *Opinion 2/92* [1995] ECR I-521, paras 7–8, where the Court specified that the participation of foreign-controlled undertakings in intra-EU trade is covered by the internal market rules.

[46] *Opinion 1/94* [1994] ECR I-5267, para 95.

[47] Ibid para 97. For the argument that the adoption of the Services Directive (Directive 2006/123 of the European Parliament and of the Council of 12 December 2006 on services in the internal market [2006] OJ L376/36) did not affect the Union's external competence under the scope of the subject matter of the GATS, including the third mode of supply, see M Krajewski, 'Of Modes and Sectors. External Relations, Internal Debates, and the Social Case of (Trade in) Services' in M Cremona (ed), *Developments in EU External Relations Law* (Oxford, Oxford University Press, 2008) 197 ff.

[48] Joined Cases C-163/94, C-165/94 and C-250/94 *Sanz de Lera* [1995] ECR I-4821, para 19; C-513/03 *van Hilten-van der Heijden* [2006] ECR I-1957, para 37.

[49] Article 64(2) TFEU stipulates that the European Parliament and the Council '[endeavour] to achieve the objective of free movement of capital between Member States and third countries to the greatest extent possible' in adopting measures on the movement of capital to and from third countries involving, inter alia, direct investment. Under Art 64(3) TFEU, 'the Council, acting in accordance with a special legislative procedure, may unanimously, and after consulting the European Parliament, adopt measures which constitute a step backwards in Union law as regards the liberalisation of the movement of capital to or from third countries'.

[50] J Karl, 'The Competence for Foreign Direct Investment, New Powers for the European Union?' (2004) 3 *Journal of World Investment and Trade* 413, 415 ff; W Shan, 'Towards a Common European Community Policy on Investment Issues' (2001) 3 *Journal of World Investment and Trade* 604, 608.

as well as with regard to their protection, this competence is in principle non-exclusive.[51]

The Union holds quite extensive external competence in the field of FDI under (now) Article 217 TFEU on association.[52] EU primary law does not define the concept of association, nor does it provide any specific criteria to this effect.[53] With regard to the association agreement with Turkey, the CJEU has, however, held that it involves the creation of:

> special, privileged links with a non-member country which must, at least to a certain extent, take part in the Community system.[54]

On that basis, the Court took the view that Article 217 TFEU:

> must necessarily empower the Community to guarantee commitments towards non-member countries in all the fields covered by the Treaty.[55]

By consequence, in the context of association there is potentially a full external dimension of any (though not every) internal Union policy. While many association agreements have been concluded with a view to future membership of the Union, they are arguably not necessarily an *antichambre* to accession.[56] Notwithstanding the issue of whether it is actually appropriate to exercise such a broad-ranging Union competence outside the context of accession,[57] there would, however, seem to be inherent limits to the exercise of this competence in the field of FDI. First, it does not provide a targeted external FDI competence, because it is inherent in the concept of association that it involves the need to include other Union policies in the agreement. It could arguably not be used to conclude external agreements that focus exclusively on investment. Secondly, the creation of

[51]   But see COM(2010)343 (above n 2) 8: 'to the extent that international agreements on investment affect the scope of the common rules set by the Treaty's Chapter on capitals [*sic*] and payments, the exclusive Union competence to conclude agreements in this area would be implied'. The Commission refers to Art 3(2) TFEU. For more analysis, see the text at I.C and accompanying notes.

[52]   Article 217 TFEU provides that 'The Union may conclude with one or more third countries or international organisations agreements establishing an association involving reciprocal rights and obligations, common action and special procedure'.

[53]   For analysis, see MA Gaudissart, 'Reflexions sur la nature et la portée du concept d'association à la lumière de sa mise en oeuvre' in MFC Tchakaloff (ed), *Le concept d'association dans les accords passés par la Communauté: essai de clarification* (Brussels, Bruylant, 1999); D Hanf and P Dengler, 'Les accords d'association' in JV Louis and M Dony (eds), *Commentaire Mégret, Le droit de la CE et de l'Union européenne*, vol 12, 2nd edn (Brussels, Édition de l'Université de Bruxelles, 2005).

[54]   12/86 *Demirel* [1987] ECR 3719, para 9.

[55]   Ibid.

[56]   F Benyon, 'Community Association Agreements: From the Sixties to the Nineties' in S Konstadinidis (ed), *The Legal Regulation of the European Community's External Relations after the Completion of the Internal Market* (Dartmouth, Aldershot, 1996). Opinion of AG Mayras of 29 June 1972 in 96/71 *Haegeman v Commission* [1972] ECR 1005, 1023: 'such a type of agreement may lead to the establishment of a very close institutional cooperation between the Community and the associated country without however going so far as the unconditional accession of that country'.

[57]   Doubted by P Eeckhout, *External Relations of the European Union: Legal and Constitutional Foundations* (Oxford, Oxford University Press, 2005) 115. See also C Lycourgos, *L'association avec union douanière: un mode de relations entre la CEE et des Etats tiers* (Paris, Presses universitaires de France, 1994) 358, who argues that the objective served by an association agreement should be the accession of the third country concerned.

special, privileged links with a third country has a political connotation that may not correspond to the reality of relations with a particular third country with which the Union wants to enter into investment-related commitments. Thirdly, Article 217 TFEU does not empower the Union to conclude investment-related commitments in multilateral settings such as the OECD or the WTO. Insofar as Article 217 TFEU empowers the Union to assume commitments in the field of FDI with third countries, which mirrors the extent to which the Union is competent to regulate intra-EU direct investment, such competence is shared.[58]

(Now) Article 352 TFEU empowers the Union to take the measures that are necessary to attain one of the objectives of the Treaties where these have not provided the Union with the necessary powers.[59] While recourse to Article 352 TFEU is justified solely where no other provision of the Treaties gives the Union the necessary power to adopt the measure in question, this provision does not at the same time allow the Union to circumvent the principle of conferral.[60] Article 352 TFEU therefore provides a procedure for determining the necessity of a measure for the achievement of one of the Union's objectives.[61] Yet, Article 352 TFEU could be of only limited relevance in the field of FDI, since the Court took the view in *Opinion 1/94* that competence conferred under the Chapter on freedom of establishment can be used in order to lay down the treatment to be accorded to

---

[58] Similarly, competence under Arts 181 and 181a EC (now Arts 211 and 212 TFEU) on cooperation with developing and other third countries is shared. Moreover, under these provisions, Union action in the field of investment has to have an explicit cooperation dimension, such as by contributing to the reduction of poverty or as an element of economic assistance. While investment-related commitments may form part of that type of cooperation with third countries, these provisions also arguably do not provide a targeted external FDI competence.

[59] Article 352 TFEU: 'If action by the Union should prove necessary, within the framework of the policies defined in the Treaties, to attain one of the objectives set out in the Treaties, and the treaties have not provided the necessary powers, the Council, acting unanimously on a proposal from the Commission and after obtaining the consent of the European Parliament, shall adopt the appropriate measures.' The possibility to take measures under Art 308 EC was more explicitly limited to action 'in the course of the operation of the common market'. For analysis, see AA Dashwood, 'Article 308 EC as the Outer Limit of Expressly Conferred Community Competence' in CS Barnard and O Odudu (eds), *The Outer Limits of European Union Law* (Oxford, Hart Publishing, 2009) 35, 36. See also R Schütze, 'Organised Change towards an "Ever Closer Union": Article 308 EC and the Limits to the Community's Legislative Competence' (2003) *Yearbook on European Law* 79; P Koutrakos, 'Legal Basis and Delimitation of Competence in EU External Relations' in M Cremona and B de Witte (eds), *EU Foreign Relations Law: Constitutional Fundamentals* (Oxford, Hart Publishing, 2008) 171 ff.

[60] *Opinion 2/94* [1996] ECR I-1759, para 30: 'That provision, being an integral part of an institutional system based on the principle of conferred powers, cannot serve as a basis for widening the scope of [Union] powers beyond the general framework created by the provisions of the [Treaties] as a whole and, in particular, by those that define the tasks and the activities of the [Union]'.

[61] Joined Opinion of AG Tizzano of 31 January 2002 in Joined Cases C-466/98 *Commission v United Kingdom* [2002] ECR I-9427; C-467/98 *Commission v Denmark* [2002] ECR I-9519; C-468/98 *Commission v Sweden* [2002] ECR I-9575; C-469/98 *Commission v Finland* [2002] ECR I-9797; C-471/98 *Commission v Belgium* [2002] ECR I-9681; C-472/98 *Commission v Luxembourg* [2002] ECR I-9741; C-475/98 *Commission v Austria* [2002] ECR I-9797; C-476/98 *Commission v Germany* [2002] ECR I-9855 ('Open Skies'), para 53: '[Article 352 TFEU] does not confine itself to requiring a measure to be necessary if Community competence is to be justified, but lays down precise conditions and procedures for the determination of that necessity and, hence, whether it is capable of founding such competence'.

third-country nationals.[62] External competence under Article 352 TFEU could, moreover, only encompass the issue of investment protection insofar as other provisions do not confer competence to do so.[63] In addition, the Court has ruled in *Opinion 1/94* that Article 352 TFEU cannot in itself vest exclusive external competence in the Union unless 'internal powers can only be effectively exercised at the same time as external powers'.[64]

This overview supports the argument that, in the pre-Lisbon era, the Community's limited external competence in the field of FDI under the EC Treaty provisions on the CCP could not satisfactorily be supplemented by having recourse to additional legal bases. While agreements covering aspects of the liberalisation of FDI could arguably be concluded under Community competence, such competence was for the most part shared with the Member States. In addition, competence in the field of investment protection remained mostly with the Member States.

C. Lisbon Reform of the Provisions on the CCP as regards FDI

The issue of extending the scope of the CCP so as to include FDI had been on the table at a number of intergovernmental conferences (IGCs) prior to Lisbon. During the negotiations that led to the Treaty of Amsterdam[65] (1997) and to the Treaty of Nice[66] (2001), the Member States were, however, not able to agree on the inclusion of FDI within the scope of the provisions on the CCP. During the Convention on the Future of Europe (2002–2003), it was proposed by the Praesidium that FDI should become part of the scope of the CCP, but this was opposed by a considerable number of participants.[67] Nevertheless, the Draft Treaty that resulted from the Convention in July 2003 contained a reference to

---

[62] *Opinion 1/94* [1994] ECR I-5267, para 90.

[63] See the text at chapter 5, II and accompanying notes for the argument that, while considerations of investment protection are not absent from EU law, it does not provide a dedicated investment protection regime.

[64] *Opinion 1/94* [1994] ECR I-5267, para 89.

[65] European Commission Opinion, 'Reinforcing political union and preparing for enlargement', COM(96)90 final, 28 February 1996, 11. The so-called Irish Draft of December 1996 referred to an extension of the Community's competence in the fields of trade in services, intellectual property and FDI. See CONF 2500/96, 77.

[66] See Commission Opinion in accordance with Art 48 of the Treaty on European Union on the calling of a Conference of Representatives of the Governments of the Member States to amend the Treaties, 'Adapting the institutions to make a success of enlargement', COM(2000)34, 26 January 2000, Brussels, 29. See also CONFER 4790/00, 23.

[67] The Preasidium proposed the inclusion of FDI in the scope of the CCP in the April Draft: CONV 685/03, 52. There have subsequently been a number of proposed amendments to the scope of the CCP during the Convention, ranging from the mere taking note of the fact that there had not been a recommendation to extend the scope of the provisions on the CCP from the working group (Earl of Stockton MEP, David Heathcoat-Amory) to the view that it would be preferable not to transfer competence to the Union in the matter of the reciprocal promotion and protection of investment (Madame Palacio, Joschka Fischer). Available at http://european-convention.eu.int/EN/amendments/amendments3dd9.html?content=866&lang=EN.

FDI as part of the provisions on the CCP.[68] It was not amended by the IGC (2003–2004) and thus found its way into the draft Constitutional Treaty, which was rejected by the French and Dutch electorates.[69] The reference to FDI was subsequently maintained in Articles 206[70] and 207(1)[71] TFEU, which eventually entered into force on 1 December 2009.

The Lisbon reform of the (now) TFEU provisions on the CCP constitutes a significant development in the history of the common commercial policy. First of all, Article 3(e) TFEU provides that the Union has exclusive competence in the field of the CCP, so that there is a general shift to exclusivity under the entire scope of the common commercial policy. Since FDI explicitly falls within the non-exhaustive range of issues of commercial policy enshrined in Article 207(1) TFEU, it follows that the Union's competence in this field, as well as in the fields of trade in services and the commercial aspects of intellectual property, is now in principle exclusive. The perceived shift to exclusivity under the entire scope of the CCP is underlined in Article 206 TFEU, where the 'Union' is now explicitly identified as the actor that conducts the CCP instead of the 'Member States', to which Article 131 EC still referred.

Illustrative of the general shift to exclusivity is, moreover, the deletion of Article 133(5)(4) EC, under which the right of the Member States to maintain and conclude agreements with third countries or international organisations was purportedly guaranteed in the fields of trade in services and the commercial aspects of intellectual property, subject to the obligation of compliance with EU law and other relevant international agreements. In addition, Article 133(6)(2) EC, which institutionalised shared competence in the field of cultural and audio-visual services, educational services, and social and human health services, has been amended. The political sensitivity of these fields is no longer reflected in the non-exclusive nature of Union competence, but in an exception to qualified majority voting (QMV) by means of unanimity voting under Article 207(4)(3) TFEU.[72] QMV is the basic voting procedure for the CCP under Article 207(4)(1) TFEU, subject to the requirement of unanimity under Article 207(4)(2) TFEU where an

[68] CONV 850/03, Art III-217.

[69] Treaty establishing a Constitution for Europe, Art III-315 [2004] OJ C310/1. For an overview of the negotiations on the provisions on the Union's external action, amongst which those on the CCP, during the Convention, see JF Brakeland, 'Politique commerciale commune, coopération avec les pays tiers et aide humanitaire' in G Amato, H Bribosia and B de Witte (eds), *Genesis and Destiny of the European Constitution* (Brussels, Bruylant, 2007) 849 ff.

[70] 'By establishing a customs union in accordance with Articles 28 to 32, the Union shall contribute, in the common interest, to the harmonious development of world trade, the progressive abolition of restrictions on international trade and on foreign direct investment, and the lowering of customs and other barriers.'

[71] 'The common commercial policy shall be based on uniform principles, particularly with regard to changes in tariff rates, the conclusion of tariff and trade agreements relating to trade in goods and services, and the commercial aspects of intellectual property, foreign direct investment, the achievement of uniformity in measures of liberalisation, export policy and measures to protect trade such as those to be taken in the event of dumping or subsidies.'

[72] It can be assumed that these exceptions to QMV still apply to the supply of services in these fields by means of a commercial presence, even if these are technically issues of FDI.

agreement contains provisions for which unanimity is required for the adoption of internal rules.

Through the inclusion of FDI within the scope of the TFEU provisions on the CCP, a certain degree of parallelism in competences between the internal and the external dimension of the Single Market has been achieved.[73] Where the Union's express external competence in the field of foreign economic relations previously contained an important blind spot in the field of establishment, it now mirrors to a larger extent the range of economic activities to which the internal market rules apply internally. At the same time, as a result of the shift to exclusivity under the comprehensive scope of the CCP, the Union's post-Lisbon FDI competence precipitates a move beyond parallelism, since the Union's internal powers in the same field are in principle shared.[74] Such a move beyond parallelism also seems to be reflected in Article 207(6) TFEU,[75] which, unlike its predecessor, Article 133(6)(1) EC,[76] it is difficult to interpret as constituting a 'parallelism clause'.[77] While Article 207(6) TFEU constitutes a limit to the exercise of the Union's FDI competence, an important difference with Article 133(6)(1) EC seems to be that Union external agreements may now in principle go beyond the powers of the Union to address such issues within the Single Market. This seems to follow from the fact that there is no explicit reference in Article 207(6) TFEU to the Union's internal powers for the purpose of which that provision (in the Nice version) specified a non-exhaustive list of measures that would go beyond such an internal power. A combined reading of the two criteria enshrined in the Lisbon version of this provision could conceivably mean that the Union's external FDI competence cannot constitute a transfer of internal competence 'through the back door'. The apparent underlying concern that the Union's limited internal competences could be circumvented by the exercise of the Union's FDI competence (giving rise to a so-

---

[73] A Dimopoulos, 'The Common Commercial Policy after Lisbon: Establishing Parallelism between Internal and External Economic Relations?' (2008) *Croatian Yearbook of European Law and Policy* 101 ff.

[74] E Neframi, 'La politique commerciale commune selon le Traité établissant une Constitution pour l'Europe' (2005) 2 *Revue trimestrielle de droit européen* 473. See also J Monar, 'Die Gemeinsame Handelspolitik der Europäischen Union im EU-Verfassungsvertrag: Fortschritte mit einigen neuen Fragezeichen' (2005) 1 *Aussenwirtschaft* 99, 113, who claims that there is no equivalent internal competence in the field of FDI. For more analysis of this proposition, see the text at III.A and accompanying notes.

[75] 'The exercise of the competences conferred by this Article in the field of the common commercial policy shall not affect the delimitation of competences between the Union and the Member States, and shall not lead to harmonisation of legislative or regulatory provisions of the Member States in so far as the Treaties exclude such harmonisation.'

[76] 'An agreement may not be concluded by the Council if it includes provisions which would go beyond the Community's internal powers, in particular by leading to harmonisation of the laws or regulations of the Member States in an area for which this Treaty rules out such harmonisation.'

[77] But see also J Ceyssens, 'Towards a Common Foreign Investment Policy? Foreign Investment in the European Constitution' (2005) 3 *Legal Issues of European Integration* 259, 279; J Dutheil de la Rochère, 'Le pouvoir des états membres de l'Union européenne de conclure des traités bilatéraux d'investissement' in C Kessedjian and C Leben (eds), *Le droit européen et l'investissement* (Paris, Éditions Panthéon-Assas, 2009) 27, 31 ff.

called 'reverse *AETR* effect')[78] supports the proposition that the Lisbon provisions on the CCP precipitate a move beyond the establishment of parallelism between the internal and the external dimension of the Single Market in this field.

The Lisbon reform of the CCP is also significant in respect of the range of instruments now available to the Union in fields other than trade in goods, with which trade in services and the commercial aspects of intellectual property (as well as FDI) have been put on an equal footing. Article 133(5)(1) EC still restricted, by way of an exception to Article 133(1) EC, the Community's competence in fields other than trade in goods to the negotiation and conclusion of external agreements, so that the Community could not take autonomous measures in those fields. The Union's competence in all fields of commercial policy, including FDI, has now been included in Article 207(1) TFEU. As a result, the Union is arguably empowered to act by means of both conventional and autonomous measures in all matters of commercial policy falling within the scope of that provision.[79]

So far as concerns the extension of the scope of the CCP to FDI, the Union is moving into relatively uncharted territory. While the issue of FDI in the services sector was already subsumed under the EC Treaty provisions on the CCP, the Union's competence now extends to FDI in other sectors of production.[80] The liberalisation of FDI in the services sector under the GATS already constituted a significant move away from the regulation of traditional issues of trade in the field of goods. The Union is now moving even further from issues to do with the external dimension of the customs union.[81] This is because services, like goods, are generally considered to be products, whereas FDI is a production factor that cannot be traded. The cross-border movement of enterprise and capital moreover gives rise to distinct regulatory issues. The international regulation of FDI not only concerns issues of liberalisation, such as the admission and non-discriminatory post-establishment treatment of FDI (including standards of treatment such as national treatment (NT) and most favoured nation (MFN) treatment) but also more specifically of investment protection, including the standard of fair and equitable treatment (FET), compensation in the case of expropriation and access to investor-state dispute settlement.

---

[78] It has been reported that the rationale of the inclusion of this provision was to assuage the fear of some Member States for a 'reverse *AETR* effect'. See Brakeland, 'Politique commerciale commune' (above n 69) 863. On the 'reverse application of the *AETR* principle', see: Dashwood and Heliskoski, 'The Classic Authorities Revisited' (above n 13) 13 ff. Under the *AETR* principle, the Member States are precluded from entering into international commitments that are capable of affecting internal Union rules. Under its reverse application, the Member States are precluded from taking internal measures as a result of international commitments entered into by the Union, since those commitments form an integral part of Union law and thus trigger the principle of primacy.

[79] For the issue of autonomous measures, see the text at III and accompanying notes. With respect to the Treaty of Rome provisions on the CCP, see *Opinion 1/75* [1975] ECR 1355, 1362: 'a commercial policy is in fact made up of the combination and interaction of internal and external measures, without priority being taken by one over the other. Sometimes agreements are concluded in execution of a policy fixed in advance, sometimes that policy is defined by the agreements themselves'.

[80] Transport services are still excluded from the scope of the CCP by virtue of Art 207(5) TFEU.

[81] Against this backdrop, it is remarkable that Art 206 TFEU still refers to the formation of the customs union as primary benchmark of the CCP.

While a Union competence in the field of FDI was originally conceived mainly to be used in the context of the WTO,[82] which is principally a vehicle for the liberalisation of cross-border trade and FDI, the extent to which the Union is now empowered to regulate other aspects of investment than the liberalisation of FDI is a thorny issue. The TFEU does not define FDI for the purpose of the provisions on the CCP. In addition, while there are widely accepted international definitions of FDI, there is no single international instrument that assumes special importance as regards its definition.[83] It therefore seems possible to argue that an interpretation of the scope of the notion of foreign direct investment under the CCP should be guided by the concept of direct investment as it is used in the law of the internal market. Article 64 TFEU on free movement of capital refers to the concept of direct investment. Moreover, Directive 366/88 provides a definition of the concept of direct investment for the purpose of the application of the TFEU provisions on free movement of capital and follows the transaction-based definitions of FDI in international instruments that serve the liberalisation of capital movements.[84] On that basis, it seems possible to argue, as the Commission does,[85] that the Union's competence in the field of FDI extends to those shareholdings that confer a lasting interest and that allow the investor to participate in the management or control of the company. This would in turn rule out the need for the investor to exercise definite and decisive influence (control) over the company, in the sense that this concept is used for the purpose of distinguishing between the substantive scope of application of Articles 49/54 and 63 TFEU.

The scope of the Union's FDI competence by the wording of the TFEU provisions on the CCP does not include foreign portfolio investment. Excluded from its scope would also be other types of assets that represent an economic value but which do not qualify as FDI, such as investments in real estate. At the same time, it can be observed that Regulation 1219/2012 containing transitional arrangements for Member State bilateral investment agreements with third countries is based exclusively on Article 207(2) TFEU, even though the transitional arrangements are purported to apply to the entire scope of the subject matter of Member State bilateral investment agreements, including the capital transfer clauses.[86] The Preamble to Regulation 1219/2012 refers to the TFEU provisions on free movement of capital as being relevant to the transitional arrangements, since 'Those rules can be affected by the international agreements relating to foreign investment concluded by Member States'. In the Explanatory Memorandum to the proposed Regulation on

---

[82]   Monar, 'Die Gemeinsame Handelspolitik' (above n 74) 112; Krajewski, 'External Trade Law and Constitutional Treaty' (above n 32) 111.

[83]   This can be contrasted with the situation in *Opinion 1/08*, where the Court pointed out that the reference to 'trade in services' in the (now) TFEU provisions on the CCP corresponds to the meaning of that concept in the context of the GATS, since that agreement assumes particular importance in the sphere of external action in that field. See *Opinion 1/08* [2009] ECR I-11129, para 121. See also C-414/11 *Daiichi Sankyo Co Ltd, Sanofi-Aventis Deutschland GmbH v DEMO Anonimos Viomikhaniki kai Emporiki Etairia Farmakon* (nyr, 2013), para 55.

[84]   For analysis, see the text at chapter 2, I.A and accompanying notes.

[85]   COM(2010)343 (above n 2) 2.

[86]   See the text at chapter 4, III.A and accompanying notes.

financial responsibility under Union investment agreements, the Commission also points to the relevance of the TFEU provisions on free movement of capital, while the proposed Regulation itself is based exclusively on Article 207(2) TFEU.[87]

Whereas the Union's FDI competence primarily concerns the external dimension of the Single Market so far as concerns the issue of establishment, the scope of international investment agreements is in fact significantly broader than FDI. According to the Court's case law, if a measure pursues two aims or has two components and if one of those aims is identifiable as the main one, whereas the other is merely incidental, the measure must be founded on a single legal basis, namely, that of the predominant aim or component.[88] By way of exception, if a measure simultaneously pursues several objectives or has a number of components, which are inseparably linked without one being secondary and indirect to the other, such a measure needs to be founded on the corresponding legal bases. Against the backdrop of this line of case law, the Commission seems to assume that foreign portfolio investment is merely incidental to foreign direct investment under the scope of the common international investment policy.[89] In view of the broad asset-based definition of investment in international investment agreements, it however seems difficult to isolate FDI as a principal component in such agreements to which foreign portfolio investment would be merely incidental. It therefore seems difficult to argue that the issue of foreign portfolio investment is incidental to the issue of FDI under the scope of the common international investment policy.[90]

Even with regard to capital transfers accompanying FDI, it seems possible to argue that they continue to fall primarily within the scope of the TFEU provisions on capital movements where provisions in external agreements apply to capital transfers, including those in relation to FDI, in a general way. In this respect, a parallel can be drawn with the operation of the internal market mechanism in relation to direct investment, where the Court has ruled that the application of the free movement of capital can in certain circumstances supersede the application of the freedom of establishment irrespective of the ownership structure underlying the transaction.[91] As a result, external competence so far as concerns

---

[87] Proposal for Regulation of the European Parliament and of the Council establishing a framework for managing financial responsibility linked to investor-state dispute settlement tribunals established by international agreements to which the European Union is a party, COM(2012)335 final, 21 June 2012, 3.

[88] *Opinion 2/00* [2001] ECR I-9713, para 23, with reference, inter alia, to C-300/89 *Commission v Council (Titanium Dioxide)* [1991] ECR I-2867, paras 13 and 17.

[89] The Commission advanced arguments in respect of the predominant purpose of the agreement concluding the GATS and the incidental nature of provisions therein, inter alia, on transport in *Opinion 1/08*, para 86. These arguments were rejected by the Court, however (para 163).

[90] See also R Vidal Puig, 'The Scope of the New Exclusive Competence of the European Union with regard to Foreign Direct Investment' (2013) 2 *Legal Issues of European Integration* 133, 141; A Dimopoulos, *EU Foreign Investment Law* (Oxford, Oxford University Press, 2012) 95; F Ortino and P Eeckhout, 'Towards an EU Policy on Foreign Direct Investment' in A Biondi, P Eeckhout and S Ripley, *EU Law After Lisbon* (Oxford, Oxford University Press, 2012) 315 ff. But see F Hoffmeister and G Ünüvar, 'From BITs and Pieces towards European Investment Agreements' in M Bungenberg, A Reinisch and C Tietje (eds), *EU and Investment Agreements, Open Questions and Remaining Challenges* (Baden-Baden, Nomos, 2013) 66 ff.

[91] See the text at chapter 2, II and accompanying notes.

capital transfers in relation to FDI is arguably granted primarily under Article 64(2) TFEU, which in principle confers shared competence in the field of capital movements to and from third countries. Shared competence would also be at issue for the other types of capital movements for which Article 64(2) TFEU confers competence. At the same time, it can be observed that Article 64(2) TFEU does not confer competence for all types of portfolio investment.

This can be contrasted with the Commission's argument for exclusivity of Union external competence under the TFEU provisions on free movement of capital in the Explanatory Memorandum of the proposed Regulation on financial responsibility under Union investment agreements. The Commission here points at Article 3(2) TFEU, which provides that the Union has exclusive competence for the conclusion of an international agreement in so far as its conclusion 'may affect common rules or alter their scope'. In the view of the Commission, the conclusion of investment agreements may affect the common rules on free movement of capital enshrined in Article 63 TFEU. It can be observed, however, that the reference in Article 3(2) TFEU in the first place concerns a codification of the *AETR* jurisprudence, under which the Union holds an exclusive external competence as a result of the *exercise* of an internal competence in the form of common rules whenever these are capable of being affected by specific international commitments. A reference to the *AETR* jurisprudence as regards a possible 'affectation' of EU primary law in the field of free movement of capital movements constitutes a departure from the classical authorities on implied exclusive competence.[92]

Given the different regulatory emphasis of the freedom of establishment and free movement of capital, it has been observed that freedom of capital movements in the Single Market has been achieved mostly at the level of EU primary law, while the freedom of establishment has required a significant amount of secondary legislation in the form of harmonisation and mutual recognition rules.[93] At the same time, it has been observed that there is Union secondary legislation in the field of capital movements, which is potentially capable of being affected by the capital transfer provisions in international investment agreements.[94] Secondary legislation in the fields of company law and capital markets has been observed to establish a harmonised regulatory framework in the field of capital movements, including provisions explicitly extending to relations with third countries.[95] However, Union secondary

---

[92]   22/70 *Commission v Council (AETR)* [1971] ECR 263, para 17: 'each time the Community, with a view to implementing a common policy envisaged by the Treaty, adopts provisions laying down common rules, whatever form these may take, the Member States no longer have the right, acting individually or even collectively, to undertake obligations with third countries which affect those rules'. See F Ortino and P Eeckhout, 'Towards an EU Policy on Foreign Direct Investment' in A Biondi, P Eeckhout and S Ripley, *EU Law After Lisbon* (Oxford, Oxford University Press, 2012) 317 ff. But see R Vidal Puig, 'The Scope of the New Exclusive Competence' (above n 90) 152 ff.

[93]   R Torrent, 'Derecho comunitario e inversiones extranjeras directas: Libre circulación de los capitales vs. regulación no discriminatoria del establecimiento. De la *golden share* a los nuevos *open skies*' (2007) *Revista Española de Derecho Europeo* 283. See the text at chapter 2, I.A and accompanying notes.

[94]   Dimopoulos, *EU Foreign Investment Law* (above n 90) 104 ff.

[95]   Dimopoulos refers, inter alia, to Directive 2001/34 of the European Parliament and of the Council of 28 May 2001 on the admission of securities to official stock exchange listing and on information to

legislation in these fields does not exhaustively cover the scope of application of the TFEU provisions on free movement of capital. As a result, the Union is arguably not vested with exclusive competence under the entire scope of the provisions on free movement of capital.[96]

It is uncontested that the Union's post-Lisbon FDI competence covers the admission of FDI. Article 133(5)(1) EC already empowered the Community to enter into 'market access' commitments so far as concerns the supply of services through a commercial presence under the GATS. The TFEU provisions on the CCP in the first place extend this competence to other sectors of production. It can also be persuasively argued that the issue of post-establishment treatment of FDI falls within the scope of these provisions. Article 206 TFEU refers to the 'progressive abolition of restrictions on . . . foreign direct investment'. While this reference has been taken as an indication that the Union's competence extends only to issues related to the pre-entry phase of FDI,[97] provisions on the post-establishment treatment of commercial presences in the form of NT and MFN treatment can also be found in the GATS.[98] Moreover, even if not all instruments of international investment law address the issue of the admission of investment, they always cover the post-establishment treatment of FDI.[99] In fact, most European BITs do not cover the admission of FDI, but only issues of post-establishment treatment. For the same reason, the Lisbon provisions on the CCP arguably empower the Union to enter into commitments with third countries as regards the standard of fair and equitable treatment (FET), which is common in international investment agreements.[100] In addition, although EU law does not contain a FET standard that can be invoked by investors in the Single Market, Article 207(6) TFEU does not in itself preclude that standard of treatment from being included in the Union's post-Lisbon external practice for that reason.

be published on those securities [2001] OJ L184/1 and Directive 2004/39 of the European Parliament and the Council of 21 April 2004 on markets in financial instruments [2004] OJ L145/1.

[96] This argument holds as long as this is not 'an area to a large extent covered by [Union] rules' in the sense of *Opinion 1/03* [2006] ECR I-1145, para 126: 'it is not necessary for the areas covered by the international agreement and the [Union] legislation to coincide fully. Where the test of "an area which is already covered to a large extent by [Union] rules" . . . is to be applied, the assessment must be based not only on the scope of the rules in question but also on their nature and content. It is also necessary to take into account not only the current state of [EU] law in the area in question but also its future development, insofar as that is foreseeable at the time of that analysis'. On the notion of 'an area covered to a large extent by Union rules', see also Opinion of AG Kokott of 27 June 2013 in C-137/12 *Commission v Council*, nyr, para 128 ff.

[97] Krajewski, 'External Trade Law and Constitutional Treaty' (above n 32) 114, who argues that only those aspects of FDI which have a direct link with international trade would be covered. See also the discussion in JA Bischoff, 'Just a Little *Bit* of "Mixity"? The EU's Role in the Field of International Investment Protection Law' (2011) 5 *CML Rev* 1527, 1539 ff.

[98] Under Art XXVIII(d)(i) GATS, the supply of services by means of a 'commercial presence' refers to any type of business or professional establishment, including through 'the constitution, acquisition or *maintenance* of a juridical person' (emphasis added).

[99] See text at chapter 4, I.A and accompanying notes.

[100] But see Ceyssens, 'Towards a Common Foreign Investment Policy?' (above n 77) 281. For an analysis of the substantive protection granted to investors under the FET standard and the extent to which that treatment is protected under EU law, see the text at chapter 5, II.C and accompanying notes. Arguably, for the same reason the Union is empowered to enter into commitments on the standard of full protection and security.

So far as the post-establishment treatment of FDI is concerned, the Union's external FDI competence seems to cover the treatment granted in connection with the initial establishment of third-country direct investors in the Single Market. For the purpose of the operation of the internal market mechanism in relation to FDI, this aspect of the post-establishment treatment of FDI was characterised as the participation of third-country direct investors in the internal economy of a Member State. Arguably, the Union's FDI competence does not, however, extend to the participation of third-country direct investors in those economic activities that are covered by the internal market mechanism. Similarly, the Court held in *Opinion 2/92* that the participation of non-EU controlled companies in trade within the Union is covered by the internal market rules and not by the common commercial policy.[101] The internal market aspects of the post-establishment treatment of FDI, ie, the issue of secondary rights of mobility for third-country direct investors, would therefore seem to be excluded from the scope of the Union's post-Lisbon FDI competence. As a result, the legal bases for an external agreement covering the post-establishment treatment of FDI in the Single Market would have to be Article 207 TFEU *and* (insofar as third-country direct investors would be able to invoke the internal market mechanism) the relevant internal market legal basis.[102] Union competence in the latter area is, moreover, non-exclusive, except insofar as the Union has exercised its internal competences.

Farthest removed from the traditionally trade-related focus of the common commercial policy is the issue of investment protection. It has been argued by some with reference to Article 345 TFEU[103] that investment protection may be excluded from the scope of the Union's FDI competence.[104] However, even if EU law does not constitute a dedicated internal investment protection regime, Article 207(6) TFEU could arguably not for that reason preclude the Union from entering into commitments with third countries in relation to investment protection.[105] A parallel could here be drawn between the Union's FDI competence and Union competence under the scope of the TRIPS Agreement, which establishes a system of intellectual property rights protection. Importantly, investment protection commitments in investment agreements do not harmonise national systems of property rights, but merely lay down particular standards of treatment. The inclusion of investment protection commitments in Union external agreements argu-

---

[101]   *Opinion 2/92* [1995] ECR I-521, para 8. See also C-414/11 *Daiichi Sankyo Co Ltd, Sanofi-Aventis Deutschland GmbH v DEMO Anonimos Viomikhaniki kai Emporiki Etairia Farmakon* (nyr, 2013), para 50: '[it] follows from [Art 207(1) TFEU], in particular the second sentence which states that the common commercial policy is within the context of "the Union's external action", that policy relates to trade with non-member countries, not to trade in the internal market'.

[102]   See also Dimopoulos, *EU Foreign Investment Law* (above n 90) 96.

[103]   'The Treaties shall in no way prejudice the rules in Member States governing the system of property ownership.'

[104]   Ceyssens, 'Towards a Common Foreign Investment Policy?' (above n 77) 279 ff. See also Bischoff, 'Just a Little *Bit* of "Mixity"?' (above n 97) 1543 ff.

[105]   But see also: Dimopoulos, 'The Common Commercial Policy after Lisbon' (above n 73) 115 f, who argues that investment protection could be excluded precisely by virtue of the principle of parallelism allegedly enshrined in Art 207(6) TFEU.

ably falls under the scope of the Union's FDI competence insofar as these provisions merely concern the *exercise* of the competence of the Member States to regulate property rights.[106] It therefore seems possible to argue that the Union's FDI competence extends to the issue of investment protection.

Similarly, the Union is arguably empowered under the TFEU provisions on the CCP to enter into commitments with third countries with the effect of establishing a system of investor-state dispute settlement. Assuming that investment protection falls within the scope of the Union's post-Lisbon FDI competence, investor-state dispute settlement would be an important aspect of the investment protection regime constituted by the investment-related provisions in Union external agreements. The Union is also already a contracting party to the Energy Charter Treaty (ECT), which contains investor-state dispute settlement provisions. The Union's competence to subject itself to international mechanisms of dispute settlement has been underlined by the CJEU when it held that the Union's competence in international relations 'necessarily entails the power to submit to the decisions of a court which is created by such an agreement as regards the interpretation and application of its provisions'.[107] The Union's competence to conclude international agreements that provide for binding dispute settlement in relation to claims not only by states, but also by individuals, is underscored by the Union's competence to accede to the European Convention on Human Rights.[108]

At the same time, the Union's competence to submit to a system of international dispute settlement needs to be exercised in a way that is compatible with the EU legal order,[109] in particular Article 19(1) TEU[110] and Article 344

---

[106] By analogy, see the case law in the field of intellectual property rights: C-30/90 *Commission v United Kingdom* [1992] ECR I-892, para 28; C-350/92 *Spain v Council* [1995] ECR I-1985. See also *Opinion 1/94* [1994] ECR I-5267, para 59, where the Court held that the (then) Community was competent, at the level of internal legislation, to harmonise national laws in the field of intellectual property on the basis of (then) Arts 100 and 100a EC. The Court also observed that the Court has indeed created new rights superimposed on national rights on the basis of (now) Art 352 TFEU in (now) Council Regulation 207/2009 of 26 February 2009 on the Community trade mark [2009] OJ L78/1. The Union now also holds an explicit competence to establish 'measures for the creation of European intellectual property rights to provide uniform protection of intellectual property rights throughout the Union and for the setting-up of centralised Union-wide authorisation, coordination and supervision arrangements' under Art 118 TFEU.

[107] *Opinion 1/91* [1991] ECR I-6079, para 40. See also more generally *Opinion 1/00* [2002] ECR I-3493; *Opinion 1/09* [2011] ECR I-1137.

[108] Article 6(2) TEU: 'The Union shall accede to the European Convention for the Protection of Human Rights and Fundamental Freedoms.'

[109] I Govaere, 'Beware of the Trojan Horse: Dispute Settlement in (Mixed) Agreements and the Autonomy of the EU Legal Order' in C Hillion and P Koutrakos (eds), *Mixed Agreements Revisited: The European Union and the Member States in the World* (Oxford, Hart Publishing, 2010); F Hoffmeister and P Ondrusek, 'The European Community in International Litigation' (2008) 1 *Revue Hellénique de Droit International* 205; N Lavranos, 'The Mox Plant and IJzeren Rijn Disputes: Which Court is the Supreme Arbiter?' (2006) 1 *Leiden Journal of International Law* 223; PFJS Strik, 'From Washington with Love: Investor-State Arbitration and the Jurisdictional Monopoly of the Court of Justice of the European Union' (2009–2010) *Cambridge Yearbook of European Legal Studies* 425. On the interplay between investor-state dispute settlement under intra-EU BITs and the autonomy of the EU legal order, see the text at chapter 5, V and accompanying notes.

[110] '[The CJEU] shall ensure that in the interpretation and application of the Treaties the law is observed.'

TFEU.[111] The Court has linked its interpretation of these provisions in various contexts to the notion of the autonomy of the EU legal order, respect for which is to be assured by the Court. A first reservation of the Court concerns the putting at risk of the uniform application of EU law by reason of the replication of EU rules in an international agreement, which allow for a different interpretation of these rules to be applied within the Union.[112] Secondly, only the Court may rule on the division of competences between the Union and the Member States.[113] Thirdly, only the Court can assess the legality of Union or Member State measures under EU law, and the Union cannot be bound to a particular interpretation of EU law.[114] So long as arbitral tribunals do not rule on the validity of Union or Member State measures under EU law, give an interpretation of EU law that is binding on the Union or the Member States, or rule on the division of competences between the Union and the Member States, it seems that the Union's FDI competence can in principle be exercised by concluding investment agreements that provide for investor-state arbitration.[115]

It has moreover been suggested that provisions in external agreements, which deal with labour, environment or technical cooperation in the field of investment, may be concluded by the Union on the basis of the TFEU provisions on the CCP, even if that could not be the main objective of such an agreement.[116] Indeed, in *Opinion 1/78*, the Court ruled that agreements concluded on the basis of (then) Article 113 EEC could include provisions on technological assistance, research programmes, labour conditions in the industry concerned and consultation in relation to national tax policies.[117] Yet, in *Opinion 2/00*,[118] the Court rejected the view that every instrument regulating a certain economic activity could be concluded on the basis of the (then) EC Treaty provisions on the CCP. The Court ruled that an international instrument cannot be concluded solely on the basis of the (now) TFEU provisions on the CCP if the primary aim of an agreement is not to regulate international trade.[119] At the same time, the Union has to respect the

---

[111] 'Member States undertake not to submit a dispute concerning the interpretation or application of the Treaties to any method of settlement other than those provided for therein.'

[112] *Opinion 1/91* (above n 107) paras 41–44.

[113] Ibid para 35.

[114] Ibid para 46; *Opinion 1/00* (above n 107), para 13; *Opinion 1/09* (above n 107), para 78.

[115] See the text at II.B(ii) for the modalities proposed by the Commission for investor-state dispute settlement under international investment agreements to which the Union is a party. For more analysis, see also SW Schill, 'Luxembourg Limits: Conditions for Investor-State Dispute Settlement under Future EU Investment Agreements' in M Bungenberg, A Reinisch and C Tietje (eds), *EU and Investment Agreements: Open Questions and Remaining Challenges* (Baden-Baden, Nomos, 2013) 37; M Burgstaller, 'Investor-State Arbitration in EU International Investment Agreements with Third Countries' (2012) 2 *Legal Issues of European Integration* 207; A Dimopoulos, 'The Compatibility of Future EU Investment Agreements with EU Law' (2012) 4 *Legal Issues of European Integration* 447; PFJS Strik, 'From Washington with Love: Investor-State Arbitration and the Jurisdictional Monopoly of the Court of Justice of the European Union' (2009–2010) *Cambridge Yearbook of European Legal Studies* 425.

[116] Ceyssens, 'Towards a Common Foreign Investment Policy?' (above n 77) 282.

[117] *Opinion 1/78* [1979] ECR 2871, para 56.

[118] *Opinion 2/00* [2001] ECR I-9713.

[119] Ibid para 23.

general objectives enshrined in Article 9 TFEU[120] in exercising its FDI competence, such as to guarantee a high level of employment and to protect human
health. Moreover, the Union's FDI competence should be exercised in accordance
with the overarching principles of the Union's external action in Article 21(2)
TEU, such as '(b) to consolidate and support . . . human rights', '(d) to foster the
sustainable economic, social and environmental development of developing
countries, with the primary aim of eradicating poverty' and '(f) to help develop
measures to preserve and improve the quality of the environment and the sustainable management of global natural resources, in order to ensure sustainable
development'.

The Union is therefore arguably empowered, pursuant to the Lisbon reform of
the CCP, to take measures that eliminate restrictions on FDI containing provisions
on certain development, social, environmental and human rights purposes.
However, pursuant to Article 207(6) TFEU, the Union will have to respect the
exclusions to harmonisation under the TFEU, such as in the fields of employment,[121]
social policy,[122] education[123] and culture.[124] Moreover, the Union cannot conclude
external agreements on the basis of Article 207 TFEU that have developmental,
social, environmental or human rights purposes as their primary aim. For agreements whose predominant purpose is to achieve those objectives, a dedicated legal
basis elsewhere in the TFEU would have to be found.

To sum up, in the pre-Lisbon era, the Community's limited external competence in the field of FDI under the EC Treaty provisions on the CCP could not
satisfactorily be supplemented by having recourse to additional legal bases. In the
post-Lisbon era, the Union holds an exclusive competence in the field of FDI. It
seems possible to argue that the Union's FDI competence empowers the Union to
assume international commitments as regards both the liberalisation and protection of FDI. As a result, the Union's action in the field of commercial policy will
move away further from the traditionally trade-related focus of the CCP. In particular, the possibility for the Union to include provisions in external agreements
on investment protection and investor-state dispute settlement would further
reinforce the autonomous character of the CCP in relation to the internal legal
organisation in the field of FDI, since EU investors do not have access to investor-
state arbitration under EU law. An important limit to the Union's FDI competence is arguably that it does not extend to the issue of secondary rights of mobility
for third-country direct investors, which remains covered by the relevant internal
market legal bases and is therefore in principle shared so far as these competences
have not been exercised. Moreover, competence for assuming investment-related

---

[120] 'In defining and implementing its policies and activities, the Union shall take into account
requirements linked to the promotion of a high level of employment, the guarantee of adequate social
protection, the fight against social exclusion, and a high level of education, training and protection of
human health.'
[121] Article 149(2) TFEU.
[122] Article 153(2)(a) TFEU.
[123] Article 165(4) TFEU.
[124] Article 166(4) TFEU.

commitments in relations with third countries so far as concerns foreign portfolio investment, as well as capital transfers in relation to FDI, seems to be shared with the Member States under the TFEU provisions on free movement of capital.

II. IMPLICATIONS OF THE LISBON REFORM OF THE CCP FOR THE UNION'S TREATY-MAKING PRACTICE IN THE FIELD OF FDI

This section examines the Union's pre-Lisbon external practice in the field of FDI, as well as the first signs of an emerging post-Lisbon practice in this field. The first part shows that, even if the (then) Community lacked a dedicated external FDI competence, pre-Lisbon external agreements did contain investment-related provisions. These focused mainly on the issue of liberalisation of FDI and have been concluded on a variety of legal bases. In an earlier stage, they were for the most part modelled on the language of the internal market concepts, such as the freedom of establishment and free movement of capital, while investment-related provisions in later agreements have been modelled on the relevant provisions in the GATS.

The second part discusses the main elements of the common international investment policy as proposed by the Commission, under which the Union will not only develop a more comprehensive market access strategy for EU companies in third countries, but will also enter into commitments with third countries on the issue of investment protection. This part first addresses the first steps and main challenges in the implementation of the common international investment policy and then discusses the proposed Regulation on financial responsibility. Under the latter instrument, the Union and the Member States will allocate financial responsibility for breaches of investment agreements to which the Union is a party and, concomitantly, determine who defends a particular measure at issue in investor-state arbitration under these agreements.

A. Pre-Lisbon External Practice in the Field of FDI

From an early stage of Community external practice, it has been the Commission's intention progressively to include more ambitious investment-related provisions in external agreements.[125] For instance, while observing a mounting competition from the United States and Japan, the Commission proposed an elaborate Community approach to encouraging European investment in developing countries in a 1978 Communication, particularly as a response to problems such as creeping expropriation measures and a resulting stagnation of European out-

---

[125] For an overview of early Commission policy and Community practice, see J Voss, 'The Protection and Promotion of European Private Investment in Development Countries – an Approach Towards a Concept for a European Policy on Foreign Investment: A German Contribution' (1981) 3 *CML Rev* 363.

bound investment.[126] Recognising that BITs were concluded by the Member States, but that their scope and coverage differed, the Commission argued that the Community seemed to offer the right dimension for action to promote investment in developing countries.[127] The Commission proposed that Community agreements would not substitute for but *complement* the network of Member State investment protection agreements. In addition, the Commission noted in 1980 the Community's interest in negotiating investment agreements with (regional) groups of developing countries.[128] In the 1996 Market Access Strategy, the Commission took the view that:

> Benefits to foreign competitors from the liberalisation of the internal market should be matched by efforts to ensure EU business opportunities on third country markets.[129]

In that Communication, the Commission emphasised the importance of achieving liberalisation commitments in the field of trade and investment, to be achieved by pursuing both bilateral and multilateral avenues.

As was pointed out in chapter 1, there has been a persistent lack of achievement in multilateral settings, such as the WTO and the OECD, on the liberalisation of FDI. As a result, the Community for the most part advanced its investment liberalisation agenda by concluding agreements with individual or smaller groups of third countries. A focus on bilateral rule-making for investment in addition to multilateral rule-making is evident from the 2006 Communication on 'Global Europe', in which the Commission has explained that these bilateral initiatives address issues, including investment, that fall outside of the multilateral trade agenda.[130] At the same time, the Community's commitment to multilateralism was underlined by stating that 'there will be no European retreat from multilateralism'.[131] The liberalisation of FDI was singled out in this Communication as a particularly important element of the Community's approach to international economic relations, for the reason that:

> Geography and proximity still matter. Establishing a 'physical' presence in a foreign country helps EU companies realise business opportunities, makes the flow of trade more

---

[126] Communication from the Commission to the Council, 'Need for Community action to encourage European investment in developing countries and guidelines for such action', COM(78)23 final, 30 January 1978, Brussels.

[127] Ibid 5.

[128] Report from the Commission to the Council, *Investment Protection and Promotion Clauses in Agreements between the Community and Various Categories of Developing Countries: Achievements to Date and Guidelines for Future Action*, COM(80)204 final, 8 May 1980, Brussels, 18.

[129] Communication from the Commission to the Council, the European Parliament, the Economic and Social Committee and the Committee of the Regions, 'The global challenge of international trade: a market access strategy for the European Union', COM(96)53 final, 14 February 1996, Brussels, 3.

[130] Communication from the Commission to the Council, the European Parliament, the European Economic and Social Committee and the Committee of the Regions, 'Global Europe: competing in the world, a contribution to the EU's growth and jobs strategy', COM(2006)567 final, 4 October 2006, Brussels, 8–10.

[131] Ibid.

predictable, and consolidates the image and reputation of the firm and of the country of origin.[132]

A need for new competitiveness-driven Free Trade Agreements (FTAs) was recognised, which aim at the highest possible degree of trade liberalisation including the far-reaching liberalisation of services and investment.[133] Therefore, the Communication called for the development of a new, ambitious model Union investment agreement in close coordination with the Member States. The 'Minimum Platform for EU FTAs', which was developed, focuses on securing additional market access commitments.[134]

Yet the Community has never concluded an external agreement exclusively devoted to investment. Community external agreements have traditionally covered a wide range of issues, such as commercial policy, development cooperation and general political dialogue, amongst which a number of investment-related provisions can occupy an important, but by no means predominant place.[135] Though Community external agreements have come in many different guises,[136] there are strong similarities so far as concerns their investment-related provisions.[137] Sharing broadly similar objectives, an important feature has persistently been that these provisions do not focus so much upon the protection of invest-

---

[132] Ibid 6–7.

[133] Ibid 9. See also Communication from the Commission to the European Parliament, the Council, the European Economic and Social Committee and the Committee of the Regions, 'On the external dimension of the Lisbon Strategy for Growth and Jobs: reporting on market access and setting the framework for more effective international regulatory cooperation', COM(2008)874 final, 16 December 2008, Brussels, 5.

[134] For an analysis of the template of investment provisions that has been developed in this context, see N Maydell, 'The European Community's Minimum Platform on Investment or the Trojan Horse of Investment Competence' in A Reinisch and C Knahr (eds), *International Investment Law in Context* (Utrecht, International Publishing, Utrecht, 2008) 73. The Minimum Platform was initially laid down in the following document, which is not accessible for the public: Note from the General Secretariat of the Council to the Article 133 Committee, *Minimum Platform on Investment for EU FTAs*, 15375/06, adopted by the Council of the European Union on 27 November 2006, Brussels. It has reportedly been finalised in early 2009 in Council doc 7242/09 of 6 March 2009. It has been used for the negotiation of the EU-CARIFORUM Economic Partnership Agreement, the EU-Korea Free Trade Agreement, the Trade Agreement with Peru and Colombia, as well as the Trade Agreement with Central America. On these agreements, see the text at II.B(i). The Minimum Platform has also been used for the negotiation of a Deep and Comprehensive Free Trade Agreement with Ukraine. See in particular Hoffmeister and Ünüvar, 'From BITs and Pieces towards European Investment Agreements' (above n 90) 61 ff.

[135] For an analysis of the substance of many types of Community bilateral agreements, see M Maresceau, *Bilateral Agreements Concluded by the European Community* (Collected Courses of the Hague Academy of International Law, 2004) 125–451. See also M Cremona, 'The European Union and Regional Trade Agreements' in C Herrmann and JP Terhechte (eds), *European Yearbook of International Economic Law* (Heidelberg, Springer, 2010) 245.

[136] For a typology, see S Peers, 'EC Frameworks of International Relations: Co-operation, Partnership and Association' in AA Dashwood and C Hillion (eds), *EC External Relations Law* (London, Sweet & Maxwell, 2000).

[137] For an analysis of the investment-related provisions in Community external agreements, see Hoffmeister and Ünüvar, 'From BITs and Pieces towards European Investment Agreements' (above n 90) 61 ff; Ceyssens, 'Towards a Common Foreign Investment Policy?' (above n 77) 265 ff; W Shan, 'Towards a Common European Community Policy on Investment Issues' (2001) 3 *Journal of World Investment and Trade* 604, 614 ff; J Karl, 'The Competence for Foreign Direct Investment: New Powers for the European Union?' (2004) 3 *Journal of World Investment and Trade* 413, 416 ff.

ments, but are geared mainly towards the liberalisation of the legal regime applicable to foreign investment. As a result, one finds provisions in different Community external agreements that commit the contracting parties to varying degrees of liberalisation, grounded however in the same concern with the free movement of production factors. In addition, there is a near-exclusive focus on assets that have some productive capacity as opposed to any kind of asset, such as those that merely serve a financial purpose. In other words, the investment-related provisions in these agreements focus on foreign direct investment rather than on foreign portfolio investment.[138]

The investment-related provisions in Community external agreements have traditionally dealt with the admission and treatment of direct investment, as well as with capital transfers in relation to such transactions. For a long time, they were drafted in the language of the law of the internal market in the sense that the basic concepts used were those of 'establishment' and 'movement of capital'. This is most clear in the Agreement establishing the European Economic Area (EEA), which stipulates that there shall be no restrictions on freedom of establishment and free movement of capital to the EEA states (Norway, Iceland and Liechtenstein) and thereby extends far-reaching investment liberalisation commitments to these countries in the same wording as the TFEU freedoms.[139] So far as concerns the provisions on 'establishment' in other Community external agreements, in most other agreements two distinct regulatory issues are addressed separately: first, the issue of the admission of direct investment and, secondly, the issue of the post-establishment treatment of direct investment. For example, the Partnership and Cooperation Agreement (PCA) with Kazakhstan distinguished between treatment with regard to the conditions affecting establishment, on the one hand, and treatment in respect of the operation of subsidiaries and branches, on the other.[140] To either of these two regulatory issues at least one of the contracting parties typically accorded national treatment (NT) or most favoured nation (MFN) treatment, or both, whether or not subject to a number of reservations for specific sectors listed in an annex.[141] The provisions in Community external agreements dealing with the free movement of capital have mostly been subsidiary to those

---

[138] Exceptions are Art 40 of the EEA Agreement [1994] OJ L1/3 and the Euro-Mediterranean Agreements (EMAs), such as Art 31 of the EMA with Israel [2000] OJ L147/3. Most Stabilisation and Association Agreements (SAAs) with the Balkan countries provide for the future liberalisation of foreign portfolio investment upon expiry of a transitional period. See, eg Art 60(2) of the SAA with Croatia [2005] OJ L26/3. Exceptionally, the SAA with Montenegro [2010] OJ L108/3 does provide for liberalisation of foreign portfolio investment (Art 63(4)). See also Art 8(2)(2) of the EU-Korea FTA [2011] OJ L127/6.

[139] [1994] OJ L1/3; Art 31(1) on establishment, Art 40 on capital movements.

[140] Article 23 [1999] OJ L196/3.

[141] For example, Art 28 of the PCA with Russia [1997] OJ L327/3 accorded (subject to a number of reservations) Russian and EU companies MFN treatment with regard to their establishment, and MFN treatment and NT to subsidiaries with regard to their operation, while in Art 23 of the PCA with Kazakhstan [1999] OJ L196/3, EU companies are also accorded NT with regard to their establishment in Kazakhstan, but not vice versa. By contrast, the Europe Agreements (EAs) contained reciprocal commitments to accord NT both to the issue of establishment and to the operation of subsidiaries, albeit subject to a specific timetable. See, eg Art 44(1), (3) of the EA with Poland [1993] OJ L348/2.

dealing with establishment, by stipulating that there should not be any restrictions (subject to possibilities for derogation explicitly mentioned in the agreements) on capital movements relating to direct investment, including the repatriation of these investments and of any profits, subject to the provisions on establishment in the agreement, and in accordance with the laws of the host state.[142]

Even if such provisions on investment in Community external agreements have for a long time mostly been drafted in the language of the law of the internal market, they arguably do not have a similar meaning as the internal market freedoms within the Single Market. The extent to which such agreements extend the internal market freedoms to relations with third countries is (for agreements other than the EEA Agreement) prima facie limited by the fact that the provisions relating to establishment are explicitly qualified. In particular, where NT and MFN treatment are accorded 'with regard to the conditions affecting establishment', this is arguably not the same as 'freedom of establishment'. The CJEU has, moreover, shown reluctance to extend internal market legal concepts to situations governed by similar language in relations with third countries. When faced with such a similarity in terms, the Court has referred to the distinguishing feature of Single Market integration, which:

> by establishing a common market and progressively approximating the economic policies of the Member States, seeks to unite national markets into a single market having the characteristic of a domestic market.[143]

The Court has interpreted the obligations flowing from specific provisions in Community external agreements differently from corresponding internal market concepts in view of the fact that the objectives and legal context of such external agreements differ from that of Single Market integration.[144]

It has been observed that the CJEU may now be more ready than previously to interpret provisions of external agreements in the same way as corresponding provisions in EU primary law.[145] The substantive scope of the free movement-related provisions in Union external agreements has indeed more recently been given the same interpretation by the Court in a number of cases[146] as identical concepts in the law of the internal market. It can be observed that this does not mean that the intensity of corresponding obligations under the free movement-

---

[142] See, eg Art 41(2) of the PCA with Kazakhstan [1999] OJ L196/3; Art 52(2) of the PCA with Russia [1997] OJ L327/3.

[143] 270/80 *Polydor* [1982] ECR 379, para 16.

[144] 270/80 *Polydor* [1982] ECR 379, paras 15–16; *Opinion 1/91* [1991] ECR I-6079, para 14; C-312/91 *Metalsa* [1993] ECR 3751, para 11. See also in the context of air transport C-547/10 P *Swiss Confederation v Commission* (nyr, 2013), paras 78–81.

[145] FG Jacobs, 'Direct Effect and Interpretation of International Agreements in the Recent Case Law of the European Court of Justice' in AA Dashwood and M Maresceau (eds), *Law and Practice of EU External Relations: Salient Features of a Changing Landscape* (Cambridge, Cambridge University Press, 2008).

[146] Ibid. See, eg C-268/99 *Jany* [2001] ECR I-8615, paras 35–42, in relation to the EAs with Poland and the Czech Republic; C-265/03 *Simutenkov* [2005] ECR I-2579, paras 30–41, in relation to the PCA with Russia (ie outside the context of enlargement).

related provisions in these agreements is interpreted identically.[147] Even if Union external agreements, so far as concerns investment, share the broadly similar objective of the liberalisation of the legal regime applicable to foreign investment, there is arguably a different intensify of their investment-related commitments. This reflects the fact that such external agreements themselves do not aim to create a single market with third countries, even if they may gradually prepare third countries for a possible accession.[148]

It can be observed that the investment-related provisions in a number of recent agreements contain a number of important innovations. First, the investment-related provisions in Union external agreements have more recently been modelled on the investment-related provisions in the GATS and, thereby, constitute a move away from the language of the internal market freedoms. Moreover, in more recent Union external agreements one can find provisions on investment behaviour and a non-lowering of standards by the public authorities, which contribute to a more balanced approach to the liberalisation of the legal framework applicable to FDI. It can be submitted that these elements collectively add to the further 'deepening' of the content of Union external agreements so far as concerns investment.[149] The following discusses a selection of the constitutive elements of these two more recent innovations in the investment-related provisions in Union external agreements.

The EU-Chile FTA[150] that was concluded as part of an association agreement, which entered fully into force in 2005, contains far-reaching investment liberalisation commitment in the form of NT commitments with regard to both the pre-establishment and post-establishment stage of FDI.[151] The respective provisions on investment liberalisation largely follow the wording of the provisions in the GATS on commercial presence in the services sector, such as by defining 'establishment' in Article 131(d) as including '(i) the constitution, acquisition or maintenance of a legal person and (ii) the creation or maintenance of a branch or a representative office, within the territory of a Party for the purpose of performing an economic activity'.[152] Moreover, it contains a departure with respect to the investment-related provisions in agreements considered thus far insofar as these commitments have been agreed for specific sectors and subsectors that are included in schedules of commitments enshrined in an annex. NT is thus granted

---

[147] See in particular C-63/99 *Gloszczuk* [2001] ECR I-6369, paras 47–53, in relation to the EA with Poland; C-257/99 *Barkoci and Malik* [2001] ECR I-6557, paras 50–56, in relation to the EA with the Czech Republic.

[148] C-63/99 *Gloszczuk* [2001] ECR I-6369, para 50; C-257/99 *Barkoci and Malik* [2001] ECR I-6557, para 53.

[149] See also Cremona, 'The European Union and Regional Trade Agreements' (above n 135) 247.

[150] [2002] OJ L352/3.

[151] Ibid, see Art 132 on establishment in non-services sectors: 'In the sectors inscribed in Annex X, and subject to any conditions and qualifications set out therein, with respect to establishment, each Party shall grant to legal and natural persons of the other Party treatment no less favourable than that it accords to its own legal and natural persons performing a like economic activity.'

[152] See Art XXVIII(d) GATS.

in accordance with a so-called positive list approach, whereby the agreement follows the type of schedules of commitments under the GATS. Two different parts of the relevant annex (X) are dedicated to the respective commitments for the Community and its Member States and for Chile. In addition, similar to the situation under the GATS, the Member States apply a number of different limitations on NT in relation to establishment.

The EU-CARIFORUM Economic Partnership Agreement (EPA),[153] which was signed in 2008 and is currently provisionally applied, contains a number of additional new elements. First, a provision can be found with the effect of creating a right of 'market access through commercial presence', albeit limited to certain sectors and subject to a number of qualifications.[154] Specifically, Article 67 on 'market access' provides that:

> With respect to market access through commercial presence, the EC Party and the Signatory CARIFORUM States shall accord to commercial presences and investors of the other Party a treatment no less favourable than that provided for in the specific commitments contained in Annex IV.

An *absolute* standard of treatment is applied to the issue of market access in the sectors enshrined in the Annex.[155] This provision moreover constitutes a departure from the language of the internal market that was used in external agreements considered thus far insofar as the terminology of 'commercial presences and investors' is used, rather than 'establishment'. The term 'commercial presence' is derived from the GATS.[156] In addition, Article 68(1) on 'national treatment' provides:

> In the sectors where market access commitments are inscribed in Annex IV and subject to any conditions and qualifications set out therein, with respect to all measures affecting commercial presence the EC Party and the Signatory CARIFORUM States shall grant to commercial presences and investors of the other Party treatment no less favourable than that they accord to their own like commercial presences and investors.

---

[153] [2008] OJ L289/I/3. See the notice concerning the provisional application of this agreement, [2008] OJ 352/62. The CARIFORUM states are Antigua and Bermuda, Bahamas, Barbados, Belize, Dominica, the Dominican Republic, Grenada, Guyana, Haiti, Jamaica, Saint Lucia, Saint Vincent and the Grenadines, Saint Kitts and Nevis, Suriname, and Trinidad and Tobago.

[154] Article 66 provides that the relevant provisions apply to all economic sectors with the exception of mining, manufacturing and processing of nuclear materials, the production of or trade in arms, munitions and war material, audio-visual services, national maritime cabotage and some national and international air transport services. Its coverage thus in principle extends to FDI in the agricultural, industrial and services sectors.

[155] Article 67(2) specifies that such market access rights preclude the maintenance or adoption of limitations on the number of commercial presences; limitation on the total value of transactions or assets; limitations on the number of operations or on the total quantity of output; limitations on the participation of foreign capital in terms of maximum percentage; and measures which restrict or require specific types of commercial presence. However, pursuant to Article 66 n 2, issues of investment protection are excluded from the scope of application of the provisions on investment treatment: 'Measures relating to expropriation and investor-to-State dispute settlement such as those covered in bilateral investment treaties are not deemed to affect commercial presence'.

[156] Article I(2)(c) GATS.

This provision follows the practice of granting NT, which is a relative standard of treatment, albeit to 'commercial presences and investors' rather than to the operation of subsidiaries and branches. The contracting parties have adopted a positive list approach to the admission and treatment of direct investors, whereby NT commitments apply only to those sectors for which market access commitments have been entered into.[157]

As in the EU-Chile FTA, the schedules of commitments in the EU-CARIFORUM EPA cover FDI in both the services and non-services sectors. However, while the schedules of commitments for the Union and the Member States in the EU-Chile FTA do not draw a strict distinction between the issue of commercial presence in the services and non-services sectors (Annexes IV.A and IV.B), in the EU-CARIFORUM EPA those for the CARIFORUM States do (Annexes IV.E and F). So far as the Union and the Member States are concerned, the Annexes list the sectors and subsectors for which a certain commitment is assumed and the scope of liberalisation to which the reservations apply, as well as both horizontal or sector Union-wide reservations and specific reservations of the Member States. As a result of the specific commitments contained in Annex IV, it can moreover be observed that the opening up to FDI is asymmetric to the extent that the Union opened up to FDI more than the CARIFORUM states, which apply more conditions and limitations, within a more limited sectoral coverage.

The EU-CARIFORUM EPA also contains provisions on investor behaviour, as well as on the need for the contracting parties to achieve certain public policy objectives. Under Article 72, the parties are to take the necessary measures to ensure, inter alia, that investors do not engage in corruption, that they act in accordance with core labour standards and do not operate in a manner that circumvents international environmental or labour conditions. Moreover, Article 73 provides that the parties shall ensure that FDI is not encouraged:

> by lowering domestic environmental, labour or occupational health and safety legislation and standards or by relaxing core labour standards or laws aimed at protecting and promoting cultural diversity.

In addition, Article 224 allows the parties to adopt measures that are necessary to achieve certain public policy objectives, such as to protect public order and secure public morals. These are important indications that the Union increasingly balances investment liberalisation commitments in external agreements with rules pertaining to the social and development dimension of FDI.[158] As a result, there is more equilibrium between the respective rights and obligations of states and investors than in the external agreements, which do not contain such provisions. At the same time, as in the other external agreements in the pre-Lisbon era, the

---

[157] At the same time, under Art 70 of the EU-CARIFORUM EPA, MFN treatment is provided for any measure affecting commercial presence, notwithstanding whether it falls under the specific schedules of commitments.

[158] For analysis, see A Dimopoulos, 'Shifting the Emphasis from Investment Protection to Liberalization and Development: The EU as a New Global Factor in the Field of Foreign Investment' (2010) 1 *JWI* 5.

investment provisions of the EU-CARIFORUM EPA do not touch upon issues of investment protection.

The investment-related provisions in the EU-Korea FTA,[159] which is provisionally applied since 1 July 2011, are drafted along the same lines as those in the agreements with Chile and the CARIFORUM states.[160] Chapter 7 of the EU-Korea FTA contains investment liberalisation commitments based on a positive list approach.[161] The Agreement also draws a distinction between the issue of market access (albeit 'through establishment', rather than 'through commercial presence'), under Article 7.11, and the issue of NT and MFN treatment 'with respect to all measures affecting establishment', which is dealt with under Articles 7.12 and 7.14. It is moreover made explicit that investment protection, including investor-state dispute settlement procedures, is not covered by the provisions dealing with establishment.[162] An important horizontal exception is that 'each Party retains the right to regulate and to introduce new regulations to meet legitimate policy objectives' under Article 7.1(4). Moreover, Article 13.3 on sustainable development recognises the right of each contracting party 'to establish its own levels of environmental and labour protection, and to adopt or modify accordingly its relevant laws and policies', while Articles 13.4 and 13.5 reaffirm the contracting parties' commitments to social and environmental standards, such as under the ILO Convention and multilateral environmental agreements to which they have subscribed. A novelty of the FTA is that a review clause has been inserted, pursuant to which the parties will assess the legal framework applicable to investment and address obstacles to investment after three years and at regular intervals thereafter.[163] Importantly, the review clause specifies that this should be done with a view to further deepening the provisions of that Chapter, including with respect to general principles of investment protection.[164]

The investment-related provisions in Union external agreements considered thus far deal mainly with issues of liberalisation and it has been shown that these provisions do not contain commitments in the field of investment protection. The issue of investment protection is not, however, entirely left unmentioned in pre-Lisbon external agreements. The investment liberalisation commitments in many, if not most, Union external agreements were complemented with provisions on the promotion of investment. These consist of best effort clauses stipu-

---

[159] [2011] OJ L127/6. Notice concerning the provisional application of the Free Trade Agreement between the European Union and its Member States, of the one part, and the Republic of Korea, of the other part [2011] OJ L168/1.

[160] In contrast with the EU-CARIFORUM EPA, the FTA with Korea does not contain provisions on investor behaviour, however.

[161] Ibid Art 7.11(1): 'With respect to market access through establishment, each party shall accord to establishments and investors of the other Party treatment no less favourable than that provided for under the terms, limitations and conditions agreed and specified in the specific commitments contained in Annex 7-A.'

[162] Ibid Art 7.10 n 14. Similarly, Art 7.14 n 21.

[163] Ibid Art 7.16(1).

[164] Ibid Art 7.16(2). But see Art 74 of the EU-CARIFORUM EPA.

lating the need for cooperation in the field of cross-border direct investment, in which the Union, the Member States and the third country in question typically expressed their willingness to extend the existing network of BITs ('where appropriate') between the Member States, on the one hand, and the third country, on the other.[165] In the recent agreements with the CARIFORUM states and Korea, there are no specific provisions with regard to the conclusion of BITs by the Member States as part of the provisions on investment promotion, and general provisions explicitly focusing on investment promotion seem to have a less prominent place. It can be observed that such clauses, however, did not in any event provide for comprehensive commitments with regard to the promotion, let alone protection, of investment. As such, they underline the *complementary* character of Union external agreements and Member State investment agreements in the pre-Lisbon era.

Exceptionally, both the Union and the Member States are contracting parties to the Energy Charter Treaty (ECT). As was discussed in chapter 1, this agreement is specifically geared towards trade and investment in the energy sector and contains investment protection provisions that are modelled after Member State BITs, including investor-state dispute settlement provisions. This agreement can be seen as an outlier in the Union's pre-Lisbon external practice. Moreover, Article 258(b) of the Lomé IV Convention stipulated a standard of fair and equitable treatment as part of the provisions on investment treatment.[166] However, dedicated investment protection provisions providing for minimum standards of treatment and specific commitments with regard to compensation for expropriation or investor-state dispute settlement, are conspicuously absent in the pre-Lisbon external practice in the field of FDI. The issue of investment protection has clearly been left to the Member States in the pre-Lisbon era.

Prior to the Lisbon reform of the (now) TFEU provisions on the CCP, most Community external agreements containing investment-related commitments have been concluded as mixed agreements on a variety of legal bases. While investment-related commitments have been concluded under (now) Article 217 TFEU (ex Article 310 EC)[167] on association, many agreements containing investment-related commitments have been concluded on different legal bases, such as ex Articles 57(2), 133, 181 or 181a, and 308 EC.[168] As a result, there is no clear link between the legal bases upon which specific external agreements have been concluded and the investment-related commitments enshrined in these agreements.

---

[165] See, eg Article 15(b) of the EU-Mexico Economic Partnership, Political Coordination and Cooperation Agreement [2000] OJ L276/44.

[166] [1991] OJ L229/3.

[167] See, eg Decision on the conclusion of the AA with Chile [2005] OJ L84/19.

[168] For example, the EPA with the CARIFORUM states has been concluded on the substantive legal bases of Arts 57(2), 71, 80(2), 133(1), 133(5), (6) and 181 EC [2008] OJ L289/1. The PCA with Russia was concluded on the substantive legal bases of Art 44(2), the last sentence of Art 47(2), and Arts 55, 57(2), 71, 80(2), 93, 133 and 308 EC (in the post-Amsterdam numbering) [1997] OJ L327/1.

B. Union Treaty-making Practice in the Field of FDI in the Post-Lisbon Era

The question arises how the Union is going to exercise its post-Lisbon FDI competence. To this effect, the Commission issued a Communication in July 2010, in which it outlined the main orientations for a Union international investment policy. Both the Council[169] and the European Parliament[170] welcomed the Commission's proposal. Pursuant to these proposed main orientations for the common international investment policy, the Union's external practice in the field of FDI may not evolve so much so far as concerns aspects of liberalisation of FDI, where a further deepening of external practice was already taking place before the entry into force of the Treaty of Lisbon. The Commission has proposed that the investment-related provisions in Union external agreements be broadened to the issue of investment protection. As a result, future Union investment agreements are envisaged to contain, inter alia, the standard of fair and equitable treatment (FET) and investor-state dispute settlement provisions. With a view to including investor-state dispute settlement provisions in Union external agreements, the Commission has moreover issued a proposal for a Regulation on financial responsibility.[171] The instrument to be adopted[172] will provide the modalities for allocating responsibility between the Union and the Member States for breaches of a Union investment agreement, as well as for the conduct of investor-state disputes under these agreements and the related system of payments.

This section discusses the main orientations for the common international investment policy as outlined by the Commission in the 2010 Communication, as well the first steps in the implementation of the common international investment policy. The section then turns to the proposed modalities for participation of the Union and the Member States in investor-state dispute settlement under Union investment agreements. The section highlights that the development of the common international investment policy gives rise to a number of challenges. In particular, while there is agreement between the Commission, the Council and the European Parliament on the need for an ambitious policy on both the liberalisation and protection of investment, there are a number of issues on which a common understanding will need to be found.[173] Moreover, the Regulation on

---

[169] Council of the European Union, 'Conclusions on a comprehensive European international investment policy', 25 October 2010, Luxembourg.

[170] European Parliament resolution of 6 April 2011 on the future European international investment policy, P7_TA(2011)0141.

[171] Proposal for a Regulation of the European Parliament and of the Council establishing a framework for managing financial responsibility linked to investor-state dispute settlement tribunals established by international agreements to which the European Union is a party, COM(2012)335 final, 21 June 2012, Brussels.

[172] See Art 207(2) TFEU: 'The European Parliament and the Council, acting by means of regulations in accordance with the ordinary legislative procedure, shall adopt the measures defining the framework for implementing the common commercial policy.'

[173] See also N Jansen Calamita, 'The Making of Europe's International Investment Policy: Uncertain First Steps' (2012) 3 *Legal Issues of European Integration* 301.

financial responsibility needs to be in place before the conclusion of the first Union external agreement under the common international investment policy that contains provisions on investment protection.

(i) Main Orientations for a Common International Investment Policy

While the Lisbon reform of the (now) TFEU provisions of the CCP is the main catalyst for the development of the common international investment policy, it is important to note that this policy does not deal exclusively with FDI. The common international investment policy deals with 'investment' in a comprehensive way and therefore includes both foreign direct investment and foreign portfolio investment. So far as concerns the liberalisation of investment, the Commission envisages that the common international investment policy will, first, seek to stimulate European investment in non-EU countries. The Commission takes the view that the Union should ensure that EU investors enjoy a level playing field in third countries, consisting in particular of 'uniform and optimal conditions for investment through the progressive abolition of restrictions on investment'.[174] Secondly, the common international investment policy aims to attract non-EU investment in the Single Market. The Commission has expressed the idea of 'openness to investment' through the progressive abolition of restrictions on investment as a 'touchstone' of the Union's international investment policy.[175] As the Commission observes, an intensified comprehensive market access approach can serve to further fill a gap in European international investment relations, since Member State investment protection agreements traditionally do not contain far-reaching commitments with regard to the liberalisation of FDI.[176]

The Commission has moreover proposed the inclusion of provisions on investment protection in future Union external agreement. The broadening of the Union's external practice in the field of investment to the issue of investment protection constitutes a departure from the Union's pre-Lisbon practice in the field of FDI. As to the specific content of the investment-related provisions in future Union external agreements, the Commission takes the view that they should be inspired by the standards of investment protection enshrined in Member State investment agreements.[177] The Commission refers to the standard of fair and equitable treatment and the standard of full security and protection, as well as the inclusion of umbrella clauses, under which contractual rights of investors are protected.[178] The Commission also envisages the inclusion of clauses in future Union external agreements governing the issue of expropriation measures, which should be non-discriminatory and proportionate in order to attain their legitimate objective, such

---

[174] COM(2010)343 (above n 2) 4.
[175] Ibid.
[176] Ibid 5. For analysis, see the text at chapter 4, I and accompanying notes.
[177] Ibid 8.
[178] Ibid.

as by providing for adequate compensation.[179] So far as the enforcement of investment commitments is concerned, the Commission has expressed the view that future Union external agreements should include provisions on investor-state dispute settlement.[180]

The Commission's Communication lays down 'broad principles and parameters for future investment agreements', which 'are to be fully developed and fleshed out in country-specific negotiating recommendations'.[181] At the same time, the Commission refers to the 'best practices' of Member State BITs as a guide to future Union investment agreements.[182] While the Commission's aim for the common international investment policy is to negotiate Union external agreements that contain state-of-the-art investment liberalisation and investment protection provisions, the Commission thus envisages a degree of flexibility in doing so. In this respect, it can be observed that a model Union investment treaty has not been developed. The country-specific, as well as asymmetric, opening up to FDI was already part of the Union's pre-Lisbon external practice in the field of FDI and it is likely to continue to be in future. Yet the ambition to include state-of-the-art investment protection provisions is arguably not served by replacing existing Member State external BITs with Union external agreements that provide for less protection to EU investors in third countries. Flexibility is therefore arguably best built into Union investment agreements so far as concerns the respective commitments on the liberalisation of investment.

The Commission envisages the following four scenarios for the Union to enter into commitments with third countries on the liberalisation and protection of investments. First, the comprehensive issue of investment can be included in ongoing negotiations with third countries, where negotiations have so far focused on issues of market access. The Commission mentions Canada, India and Singapore in this respect.[183] Secondly, stand-alone investment agreements could be negotiated in the short to medium term. The investment-related provisions in such agreements would not be part of a more comprehensive agreement that additionally deals with other issues of economic and non-economic cooperation, but would consist of self-standing investment deals. In this context, the Commission explicitly mentions China and Russia. Thirdly, sectoral agreements could be negotiated with third countries where the conclusion of a comprehensive investment agreement proves unfeasible. An example here is the multilateral ECT in the energy sector. Fourthly, the Commission takes the view that a multilateral initiative could be considered in the long run. Here one can think of

---

[179] Ibid 9. The Commission refers to Art 345 TFEU and the issue of compensation for expropriation under the fundamental freedoms. For a comparison of aspects of the investment protection regime in EU law and Member State investment agreements, see the text at chapter 5, II and accompanying notes.

[180] Ibid10.

[181] Ibid 6.

[182] Ibid 11.

[183] See below for the issue of the extension to investment protection of the mandates for ongoing negotiations with Canada, India and Singapore, as well as the mandates for the negotiation of investment agreements with other third countries.

multilateral settings such as the OECD or the WTO, where no specific negotiations with regard to a comprehensive agreement on investment are ongoing at the moment.

The Commission also points to a number of specific challenges in shaping the common international investment policy. The Commission has highlighted that Union investment agreements should be consistent with other policies of the Union and the Member States, such as on the protection of the environment, health and safety at work, consumer protection, cultural diversity, development policy and competition policy.[184] The Commission recalls that a common international investment policy should be guided by the overarching principles and objectives of the Union's external action, including the promotion of the rule of law, human rights and sustainable development.[185] By being subject to the general principles of external action enshrined in the TEU, the post-Lisbon provisions on the CCP are now arguably less isolated as part of the Union's external practice.[186] In this context, the Commission points to the need to balance the rights and responsibilities of investors, such as in the OECD Guidelines for Multinational Enterprises. So far as the challenge of designing state-of-the-art investor-state dispute settlement provisions in Union investment agreements is concerned, the Commission points, inter alia, to the need for transparency of investor-state dispute settlement with regard to requests for arbitration, submissions, open

---

[184] COM(2010)343 (above n 2) 9. See Art 21(3)(2) TEU, which provides that 'The Union shall ensure consistency between the different areas of its external action and between these and its other policies'. That this provision applies equally to the TFEU provisions on the CCP follows from Art 205 TFEU, which provides that 'The Union's action on the international scene, pursuant to this Part, shall be guided by the principles, pursue the objectives and be conducted in accordance with the general provisions laid down in Chapter 1 of Title V of the Treaty on European Union'. For a discussion of the linguistic ambiguity between the notions of consistency and of coherence in the different language versions of the TEU, see C Hillion, '*Tous pour un, un pour tous!* Coherence in the External Relations of the European Union' in M Cremona (ed), *Developments in EU External Relations Law* (Oxford, Oxford University Press, 2008).

[185] See Art 21(1) TEU, which provides that 'The Union's action on the international scene shall be guided by the principles which have inspired its own creation, development and enlargement, and which it seeks to advance in the wider world: democracy, the rule of law, the universality and indivisibility of human rights and fundamental freedoms, respect for human dignity, the principles of equality and solidarity, and respect for the principles of the United Nations Charter and international law'. See also Art 21(2) TEU, which provides that '[the Union] shall define and pursue common policies and actions . . . in order to: . . . (b) consolidate and support democracy, the rule of law, human rights and the principles of international law; . . . (d) foster the sustainable economic, social and environmental development of developing countries, with the primary aim of eradicating poverty; (e) encourage the integration of all countries into the world economy, including through the progressive abolition of restrictions on international trade; (f) help develop international measures to preserve and improve the quality of the environment and the sustainable management of global natural resources, in order to ensure sustainable development'.

[186] In the view of Krajewski, the post-Lisbon provisions on the CCP even aim at 'new' trade policy objectives, such as human rights, equality and solidarity, sustainable development and the preservation and improvement of the quality of the environment, with the effect that the reduction and abolition of restrictions to trade and investment should not serve as an objective of the CCP unless it contributes to those goals. See Krajewski, 'External Trade Law and Constitutional Treaty' (above n 32) 107 ff. See also M Cremona, 'The Draft Constitutional Treaty: External Relations and External Action' (2003) 6 *CML Rev* 1347, 1349, who takes the view that 'the CCP will in the future also have an explicit sustainable development and human rights mandate'.

hearings, *amicus curiae* briefs and publication of the awards.[187] Moreover, the Commission refers to the possible use of quasi-permanent arbitrators and/or appellate mechanisms in order to enhance the consistency and predictability of investor-state arbitration under Union investment agreements.

In response to the Commission's Communication, the Council has expressed support in its Conclusions of 25 October 2010 for a comprehensive international investment policy that creates a level playing field for EU investors in third countries and for investors from third countries in the Union. The Conclusions reiterate the Union's commitment to maintain an open investment environment and underline the importance of a broad scope for the Union's international investment policy by covering all types of investment.[188] The Council has identified as a priority that the new legal framework should not negatively affect investor protection and guarantees enjoyed under existing Member State BITs, but should increase the level of protection and legal security for EU investors in third countries.[189] As for the criteria to select priority partners, the Council suggests to look specifically at the economic climate in third countries, their market size and growth, the strategic importance of the economic relations of the Union with them, the opportunities offered by these countries in terms of investment, their political and institutional stability, the degree of local legal protection for EU investors, the BITs concluded by Member States with these countries, and at the potential added value of a Union investment agreement with them.[190]

So far as the substance of future Union investment agreements is concerned, the Council's views generally align well with the Commission's proposed main orientations for the Union's international investment policy. The Council has recognised the need for the inclusion in Union investment agreements of the standards of non-discrimination (NT and MFN treatment), fair and equitable treatment, full protection and security, and the protection against expropriation (including the right to prompt, adequate and effective compensation), free capital transfers, as well as an effective investor-state dispute settlement mechanism.[191] Moreover, the Council underlines the importance of the social and environmental dimension of investment, as well as the issue of corporate social responsibility.[192] In addition, the Council highlights that the Union's international investment policy must continue to allow both the Union and the Member States to adopt measures necessary to pursue public policy objectives.[193]

---

[187] COM(2010)343 (above n 2) 10.

[188] Council Conclusions (above n 169) paras 6 and 7.

[189] Ibid para 8. In this context, the Conclusions refer to the importance of transitional arrangements for the replacement of existing BITs by Union investment agreements (ibid para 9). These transitional arrangements, which will be discussed at chapter 4, III, were at the time of the publication of these Conclusions still to be adopted.

[190] Ibid para 12.

[191] Ibid para 14.

[192] Ibid para 16.

[193] Ibid para 17.

The European Parliament (EP) has welcomed the Commission's Communication in its Resolution on the Union's international investment policy and agrees that investment protection should be a key priority.[194] However, the EP has highlighted a number of concerns with regard to the substance of future Union investment agreements, which can be contradistinguished from the broadly concurring views of the Commission and the Council on the main orientations for the Union's international investment policy. Importantly, the EP stresses that the Union's international investment policy should better address the right to protect the public capacity to regulate and to meet the Union's obligation to exercise policy coherence for development, instead of focusing solely on the issue of investment protection.[195] According to the EP, a balance needs to be struck between the objective of investment protection and the preservation of the right of public authorities to regulate in the public interest. In this context, the EP notes the issue of vague language in investment agreements, which are subsequently left open for interpretation by arbitral tribunals.[196] This is a problem for the EP insofar as it opens up the possibility of conflict between private interests and the regulatory tasks of public authorities, particularly under the FET standard. The EP moreover calls for a clear definition of investments to be protected, including both FDI and portfolio investment, with the exclusion, however, of purely 'speculative forms of investment'.[197] It can be observed that the EP does not give further guidance on how to distinguish between 'speculative' and 'non-speculative' forms of investment.

Against the backdrop of these concerns, the EP has identified a number of features as necessary elements of future Union investment agreements. First, in the view of the EP, the standards of non-discriminatory treatment (NT and MFN treatment) need to contain a definition referring to foreign and national investors as operating 'in like circumstances' so as to preserve policy space for the public authorities to regulate in the public interest. Secondly, the standard of FET treatment would need to be defined on the basis of the level of treatment established under customary international law. Thirdly, the provisions on protection against direct and indirect expropriation need to establish a 'clear and fair balance between public welfare objectives and private interests, and allowing for adequate compensation in accordance with the damages occurred in the event of illegitimate expropriation'.[198] The EP also calls for the inclusion of specific clauses stipulating the right of the parties to a Union investment agreement to regulate in the public interest, such as in the areas of protection of national security, the environment, public health, workers' and consumers' rights, industrial policy and cultural diversity.[199] The EP moreover points to the need to promote sustainable

---

[194] European Parliament resolution of 6 April 2011 on the future European international investment policy (P7-TA(2011)0141).
[195] Ibid para 6.
[196] Ibid Preamble para G.
[197] Ibid para 11.
[198] Ibid para 19.
[199] Ibid para 25.

investment and therefore suggests a reference to the OECD Guidelines for Multinational Enterprises in Union investment agreements, as well as the inclusion of a corporate social responsibility clause and effective social and environmental clauses.[200] In addition, the EP highlights the importance of including obligations for investors in terms of compliance with human rights and anti-corruption standards.[201]

The EP endorses the principle that priority partners for Union investment agreements should be countries with great market potential but where improved protection of investments is needed.[202] So far as concerns the issue of investment liberalisation, the EP calls for reciprocity in the negotiation of market access commitments with developed countries. At the same time, it underlines the need to exclude sensitive sectors and to maintain asymmetry in the Union's trading relations with developing countries.[203] So far as investment protection is concerned, the EP recognises that investor-state arbitration is an important asset of investment agreements, but believes that changes need to be made to current investor-state dispute settlement systems.[204] Importantly, the EP suggests in this context including in Union investment agreements the obligation to exhaust local judicial remedies where they are reliable enough to guarantee due process. Moreover, the EP takes the view that investor-state dispute settlement under Union investment agreements should allow for greater transparency, the opportunity for parties to appeal, the possibility to use *amicus curiae* briefs and the obligation to select one single place of investor-state arbitration.

The Commission has issued a response to the European Parliament's Resolution on the common international investment policy.[205] It notes the degree of convergence between the EP's views on the common international investment policy and that outlined by the Commission in its Communication, in particular on the need for a coordinated and comprehensive Union framework on investment, which provides legal certainty and a high level of protection for EU investors, whilst at the same time respecting the Union's broader economic interests and external policy objectives. Moreover, the Commission notes the agreement between the two Union institutions on the potential of foreign investment to promote growth and development of the host state, including the transfer of skills and technology, as well as on the criteria for selecting priority negotiating partners for Union investment agreements. The Commission has endorsed the EP's request to ensure reciprocity when negotiating market access with the Union's main developed trading partners and emerging markets, while excluding sensitive sectors and maintaining asymmetry in the Union's trading relations with devel-

---

[200]   Ibid paras 27–28.
[201]   Ibid para 37.
[202]   Ibid para 36.
[203]   Ibid para 21.
[204]   Ibid para 31.
[205]   Follow-up to the European Parliament's Resolution on the future European international investment policy, adopted by the European Commission on 5 July 2011, available at www.europarl.europa.eu/oeil/spdoc.do?i=19829&j=0&l=en.

oping countries. The Commission points out that this is in fact current practice as regards the market access commitments in negotiations on free trade agreements and it intends to adopt the same approach in the context of negotiations on investment protection. The Commission highlights that it does not envisage the adoption of a Union model investment treaty, which would consolidate the best practices of the Member States, because such a one-size-fits-all model does not serve the objective of customising the Union's approach to each individual third country.

However, the Commission also notes a number of points of divergence between the proposed main orientations for a common international investment policy and the views expressed by the EP in its resolution in response to that. As regards the right to regulate, the Commission takes note of the EP's request for the establishment of clear definitions of the standards of investment protection in Union investment agreements. Yet the Commission observes that all these standards are in fact subject to a common understanding among experts in the field. So far as concerns the EP's request for the inclusion in all future Union investment agreements of specific clauses laying down the right to regulate, the Commission points out that these are consistent with the current practice of the Union in negotiating market access commitments with third countries, which will be replicated in the context of negotiating investment protection commitments. So far as the issue of purely speculative forms of investment is concerned, the Commission points out that it agrees with the EP's views on this matter but that these do not fall within the scope of existing Member State BITs either. In particular, the Commission refuses to equate foreign portfolio investment with mere speculation. In the view of the Commission, BITs focus on the contribution and the commitment within the host state of substantial resources for the longer term, distinguishing between investment and ordinary commercial transactions for the purpose of protecting established investors within the host state. While the Commission considers that Member State BITs have not led to abusive practices, such as providing protection for mailbox companies or speculative investments, it leaves open the possibility of including more explicit language to this effect in future Union investment agreements.

It can thus be observed that the development of the common international investment policy gives rise to a number of challenges. While there is agreement between the Commission, Council and the EP on the need for an ambitious policy in the common interest[206] on both the liberalisation and protection of

---

[206] That the Union needs to act 'in the common interest' under its post-Lisbon FDI competence follows from Art 206 TFEU, which stipulates that 'the Union shall contribute, *in the common interest*, to . . . the progressive abolition of restrictions on foreign direct investment' (emphasis added). The concept of Union interest is grounded in Art 4(3) TEU, which provides that 'Pursuant to the principle of sincere cooperation, the Union and the Member States shall, in full mutual respect, assist each other in carrying out the tasks which flow from the Treaties. The Member States shall take any appropriate measure, general or particular, to ensure fulfilment of the obligations arising out of the Treaties or resulting from the acts of the institutions of the Union. The Member States shall facilitate the achievement of the Union's tasks and refrain from any measure which could jeopardise the attainment of the Union's objectives'. In the words of Cremona, the concept of Union interest is linked closely to the tasks

investment, there are a number of issues on which agreement will need to be found. The broadening of the Union's investment policy to the issue of investment protection precipitates the need for a balancing act of the Commission between the views of the different institutions. In particular, the requirement of high standards of investment protection, including access to investor-state dispute settlement, on the one hand, and the recognition of the importance of the right for public authorities to regulate in the public interest, on the other hand, is a controversial issue in the development and implementation of the common international investment policy. A common understanding between the Union institutions will need to be found on a number of issues, such as on the precise formulation of the standards of investment treatment, the issue of the right to regulate in the public interest, the obligations of investors and the specific features of investor-state dispute settlement under Union investment agreements.

Against the backdrop of this dialogue between the Union institutions on the main orientations for the common international investment policy, it is instructive to turn to the first steps in the exercise of the Union's post-Lisbon FDI competence. The investment liberalisation commitments in the Union's post-Lisbon external agreements are arguably likely to be quite similar to those in the most recent external agreements, such as the EU-CARIFORUM EPA and the EU-Korea FTA. In this respect, it can be observed that a number of innovations in the Community's external practice with regard to the liberalisation of FDI were perhaps already in anticipation of the Union's post-Lisbon FDI competence. The exercise of the Union's post-Lisbon FDI competence in the field of the liberalisation of investment is evidenced by the trade agreement that was signed with Colombia and Peru in 2012, and which has been provisionally applied between the Union and Peru from 1 March 2013 and between the Union and Colombia from 1 August 2013.[207] While it

---

and objectives of the Union and is not simply an expression of the collective interest of the Member States. See M Cremona, 'Defending the Community Interest: The Duties of Cooperation and Compliance' in M Cremona and B de Witte, *EU Foreign Relations Law: Constitutional Fundamentals* (Oxford, Hart Publishing, 2008) 127.

[207] [2012] OJ L354/3. Art 112(1) on market access, and Art 113(1) for Colombia and Art 113(2) for Peru on the standard of NT, have the same type of wording as the corresponding provisions in the EU-Korea FTA. An interesting feature of the trade agreement with Peru and Colombia is Art 116 on investment promotion and review, which however does not refer to the protection of investment. See Art 116(1): 'With a view to a progressive liberalisation of investments, the European Union and the signatory Andean Countries shall seek to promote an environment attractive for reciprocal investment within their respective spheres of competence'; Art 116(2) 'The promotion referred to in paragraph 1 shall lead to cooperation that shall include, among others, the review of the investment legal framework, the investment environment and the flow of investment between the Parties, consistent with their commitments under international agreements. Such review shall take place no later than five years following the entry into force of this Agreement and subsequently at regular intervals.' On the provisional application of this agreement, see Notice concerning the provisional application between the European Union and Peru of the Trade Agreement between the European Union and its Member States, of the one part, and Colombia and Peru, of the other part [2013] OJ L56/1; Notice concerning the provisional application between the European Union and Colombia of the Trade Agreement between the European Union and its Member States, of the one part, and Colombia and Peru, of the other part [2013] OJ 201/7.

was concluded after the entry into force of the Treaty of Lisbon, it largely follows the more recent pre-Lisbon practice in the field of FDI. Moreover, and along similar lines so far as concerns the issue of liberalisation of investment, the Union has signed a trade agreement with Central America (Costa Rica, El Salvador, Guatemala, Honduras, Nicaragua and Panama) in 2012, which has been provisionally applied between the Union and Honduras, Nicaragua and Panama from 1 August 2013.[208] A significant development is that the Union has chosen a negative list approach for the liberalisation of services in the ongoing negotiations with Canada for a Comprehensive Economic and Trade Agreement (CETA), under which liberalisation commitments apply to all services sectors except those which have been explicitly carved out from the agreement.[209]

Marked changes with regard to the Community's pre-Lisbon external practice in the field of FDI are to be expected rather in the implementation of the common international investment policy so far as concerns the issue of investment protection.[210] Meanwhile, the negotiating directives for the ongoing negotiations with Canada (CETA), India (FTA) and Singapore (FTA) have been revised and now include investment.[211] The Union is currently negotiating investment protection commitments with these third countries as part of a broader package of commitments.[212] The negotiating directives for negotiations towards the conclusion of Deep and Comprehensive Free Trade Areas (DCFTAs) with Tunisia, Morocco, Jordan and Egypt also cover investment protection.[213] The Council has moreover approved a mandate for the Commission to open negotiations on a FTA with Japan.[214] Importantly, the Council has also adopted a decision authorising the Commission to negotiate a Transatlantic Trade and Investment Partnership (TTIP) with the United States.[215] In addition, the Commission has presented a

---

[208] [2012] OJ L346/3. See Art 164 on market access and Art 165 on national treatment. On the provisional application of this agreement, see Notice concerning the provisional application of Part IV (trade matters) of the Agreement establishing an Association between the European Union and its Member States, on the one hand, and Central America on the other (Nicaragua, Panama, Honduras) [2013] OJ L204/1.

[209] See, eg European Parliament resolution of 8 June 2011 on EU-Canada trade relations (P7-TA(2011)0257).

[210] See the overview at http://ec.europa.eu/trade/policy/accessing-markets/investment/. See also Hoffmeister and Ünüvar, 'From BITs and Pieces towards European Investment Agreements' (above n 90) 84 ff.

[211] Press release for the 3109th meeting of the General Affairs Council, 12 September 2011, doc no 13587/11, 13.

[212] On the main challenges in the negotiations of the EU-Canada CETA, see C Lévesque, 'The Challenges of "Marrying" Investment Liberalisation and Protection in the Canada-EU CETA' in M Bungenberg, A Reinisch and C Tietje (eds), *EU and Investment Agreements, Open Questions and Remaining Challenges* (Baden-Baden, Nomos, 2013) 121–44.

[213] Press release for the 3136th meeting of the Foreign Affairs Council, 14 December 2011, doc no 18685/11, 8.

[214] Press release for the 3203rd meeting of the Foreign Affairs Council, 29 November 2012, doc no 16943/12, 9.

[215] Press release for the 3245th meeting of the Foreign Affairs Council, 14 June 2013, doc no 10862/13, 6. On the Union's investment policy with regard to the United States, see also Statement of the European Union and the United States on Shared Principles for International Investment, 10 April 2012, available at http://trade.ec.europa.eu/doclib/docs/2012/april/tradoc_149331.pdf.

recommendation for a Council Decision authorising it to negotiate a stand-alone investment agreement with China.[216]

An important question is whether Union investment agreements under the common international investment policy will be concluded with third countries by the Union or jointly by the Union and the Member States. For the investment-related provisions in more comprehensive agreements, the scope of the entire agreement will not fall under the Union's FDI competence. These type of agreements are likely to continue to be concluded as mixed agreements irrespective of their investment-related commitments. Whether or not stand-alone investment agreements will be concluded as mixed agreements depends on whether the Union holds exclusive competence under its post-Lisbon FDI competence in respect of all investment-related provisions in such agreements. As has been shown above (I.C), it is possible to argue that the Union's FDI competence extends to both the liberalisation and the protection of FDI. However, competence for assuming investment-related commitments in relations with third countries so far as concerns foreign portfolio investment, as well as capital transfers in relation to FDI, is arguably shared with the Member States under the TFEU provisions on free movement of capital. Moreover, an important limit to the Union's FDI competence is arguably that it does not extend to the issue of secondary rights of mobility for third-country direct investors, which remains covered by the relevant internal market legal bases and is in principle shared insofar as these competences have not been exercised.

To sum up the discussion in this section, there is agreement between the Commission, the Council and the EP on the need for an ambitious policy on both the liberalisation and protection of investment. The exercise of the Union's post-Lisbon FDI competence is therefore likely to lead to a further deepening of the Union's external practice so far as concerns the liberalisation of FDI. It will moreover lead to a broadening of the Union's external practice to the issue of investment protection. The Commission envisages the conclusion of state-of-the-art investment protection provisions modelled after the standards of protection in Member State investment agreements, including investor-state dispute settlement provision, and has been authorised to negotiate Union investment agreements with a number of third countries. Importantly, unlike the pre-Lisbon external practice in the field of FDI, Union agreements will not complement Member State investment agreements, but are likely to gradually *replace* at least some of them.[217] At the same time, there are a number of issues on which a common understanding between the Union institutions will need to be found, such as on the precise

---

[216]   Ibid 9. See also DG Trade, 'Roadmap of EU-China investment relations' of 21 March 2012, available at http://ec.europa.eu/governance/impact/planned_ia/docs/2012_trade_03_china_investment_agreement_en.pdf. For historical background and analysis of the legal challenges, see in particular W Shan and S Zhang, 'The Potential EU-China BIT: Issues and Implications' in M Bungenberg, A Reinisch and C Tietje (eds), *EU and Investment Agreements: Open Questions and Remaining Challenges* (Baden-Baden, Nomos, 2013) 87–119; W Shan, *The Legal Framework of EU-China Investment Relations: A Critical Appraisal* (Oxford, Hart Publishing, 2005).

[217]   See the text at chapter 4, III and accompanying notes.

formulation of the standards of investment treatment, the issue of the right to regulate in the public interest, the obligations of investors and the specific features of investor-state dispute settlement under Union investment agreements. Moreover, the common international investment policy needs to be implemented consistently with the overarching principles of the Union's external action.

(ii) Modalities for Investor-State Dispute Settlement under Union Investment Agreements

The Commission is currently negotiating provisions on investment protection with a number of third countries. The outcome of these negotiations is likely to be a set of agreements, which will contain standards of investment protection and investor-state dispute settlement provisions, modelled on existing Member State BITs.[218] Since the ECT constitutes the only precedent of the Union subscribing to an investor-state dispute settlement mechanism, the Union enters relatively uncharted territory. The Union has, moreover, never been challenged by a third-country investor under the ECT. It has been questioned whether the Union could include investor-state dispute settlement provisions in Union investment agreements with third countries without arbitral tribunals being able to refer questions for a preliminary ruling to the CJEU.[219] The participation of the Union and the Member States in investor-state dispute settlement under future Union investment agreements also presents a number of specific challenges. Some of these will need to be taken up in the respective commitments on investment protection to be entered into with the third countries concerned. Others will need to be addressed internally between the Union and the Member States.

[218] The Commission has prepared provisions on investor-state dispute settlement for the purpose of ongoing negotiations, which are confidential. For a discussion of the issues arising in this context, see in particular Hoffmeister and Ünüvar, 'From BITs and Pieces towards European Investment Agreements' (above n 90) 70 ff; C Brown and I Naglis, 'Dispute Settlement in Future EU Investment Agreements' in M Bungenberg, A Reinisch and C Tietje (eds), *EU and Investment Agreements: Open Questions and Remaining Challenges* (Nomos, Baden-Baden, 2013) 25 ff; A Reinisch, 'The Future Shape of EU Investment Agreements' (2013) 1 *ICSID Review* 185 ff.

[219] See in particular M Burgstaller, 'Investor-State Arbitration in EU International Investment Agreements with Third Countries' (2012) 2 *Legal Issues of European Integration* 207, who argues that the Union could submit to investor-state arbitration only following a change in EU primary law so that investment tribunals could be deemed 'courts or tribunals of a Member State' within the meaning of Art 267 TFEU. See also N Lavranos, 'Is an International Investor-to-State Arbitration System under the Auspices of the ECJ Possible?', available at http://papers.ssrn.com/sol3/papers.cfm?abstract_id=1973491. For analysis of some of the issues pertaining to the exercise of the Union's competence by submitting to a system of international dispute settlement in a way that is compatible with the autonomy of the EU legal order, see the text at I.C. For an analysis of the interplay between investor-state dispute settlement under intra-EU BITs and the autonomy of the EU legal order, see the text at chapter 5, V. See also A Dimopoulos, 'The Compatibility of Future EU Investment Agreements with EU Law' (2012) 4 *Legal Issues of European Integration* 447, 467 ff; PFJS Strik, 'From Washington with Love: Investor-State Arbitration and the Jurisdictional Monopoly of the Court of Justice of the European Union' (2009–10) *Cambridge Yearbook of European Legal Studies* 425; Hoffmeister and Ondrusek, 'The European Community in International Litigation' (above n 109); N Lavranos, 'The Mox Plant and IJzeren Rijn Disputes: Which Court is the Supreme Arbiter?' (2006) 1 *Leiden Journal of International Law* 223.

One of the issues arising in this context concerns the choice of forum for investor-state dispute settlement under Union investment agreements. In this respect, it can be observed that the options for the Union are limited in comparison with the Member States. Importantly, the ICSID Convention is currently open only to states, and not to international organisations.[220] While the Commission has indicated in its 2010 Communication on the common international investment policy that it will explore the possibilities for the Union's accession to the ICSID Convention, the necessary amendment of the ICSID Convention may be difficult to achieve in view of the fact that it needs to be approved and ratified by all contracting parties. At the same time, the UNCITRAL arbitration rules could arguably be resorted to by the Union in investor-state dispute settlement, since these refer in general terms to the 'parties' to a dispute.[221] The same seems to apply to the arbitration rules of the International Chamber of Commerce (ICC) in Paris, the Stockholm Chamber of Commerce (SCC) and the London Court of International Arbitration (LCIA). The Permanent Court of Arbitration does provide for specific rules of procedure for arbitration between international organisations and private parties.[222] Another possibility would be for the Union and the Member States to include more detailed, and customised, arbitration rules in the investment agreements themselves.

There are also a number of distinct challenges with regard to the issue of allocation of responsibility for breaches of a Union investment agreement. In the event that investment agreements under the common international investment policy will be concluded by the Union to the exclusion of the Member States, the situation arises that only the Union can be challenged directly for a breach of a Union investment agreement flowing from treatment by a Member State. Where investment agreements under the common international investment policy are concluded as mixed agreements, the situation could in principle arise that a Member State will be challenged for treatment granted by the Union, as well as vice versa. In view of the financial stakes potentially involved in litigating over alleged breaches of Union investment agreements, the Commission has proposed a specific internal arrangement with a view to shaping the modalities for the Union and the Member States' participation in investor-state dispute settlement under Union investment agreements. The proposed Regulation on financial responsibility contains internal arrangements both for the allocation of responsibility between the Union and the Member States for breaches of a Union investment agreement and, concomitantly, for the conduct of disputes under these agreements, as well the system of payment.[223]

---

[220] Article 67 of the ICSID Convention. A list of contracting states to the ICSID Convention is available at https://icsid.worldbank.org/ICSID/FrontServlet?requestType=ICSIDDocRH&actionVal=Show Document&language=English. It can be observed that Poland is not a contracting state to the ICSID Convention.

[221] Article 1(1) of the UNCITRAL Arbitration Rules.

[222] Permanent Court of Arbitration Optional Rules for Arbitration between International Organisations and Private Parties, available at www.pca-cpa.org/showpage.asp?pag_id=1188.

[223] COM(2012)335 (above n 171). In view of the fact that the proposed Regulation is purported to apply to all agreements that contain provisions on investor-state dispute settlement and to which the

As a matter of international law, the Union can be considered as an international organisation for the issue of determining responsibility for breaches of international law.[224] While a state is responsible under international law for actions of subdivisions like regional governments,[225] Union responsibility for actions of Member States could be conceptualised as providing for an additional layer of responsibility for such breaches, in particular whenever the Union were to aid or assist, direct or control, or coerce the acts of a Member State, or circumvent international obligations through decisions and authorisations addressed to the Member States.[226] At the same time, it has been observed that EU law may provide for 'special rules' on the allocation of responsibility between the Union and the Member States,[227] with the effect that Union responsibility for breaches of international law is not merely concurrent with Member State responsibility for breaches of international law but may also replace Member State responsibility.[228]

As regards the issue of responsibility for breaches of a Union investment agreement, the Commission has advanced the view that this in principle has to be decided, as a matter of EU law, not by the author of the treatment at issue, but on the basis of the competence for the subject matter of the international rules in question.[229] It would be immaterial whether the Union or a Member State has granted a particular treatment to an investor while acting under its competence to legislate internally under the rules of the internal market. In the view of the Commission, responsibility for a breach of a Union external agreement has to

European Union is a contracting party, it can be observed that the proposed Regulation is intended to apply not only to future Union investment agreements, but also to dispute settlement under the ECT.

[224] See generally PJ Kuijper, 'International Responsibility for EU Mixed Agreements' in C Hillion and P Koutrakos (eds), *Mixed Agreements Revisited: The EU and the Member States in the World* (Oxford, Hart Publishing, 2010); F Hoffmeister, 'Litigating Against the European Union and its Member States: Who Responds under the ILC's Draft Articles on International Responsibility of International Organizations?' (2010) 3 *EJIL* 723; Directorate-General for External Policies of the European Parliament, *Responsibility in Investor-State Arbitration in the EU: Managing Financial Responsibility Linked to Investor-State Dispute Settlement Tribunals Established by EU's International Investment Agreements* (2012), available at www.europarl.europa.eu/committees/en/inta/studiesdownload.html?languageDocument=EN&file=79450.

[225] ILC Draft Articles on State Responsibility for Internationally Wrongful Acts, 2001, available at http://untreaty.un.org/ilc/texts/instruments/english/commentaries/9_6_2001.pdf. See Art 4(1): 'The conduct of any State organ shall be considered an act of that State under international law, whether the organ exercises legislative, executive, judicial or any other functions, whatever position it holds in the organization of the State, and whatever its character as an organ of the central Government or of a territorial unit of the State.'

[226] Articles 14–19 of the ILC Draft Articles on the Responsibility of International Organizations, 2011, available at http://untreaty.un.org/ilc/texts/instruments/english/draft%20articles/9_11_2011.pdf.

[227] Ibid art 64: 'These draft articles do not apply where and to the extent that the conditions for the existence of an internationally wrongful act or the content or implementation of the international responsibility of an international organization, or of a State in connection with the conduct of an international organization, are governed by special rules of international law. Such special rules of international law may be contained in the rules of the organization applicable to the relations between an international organization and its members.'

[228] See in particular Hoffmeister, 'Litigating Against the European Union and its Member States' (above n 224).

[229] Ibid 4.

flow principally from the division of competences between the Union and the Member State under the subject matter of the international agreement in question. The Commission finds support for this view in *Opinion 1/91*.[230] In relation to dispute settlement under the EEA Agreement, which was to be concluded as a mixed agreement, the CJEU took the view in respect of the expression 'Contracting Parties' in the Agreement that:

> As far as the Community and its Member States are concerned, it covers the Community and the Member States, or the Community, or the Member States, depending on the case. Which of the three possibilities is to be chosen is to be deduced in each case from the relevant provisions of the agreement and *from the respective competences* of the Community and the Member States as they follow from the EEC Treaty and ECSC Treaty. (emphasis added)[231]

In other words, the Court seemed to suggest that the allocation of responsibility under the EEA Agreement follows the division of competence between the (then) Community and Member States under the respective provisions in the agreement. The Commission notes that, as a matter of international law, it is moreover accepted that such 'special rules' may be applied to the issue of the allocation of responsibility between the Union and the Member States.

By consequence, if a Union investment agreement falls entirely under the Union's exclusive competence and is therefore concluded solely by the Union, then only the Union is internationally responsible and can be challenged for a breach of the agreement. When both the Union and the Member States are contracting parties to a Union investment agreement, responsibility for a breach of the agreement in principle would need to be determined by the division of competence between the Union and the Member State for entering into the specific international commitments at issue.[232] This competence-based analysis of the issue of responsibility of the Union and the Member States for breaches of mixed Union investment agreements can be contrasted with case law in which the CJEU took the view that the Union and the Member State are jointly responsible for fulfilling the obligations under a mixed agreement, in the absence of a public declaration on the division of powers.[233] For example, the Court has ruled that the (then) Community and the Member States were jointly liable for every commit-

---

[230] *Opinion 1/91* [1991] ECR I-6079.

[231] Ibid para 33.

[232] It can be observed that a statement was issued by the (now) Union upon the conclusion of the Energy Charter Treaty as regards investor-state dispute settlement by the Union and the Member States. The statement provides that 'The Communities and the Member States will, if necessary, determine among them who is the respondent party to arbitration proceedings initiated by an Investor of another Contracting Party. In such a case, upon the request of the Investor, the Communities and the Member States will make such determination within a period of 30 days'. As a result, the Union and the Member States are able to determine to whom international responsibility should be attributed for the fulfilment of the obligations contained in the ECT in accordance with their respective competences under the agreement. See Statement submitted by the European Communities to the Secretariat of the Energy Charter pursuant to Article 26(3)(b)(ii) of the Energy Charter Treaty [1998] OJ L69/115.

[233] For analysis, see in particular Kuijper, 'International Responsibility for EU Mixed Agreements' (above n 224) 209 ff; Bischoff, 'Just a Little *Bit* of "Mixity"?' (above n 97) 1562 ff.

ment under the fourth EEC-ACP Convention, in the absence of derogations expressly laid down in the Convention.[234] At the same time, the agreement in question had been concluded under parallel competences of the Union and the Member States in the sense of Article 4(4) TFEU.[235]

In view of the fact that the sole legal basis of the proposed Regulation on financial responsibility is Article 207(2) TFEU, the exclusivity of Union competence in the field of investment protection as regards both foreign direct investment and foreign portfolio investment seems to be assumed as is, consequently, the non-mixed nature of Union investment agreements. In light of the Commission's competence-based analysis of responsibility of the Union and the Member States for breaches of a Union investment agreement, the Union would be responsible for any Member State treatment of non-EU investment in the Single Market under a Union investment agreement. In view of the financial stakes potentially involved in investor-state arbitration under Union investment agreements, the Commission therefore proposes to provide, as a matter of EU law, for a specific attribution of financial responsibility between the Union and the Member States in a manner that reflects whether the Union or a Member State provides the treatment in question instead of the underlying division of competence under the Union investment agreement at issue. In other words, the proposed Regulation provides for an internal disconnection between the issue of international responsibility for a breach of the agreement, on the one hand, and the attribution of financial responsibility based on who is the author of the treatment in question, on the other.

The Commission also proposes to empower a Member State in the sense of Article 2(1) TFEU to act as a respondent in investor-state dispute settlement in appropriate circumstances when it has granted a particular treatment in areas under a provision of a Union investment agreement for which the Union holds exclusive competence. The envisaged approach is that a Member State should be permitted to act as respondent in order to defend its own action under a provision of a Union investment agreement that falls under the exclusive competence of the Union, except in circumstances where the Union interest requires otherwise. This in principle seems to be an adequate and pragmatic way of dealing with the issues at hand, which reflects the financial stakes potentially involved in litigating over a breach of a Union investment agreement. At the same time, it can be observed that an internal mechanism by which the Union and the Member States unilaterally decide who is financially responsible for a possible breach of a Union investment agreement and who is the respondent in investor-state disputes under such an agreement needs to be complemented by a corresponding assertion in the respective dispute settlement provisions in the investment agreement.

---

[234] C-316/91 *European Parliament v Council* [1994] ECR I-625, para 24 ff.

[235] 'In the areas of development cooperation and humanitarian aid, the Union shall have competence to carry out activities and conduct a common policy; however, the exercise of that competence shall not result in Member States being prevented from exercising theirs.'

The central organising principle of the proposed Regulation on financial responsibility is therefore that financial responsibility for a breach of the investment protection provisions in a Union investment agreement should be attributed to the Union or the Member State that has afforded the treatment at issue.[236] The proposed Regulation has three other organising principles. First, it is suggested that the allocation of financial responsibility must be budget neutral so that the Union only bears those costs which are triggered by acts of Union institutions. Secondly, the Commission underlines that third-country investors must not be disadvantaged by the need for the Union and the Member States to manage the allocation of financial responsibility within the Union. Thirdly, the Commission points out that the mechanism for the allocation of financial responsibility and the subsequent conduct of disputes must respect the fundamental principles governing the Union's external action and the case law of the CJEU, in particular as regards the requirement of unity of external representation and the duty of sincere cooperation. These organising principles arguably constitute sound parameters for the proposed framework for managing financial responsibility and the conduct of disputes under Union investment agreements.

More specifically, the issue of allocation of financial responsibility is dealt with in Chapter II of the proposed Regulation. Chapter II consists of a single Article 3, the first paragraph of which provides the following criteria for the apportionment of financial responsibility arising from a dispute under a Union investment agreement:

(a) the Union shall bear the financial responsibility arising from treatment afforded by the institutions, bodies or agencies of the Union;
(b) the Member State concerned shall bear the financial responsibility arising from treatment afforded by that Member State, except where such treatment was required by the law of the Union.

While these criteria seem straight-forward, it might not be easy in practice to determine to what extent specific treatment by a Member State was required by EU law.[237] EU law may prescribe a certain result to be achieved by a Member State while leaving discretion to the Member State as to the way in which to achieve this result. The situation can occur that the Union and a Member State are in fact jointly responsible for the treatment in question. In addition, Article 3 of the proposed Regulation provides expressly that a Member State is financially responsible when it is required to act under EU law in order to remedy an inconsistency of a prior act with EU law, unless the adoption of the prior act was required by EU law. Article 3(2) of the proposed Regulation provides that the Commission takes a decision on the financial responsibility of a Member State on the basis of the criteria in Article 3(1). The Member States could challenge such a decision before the CJEU under Article 263 TFEU.

---

[236] Ibid 2.
[237] For more analysis, see Directorate-General for External Policies, *Responsibility in Investor-State Arbitration in the EU* (above n 224) 6.

Chapter III of the proposed Regulation deals with the conduct of disputes. It can be observed that the proposal is based on a single respondent mechanism. The proposal does not provide for a co-respondent mechanism under which disputes could be brought simultaneously against both the Union and a Member State. According to the Commission, such a mechanism is not well adapted to investor-state arbitration.[238] First, it does not adequately provide for a mechanism for the allocation of financial responsibility between the Member State concerned and the Union. Secondly, the Commission takes the view that it could lead to inconsistencies in the defence of the claim, with each co-respondent presenting conflicting or diverging arguments. Thirdly, it could allegedly result in the tribunal having to make a pronouncement on the division of competences between the Union and Member States, in circumstances where the two co-respondents present different positions on this issue to the tribunal. And finally, the Commission submits that it is unlikely that a tribunal would permit the Union and the Member State concerned both to recover costs in the event that a case is successfully defended. For those reasons, the Commission does not propose any modalities for dispute settlement of the Union and the Member States under Union investment agreements by means of a co-respondent mechanism.[239]

Article 4 of the proposed Regulation on financial responsibility provides that the Union shall act as respondent where the Union has afforded the treatment in question. The remainder of Chapter III applies to disputes which concern 'fully or partially' treatment by a Member State. While a Member State shall in principle defend its own measures, the Commission may decide under Article 8(2) that the Union shall act as respondent if any of the following circumstances arise:

(a) it is likely that the Union would bear at least part of the potential financial responsibility arising from the dispute in accordance with the criteria laid down in Article 3;

(b) the dispute also concerns treatment afforded by the institutions, bodies or agencies of the Union;

(c) it is likely that similar claims will be brought under the same agreement against treatment afforded by other Member States and the Commission is best placed to ensure an effective and consistent defence; or,

(d) the dispute raises unsettled issues of law which may recur in other disputes under the same or other Union agreements concerning treatment afforded by the Union or other Member States.

It can be observed that these situations generally reflect the organising principles of the proposed Regulation. In particular, the principle of budget neutrality, under which the Union will only bear financial responsibility for treatment by the Union, seems to be at stake in the situations under subparagraphs (a) and (b), and

---

[238] Ibid 7.

[239] But see the co-respondent mechanism that is envisaged in the context of the Union's future accession to the European Convention on Human Rights at www.coe.int/t/dghl/standardsetting/hrpolicy/accession/Meeting_reports/Web_47_1(2013)R05_EN.pdf.

requires the involvement of the Commission in disputes that may impact on the Union budget. Moreover, the circumstances under subparagraphs (c) and (d) are likely to impinge on the obligation to comply with the requirement of unity of external representation. Yet it can be observed that the phraseology of Article 8(2) leaves the Commission a considerable amount of discretion as to whether it will defend a particular Member State measure and may have as a consequence that the Commission will be defending a particular treatment, while a Member State will remain (at least in part) financially responsible in the event that a breach is found by an arbitral tribunal.

The four circumstances identified under Article 8(2) seem to provide important references for the interpretation of the more general criteria under which the Commission can require a Member State to take a particular position when the Member State is defending treatment granted by that Member State. In this respect, Article 9(2) on the conduct of arbitration proceedings by a Member State provides that:

> The Commission may, at any time, require the Member State concerned to take a particular position as regards any point of law raised by the dispute or any other element having a Union interest.

So far as concerns specific points of law raised by a dispute, the proposal caters for the need to safeguard the unity of external representation and the Commission's task in upholding this requirement. It is for the same reason that the Commission may require a Member State under Article 9(3) of the proposed Regulation to lodge an application for annulment, appeal or review of an arbitration award 'where it considers that the consistency or correctness of the interpretation of the agreement so warrant'.

It can moreover be observed that the phraseology of 'any other element having a Union interest' comes back in slightly altered form in Article 13(3) of the proposed Regulation. Under that provision, the Commission may settle a dispute where the Union is respondent in respect of treatment afforded by a Member State, even when a Member State does not consent to settle, 'where overriding interests of the Union so require'.[240] Similar to the situation under Article 8(2), the Commission has a considerable amount of discretion under Articles 9(2) and 13(3) of the proposed Regulation. Arguably, the circumstances that are identified in Article 8(2), such as an impact on the Union budget and questions of consistency of interpretation of a Union investment agreement, should closely guide the application of the broad notions of 'any element having a Union interest' under Article 9(2) and that of 'overriding interests of the Union' under Article 13(3).

---

[240] See also Art 14(1)(3): 'Where the Union is a respondent in a dispute concerning exclusively treatment afforded by a Member State, the Member State may settle a dispute where: (a) the Member State concerned accepts any financial responsibility arising from the settlement; (b) any settlement arrangement is enforceable only against the Member State concerned; (c) the terms of the settlement are compatible with the law of the Union; and, (d) there is no *overriding interest of the Union* against the settlement' (emphasis added).

In addition to the specific modalities for the attribution of financial responsibility and the conduct of investor-state disputes by the Union and the Member States under Union investment agreements, the successful implementation of the proposed framework will depend to a large extent on close cooperation between the Commission and the Member States. To this effect, Articles 6 and 7 of the proposed Regulation provide for obligations for both the Commission and the Member States to notify each other and share information in case of a request for consultations by a third-country investor, and where a notice is issued by which a claimant states its intention to initiate arbitration proceedings. Articles 9 and 10 provide for obligations of close cooperation between the Union and the Member States in the conduct of proceedings by both the Union and the Member States, such as to share documents (Articles 9(1)(a) and 10(c)) and to prepare a defence in close cooperation such as by permitting representatives of the Commission to form part of the delegation representing the Member State (Article 9(1)(c)) and by permitting representatives of the Member State to form part of the Union delegation in the proceedings (Article 10(d)). The proposed Regulation moreover contains obligations for the Member States to inform the Commission of all significant procedural steps (Article 9(1)(b)) and to enter into regular consultations and provide all necessary assistance to the Commission (Articles 9(1)(b) and 10(b)). The Commission shall take all necessary measures to defend the treatment of a Member State (Article 10(a)). These proposed provisions reflect the general duty of loyal cooperation between the Union and the Member States as stipulated in Article 4(3) TEU.

To sum up the findings of this part, the development and implementation of a common international investment policy therefore gives rise to a number of challenges. While there is agreement between the Commission, the Council and the EP on the need for an ambitious policy on both the liberalisation and protection of investment, there are a number of additional issues on which a common understanding will need to be found. The Commission has been authorised to negotiate Union investment agreements with a number of third countries and envisages the conclusion of state-of-the-art investment protection provisions modelled after the standards of protection in Member State investment agreements, including investor-state dispute settlement provision. The proposed Regulation on financial responsibility is grounded on the principle that financial responsibility for a breach of the investment protection provisions in a Union investment agreement should be attributed to the Union or the Member State that has afforded the treatment at issue. This constitutes a sound and pragmatic central organising principle for the proposed arrangement that needs to be balanced with the other organising principles and has to be reflected in the circumstances in which the Commission may intervene in disputes which concern 'fully or partially' treatment by a Member State. Importantly, the arrangement that shapes the modalities for investor-state dispute settlement under Union investment agreements needs to be in place before the conclusion of the first Union agreement under the common international investment policy that contains provisions on investment protection.

III. THE LISBON REFORM OF THE CCP AND INWARD FDI
INTO THE SINGLE MARKET

The previous section has focused on the impact of the Lisbon reform of the CCP on the Union's treaty-making practice in the field of FDI. While the common international investment policy is likely to create additional opportunities for EU investors in third countries in the form of market access, investment treatment and investment protection rights, it will also have implications for the admission and treatment of third-country direct investment in the Single Market. With a view to the need for the Union's external action to be consistent[241] with the internal legal organisation as regards direct investment, this section conceptualises a number of issues of EU legal integration in relation to the primary and secondary rights of mobility of third-country direct investors in the Single Market under the common international investment policy. In doing so, it builds on the analysis in the previous chapter on the post-establishment treatment of FDI from the perspective of the law of the internal market.

Whereas the Lisbon reform of the (now) TFEU provisions on the CCP may increase the degree to which it constitutes an ever more autonomous policy area with independent objectives, the analysis that follows on the interplay of the common international investment policy with the law of the internal market underscores the need for an integral approach to the EU legal organisation in the field of FDI. This section highlights that the further development of the external dimension of the Single Market in the field of FDI pursuant to the common international investment policy is likely to increase the extent to which the Single Market constitutes a truly 'single' market for third-country direct investors. The issue of the post-establishment treatment of FDI under the common international investment policy is approached from the perspective of the scope of NT and MFN obligations in future Union investment treaties and their interaction with the law of the internal market.

A. The Common International Investment Policy and the Initial Establishment of Third-Country Direct Investors in the Single Market

It was observed in chapter 2 that, while there are provisions in Union secondary legislation and in external agreements that address the admission and treatment of FDI, there is no comprehensive Union external FDI regime. The Lisbon amendments to the TFEU provisions on the CCP could further contribute to the progressive shaping of the external dimension of the Single Market in the field of FDI. At the same time, the Union's post-Lisbon FDI competence gives rise to a number

---

[241] Article 207(3)(2) TFEU provides that 'The Council and the Commission shall be responsible for ensuring that the agreements negotiated are compatible with internal Union policies and rules'.

of institutional and substantive issues in relation to the initial establishment of third-country direct investment in the Single Market.

The Union's post-Lisbon FDI competence with regard to the initial establishment of third-country direct investors gives rise to two issues in relation to the Union's internal market competences in the field of intra-EU direct investment. In the first place, as a result of the Lisbon reform of the CCP, the Union has an exclusive competence in the field of FDI, while unexercised Union competence as regards intra-EU direct investment is shared. For instance, under Article 50(1) TFEU, which provides for Union legislative competence in the field of freedom of establishment, and Article 114 TFEU, under which the Union may adopt measures with a view to the establishment and functioning of the internal market, Union competence is shared until it has been exercised. As such, the exclusive nature of the Union's FDI competence can be contrasted with the more substantial competences that the Member States still hold to regulate the admission of intra-EU direct investment, subject to the need for the exercise of such competences to be compatible with the law of the internal market.

In the second place, while Lisbon reform of the CCP has arguably empowered the Union to conclude external agreements that, inter alia, contain a standard of fair and equitable treatment and investor-state dispute settlement provisions, EU direct investors cannot invoke an FET standard or the standard of full protection in investment arbitration against a host Member State within the Single Market under EU law. As a result, non-EU direct investors would hold rights under Union investment agreements when investing in the Single Market that EU direct investors do not hold in the same form under EU law. By consequence, the so-called rule of reason for determining the scope of EU external competences, which has been coined by Timmermans, would not find application in the context of the EU legal organisation in the field of FDI, since the Union's external competence in the field of FDI would then be interpreted so as to go partially beyond the substantive scope of the existing intra-EU regime as regards direct investment.[242] There also seems to be no targeted internal competence in the field of direct investment within the Single Market, which serves as the substantive internal equivalent of the Union's FDI competence under the TFEU provisions on the CCP.[243]

So far as concerns the precise nature of the measures potentially to be adopted under the Union's post-Lisbon FDI competence, an important question is whether the TFEU provisions on the CCP empower the Union mainly to liberalise or also to regulate FDI. So far as concerns the Union's competence to regulate the internal market, the CJEU has indicated in a number of cases that there

---

[242] CWA Timmermans, 'Common Commercial Policy (Article 113 EEC) and International Trade in Services' in F Capotorti, CD Ehlermann et al (eds), *Du droit international au droit d'intégration: Liber Amicorum Pierre Pescatore* (Baden-Baden, Nomos, 1987) 678, 679.

[243] See J Monar, 'Die Gemeinsame Handelspolitik der Europäischen Union im EU-Verfassungsvertrag: Fortschritte mit einigen neuen Fragezeichen' (2005) 1 *Aussenwirtschaft* 99, 113.

are limits to that competence.[244] For instance, in the 'Tobacco Advertising' case,[245] the Court held that the (then) Community could not issue a Directive banning tobacco advertising[246] under Articles 47(2), 55 and 95 EC where such a regulatory measure does not genuinely aim at removing obstacles to free movement and rectifying disparities between national laws that amount to an appreciable distortion of competition.[247] The measure appeared to be linked, rather, to public health policy objectives. Along the same lines, there are limits to the Union's internal competence to regulate the internal market in the field of direct investment. Regulatory measures in this field also arguably genuinely need to aim at removing obstacles to free movement. As has been pointed out above, there are moreover a number of TFEU provisions that specifically rule out the possibility of harmonisation in particular fields, such as education (Article 165(4) TFEU), public health (Article 168(5) TFEU) and culture (Article 167(5) TFEU).

So far as Union competence under the TFEU provisions on the CCP is concerned, it seems to be circumscribed by the explicit aim in Article 206 TFEU of the progressive abolition of restrictions on international trade and foreign direct investment. In this regard, it can be observed that the CJEU took a broad approach to the notion of progressive abolition of restrictions on international trade in the early years of the CCP in *Opinion 1/78*. In relation to an international agreement on natural rubber, which aimed at the organisation of the world market rather than the mere operation of customs duties and quantitative restrictions, the Court took the view that:

> It is . . . not possible to lay down, for [(now) Article 207 TFEU], an interpretation the effect of which would be to restrict the common commercial policy to the use of instruments intended to have an effect only on the traditional aspects of external trade to the exclusion of more highly developed mechanisms such as appear in the agreement envisaged. A 'commercial policy' understood in that sense would be destined to become nugatory in the course of time.

The Court then observed that:

> Although it may be thought that at the time when the Treaty was drafted liberalisation of trade was the dominant idea, the Treaty nevertheless does not form a barrier to the possibility of the Community's developing a commercial policy aiming at a *regulation*

---

[244] DA Wyatt, 'Community Competence to Regulate the Internal Market' in M Dougan and S Curie (eds), *50 Years of the European Treaties: Looking Back and Thinking Forward* (Oxford, Hart Publishing, 2009).

[245] C-376/98 *Germany v Parliament and Council* [2000] ECR I-8419.

[246] Directive 98/43 of the European Parliament and of the Council of 6 July 1998 on the approximation of the laws, regulations and administrative provisions of the Member States relating to the advertising and sponsorship of tobacco products [1998] OJ L213/9.

[247] *Germany v Parliament and Council* (above n 245) paras 83–84. For analysis, see G de Búrca, 'The Tobacco Judgment: Political Will versus Constitutional Limits' in University of Cambridge Centre for European Legal Studies, *The ECJ's Tobacco Advertising Judgment*, Occasional Paper No 5 (July 2001); DA Wyatt, 'Constitutional Significance of the Tobacco Advertising Judgment of the European Court of Justice' in University of Cambridge Centre for European Legal Studies, *The ECJ's Tobacco Advertising Judgment*, Occasional Paper No 5 (July 2001).

of the world market for certain products rather than at a mere *liberalisation* of trade. (emphasis added)[248]

In *Opinion 1/78*, the Court therefore adopted a wide approach to the type of international instruments, which the (now) Union may become a contracting party to under the commercial policy. Along the same lines, it can be argued that the Union's post-Lisbon FDI competence includes the competence to enter into detailed commitments on the admission, treatment and protection of FDI.

At the same time, the primary aim of Union measures under Article 207 TFEU in the field of FDI should arguably be to address restrictions to FDI.[249] It was argued in the previous section that the Union cannot conclude an external agreement exclusively on that legal basis that contains provisions aiming at certain developmental, social, environmental or human rights purposes as a primary aim in themselves. Provisions to this effect can arguably, however, be included in Union investment agreements in light of the overarching principles of EU external action in Article 21(1) and (2) TEU. In addition, a limit to the Union's FDI competence is Article 207(6) TFEU, which stipulates, inter alia, that the exercise of the Union's FDI competence:

> shall not lead to harmonisation of legislative or regulatory provisions of the Member States in so far as the Treaties exclude such harmonisation.

This provision is supposed to preclude harmonisation under Article 207 TFEU in the fields where this is explicitly excluded elsewhere in the EU Treaties. However, apart from this explicit limit, as was explained above (I.C), it seems possible to argue that the regulatory scope of measures adopted under the Union's post-Lisbon external FDI competence may now in principle surpass the regulatory scope of internal measures in certain cases in view of the absence of an explicit parallelism clause.

The inclusion of provisions on investment protection in future Union external agreements underscores a relative independence of the Union's action under the post-Lisbon TFEU provisions on the CCP in relation to the legal organisation of direct investment within the Single Market. At the same time, the exercise of the Union's FDI competence is potentially an important complement to the Union's internal legal organisation in the field of direct investment. As was shown in chapter 2, there was a close link between the principle of free circulation of goods originating in third countries and the establishment of the CCP. The assimilation of goods in 'free circulation' to products originating within the Member States was even conditional upon the creation of a common commercial policy. A uniform regime for the importation of goods was created in order to prevent goods being imported into a Member State via another Member State so as to benefit from the latter's more advantageous import regime. By contrast, no such uniform

---

[248] *Opinion 1/78* [1979] ECR 2871, para 44.
[249] *Opinion 2/00* [2001] ECR I-9713, para 23, with reference, inter alia, to C-300/89 *Commission v Council (Titanium Dioxide)* [1991] ECR I-2867, paras 13 and 17.

admission regime has been created in the field of FDI, so that the concern had been voiced that third-country direct investors could circumvent certain restrictions of a Member State vis-à-vis third-country direct investment by first incorporating in a Member State with a liberal admissions policy and subsequently invoking Articles 49/54 TFEU in order to become economically active as a legal person in another Member State.

In the field of establishment, uniformity is a less prominent feature of the Union's legislative approach internally than in the field of trade in goods. Nevertheless, future Union external agreement may indeed foster the uniformity of the conditions of admission of FDI in the Single Market under the rights in such agreements with regard to the admission and treatment of FDI. As was argued above (I.C), the TFEU provisions on the CCP empower the Union not only to conclude international agreements in the field of FDI, but also to take autonomous measures under Article 207(2) TFEU. In this respect, the TFEU provisions on the CCP arguably do not only empower the Union to adopt measures for the implementation of the CCP, but also to adopt autonomous measures as a tool for the establishment of a more comprehensive policy on the admission and treatment of third-country direct investors in the Union, consisting of substantive rules if needed.[250] In addition, Article 207(1) TFEU now lays down a requirement for future Union measures shaping the external dimension of the Single Market in the field of FDI to be premised upon 'uniform principles'. In this regard, the Union's exclusive FDI competence thus potentially has a gap-filling role.

The Commission in its July 2010 Communication does not explicitly envisage the adoption of autonomous measures laying down specific requirements for the admission and treatment of FDI in specific sectors. It emphasises the need for openness to FDI.[251] At the same time, requirements for the admission and treatment of direct investment in specific sectors, including by third-country direct investors, continue to exist and can still be adopted under the relevant Union internal market competences. Non-EU investors will have to comply with Union secondary legislation when investing in the Single Market. So far as Union autonomous measures are concerned, sole recourse to the relevant internal market legal basis such as Article 50(1) TFEU is arguably still preferable where a measure does not apply exclusively to third-country direct investment, but applies to both EU and third-country direct investment.[252] This is because provisions on third-country direct investment in such measures are normally secondary to the predominant aim of the measure. As was explained in chapter 2, Union secondary legislation pre-dating the Treaty of Lisbon contains such provisions and future legislation may continue to do so. In the case that the provisions on third-country direct investment in Union secondary legislation are not merely incidental, it may be necessary to enact separate measures for EU and third-country direct invest-

---

[250] Dimopoulos, 'The Common Commercial Policy after Lisbon' (above n 73) 107.
[251] COM(2010)343 (above n 2) 4.
[252] See also Puig, 'The Scope of the New Exclusive Competence' (above n 90) 144 ff.

ment, since Article 207(2) TFEU provides for the adoption of regulations while Article 50(1) TFEU provides for the adoption of directives.

So far as Union competence to adopt autonomous measures on FDI is concerned, it can also be observed that Article 64(1) TFEU grandfathers restrictions under national and Union law in respect of capital movements to and from third countries involving direct investment, as well as establishment, which existed on 31 December 1993.[253] Moreover, Article 64(2) and (3) TFEU provides for the possibility to adopt measures with regard to the same categories of capital movements to and from third countries. In view of the possibilities for overlap between the substantive scope of the TFEU provisions on the CCP and on capital movements to and from third countries involving direct investment, it has been suggested that Article 64(2) and (3) TFEU should be used for the adoption of autonomous measures that specifically address those restrictions on foreign direct investment, which have been grandfathered under Article 64(1) TFEU.[254] Autonomous measures applying indistinctly to all foreign direct investment should instead be based on Article 207(2) TFEU. This interpretation has the virtue of being consistent with the reference to capital movements to and from third countries 'involving direct investment', whilst preserving the possibility of recourse to Article 207(2) TFEU as a legal basis for autonomous measures applying generally to all foreign direct investment.

Article 206 TFEU specifies that the CCP should be implemented 'in the common interest' and Article 207(1) TFEU stipulates that there is a need for the Union's FDI competence to be exercised 'upon uniform principles'. A strict reading of these provisions could conceivably make it seem more difficult to take into account any special interests of the Member States under the common international investment policy in the adoption of both conventional and autonomous measures as regards the admission of third-country direct investment in the Single Market. An example of accommodating a special interest of a Member State is if an authorisation to invest is only granted if the investment passes a so-called economic needs test for the economy of that specific Member State.[255] This would then need to be contrasted with the situation in the early days of the CCP, when special interests of the Member States were protected by way of the subdivision of the Community quota for certain products into a number of national sub-quotas for individual Member States.[256] As Cremona has observed in the context of the Single Market Programme in the late 1990s, it became increasingly

---

[253] In the case of Bulgaria, Estonia and Hungary, the relevant date is 31 December 1999. For Croatia, the relevant date is 31 December 2002. See Art 12 of the Act concerning the conditions of accession of the Republic of Croatia and the adjustments to the Treaty on European Union, the Treaty on the Functioning of the European Union and the Treaty establishing the European Atomic Energy Community [2012] OJ L112/21.

[254] See in particular: Puig, 'The Scope of the New Exclusive Competence' (above n 90) 148 ff.

[255] Such an economic needs test was mentioned in *Opinion 1/08* [2009] ECR I-11129, para 60.

[256] The preservation of national sub-quotas was initially approved, although such a division was subject to the condition that it did not hinder the free movement of the goods forming part of the quota after they had been released into free circulation in the territory of one of the Member States. See 59/84 *Tezi Textiel v Commission* [1986] ECR 887, para 28.

hard to justify measures that 'perpetuate the division of the Community market into separate national markets'.[257] Similarly, it may seem to be increasingly more difficult to justify any special requirements for the admission of FDI in specific Member States if such requirements would be at odds with the common interest of the Union in implementing an international investment policy or in clear conflict with the need for this policy to be premised upon 'uniform principles'. Yet, as was discussed in the previous section, it can be observed that specific Member State commitments in addition to Union commitments continue to be included in the schedules of commitments under post-Lisbon external agreements and it may not seem feasible or desirable no longer to have such differentiated schedules of commitments for the Member States.

Have the Member States, pursuant to the Union's post-Lisbon FDI competence, lost the competence to regulate FDI not only by conventional measures, but also by autonomous measures? In view of the exclusive nature of the Union's FDI competence, the Member States seemingly no longer have the competence to take autonomous measures in all the fields covered by the CCP, unless they are empowered to do so by the Union in the sense of Article 2(1) TFEU.[258] At the same time, Article 207(6) TFEU provides, inter alia, that the exercise of the Union's post-Lisbon FDI competence 'shall not affect the delimitation of competences between the Union and the Member States'. As was argued above (I.C), pursuant to Article 207(6) TFEU, the exercise of the Union's FDI competence cannot give rise to an exclusive competence so far as concerns intra-EU direct investment 'through the back door'. Moreover, it seems that it is still possible for the Member States to adopt measures that apply indistinctly to EU and non-EU direct investment in areas where the Union has not yet exercised its competence, subject to the obligation of compliance with EU law. However, it arguably follows from the Union's post-Lisbon exclusive FDI competence that the Member States can no longer adopt autonomous measures that deal specifically with issues covered by the CCP, such as the admission of third-country direct investment, unless a Member State is empowered to do so by the Union.[259]

There is also the question whether the Union's post-Lisbon FDI competence affects the application of existing national investment codes, under which a Member State may or may not authorise third-country direct investment with implications for public policy, public security or national defence.[260] In this regard, the TFEU provisions on the CCP arguably do not in themselves lay down any specific substantive obligations on the Member States so far as their existing arrangements are concerned. This may be contrasted with the 12-year transitional

---

[257] M Cremona, 'The Completion of the Internal Market and the Incomplete Commercial Policy of the European Community' (1990) 4 *EL Rev* 283, 287.

[258] See also E Neframi, 'La politique commerciale commune selon le Traité établissant une Constitution pour l'Europe' (2005) 2 *Revue trimestrielle de droit européen* 473, 485.

[259] See the text at chapter 4, III and accompanying notes on the issue of authorisation of Member State measures by the Union.

[260] See the text at chapter 2, III and accompanying notes on the recently adopted German and French investment codes.

period enshrined in the Treaty of Rome for the establishment of the CCP in the field of trade in goods.[261] The Member States were then free to regulate external trade by means of both conventional and autonomous measures until 'full responsibility' for the CCP was transferred to the Community, after which there was a requirement of authorisation by the Council of existing commercial policy measures of the Member States.[262] If the Union would have acquired a similarly defined 'full responsibility' pending the lapse of a transitional period in the field of FDI pursuant to the Lisbon reform of the CCP, the Member States would equally need to be authorised to maintain existing legislation or else there would be a sudden legislative vacuum in the field of FDI.[263] However, even then the Member States in fact retained their existing arrangements with regard to non-tariff barriers to trade in goods until there were Community rules or a Community trade agreement, even if they needed authorisation to do so by the Community.[264]

With respect to the post-Lisbon situation in the field of FDI, in view of the absence of a transitional period enshrined in EU primary law, only the *exercise* by the Union of its post-Lisbon FDI competence could arguably affect the application of existing Member State regulation in the same field. The adoption of such measures by the Union could affect the application of national investment codes by virtue of the application of the principle of primacy, which is the substantive conflict rule that governs the interplay between EU law and Member State measures. It is not very likely, however, that the Union will adopt such measures. While the Commission has earlier said that it may want to formulate a common response to inward investment by sovereign wealth funds (SWFs), possibly by restricting such investment,[265] the Commission emphasises the importance of an open admission regime for FDI, which would seem to indicate that it does not envisage the creation of any type of screening or authorisation mechanism for the admission of FDI into the Single Market.[266] In addition, it seems possible to argue that the Member States need authorisation from the Union for the *amendment* of existing legislation that applies exclusively to third-country direct investment, since such measures fall under the subject matter of the TFEU provisions on the CCP.

---

[261] See the text at chapter 4, III on the substantive obligations flowing from this transitional period.

[262] 41/76 *Donckerwolcke* [1976] ECR 1921, para 32.

[263] See Joined Cases 37/73 and 38/73 *Diamantarbeiders* [1973] ECR 1609. With regard to the requirement for the common commercial policy to be based on uniform principles, the Court took the view that 'The definition of these uniform principles involves, as does the common tariff itself, the *elimination of national disparities*, whether in the field of taxation or of commerce, affecting trade with third countries' (para 16) (emphasis added). As a result, subsequent to the introduction of the common customs tariff, the Member States were not only prohibited from introducing, on a unilateral basis, any new charges or from raising the level of those already in force, but evaluation by the Community was needed as regards charges already in existence in order to establish their compatibility with the EC Treaty (paras 18–19).

[264] Cremona, 'The Completion of the Internal Market' (above n 257) 286.

[265] Communication from the Commission to the European Parliament, the Council, the European Economic and Social Committee and the Committee of the Regions, 'A common European approach to Sovereign Wealth Funds', COM(2008)115 final, 26 February 2008, Brussels, 5. See the text at chapter 1, II and accompanying notes.

[266] COM(2010)343 (above n 2) 4.

Notwithstanding the Union's post-Lisbon FDI competence, the Member States will still be able to engage in investment promotion measures in order to attract third-country investment, such as investment assistance and support schemes. That has also been explicitly recognised by the Commission in its 2010 Communication, in which it claims that:

> While it is the Union's responsibility to promote the European model and the single market as a destination for foreign investors, it seems neither feasible nor desirable to replace the investment promotion efforts of Member States, as long as they fit with the common commercial policy and remain consistent with EU law.[267]

Even if there remains scope for the Member State to pursue their investment promotion policies, the Commission has indicated that these efforts may not go against the policies of the Union. The Commission emphasises the importance of cooperation and coordination among the Union and the Member States in this context. These obligations flow from the principle of sincere cooperation that is laid down in Article 4(3) TEU.

B. The Common International Investment Policy and Secondary Rights of Mobility for Third-Country Direct Investors in the Single Market

The Lisbon reform of the CCP may further contribute to the progressive shaping of the external dimension of the Single Market in the field of FDI. In this respect, there is an important link between the development of the common international investment policy and the issue of the distinction between EU and non-EU direct investment for the purpose of the treatment that is granted to such investment in the Single Market. In Eeckhout's view, there would in fact be no need for a common policy in the case that non-EU direct investment automatically receives the same post-establishment treatment as EU direct investment.[268] In other words, it is the very matter of differential treatment of non-EU controlled legal entities that opens up the need to negotiate national treatment commitments with third countries. Upon this view, only when there is preferential treatment of EU direct investment in the Single Market would there be a need for a common international investment policy with regard to the post-establishment treatment of third-country direct investment in the Single Market.

There is a certain difficulty conceptually to separate the issue of post-establishment treatment of FDI pursuant to the exercise of the Union's post-Lisbon FDI competence, on the one hand, and the issue of post-establishment treatment of FDI under the internal market mechanism, on the other. As a result of the inward-looking nature of the TFEU freedom of establishment, there is in

---

[267] Ibid 6.

[268] P Eeckhout, 'The External Dimension of the Internal Market and the Scope and Content of a Modern Commercial Policy' in M Maresceau (ed), *The European Community's Commercial Policy After 1992: The Legal Dimension* (Dordrecht, Martinus Nijhoff, 1993) 86.

principle not much interaction between the common international investment policy and the operation of the internal market mechanism as regards the issue of admission of FDI in the Single Market, except for those elements that fall primarily within the scope of the TFEU provisions on free movement of capital. At the same time, while third-country direct investors cannot invoke the TFEU freedom of establishment upon their initial establishment in the Single Market, NT and MFN treatment commitments in specific Union investment agreements raise the issue of whether the treatment accorded by a Member State to direct investors from another Member State needs to be extended to third-country direct investors upon their initial establishment. Depending on the specific rights flowing from the NT and MFN commitments in Union investment agreements, third-country direct investors may be given all the benefits in relation to their initial establishment that they are granted under the internal market mechanism in relation to their secondary rights of mobility.

In this regard, it has been observed above (II.A) that the CJEU focuses on the objectives of the agreement for an interpretation of the intensity of commitments under the free movement-related provisions in Union external agreements, which it contradistinguishes from the objectives of Single Market integration. As a result, the Court did not extend obligations under the law of the internal market to relations with third countries under Union external agreements, even when there is a similarity in wording. In this respect, it is important that the internal market freedoms essentially operate *between the Member States* as part of a process of economic integration. The operation of the internal market freedoms is moreover flanked by the adoption of measures of positive integration in order to facilitate to the greatest extent possible the conditions for fusing the national markets of the Member States into a Single Market. The objective served by the internal market freedoms is therefore markedly different from the objective served by the investment-related commitments assumed by the Union in agreements with third countries.

An integral approach to the issue of the interaction between the NT and MFN obligations under Union investment agreements and the internal market freedoms, which fits both with the objectives of Single Market integration and the objectives of the common international investment policy, could be conceived along the following lines. The application of NT commitments in Union external agreements gives rise to actual 'EU treatment' of third-country direct investors insofar as those investors would be subject to Union measures. Yet the application of NT commitments in Union external agreements with regard to Member State measures is arguably confined to a comparison with the treatment by that Member State of its own nationals, and not with the (potentially better) treatment of nationals from other Member States by virtue of the free movement rights enjoyed by the latter under the internal market mechanism. In addition, the scope of application of MFN treatment commitments would be limited to the post-establishment treatment commitments under other agreements concluded by the Union (with or without the Member States) with other third countries.

It can be asked whether a similar approach would be adopted to this issue when questions on the interpretation of the provisions on NT and MFN treatment arise in investor-state dispute settlement under a Union investment agreement. The point of departure for arbitral tribunals in interpreting the NT and MFN commitments in Union investment agreements will be the wording of the respective provisions, which may or may not specify the interpretation to be given to those commitments in the light of the law of the internal market. In order to encapsulate the approach to the post-establishment treatment of FDI, which fits both with the objectives of the Single Market and of the common international investment policy, a regional economic integration organisation (REIO) clause would arguably need to be included in Union investment agreements.[269] Under such a provision, MFN treatment would be expressly limited to the post-establishment treatment commitments under other agreements concluded by the Union (with or without its Member States) with other third countries.

An important precedent in respect of investment can be found in Article 25(1) of the ECT, which provides that:

> The provisions of this Treaty shall not be so construed as to oblige a Contracting Party which is a party to an Economic Integration Agreement (hereinafter referred to as 'EIA') to extend, by means of most favoured nation treatment, to another Contracting Party which is not a party to that EIA, any preferential treatment applicable between the parties to that EIA as a result of their being parties thereto.

On the concept of an Economic Integration Agreement (EIA), Article 25(2) ECT specifies that:

> For the purposes of paragraph (1), 'EIA' means an agreement substantially liberalizing, inter alia, trade and investment, by providing for the absence or elimination of substantially all discrimination between or among parties thereto through the elimination of existing discriminatory measures and/or the prohibition of new or more discriminatory measures, either at the entry into force of the agreement or on the basis of a reasonable time frame.

In addition, a declaration issued by the (now) Union with regard to Article 25 upon the conclusion of the ECT clarified that:

> the application of [that] provision will allow only those derogations necessary to safeguard the preferential treatment resulting from the wider process of economic integration resulting from the Treaties establishing the European Communities.[270]

---

[269] Member States have carved out benefits arising from Single Market integration from the commitments on investment treatment in BITs by including a REIO exception. See eg Art 7 of the United Kingdom-Moldova BIT, which provides that 'The provisions of this Agreement relative to the grant of treatment not less favourable than that accorded to the nationals or companies of either Contracting Party or of any third State shall not be construed so as to oblige one Contracting Party to extend to the nationals or companies of the other the benefit of any treatment, preference or privilege resulting from: (a) any existing or future customs union or similar international agreement to which either of the Contracting Parties is or may become a party'.

[270] See 'Energy Charter Treaty and Related Documents', 32, available at www.encharter.org/fileadmin/user_upload/document/EN.pdf.

Under this type of provision, MFN treatment under a Union investment agreement is limited to the treatment by the Union and its Member States of direct investment from other third countries and does not include the treatment granted by a Member State to direct investment from another Member State.[271]

In the case that a REIO exception to MFN treatment is included in future Union investment agreements, the NT commitments under a Union investment agreement, so far as concerns treatment of third-country direct investors by a Member State, should arguably be interpreted so as to involve a comparison of the treatment of third-country direct investment with the treatment by a specific Member State of its own nationals and not of other EU nationals that are economically active in that Member State. Otherwise, the commitments carved out by the REIO exception to MFN treatment would be imported into the agreement via the provisions on national treatment. The REIO exception to the MFN clause would consequently be defunct. It is arguably only by including both elements that it is possible to encapsulate the approach to the issue of initial post-establishment treatment of FDI, which is consistent with both the objectives of Single Market integration in the field of direct investment and with those under the common international investment policy so far as concerns the shaping of the external dimension of the Single Market in that field.

At the same time, the common international investment policy has potential implications for the extent to which the Single Market is increasingly a single investment area for non-EU investors. As was argued in chapter 2, the treatment of FDI in respect of the initial establishment of third-country investors is subject to Member State legislation, as well as, inter alia, the free movement of capital, Union secondary legislation in specific sectors and the investment-related provisions in Union external agreements. The treatment of FDI in the Single Market is likely to be increasingly subject to EU law in the form of both autonomous and conventional measures pursuant to the common international investment policy. The Lisbon reform of the CCP may thus contribute to the extent to which the Single Market constitutes a truly single investment area for non-EU investors. Even if such investors would still not be able to invoke the TFEU freedom of establishment, the extent to which they actually participate in the economy of the Single Market rather than in the internal economy of a Member State could increase as a result of the Union regulatory framework, to which non-EU investors can be expected to be increasingly subject.

So far as the secondary rights of mobility of third-country direct investors are concerned, the question moreover arises to what extent Article 54 TFEU, under which such rights are automatically granted to third-country investors,

---

[271] Another example is the EU-Russia PCA, Art 44 of which provides that 'For the purposes of [the provisions affecting the establishment and operation of companies], no account shall be taken of treatment accorded by the Community, its Member States, or Russia pursuant to commitments entered into in economic integration agreements'. See also Art V GATS, under which the treatment that is accorded in respect of services under economic integration agreements is exempted from the scope of the MFN treatment clause.

circumscribes the exercise of the Union's FDI competence. As was discussed in chapter 2, the internal market mechanism (with the exception of the free movement of capital) can only be invoked by third-country direct investors so far as concerns the issue of rights of intra-EU mobility. It has also been argued in the previous section that the exercise of the Union's post-Lisbon FDI competence is arguably circumscribed by the need to include an internal market legal basis for the negotiation of commitments with third countries on the post-establishment treatment of FDI for the issue of rights of intra-EU mobility of third-country direct investors in the Single Market. The issue of the rights of intra-EU mobility of third-country direct investors in the Single Market is thus primarily an internal market issue, even if it is technically also an aspect of the post-establishment treatment of FDI.

The question arises whether third-country direct investors can invoke Article 54 TFEU in respect of restrictions in Union external agreements on FDI flowing into the Single Market. The problem is analogous to the issue of discriminatory treatment of non-EU direct investment under Union secondary legislation and Member State national investment codes, which has been discussed in the previous chapter. A recent example is the Air Transport Agreement[272] that was concluded as a mixed agreement with the United States in 2007. One of the much debated issues was the reciprocal opportunities for market access in the agreement, particularly as regards ownership and control of airlines. The negotiations purportedly had the objective to create a single market for air transport between the Union and the United States in which investment can flow freely.[273] Yet, the Air Transport Agreement stipulates that:

> Ownership by US nationals of a Community airline shall be permitted subject to two limitations. First, the airline must be majority owned by Member States and/or by nationals of Member States. Second, the airline must be effectively controlled by such States and/or such nationals.[274]

The Union has thus reserved the right to limit investment by US nationals in the voting equity of an EU airline. For that purpose, the Union uses a definition of corporate nationality based on ownership and control under which a legal person in the Union, which is owned or controlled by US nationals, would not necessarily qualify as an EU company for the purpose of exercising any secondary rights of mobility such as by subsequently purchasing a stake in an EU airline in another Member State.

---

[272] [2007] OJ L134/4.

[273] DG Energy and Transport, Information note of 6 March 2007, 1–2, available at http://ec.europa.eu/transport/air/international_aviation/country_index/doc/2007_03_05_us_information_note.pdf.

[274] Air Transport Agreement, Annex 4 on ownership, investment and control, Art 1(2). See also Art 1(4): 'Notwithstanding paragraph 2, the European Community and its Member States reserve the right to limit investments by US nationals in the voting equity of a Community airline made after the signature of this Agreement to a level equivalent to that allowed by the United States for foreign nationals in US airlines, provided that the exercise of that right is consistent with international law.'

The question that arises is whether this type of provision gives rise to an issue of compatibility with Article 54 TFEU. In particular, does Article 54 TFEU override the market access restrictions in the new Air Transport Agreement with the United States, insofar as these pertain to the secondary rights of mobility enjoyed by US direct investors in the Single Market?[275] And does Article 54 TFEU therefore restrict the scope of manoeuvre for the Union when it enters into commitments with third countries with regard to the external dimension of the Single Market in the field of FDI? It can in fact be observed that many instruments of international economic law, of which both the Union and the Member States are contracting parties, use a definition of corporate nationality on the basis of control.[276]

In this context, a parallel can be drawn with the practice of national sub-quota in the early years of the CCP, where the Member States could not restrict the importation of goods that were in free circulation in the Single Market unless an express provision to the contrary had been adopted by the competent Community institution.[277] At the same time, however, the Commission could authorise a Member State under Article 115 EEC to take 'necessary protective measures' in the case that goods originating from third countries were imported indirectly via another Member State and thus obstructed a Member State's commercial policy. This was a problem specifically when the conditions for importation of goods from third countries had not yet entirely been harmonised, whereas this provision was effectively redundant once there were uniform conditions of importation.[278] Unlike in the field of trade, rights of intra-EU mobility for third-country direct investors are not conditional upon the creation of uniform conditions for the admission of FDI, but were automatically extended to non-EU direct investors. This underscores the relative independence of the common international investment policy from the legal organisation of direct investment within the Single Market.

At the same time, the exercise of the Union's post-Lisbon FDI competence potentially has an important bearing on the issue of secondary rights of mobility for non-EU direct investors in the Single Market. From the perspective of international economic relations, it is up to the discretion of the Union whether it wants to include in its commitments with third countries the rights unilaterally given to third-country direct investors under the internal market mechanism. Where the Union does not extend such rights to third-country investors under an external agreement, the Union does not necessarily rescind on the rights granted to third-country direct investors under the internal market mechanism. Under

---

[275] For critical analysis in the context of the reciprocity provisions in secondary legislation in the financial services sector in the early 1990s, see P Eeckhout, *The European Internal Market and International Trade: A Legal Analysis* (Oxford, Clarendon Press, 1994) 64 ff. This policy was conducted upon the principle that, where there were no multilateral rules, the Community was not prepared unilaterally to extend the benefits of the Single Market to third-country direct investors if European firms were not afforded similar opportunities abroad.

[276] See Art XXVIII(m)(ii) GATS; Art 1(6) ECT.

[277] 288/83 *Commission v Ireland* [1985] ECR 1761, para 25.

[278] Cremona, 'The Completion of the Internal Market' (above n 257) 294.

EU law, commitments in Union external agreements prevail over secondary legislation, but not over primary law.[279] From the perspective of international economic relations, the main consequence will be that a third country cannot oppose those rights to the Union under the agreement in question.

On the other hand, there may be situations where the Union wants to effectively restrict the rights of admission of third-country direct investment in particular sectors. In order to be able to do that effectively, it may be expedient to limit the rights of intra-EU mobility of third-country direct investors in derogation from the rights of intra-EU mobility conferred on non-EU direct investors under Article 54 TFEU. In this respect, it has been pointed out in chapter 2 that, in view of the application of the formalistic criteria enshrined in Article 54 TFEU, it is arguable that restrictions on the intra-EU mobility of non-EU controlled companies could in some instances be easier to justify than in relation to EU companies under Article 52(1) TFEU, such as on grounds of public policy or public security.[280] It was suggested that a parallel could here perhaps be drawn with the case of *A v Skatteverket*, where the CJEU ruled that restrictions on extra-EU capital transfers may be easier to justify than restrictions on intra-EU capital transfers.

It may seem that the same type of reasoning could be applied to restrictions on the secondary rights of mobility of third-country direct investors, insofar as they are effectively part of a third-country situation. Pursuant to the implementation of the common international investment policy, it also seems possible to argue that there is more scope for the justification of differential treatment of non-EU investors *by the Union*, while there seems to be less scope *for the Member States* to do so. The development of a common international investment policy upon uniform principles does not seem to be served by Member State legislation to the same extent as by Union measures, which provide for the differential treatment of non-EU investors so far as concerns their rights of intra-EU mobility. Such differential treatment by the Union could therefore perhaps be justified more easily than differential treatment by a Member State.

In sum, the Lisbon reform of the CCP may contribute to the progressive shaping of the external dimension of the Single Market in the field of FDI. The Union is empowered to adopt both conventional and autonomous measures in order to implement the common international investment policy. The exercise of the Union's FDI competence may have implications for existing Member State legislation. While the Lisbon reform of the TFEU provisions on the common commercial policy may contribute to the CCP as an autonomous policy area with independent objectives, the Union's international investment policy will at the same time interact with the *internal* legal organisation in the Single Market in the field of FDI. Notwithstanding the inward-looking character of the TFEU freedom of establishment, the admission of FDI is likely to be increasingly subject to both

---

[279] C-61/94 *Commission v Germany* [1995] ECR I-3989, para 52.

[280] See, by analogy, the case law on requirements of public security and overriding reasons of public interest as justification for restrictions on the free movement of capital: C-171/08 *Commission v Portugal* [2010] ECR I-6817, para 69; C-274/06 *Commission v Spain* [2008] ECR I-26, paras 35–39.

conventional and autonomous Union measures. The common international investment policy moreover interacts with the issue of intra-EU rights of mobility of third-country investors when the Union negotiates commitments with third countries on the post-establishment treatment of FDI. This section has highlighted the importance of the intensity of commitments undertaken under the NT and MFN standards in Union external agreements, as well as the interplay of such commitments with Article 54 TFEU.

IV. CONCLUSION

Pursuant to the Lisbon reform of the CCP, the Union has acquired an exclusive FDI competence. It seems possible to argue that the scope of the Union's FDI competence extends to both the liberalisation and protection of FDI. There are, however, limits to the scope of the Union's FDI competence, such as with regard to foreign portfolio investment and capital transfers in relation to direct investment. The common international investment policy is likely to have far-reaching implications for the Union's treaty-making practice. While the proposed further deepening of investment liberalisation commitments builds on the Community's external practice in the pre-Lisbon era, the broadening of the Union's treaty-making practice to the issue of investment protection would mean that the Union enters into relatively new territory. A number of building blocks for the Union's international investment policy are gradually taking shape. In addition to the main orientations for the common international investment policy, negotiations with third countries in the field of investment protection are currently ongoing. The Union is also putting in place the modalities for the attribution of financial responsibility between the Union and the Member States for breaches of investment agreements to which the Union is a party and the conduct of investor-state dispute settlement under these agreements. Further external legal integration will transform the CCP into a more autonomous policy area with independent objectives while being less isolated from Union external action in other fields.

In the words of Eeckhout, 'the [CCP] is the external side of the establishment of the internal market. If the latter were a building, the CCP would be its façade.'[281] This façade is gradually taking shape so far as concerns direct investment from and into the Single Market. An important consequence of an ambitious common international investment policy is that the Single Market will increasingly become a more truly 'single' market for third-country investors. At the same time, the inclusion of the FET standard and investor-state dispute settlement provisions in Union external agreements has the important consequence that non-EU investors will be able to invoke rights that are not granted in the same form to EU investors under EU law. The external dimension of the Single Market will thus not merely run parallel with the internal dimension of the EU legal organisation in the field

---

[281] Eeckhout, *The European Internal Market and International Trade* (above n 275) 344.

of direct investment. Notwithstanding the inward-looking nature of the freedom of establishment, the post-establishment treatment of FDI under Union investment agreements interacts with the law of the internal market. The interplay of the common international investment policy and the internal market mechanism underscores the need for an integral approach to the EU legal organisation in the field of FDI.

4

The Interplay between EU Law and Member State Bilateral Investment Agreements with Third Countries

> In the long run, we should achieve a situation where investors from the EU and from third countries will not need to rely on BITs entered into by one or the other Member State for an effective protection of its investments.[1]

FROM THE EARLY years of Single Market integration, the (now) Union has concluded a significant number of external agreements (together with the Member States) containing investment-related provisions. Contemporaneously, the Member States have concluded numerous bilateral investment treaties (BITs) with third countries. The latter practice, which initially served mainly to protect European outward investment, has developed into a dense network of external BITs. The Member States have concluded BITs independently from Union initiatives in helping to shape the external dimension of the Single Market in the field of foreign direct investment (FDI). Nevertheless, they cannot be seen in isolation from EU law, because these agreements interact in a number of ways with EU law.

Furthermore, the Union's post-Lisbon FDI competence and the development of the common international investment policy raise questions with regard to the continued existence and application of Member State BITs with third countries. On 9 January 2013, Regulation 1219/2012 establishing transitional arrangements for BITs between Member States and third countries entered into force.[2] Regulation 1219/2012 establishes both a replacement mechanism for existing Member State BITs with third countries and an authorisation mechanism for the amendment of existing Member State BITs and for the conclusion of new BITs. First and foremost, it therefore confirms the status quo of existing BITs with third countries. These transitional arrangements constitute an important step in the

---

[1] Communication from the Commission to the Council, the European Parliament, the European Economic and Social Committee and the Committee of the Regions, 'Towards a comprehensive European international investment policy', COM(2010)343 final, 7 July 2010, Brussels, 5–6.

[2] Regulation 1219/2012 of the European Parliament and of the Council of 12 December 2012 establishing transitional arrangements for bilateral investment agreements between Member States and third countries [2012] OJ L351/40.

shaping of the external dimension of the Single European Market in the field of FDI.

This chapter explores a number of the EU legal aspects of the interplay between EU law and Member State investment agreements with third countries. The chapter looks first at the historical background to the Member States' practice of concluding BITs with third countries, as well as at various ways in which these agreements interact substantively with EU law. The second section discusses a number of aspects of the EU legal framework that governs the interplay between EU law and Member State BITs with third countries and focuses on how the EU legal order deals with conflicts between EU law and the legal commitments of the Member States in relations with third countries. Against this backdrop, the third section looks in detail at Regulation 1219/2012 establishing transitional arrangements for Member States' BITs with third countries. The chapter shows that the EU legal framework that governs the interplay between EU law and Member State agreements with third countries focuses on issues of substantive compatibility and has potential implications for existing BITs. Moreover, it is submitted that Regulation 1219/2012 does not affect the level of protection currently offered to investors under Member States' BITs with third countries, while the precise implications of the transitional arrangements will depend on the Union's success in the implementation of the common international investment policy.

I. MEMBER STATE PRACTICE OF CONCLUDING BITS AND THEIR SUBSTANTIVE INTERACTION WITH EU LAW

This section explores the substantive interaction with EU law of Member State BITs with third countries. In view of the historical background to the Member States' practice of concluding such agreements, the section emphasises that Union external agreements and Member State BITs have traditionally served different purposes and demonstrate a different approach to the issue of FDI, as well as that these parallel patterns of external action have historically developed without a preconceived division of function between them. After having highlighted that Union external agreements and Member State BITs nonetheless contain overlapping and conflicting provisions, the section shows that Member State BITs with third countries interact in various ways with the EU Treaties and with Union secondary legislation.

A. Historical Background to the Conclusion of BITs by the Member States

During the early years of European integration, the Member States were mainly exporters of FDI to the many new states that had just come into being as a result of the process of decolonisation. At the same time, the international investment climate in these early years of the Community was subject to considerable change, uncertainty and controversy. Multilateral developments were characterised by the persistent dismantling of standards of international customary law for the protection of investment.[3] As part of the post-colonial struggle for economic sovereignty, discussions within UNCTAD led up to the 1974 Resolution calling for a new international economic order, which proclaimed that every state enjoys full permanent sovereignty over its natural resources and all economic activities, and that each state thus has the right to nationalise foreign property.[4] In that context, European investment in third countries faced an increased risk not only of explicit forms of expropriation but also of so-called 'creeping expropriation', which refers to a series of measures or events attributable to the host country that, taken together, dilute or even destroy the economic substance of the investment.[5]

The politicised clash between developed countries, including the Member States of the (then) European Economic Community, and the newly independent developing countries gave rise to the need for agreements to protect European investment in such third countries.[6] Even though many developing countries opposed property right commitments at a multilateral level, they were pressured into restoring them via bilateral investment agreements by the competition for foreign capital.[7] In this international context, BITs were understood as striking a balance between the rights of third countries to decide on the admission of investment and to expropriate investors, while conferring upon European investors the right to a certain treatment of their investments and adequate compensation in case of expropriation.[8] Although the Member States still had competence to assume commitments with third countries with regard to the admission of investment,[9] they have expressly limited the scope of their BITs to issues of post-establishment treatment in response to the specific problem of investment security.

Whereas West Germany spearheaded the practice of concluding BITs in the late 1950s, France, the Belgo-Luxembourg Economic Union (BLEU) and the

---

[3] J Voss, 'The Protection and Promotion of Foreign Direct Investment in Developing Countries: Interests, Interdependencies, Intricacies' (1982) 4 *ICLQ* 686, 692.

[4] UN Resolution 3201 (S-VI), 1 May 1974 (Declaration on the Establishment of a New International Economic Order). See also UN Resolution 3202 (S-VI), 1 May 1974 (Programme of Action on the Establishment of a New International Economic Order). Under the Hull Rule, which had ceased to be a rule of international customary law by the mid-1970s, expropriating states owed 'prompt, adequate and effective' compensation to investors. For an analysis of the extent to which traditional rules pertaining to the protection of foreign property have been replaced, see WD Verwey and NJ Schrijver, 'The Taking of Foreign Property under International Law: A New Legal Perspective?' (1984) *Netherlands Yearbook of International Law* 3.

[5] Voss, 'The Protection and Promotion of Foreign Direct Investment' (above n 3) 703.

[6] T Pollan, *Legal Framework for the Admission of FDI* (Utrecht, Eleven International Publishing, 2006) 3 ff.

[7] J Voss, 'The Protection and Promotion of European Private Investment in Development Countries – An Approach Towards a Concept for a European Policy on Foreign Investment: A German Contribution' (1981) 3 *CML Rev* 363, 372; AT Guzman, 'Why LDCs Sign Treaties that Hurt Them: Explaining the Popularity of Bilateral Investment Treaties' (1998) 4 *Virginia Journal of International Law* 639.

[8] P Juillard, *L'évolution des sources du droit des investissements* (Collected Courses of the Hague Academy of International Law, 1994) 24.

[9] See text at chapter 3, I and accompanying notes.

Netherlands followed suit by initiating their BIT programmes in the late 1960s and early 1970s. These early investment treaties have all been entered into by the original signatories of the Treaty of Rome after the entry into force of the Community's founding treaty.[10] Most Member States joining the Union in successive accession rounds have concluded BITs both before and after accession. By the late 1990s Germany, France and Britain had established an extensive network of BITs. Germany was the frontrunner with more than 120 BITs, while a significant group of other Member States (including Italy, the Netherlands and the BLEU states) had concluded more than 60 BITs.[11] Some BITs have been concluded with countries that would later accede to the Union. For instance, Germany concluded investment treaties with Greece[12] and Portugal[13] prior to their accession to the Community, and many Member States concluded BITs with Central and Eastern European states within a few years after the collapse of the Soviet Union. The total number of extra-EU BITs, currently amounting to more than 1,000 treaties, has become a constituent element in shaping the external dimension of the Single Market in the field of investment.

The BITs of the Member States have for the most part followed the 1967 OECD Draft Convention on the Protection of Foreign Property.[14] This model treaty has never been binding on OECD countries, but has provided general guidelines for the negotiation of BITs by the Member States, particularly by informing the substance of these agreements so as to focus on issues of post-establishment treatment. As a result, the scope of application of the notion of 'treatment' of investment in European BITs differs from that in US BITs, since it is restricted to post-establishment treatment in the former, whereas in the latter it extends to the issue of the admission of investment.[15] BITs concluded by different Member States generally follow the same approach to investment, focusing upon the protection of assets in a third country, as opposed to the liberalisation of more specific types of capital movements. So far as concerns the definition of investment, the OECD Draft Convention refers to 'property', which includes, but is not limited to, investments. Pursuant to Article 9(c) of the OECD Draft, 'property' means 'all property, rights and interests, whether held directly or indirectly, including the interest which a member of a company is deemed to have in the property of the company'.

For the purpose of offering the broadest protection possible to their companies' cross-border transactions, capital exporting Member States have tried to ensure that these agreements contain a wide and inclusive 'asset-based' definition of

---

[10] The first BIT ever concluded was that between West Germany and Pakistan (signed 25 November 1959, entered into force 28 April 1962).

[11] See UNCTAD, *Bilateral Investment Treaties, 1959–1999*, UNCTAD/ITE/IIA/2, 2000.

[12] Germany-Greece BIT (signed 27 March 1961, entered into force 15 July 1963).

[13] Germany-Portugal BIT (signed 16 September 1980, entered into force 23 April 1982).

[14] Available at www.oecd.org/dataoecd/35/4/39286571.pdf. The 1967 Draft Convention on the Protection of Foreign Property is a revised version of the 1962 Draft, which in turn followed the 1959 Abs-Shawcross Draft Convention on Foreign Investment (reprinted in UNCTAD, *International Investment Instruments: A Compendium* (New York, United Nations, 2000) vol V, 395).

[15] On US BITs, see KJ Vandevelde, *U.S. International Investment Agreements* (Oxford, Oxford University Press, 2009).

investment.[16] There is little variation in Member State BITs as to their scope of application to the exclusion of some (or all) kinds of portfolio investments.[17] So far as investment treatment is concerned, which in European BITs exclusively refers to the legal regime applicable to an investment after the host state has allowed the investment to be made, there are two types of standards. The first is the standard of fair and equitable treatment (FET), which is an 'absolute standard'. The second is the standard of non-discriminatory treatment, articulated as a combination of national treatment (NT) and most favoured nation (MFN) treatment, which are 'relative standards'; that is, relative to the treatment of national companies or those of other third countries.

Whereas the investment-related provisions in Union external agreements have so far focused on the issue of investment mobility through effective market access, the provisions of Member State BITs predominantly deal with issues of investment security (the protection of rights *in rem*). Member State BITs and the investment-related provisions in Union external agreements have thus traditionally served different objectives. There is, moreover, no real preconceived functional division of labour between these two patterns of external action, which have for the most part developed in parallel to each other. One of the few instances indicating an intention to secure a degree of coordination between these two patterns of external action is a 1978 Communication, in which the European Commission argued that Community agreements should complement the network of Member State investment protection agreements.[18] An attempt at coordination of the protection of European investments in third countries that the author has been able to find was in the context of the conclusion of Lomé IV, when the Council issued a statement pursuant to which the Community and the Member States agreed to undertake concerted action in formulating a common approach to the issue of the promotion and protection of investment.[19] These two parallel patterns of external action can therefore be understood as constituting complementary layers of rules on investment.[20]

---

[16] For the asset-based definition of 'investment' in Member State BITs, see the United Kingdom-Ukraine BIT, Art 1(a), quoted in text at chapter 1, IV. Note moreover that, inter alia, the Germany-Nigeria BIT adds to these 'rights arising out of a leasing agreements' as a sixth non-exhaustive category (Art 1(1)(d)). The Italy-Nicaragua BIT adds to these five examples of investments 'any increase in value of the original investment' as a sixth non-exhaustive category (Art 1(1)(f)).

[17] Eg, pursuant to Art 1(a) of the Germany-Israel BIT the term 'investment' means either investment in an enterprise involving active participation therein and the acquisition of assets ancillary thereto, or the enterprise or assets acquired as a result of such investment. Article 1(2) of the Czech Republic-Mexico BIT stipulates that the term 'investment' comprises only investments with regard to economic activities and excludes short-term loans. Article 1(1)(c)(i) of the Portugal-Mexico BIT excludes 'credits with a maturity of less than three years' from the scope of application of the treaty. These restrictions to the scope of the subject matter of Member State BITs constitute the exception rather than the rule, however.

[18] Communication from the Commission to the Council, 'Need for Community Action to Encourage European Investment in Developing Countries and Guidelines for such Action', COM(78)23 final, 30 January 1978, Brussels, 5.

[19] EC Council, *Position communautaire sur les principes de protection des investissements dans les états acp*, ACP-EEC 2172/92, 3 November 1992, Brussels.

[20] COM(2010)343 (above n 1) 4 ff.

The external dimension of the Single Market in the field of FDI is thus shaped in part by two separate patterns of external activity, which have predominantly been complementary while serving different objectives. Nevertheless, instances of overlapping commitments in relations with third countries can be found in these different patterns of external action. For example, while Member State investment agreements have traditionally left the decision to admit investments to the third country in question, market access commitments can now also be found in some of these agreements. As a result of the accession of a number of Central and Eastern European countries to the Union in 2004, the market access commitments enshrined in BITs between these countries and the United States, which are based on the United States model BIT and thus extend the standard of non-discriminatory treatment to pre-establishment issues, have been imported into the Member States' external BIT network.[21] It can also be observed that Italy has included market access commitments in its most recent BITs.[22]

In addition to the provisions on market access in some Member State BITs, there is moreover clearly a degree of overlap between the provisions in pre-Lisbon Union external agreements and the provisions in Member State BITs dealing with the treatment of investments. The investment-related provisions in both Member State BITs and Union external agreements typically contain provisions on NT and MFN treatment. Member State BITs also contain provisions on FET and full protection and security. In addition to this overlap in coverage, it can be observed that Member State BITs provide for unlimited NT and MFN commitments, subject to exceptions as a result of preferential treatment under a regional integration organisation and international taxation agreements.[23] By contrast, Union external agreements contain lists of exceptions to the application of NT and MFN commitments to specific sectors.[24]

---

[21] For analysis, see the text at I.B.

[22] Pollan, *Legal Framework for the Admission of FDI* (above n 6) 75. Article II(2) of the Italy-DR Congo BIT, which was signed in 2006, stipulates that 'Les investisseurs des deux Parties Contractantes auront un droit d'accès aux activités d'investissement dans le territoire de l'autre Partie Contractante non moins favorable que celui prévu à l'Article III, paragraphe 1', which provides that 'Chacune des Parties Contractantes accorde aux investissements realisés sur son territoire par l'investisseur de l'autre Partie Contractante et aux revenus y afférents, un traitement non moins favorable que celui réservé aux investissements realisés par ses propres nationaux ou ceux de pays tiers et aux revenus y afférents. Le même traitement s'étend aux activités liées à l'investissement' ['Investors from the two contracting parties will have a right of access to investment activities on the territory of the other contracting party, which is not less favourable to that provided in Article III, first paragraph', which provides that 'both of the contracting parties shall accord to investments realised on its territory by an investor of the other contracting party and to revenues in relation to those, treatment not less favourable than that which is reserved to investments by its own nationals or nationals from third countries and to revenues in relation to those. The same treatment is extended to activities in relation to investment' trans]. Yet, not all recent Italian BITs contain provisions stipulating a right to invest. See, eg the Italy-Libya BIT (signed 13 December 2000, entered into force 20 October 2004). Moreover, the inclusion of market access commitments in Italian BITs is not an entirely new phenomenon. See, eg, Art 2(2) of the Italy-Kazakhstan BIT (signed 22 September 1994, entered into force 12 July 1996).

[23] See, eg Arts 3 and 4 of the United Kingdom-Ukraine BIT. See also R Torrent, 'The Contradictory Overlapping of National, EU, Bilateral, and the Multilateral Rules on Foreign Direct Investment: Who is Guilty of Such a Mess' (2011) 5 *Fordham International Law Journal* 1377, 1384.

[24] See the text at chapter 3, II.A and accompanying notes.

Instances of overlapping, and even inconsistent, commitments in these two patterns of external action can perhaps most clearly be found in the respective provisions dealing with capital transfers. Such provisions allow an investor, once it has been given permission by the host state to invest, to bring in the funds necessary for the investment. States, however, are also responsible for financial stability and monetary policy, and can perceive the need to restrict these transfers of capital. While the provisions in Union external agreements that deal with movements of capital need to reserve the possibility for the Council to impose restrictions on capital movements to and from third countries in accordance with Articles 64(3), 66 and 75/215 TFEU,[25] the provisions dealing with capital transfers in Member State BITs often do not explicitly provide the contracting parties with the possibility of introducing restrictions on capital transfers in relation to investments.[26] As a result, a third country could restrict the repatriation of European capital in case of serious financial or monetary difficulties in accordance with its commitments under a Union external agreement, but could subsequently be sued under one of the BITs with an EU Member State, under which this is not allowed. At the same time, it can be observed that both the Union and the Member States are contracting parties to the Energy Charter Treaty (ECT), Article 14 of which guarantees free transfers of capital in relation to investment in the energy sector, which also does not explicitly provide for such a possibility of derogation.

B. Substantive Interaction of Member State External BITs with EU Law

Member State BITs demonstrate a different approach to the issue of investment from the investment-related provisions in pre-Lisbon Union external agreements. Nonetheless, these two parallel patterns of external action contain overlapping and even inconsistent provisions. Member State external BITs, moreover, give rise to various possibilities for substantive interaction with the EU Treaties and

[25] Eg, Art 30 of the EU-Mexico Joint Council Decision 2/2001 of 27 February 2001 [2001] OJ L70/7, provides for the possibility of restricting payments related to investments between the parties where they cause or threaten to cause serious difficulties for the operation of the exchange rate policy or monetary policy of a party. Article 31 provides for a similar safeguard in the case of serious balance of payments difficulties.

[26] A fairly typical provision on transfers of capital is Art 6(1) of the Germany-Nigeria BIT, which provides that 'Each Contracting Party shall guarantee to investors of the other Contracting Party the free transfer of payments in connection with an investment, in particular (a) the principal and additional amounts to maintain or increase the investment; (b) the returns; (c) the repayments; (d) the proceeds from the liquidation or the sale of the whole or any part of the investment; (e) the compensation provided for in Article 5'. But see Art 6(4) of the Portugal-Mexico BIT: 'In case of serious balance of payments difficulties or the threat thereof, each Contracting Party may temporarily restrict transfers, provided that such a Contracting Party implements measures or a programme in accordance with the International Monetary Fund's standards. This restriction would be imposed on an equitable, non-discriminatory and in good faith basis, and may not go beyond what is necessary to remedy the balance of payments situation.'

Union secondary legislation.[27] While Member State BITs have been concluded independently of Union external agreements, they cannot therefore be seen in isolation from EU law.

The first instance in which the CJEU has ruled on the compatibility of Member State external BITs with EU law are the 'BITs' judgments from 2009 against Austria, Sweden and Finland.[28] The Court held that there was an incompatibility between the capital transfer clauses in a number of pre-accession BITs of these Member States with third countries and the provisions on free movement of capital in the (then) EC Treaty. The relevant clauses in the BITs at issue guarantee the free transfer of capital, which in the view of the Court revealed an incompatibility with Articles 57(2), 59 and 60(1) EC (Articles 64(3), 66 and 75/215 TFEU), under which the Council is empowered to take restrictive measures with regard to capital transfers to and from third countries.[29] While the 'BITs' judgments have been criticised for addressing an issue unlikely to arise in practice,[30] it was not the first time that the compatibility of these transfer clauses with EU law had been at issue. In the context of the adoption under Article 60(1) EC of a ban on investment in relation to the Federal Republic of Yugoslavia, Germany had previously declared that it was unable to impose the sanction as a result of commitments under its BIT with that country.[31] It was moreover recognised in the 'BITs' case against Sweden that the Commission had earlier not commenced infringement proceedings against that Member State when sanctions under Article 60(1) EC were applied against the Republic of Côte

---

[27]   See generally A Radu, 'Foreign Investors in the EU: Which "Best Treatment"? Interactions between Bilateral Investment Treaties and EU Law' (2008) 2 *European Law Journal* 237.

[28]   Joined Cases C-205/06 *Commission v Austria* [2009] ECR I-1301; C-249/06 *Commission v Sweden* [2009] ECR I-1335; C-118/07 *Commission v Finland* [2009] ECR I-10889.

[29]   Under Art 64(3) TFEU, 'the Council, acting in accordance with a special legislative procedure, may unanimously, and after consulting the European Parliament, adopt measures which constitute a step backwards in Union law as regards the liberalisation of the movement of capital to or from third countries'. Article 66 TFEU provides that 'Where, in exceptional circumstances, movements of capital to or from third countries cause, or threaten to cause, serious difficulties for the operation of economic and monetary union, the Council, on a proposal from the Commission and after consulting the European Central Bank, may take safeguard measures with regard to third countries for a period not exceeding six months if such measures are strictly necessary'. Article 75 TFEU provides that 'Where necessary to achieve the objectives set out in Article 67, as regards preventing and combating terrorism and related activities, the European Parliament and the Council, acting by means of regulations in accordance with the ordinary legislative procedure, shall define a framework for administrative measures with regard to capital movements and payments, such as the freezing of funds, financial assets or economic gains belonging to, or owned or held by, natural or legal persons, groups or non-State entities'. See also Art 215(1) TFEU, which provides that 'Where a decision, adopted in accordance with Chapter 2 of Title V of the Treaty on European Union, provides for the interruption or reduction, in part or completely, of economic and financial relations with one or more third countries, the Council, acting by a qualified majority on a joint proposal from the High Representative of the Union for Foreign Affairs and Security Policy and the Commission, shall adopt the necessary measures'.

[30]   E Denza, 'Bilateral Investment Treaties and EU Rules on Free Transfer: Comment on Commission v Austria, Commission v Sweden and Commission v Finland' (2010) 2 *EL Rev* 263.

[31]   European Commission Directorate General Economic and Financial Affairs, Note of the Economic and Financial Committee, Bilateral Investment Treaties, Further Background Requested by Alternates, Brussels, ECFIN/574/02-EN Rev 2, 8–9. The Regulation in question was eventually adopted, and no formal reservation was entered into by Germany. See Council Regulation 1294/1999 of 15 June 1999 concerning freezing of funds [1999] OJ L153, repealing Regulations 1295/98 and 1607/98.

d'Ivoire and the Socialist Republic of Yugoslavia, which had similarly revealed an incompatibility with Sweden's obligations under its BITs with these two countries.[32]

The Court held in the 'BITs' judgments that the transfer clauses in these agreements did not reserve the possibility for the Council to adopt restrictive measures on capital movements from and into the Single Market. The Court ruled that Austria, Sweden and Finland had failed to fulfil their obligations under Article 307(2) EC (Article 351(2) TFEU), since they had not taken appropriate steps to eliminate the incompatibilities between the capital transfer clauses in the external BITs in issue, on the one hand, and the EC Treaty provisions that empower the Council to take restrictive measures with regard to capital transfers to and from third countries, on the other. The Court noted, in particular, that the investment agreements do not contain any provision, so far as these transfer clauses are concerned, allowing those Member States to exercise their rights and to fulfil their obligations as a member of the (then) Community.[33] The Court took the view that there is also no international law mechanism which makes that possible.[34] This was ruled to be incompatible with the effectiveness of the TFEU provisions under which the Council can take the restrictive measures concerned.[35]

The text below (II.A) comments in more detail on a number of aspects of the 'BITs' judgments, such as the nature of the incompatibilities in issue.[36] For the present purpose, however, it is important that the 'BITs' judgments have implications beyond the specific investment agreements at issue in these cases. Many of the Member States are contracting parties to investment agreements with third countries that do not explicitly reserve the right for the Member State at issue to restrict capital transfers in accordance with their obligations under EU law when the Council decides to take restrictive measures. Similarly, the Member States, as well as the Union, are contracting parties to the Energy Charter Treaty (ECT), Article 14 of which guarantees free transfers of capital in relation to investment in the energy sector without explicitly providing for such a possibility of derogation.

The scope for substantive interaction between external BITs and EU law is not confined to the capital transfer clauses in BITs and the TFEU provisions on free movement of capital. This is illustrated by *Commission v Slovakia*,[37] in which the Commission challenged Slovakia for not fulfilling its obligations under Articles 9(e) and 20(1) of Directive 2003/54 concerning the common rules for the internal market in electricity[38] by not granting non-discriminatory access to its transmission

---

[32] *Commission v Sweden* (above n 28) para 21.
[33] *Commission v Austria* (above n 28) para 37.
[34] Ibid.
[35] Ibid para 36.
[36] See also P Koutrakos in (2009) 6 *CML Rev* 2059; T Eilmansberger, 'Bilateral Investment Treaties and EU Law' (2009) 2 *CML Rev* 383; M Burgstaller, 'European Law and Investment Treaties' (2009) 2 *Journal of International Arbitration* 181; PFJS Strik, 'Transferclausules in bilaterale investeringsovereenkomsten in strijd met het EG-Verdrag' (2009) 6 *Nederlands Tijdschrift voor Europees Recht* 193.
[37] C-264/09 *Commission v Slovakia* [2011] ECR I-08065.
[38] Directive 2003/54 of 26 June 2003 concerning the common rules for the internal market in electricity [2003] OJ 2003 L176/37.

system. In particular, the state-owned Slovak transmission system operator had granted by contract a preferential right of transmission to a Swiss undertaking, a commitment which predated accession of Slovakia to the Union on 1 May 2004. Against the alleged breach of Directive 2003/54, Slovakia invoked the need to comply with the right to fair and equitable treatment and the provisions governing expropriation in the ECT and the Slovakia-Switzerland BIT, which also predated accession of Slovakia to the Union.[39] The Court approached the matter exclusively in light of the Slovakia-Switzerland BIT and not of the ECT. The Court took the view that the preferential access granted to the Swiss undertaking was an investment covered by the BIT, which in the view of the Court precluded the contract at issue from being adjusted.[40] The Slovakia-Switzerland BIT moreover fell within the scope of (now) Article 351(1) TFEU, so that its application could not be affected by the EU law obligations of Slovakia.[41]

Various ways in which Member State BITs and EU law interact in helping to shape the external dimension of the Single Market have also been at issue in the context of accession to the Union by eight Central and Eastern European countries in 2004.[42] In particular, the compatibility with the *acquis* of pre-existing BITs between the United States and eight acceding countries has been the subject of discussions between the European Commission, the eight acceding and candidate countries and the United States. A non-binding Memorandum of Understanding (MoU) was signed by the parties on 22 September 2003 outlining a number of interpretations and specific amendments to these BITs having regard to the EU law obligations to be assumed by these countries.[43] The MoU takes account of a number of areas in which rights held by investors under investment treaties between the United States and the Central and Eastern European countries concerned may conflict with the latter's EU law obligations.

The MoU first notes the incompatibility between the transfer clauses in these BITs and the EC Treaty provisions that empower the Council to take restrictive measures with regard to capital movements to and from third countries. Secondly, the MoU addresses the interaction between the performance requirements enshrined in Union secondary legislation in particular sectors and the obligations of acceding countries under their BITs with the United States in this field.[44] Such performance requirements are conditions set by the host state on foreign investments so as to assure the economic and social utility of an investment to the host country, typically by trying to influence the way in which investors use resources by local sourcing or content requirements. They may also require a foreign firm

---

[39]   *Commission v Slovakia* (above n 37) paras 22–24.

[40]   Ibid paras 47–50.

[41]   Ibid para 51. For analysis, see text at II and accompanying notes.

[42]   Poland, Estonia, Latvia, Lithuania, Czech Republic, Slovakia, Bulgaria and Romania. Bulgaria and Romania were then officially still candidate countries for accession.

[43]   Understanding Concerning Certain US Bilateral Investment Treaties, signed by the United States, the European Commission, and candidate countries for accession to the European Union, 22 September 2003, available at www.state.gov/s/l/2003/44366.htm.

[44]   For examples, see Radu, 'Foreign Investors in the EU' (above n 27) 252 ff.

to employ nationals or ask firms to export a number of its products.[45] In this regard, the parties agreed that the BITs in force between the United States and these Central and Eastern European countries cannot prejudice the application of Union measures laying down performance requirements. Thirdly, the MoU deals with the issue of non-discriminatory treatment in the Single Market. The MoU states that where Union measures in sensitive sectors would conflict with the non-discrimination obligations of these Central and Eastern European countries under their BITs with the United States, the governments of the acceding countries would retain the right to make or maintain exceptions to NT (such as in the fields of agriculture, transport, financial services and subsidies) and MFN treatment (such as in the field of audio-visual services).

Fourthly, the parties acknowledged that the general exception to the non-discrimination obligations for advantages accorded to nationals or companies from a third country as a member of a free trade area or customs union extends to the advantages to be accorded by the acceding Member States under EU law to investors from other Member States. The MoU, fifthly, stipulates that there is to be consultation between Commission and US officials with regard to future developments in EU law, in particular when new Union measures affecting foreign investment are under consideration that could raise questions of compatibility with pre-existing investment agreements. Sixthly, the MoU elaborates on the scope and operation of (then) Article 48 EC[46] (Article 54 TFEU) and, seventhly, the Central and Eastern European countries agreed to refrain from applying new discriminatory measures with regard to the protection of existing investments.

Signature of the MoU was followed by the adoption of amending protocols for the BITs concerned.[47] These protocols reflect the various issues raised in the MoU. Article I of the amending protocols stipulates that the BITs concerned shall not limit the possibility of these countries to impose performance requirements in the agricultural sector or in the audio-visual sector when necessary under EU law. Pursuant to Article II, the terms of the customs union or free trade area exception of these BITs apply to all obligations of a party by virtue of its membership of an economic integration agreement that includes a free trade area or customs union, such as the European Union. Under Article III, the parties agreed to consult promptly whenever a party believes that steps are necessary to assure compatibility between the BIT and the (then) EC Treaty. Article IV makes provision for exceptions to NT in the sectors of agriculture, audio-visual, securities, investment services and other financial services, fisheries, hydrocarbons, subsidies, transport (air carriers, inland waterways, maritime), as well as for exceptions to MFN treatment in the agricultural, audio-visual and hydrocarbon sectors, whenever such reservations are necessary for these countries to comply with EU law. It is specified, however, that existing US

---

[45] See Pollan, *Legal Framework for the Admission of FDI* (above n 6) 215 ff.

[46] For analysis, see the text at chapter 2, III and accompanying notes.

[47] They can be found at http://tcc.export.gov/Trade_Agreements/Bilateral_Investment_Treaties/index.asp. It can be observed that this website does not provide any information about the United States-Croatia BIT in view of accession of Croatia to the Union.

investments remain protected for at least 10 years from the date at which the relevant law or regulation adopted by (or Union measure directly applicable within) the country concerned takes effect. The United States' BITs with the Member States concerned have been amended accordingly.

The Central and Eastern European countries concerned have also had discussions with Canada in order to ensure the compatibility with EU law of pre-accession BITs with that country. In the end, the Commission supported the results of the discussions between Canada, on the one hand, and the Czech Republic, Slovakia, Poland, Hungary, Latvia and Romania, on the other.[48] Amended BITs have subsequently been concluded with Canada by Latvia (5 May 2009), the Czech Republic (6 May 2009), Romania (8 May 2009) and Slovakia (20 July 2010).[49] The negotiations with Hungary have been successfully concluded, while talks with Poland are reportedly still ongoing.

The amended provisions of these BITs with Canada generally reflect the concerns that have been addressed in the context of the pre-existing BITs of these Member States with the United States. They now contain specific provisions on the issue of consultation and exchange of information.[50] Moreover, with regard to the interplay between the investment treatment provisions in these BITs and the benefits accorded to EU investors by virtue of EU law, Article IV(2) of the Canada-Czech Republic BIT provides that:

> The National Treatment and Most-Favoured-Nation Treatment provisions of this Agreement shall not apply to advantages accorded by a Contracting Party pursuant to its obligations as a member of a customs, economic or monetary union, a common market or a free trade area. In addition, the National Treatment and Most-Favoured-Nation Treatment provisions to this Agreement shall not apply to subsidies or grants provided by a Contracting Party or a state enterprise, including government-supported loans, guarantees and insurance.[51]

To this, Article IV(3) of the Canada-Czech Republic BIT adds that:

> The Contracting Parties understand the obligations of a Contracting Party as a member of a customs, economic or monetary union, a common market or a free trade area to include obligations arising out of an international agreement or reciprocity arrangement of that customs, economic or monetary union, common market or free trade area.

---

[48] Commission press release of 29 September 2004, IP/04/1156.

[49] The relevant information is available at www.international.gc.ca/trade-agreements-accords-commerciaux/agr-acc/fipa-apie/eu6-ue6.aspx.

[50] Eg, Art XIV of the Canada-Latvia BIT and the Canada-Romania BIT provides: '(1) Either Contracting Party may request consultations on the interpretation or application of this Agreement. The other Contracting Party shall give sympathetic consideration to the request. Upon request by either Contracting Party, information shall be exchanged on the measures of the other Contracting Party that may have an impact on new investments, investments or returns covered by this Agreement. (2) The consultations provided for by this Article shall include consultations concerning any step that a Contracting Party may consider are necessary to ensure compatibility between this Agreement and the Treaty Establishing the European Community'. But see Art XI of the Canada-Czech Republic BIT.

[51] But see also Art IV(2) of the modified Canada-Romania BIT and Canada-Latvia BIT, which does not refer to the issue of subsidies. With regard to subsidies, see however Art VI(2) of these BITs.

So far as the issue of capital transfers is concerned, Article VII(3) of the same BIT provides that:

> a Contracting Party may prevent a transfer through the equitable, non-discriminatory and good faith application of its laws relating to: (a) bankruptcy, insolvency or the protection of the rights of creditors; (b) issuing, trading or dealing in securities; (c) criminal or penal offences; (d) reports of transfers of currency or other monetary instruments; or (e) ensuring the satisfaction of judgments in adjudicatory proceedings.[52]

Specific provisions on performance requirements can moreover be found in the BITs with Canada of Romania and Latvia. Article V(2) of these agreements prohibits the imposition of performance requirements, such as to export a given level or percentage of goods, the achievement of a given level or percentage of domestic content and the transfer of technology.[53]

That the concerns addressed in the amended BITs with Canada and the United States are real is underscored by the fact that Union secondary legislation has been invoked in a number of investment arbitrations.[54] While in some cases a Member State has invoked the need to comply with Union secondary legislation in defence to a claim under a BIT,[55] in other investment arbitrations an investor has claimed that a Member State had violated its obligations under Union secondary legislation, which was allegedly constitutive of a breach of the standards of investment treatment enshrined in a BIT.[56] Yet the implications of the potential application of EU law in dispute settlement under Member State BITs with third countries is not part of the arrangements with the United States and Canada for the BITs of these eight acceding Eastern and Central European Member States. The many possibilities for substantive interaction that have been addressed with regard to these BITs of a number of Central and Eastern European Member States with the United States and Canada also seem to arise in the context of many BITs with other third countries. That these BITs have been explicitly addressed may be because they contain more far-reaching pre-establishment obligations than the BITs that have been concluded with other third countries, as well as because of the strong influx

---

[52] This provision can be read in conjunction with Art IX(3)(a) of the same agreement, which provides that 'Nothing in this Agreement shall be construed to prevent a Contracting Party from adopting or maintaining measures that restrict transfers where the Contracting Party experiences serious balance of payments difficulties, or the Threat thereof, and such restrictions are consistent with subparagraph (b)'. Relevant in this context is also Art XV(3), which provides that 'All references in this Agreement to measures of a Contracting Party shall include measures applicable in accordance with European Union law in the territory of that Contracting Party pursuant to its membership in the European Union. References to "serious balance of payments difficulties, or the threat thereof", shall include serious balance of payments difficulties, or the threat thereof, in the economic or monetary union of which a Contracting Party is a member'. See also Art XVII(4) of the Canada-Romania BIT and Canada-Latvia BIT.

[53] Article V(3) of the Canada-Latvia BIT and Canada-Romania BIT adds to this that 'The provisions of paragraph 2 shall not be interpreted to prohibit [Latvia/Romania] from adopting or maintaining performance requirements necessary to meet [Latvia/Romania]'s obligations as a member of the European Union pursuant to measures that are adopted or maintained by the European Union with respect to the production, processing and trade of agricultural and processed agricultural products'.

[54] See the text at chapter 5, V and accompanying notes.

[55] See, eg *ADC v Hungary*, ICSID Case No ARB/03/16, Award of 2 December 2006.

[56] See, eg *Telenor v Hungary*, ICSID Case No ARB/04/15, Award of 13 September 2006.

of FDI into the Single Market from the United States and Canada, which increases the likelihood of problems of conflicting legal obligations emerging in practice.

Arguably, at least two types of clauses need to be included in existing external BITs. First, an Article 49 TFEU clause needs to be included in view of the 'Open Skies' judgments,[57] which are discussed in more detail in chapter 5. In those judgments, the CJEU took the view that it is incompatible with the TFEU freedom of establishment not to extend the benefits enshrined in a bilateral aviation agreement with a third country to EU airlines that operate in that third country through a subsidiary in the Member State that is a contracting party to the agreement in question. This obligation seems to apply by analogy to Member State BITs with third counties to which an EU investor channels an investment through a subsidiary in the Member State in question. An Article 49 TFEU clause extends the benefits in the agreement to investors in the third country in question from other EU Member States, when they channel their investment through a subsidiary in the Member State that is a contracting party to the BIT. Secondly, in order to be consistent with the relevant practice in relation to the United States and Canada, discussed above, it seems that a regional economic integration organisation (REIO) clause would need to be included in other external BITs, which exempts Member States from having to extend to non-EU investors the benefits of Single Market integration under the MFN clause of a BIT.[58]

II. THE EU LEGAL FRAMEWORK THAT GOVERNS THE INTERPLAY BETWEEN EU LAW AND MEMBER STATE BITS WITH THIRD COUNTRIES

It has been shown that Member State BITs with third countries interact in various ways with EU law. This raises the question how the EU legal order deals with conflicts between EU law and the legal obligations of the Member States in relations with third countries.[59] This section investigates the potential implications of the

---

[57] Joined Cases C-466/98 *Commission v United Kingdom* [2002] ECR I-9427; C-467/98 *Commission v Denmark* [2002] ECR I-9519; C-468/98 *Commission v Sweden* [2002] ECR I-9575; C-469/98 *Commission v Finland* [2002] ECR I-9797; C-471/98 *Commission v Belgium* [2002] ECR I-9681; C-472/98 *Commission v Luxembourg* [2002] ECR I-9741; C-475/98 *Commission v Austria* [2002] ECR I-9797; C-476/98 *Commission v Germany* [2002] ECR I-9855 ('Open Skies'). See also C-523/04 *Commission v Netherlands* [2007] ECR I-3267.

[58] An example of a REIO-clause outside the context of the amended BITs with the United States and Canada is Art 7 of the United Kingdom-Moldova BIT, which provides that 'The provisions of this Agreement relative to the grant of treatment not less favourable than that accorded to the nationals or companies of either Contracting Party or of any third State shall not be construed so as to oblige one Contracting Party to extend to the nationals or companies of the other the benefit of any treatment, preference or privilege resulting from: (a) any existing or future customs union or similar international agreement to which either of the Contracting Parties is or may become a party'. For more analysis on the application of a REIO-clause in the external treaty relations of the Union and the Member States, see the text at chapter 3, III.B.

[59] For an analysis of the application of public international law principles that govern the interplay between EU law and Member State BITs with third countries, see R Volterra, 'Le point de vue des états tiers' in C Kessedjian and C Leben (eds), *Le droit européen et l'investissement* (Paris, Éditions Panthéon-Assas, 2009).

EU legal framework that governs the interplay between EU law and Member State agreements with third countries for existing external BITs, as well as for the conclusion of external BITs under the remaining investment-related competences of the Member States. In the discussion that follows, a distinction will be drawn between pre-accession and post-accession BITs. The acceding Member States concerned did not only have to comply with specific stipulations in the Acts of Accession with regard to their pre-accession BITs. After accession, the interplay between the EU law obligations of the Member States, on the one hand, and pre-accession agreements with third countries, on the other hand, is governed by Article 351 TFEU. So far as post-accession agreements are concerned, the EU law obligations of the Member States in the conclusion and application of these agreements – commitments that have partly been assumed under shared competences – consist of the duties of compliance and of sincere cooperation. The specific obligations under Regulation 1219/2012 establishing transitional arrangements for Member State BITs with third countries will be analysed in section III.

A. Pre-accession BITs and Article 351 TFEU

For all acceding Member States, it was part of the accession process to bring their international agreements with third countries into compliance with the obligations to be assumed by them under EU law. This process of adjustment was subject to specific provisions in the Acts of Accession and monitored by the European Commission. Article 6(10) of the 2003 Act of Accession[60] provided that:

> To the extent that agreements between one or more of the new Member States on the one hand, and one or more third countries on the other, are not compatible with the obligations arising from this Act, the new Member State shall take all appropriate steps to eliminate the incompatibilities established.[61]

The same provision in the 2003 Act of Accession moreover stipulated that:

> If a Member State encounters difficulties in adjusting an agreement concluded with one or more third countries before accession, it shall, according to the terms of the agreement, withdraw from that agreement.

Acceding Member States were thus required to remove the incompatibilities concerned not only by way of amending external BITs, but also by terminating them, if needed, within the terms of the agreements in issue. That the European Commission

---

[60] Concerning the conditions of accession of the Czech Republic, the Republic of Estonia, the Republic of Cyprus, the Republic of Latvia, the Republic of Lithuania, the Republic of Hungary, the Republic of Malta, the Republic of Poland, the Republic of Slovenia and the Slovak Republic [2003] OJ L236/33.

[61] See also Art 6(10) of the 2005 Protocol concerning the conditions and arrangements for admission of the Republic of Bulgaria and Romania to the EU [2005] OJ L157/29; Art 6(9) of the Act concerning the conditions of accession of the Republic of Croatia and the adjustments to the Treaty on European Union, the Treaty on the Functioning of the European Union and the Treaty establishing the European Atomic Energy Community [2012] OJ L112/21.

monitored this process of adjustment is evidenced not only by the MoU that was signed with the United States and the renegotiation, with involvement of the Commission, of a number of pre-existing BITs of the Central and Eastern European Member States with Canada, but also by the periodic reports of the Commission on the progress of acceding countries in relation to their agreements with third countries.[62]

Newly acceded Member States are subject to the comprehensive body of EU primary and secondary law, as well as Union external agreements, pending the lapse of any transitional arrangements. This not only vastly increases the number of substantive obligations for those states flowing from EU law, but also changes the intensity of those obligations. Member State legislation and conventional measures become subject to the organising principles of the Union's constitutional order, such as the principle of primacy. While treaty conflicts under international law are in principle subject to a single set of rules laid down in the 1969 Vienna Convention on the Law of Treaties (VCLT), in the eyes of EU law a distinction ought to be drawn between agreements that have been concluded by a Member State with a third country before the former acceded to the Union, and agreements with third countries that have been concluded by a Member State after it has assumed its obligations under the EU Treaties. The main difference is that Article 351 TFEU lays down a number of specific rules that govern the relationship between Member State obligations under EU law and their pre-accession agreements with third countries, but it is not applicable to post-accession agreements.

Article 351(1) TFEU confirms the rights of third countries derived from agreements concluded by Member States before the entry into force of the Treaty of Rome, or before accession. It provides that:

> The rights and obligations arising from agreements concluded before 1 January 1958 or, for acceding States, before the date of their accession, between one or more Member States on the one hand, and one or more third countries on the other, shall not be affected by the provisions of the Treaties.

It is an expression of the *pacta tertiis* rule of international law by recognising that, for a third country, the EU Treaties and Union secondary law are *res inter alios acta*.[63] Article 351(1) TFEU therefore suspends the principle of primacy in order to allow for the satisfaction of prior international obligations of Member States with third states.[64] Member State national authorities and national courts are thus

---

[62] *Towards the Enlarged Union*, Strategy Paper and Report of the European Commission on the progress towards accession by each of the candidate countries, COM(2002)700 final, 9 October 2002, Brussels, 20. See also the period reports on the progress made by Croatia on its way to accession, eg *Screening Report for Croatia, Chapter 4 – Free Movement of Capital*, 4 July 2006, 8.

[63] Art 34 VCLT: 'A treaty does not create either obligations or rights for a third State without its consent.'

[64] B de Witte, 'Internationale verdragen tussen lidstaten van de Europese Unie' in RA Wessel and B de Witte, *De plaats van de Europese Unie in het veranderende bestel van de volkenrechtelijke organisatie, Mededelingen van de Nederlandse Vereniging voor Internationaal Recht* (The Hague, TMC Asser Press, 2001) 119; R Schütze, 'EC Law and International Agreements of the Member States: An Ambivalent Relationship?' (2006–2007) *Cambridge Yearbook of European Legal Studies* 391 ff.

allowed (at least provisionally) to apply a measure of national law that conflicts with its obligations under EU law. If the conditions for its application have been satisfied, Article 351(1) TFEU could allow for derogations from EU primary law, such as Article 207 TFEU on the common commercial policy (CCP), as well as from Union secondary legislation.[65] However, the CJEU has also ruled that:

> Article [351 TFEU] may in no circumstances permit any challenge to the principles that form part of the very foundations of the [Union] legal order, one of which is the protection of fundamental rights, including the review by the [Union] judicature of the lawfulness of [Union] measures as regards their consistency with those fundamental rights.[66]

In addition, Member States are only allowed to provisionally apply incompatible prior agreements with third countries to the extent that a particular measure is required by such an agreement, so that:

> when an international agreement allows, but does not require, a Member State to adopt a measure which appears to be contrary to Community law, the Member State must refrain from adopting such a measure.[67]

Since Article 351(1) TFEU focuses on the *obligation* imposed upon a Member State by a pre-existing agreement, it does not allow Member States to exercise *rights* conferred upon them by such agreements in violation of EU law.[68] The Court has also ruled that the Union institutions may not impede the Member States in the performance of their pre-existing treaty obligations.[69]

Insofar as pre-existing agreements reveal an incompatibility with EU law, Article 351(2) TFEU provides that:

> the Member State or States concerned shall take all appropriate steps to eliminate the incompatibilities established.

The obligations of Member States under Article 351(2) TFEU are far-reaching, since the Court has ruled that Member States can fail to fulfil this duty by not denouncing prior international agreements.[70] In two infringement proceedings brought against Portugal for failure to adjust or denounce pre-accession agreements with the Federal Republic of Yugoslavia and several African states, the issue came up whether Article 351(2) TFEU is an obligation of result, or merely a 'best efforts' obligation.[71] Portugal argued that Article 351(2) TFEU does not require Member States to eliminate incompatible provisions in pre-existing agreements regardless of the legal consequences and political price. The constitutional duty to denounce an

[65] C-124/95 *Centro-Com* [1997] ECR I-0081, para 61.

[66] Joined Cases C-402/05 P and C-415/05 *Kadi and Al Barakaat v Council and Commission* [2008] ECR I-6351, para 304.

[67] C-324/93 *Evans Medical* [1995] ECR I-563, para 32. See also Joined Cases C-364/95 and C-365/95 *Hamburg-Jonas* [1998] ECR I-1023, paras 59–61.

[68] C-158/91 *Levy* [1993] ECR I-4287, para 12, with reference to 10/61 *Commission v Italy* [1962] ECR 1, para 10.

[69] 812/79 *Burgoa* [1980] ECR 2787, para 9.

[70] C-170/98 *Commission v Belgium* [1999] ECR I-5493, para 42.

[71] C-62/98 *Commission v Portugal* [2000] ECR I-5171 and C-84/98 *Commission v Portugal* [2000] ECR I-5215. See C Hillion in (2001) 5 *CML Rev* 1269.

agreement would arise only 'exceptionally and in extreme situations'.[72] The Court ruled that the Member States might have a choice as to what steps to take, but they are 'nevertheless under an obligation to eliminate any incompatibilities existing between a pre-Community convention and the [Treaties]'.[73] The Court held that 'if a Member State encounters difficulties which make adjustment of an agreement impossible, an obligation to denounce the agreement cannot be excluded'.[74] Notwithstanding the fact that the agreements at issue contained clauses that expressly enabled Portugal to denounce the agreements, it follows from the Court's reasoning that the obligation to eliminate incompatibilities between pre-existing agreements and the EU Treaties by taking all appropriate measures is an obligation of result.

While Article 351(1) TFEU suspends the principle of primacy by allowing Member States to give preference to pre-accession agreements with third countries over conflicting obligations under EU law, it follows from the obligation under Article 351(2) TFEU for the Member States to eliminate such incompatibilities that Article 351(1) TFEU does not provide for a general derogation from the principle of primacy.[75] Whereas the Member States do not need to disapply or set aside incompatible commitments in relations with third countries that pre-date accession, Article 351(2) TFEU contains the more far-reaching obligation to take all appropriate measures to eliminate such incompatibilities. The latter obligation reflects the fact that Article 351 TFEU deals with pre-existing agreements of the Member States *with third countries*, which under international law cannot be disapplied in view of the *pacta tertiis* rule. It does not seem helpful to qualify Article 351(1) TFEU as providing in any way for a derogation from the exclusivity of Union competence.[76] The reason is that Article 351 TFEU does not address an issue of competence, but of compatibility. In other words, it does not deal with whether the Union or the Member States are empowered to adopt a specific measure, or even whether a Member State adopted a measure that could only have been adopted by the Union. The issue under Article 351 TFEU is that of the substantive compatibility of pre-existing agreements of the Member States with third countries, on the one hand, with the latter's obligations under EU law, on the other.

Article 351(2) TFEU is triggered only in the case that an incompatibility is sufficiently clearly established.[77] The CJEU has taken a potentially wide view of what

---

[72] C-62/98 *Commission v Portugal* (above n 71) para 28; C-84/98 *Commission v Portugal* (above n 71) para 33.

[73] C-62/98 *Commission v Portugal* (above n 71) para 49; C-84/98 *Commission v Portugal* (above n 71) para 58.

[74] Ibid.

[75] But see E Neframi, 'The Duty of Loyalty: Rethinking its Scope Through its Application in the Field of EU External Relations' (2010) 2 *CML Rev* 323, 344.

[76] Ibid 347.

[77] See C-203/03 *Commission v Luxembourg* [2005] ECR I-935, para 62, where the Court ruled that the incompatibility of the prohibition laid down by Convention No 45 of the ILO with a specific provision of Union secondary legislation had not been sufficiently clearly established for that Member State to be bound by the obligation to denounce the Convention.

constitutes an incompatibility with EU law for the purpose of Article 351 TFEU. In *Burgoa*, the Court held that Article 351 TFEU is 'of general scope and it applies to any international agreement, irrespective of subject-matter, which is *capable of affecting* the application of the Treaty' (emphasis added).[78] The Court has further addressed the scope of the notion of 'incompatibility' under Article 351 TFEU in the 'BITs' judgments.[79] In these cases, since the Community had not yet adopted restrictive measures with regard to capital transfers to or from third countries that were liable to be affected by the transfer clauses in the investment agreements at issue, it was submitted that the incompatibility of these transfer clauses with the EC Treaty was thus only potential and the failure to fulfil obligations under the Treaty merely hypothetical.[80] The Member States particularly feared that the finding of an incompatibility by the Court would confer on Article 351(2) TFEU an unlimited scope by extending to potential future incompatibilities with Union secondary legislation.

In the view of some, the CJEU has indeed applied a general 'hypothetical incompatibility' test in the 'BITs' judgments, to the effect that 'even a perceived – but not yet materialised – conflict between pre-accession treaties and EU law obligations is sufficient to constitute a violation of Article [351 TFEU]'.[81] This aspect of the 'BITs' judgments has been argued to reflect an 'obligation to prevent conflict'.[82] Yet it can be observed that the Court was careful to situate the incompatibilities at issue firmly in the specific context of the precise measures to be taken by the Council under the EC Treaty provisions in question. The Court took the view that:

> In order to ensure the effectiveness of [Articles 57(2), 59 and 60(1) EC], measures restricting the free movement of capital must be capable, where adopted by the Council, of being applied immediately with regard to the States to which they relate.[83]

The Court then held that the powers of the Council to take restrictive measures with regard to the movement of capital to and from third countries, insofar as this involves a matter which is identical to, or connected with, that covered by an earlier agreement concluded between a Member State and a third country:

> reveal an incompatibility with that agreement where, first, the agreement does not contain a provision allowing the Member State concerned to exercise its rights and to fulfil its obligations as a member of the Community and, second, there is also no international-law mechanism which makes that possible.[84]

---

[78]   812/79 *Burgoa* [1980] ECR 2787, para 6.
[79]   As regards the compatibility of a Member State BIT with EU law, see also C-264/09 *Commission v Slovakia* [2011] ECR I-08065.
[80]   *Commission v Austria* (above n 28) paras 18–19; *Commission v Sweden* (above n 28) paras 17–18 and para 20.
[81]   N Lavranos in (2009) 4 *AJIL* 716, 717; N Lavranos, 'Protecting European Law from International Law' (2010) 2 *European Foreign Affairs Review* 265, 278.
[82]   Neframi, 'The Duty of Loyalty' (above n 75) 374.
[83]   *Commission v Austria* (above n 28) para 36.
[84]   Ibid para 37; *Commission v Sweden* (above n 28) para 38.

The Court was thus primarily concerned with the practical effectiveness of the provisions under which the Council is empowered to take restrictive measures with a view to their specialised purpose. The Court took the view that, in order to guarantee the effectiveness of these provisions, the restrictive measures that can be taken by the Council with regard to capital movements to and from third countries must be capable of being applied immediately. In that specific context, the Court held that international commitments of Member States with a third country that grant investors an unconditional right to transfer capital would seriously undermine the possibility of the Council to take such restrictive measures.

There was thus a clear incompatibility between the transfer clauses in the investment agreements at issue, which guarantee the free transfer of capital, and the power of the Council to take restrictive measures with regard to such capital transfers, which was apparent on the face of the EC Treaty. In this respect, it particularly needs to be borne in mind that the provisions under which the Council is empowered to take restrictive measures that need immediate application do not constitute a legislative competence that could be exercised by taking a wide range of actions. The Treaty provisions in question confer upon the Council not a general legislative competence, but a specific power to take a certain type of urgent executive measures in exceptional circumstances. It has therefore been correctly observed that the Court could perhaps have differentiated between (then) Article 57(2) EC, on the one hand, and Articles 59 and 60(1) EC, on the other hand.[85] While measures constituting a 'step back' to the liberalisation of capital movements under (then) Article 57(2) EC Treaty would presumably be similarly exceptional as measures under the latter two provisions, they would not necessarily evidence the same degree of urgency. Nevertheless, the incompatibilities established in the 'BITs' judgments are arguably confined to the context of the specific EC Treaty provisions at issue and the Court therefore did not endorse the application of a general 'hypothetical incompatibility' test in relation to Article 351 TFEU.[86]

Importantly, the Court did not recognise a possible role for principles of international law in reducing the scope for incompatibilities between pre-accession agreements and EU law. The Member States in question had argued that international law offers mechanisms to deal with instances of an actual conflict between these BITs and possible restrictive measures taken by the Council. The Court was, inter alia, faced with the argument that the Member States in question could rely on the principle of *rebus sic stantibus*[87] and provisionally suspend the capital transfer provisions in the BITs in the event that the Council adopts restrictive measures.[88] Under that principle, a contracting party to an agreement may invoke a fundamental change of circumstances that has occurred with regard to those existing at the time

---

[85]   P Koutrakos in (2009) 6 *CML Rev* 2059, 2068.

[86]   But see Lavranos, 'Protecting European Law from International Law' (above n 81) 281, who takes the view that there is nothing to suggest that the Court would not apply the 'hypothetical incompatibility' test to 'all types of pre-accession treaties'.

[87]   The literal translation is 'things thus standing'.

[88]   *Commission v Finland* (above n 28) para 17.

of the conclusion of the agreement, and which was unforeseen by the parties, in order to terminate or suspend the operation of an agreement if: (a) the existence of those circumstances constituted an essential basis of the consent of the parties to be bound by the treaty; and (b) the effect of the change is radically to transform the extent of obligations still to be performed under the treaty.[89] Advocate General (AG) Maduro observed that the principle of *rebus sic stantibus* only finds application in very limited circumstances.[90] He found that the application of Article 351 TFEU could not depend on the application of the principle of *rebus sic stantibus*, which he referred to as 'a controversial point of international law'.[91]

While the CJEU had shown some deference in the past to the application of the principle of *rebus sic stantibus* to the suspension or termination of an external agreement of the Community,[92] it did not explicitly consider the possible application of the principle of *rebus sic stantibus* to the transfer clauses at issue in the 'BITs' judgments. It did point to the general uncertainties involved in relying on international law mechanisms such as the suspension or even the denunciation of the agreements at issue.[93] In the view of the Court, the Member States in question could not guarantee that they would be able to fulfil their obligations under EU law if the Council took restrictive measures. Indeed, it is questionable whether the taking of restrictive measures by the Council would in itself qualify as a fundamental change of circumstances for the purpose of the application of the BITs in issue.[94] Rather, it is precisely the need for the Member States in question to comply with these restrictive measures which would have to be justified with reference to the principle of *rebus sic stantibus*. In this, the taking of such restrictive measures is prima facie incompatible with the objective of free capital transfers and does not in itself seem to affect the obligation that would need to be performed by a Member State under the BITs in issue.

Another international law principle that was invoked in the 'BITs' judgments with a view to reducing the scope for incompatibilities between pre-accession BITs and EU law was the principle of systemic interpretation, which requires, for the interpretation of an international agreement, the taking into account of

---

[89]   Article 62 VCLT.

[90]   Opinion of AG Maduro of 10 July 2008 in *Commission v Austria* and *Commission v Sweden* (above n 28) para 61.

[91]   Ibid para 62.

[92]   See C-162/96 *Racke* [1998] ECR I-3655, paras 55–56, in which the Court recognised the effect of changing circumstances as a result of the disintegration of Yugoslavia on the Association Agreement with that country in view of the outbreak of hostilities and the absence of institutions that could guarantee the implementation of the agreement. At the same time, while the decision to suspend the agreement was taken by the Council and not by a Member State, the Court only scrutinised whether a 'manifest error of assessment' had been made. For analysis, see PJ Kuijper, 'The Court and the Tribunal of the EC and the Vienna Convention on the Law of Treaties 1969' (1998) 1 *Legal Issues of European Integration* 1, 18 ff.

[93]   *Commission v Austria* (above n 28) paras 39–40; *Commission v Sweden* (above n 28) paras 40–41; *Commission v Finland* (above n 28) para 32.

[94]   But see Lavranos, 'Protecting European Law from International Law' (above n 81) 280 ff, who suggests that the Member States would be able to successfully invoke the *rebus sic stantibus* principle in order to renegotiate their BIT in the case that the Council considers adopting restrictive measures.

'any relevant rules of international law applicable in the relations between the parties'.[95] With regard to Article 351(2) TFEU, the CJEU had already recognised in *Budvar* that national courts have a role in:

> [ascertaining] whether a possible incompatibility between the [Treaties] and [a] bilateral convention can be avoided by interpreting that convention, to the extent possible and in compliance with international law, in such a way that it is consistent with Community law.[96]

The Court moreover took the view that:

> If it proves impracticable to interpret an agreement concluded prior to a Member State's accession to the European Union in such a way that it is consistent with Community law then, within the framework of Article 307 EC, it is open to that State to take the appropriate steps, while, however, remaining obliged to eliminate any incompatibilities existing between the earlier agreement and the Treaty.[97]

While the Court did not expressly consider the potential relevance of the principle of systemic interpretation in the *BITs* judgments against Austria and Sweden, it did do so in the case against Finland, which had pointed to a specific clause in some of its BITs guaranteeing investment protection within the limits of the national legislation of the contracting party.[98] Finland had argued that the restrictive measures adopted by the Council could be applied under the BIT because they would be part of Finnish law within the meaning of those provisions by virtue of the direct effect of EU law.[99]

The Court observed, in the first place, that it was not clear whether such measures could be regarded as part of Finnish law in the sense of the BITs in issue.[100] The Court then turned to Article 31 VCLT. In view of the aim of the agreements concerned, which is to ensure freedom of capital transfers in relation to investments, the Court took the view that it is:

> debatable whether the provision which guarantees the protection of investments within the limits authorised by the laws of the Contracting Party contained in the bilateral agreements concerned would allow a party to limit payment entitlement pursuant to decisions – whether national or otherwise – taken after the entry into force of the agreements, especially as in some agreements it is also stated that each Contracting Party is required to act 'in accordance with international law'.[101]

---

[95] Article 31(3)(c) VCLT. From an international law point of view, see C McLachlan, 'The Principle of Systemic Integration and Article 31(3)(c) of the Vienna Convention' (2005) 2 *ICLQ* 279. For a precedent in investment treaty arbitration where the principle of systemic interpretation was invoked in relation to the obligations of a contracting Member State under EU law, see *Saluka v Czech Republic*, Partial Award of 17 March 2006, para 254.

[96] C-216/01 *Budvar* [2003] ECR I-13617, para 169.

[97] Ibid para 170.

[98] See, eg Art 3 of the Finland-Sri Lanka BIT: 'Every contracting Party guarantees under all circumstances, within the limits authorised by its own laws and decrees and in conformity with international law, a reasonable and appropriate treatment of investments made by citizens or companies of the other contracting party.'

[99] *Commission v Finland* (above n 28) para 37.

[100] Ibid para 38.

[101] Ibid para 41.

The Court therefore held that the specific interpretation of the provisions of the BITs relied on by Finland was too uncertain.[102] It follows from the 'BITs' judgment against Finland that the issue of compatibility between EU law and a pre-accession BIT of a Member State cannot depend on a disputed interpretation of a specific provision in the agreement and it suggests a potentially limited role for the international law principle of systemic integration in reducing the scope for incompatibilities between EU law and pre-accession BITs of the Member States with third countries.

The application of Article 351 TFEU with regard to Member State BITs can be contrasted with the application of that provision in the context of the ECT. As was mentioned above (I.B), the ECT contains capital transfer clauses that are similar to the ones to be found in Member State BITs. Article 351(1) TFEU seems to be applicable in relation to the obligations of the Member States that acceded to the Union after becoming a contracting party to the ECT, but not for the other Member States. The ECT gives rise to the additional complication that it was concluded by both the Member States and the Union. The obligation of harmonious interpretation under EU law therefore applies in the context of the ECT, with the effect that EU law should be interpreted in the light of this binding international agreement. In *Poulsen*, the CJEU observed that the European Community must respect international law in the exercise of its powers.[103] In *Safety Hi-Tech*, the Court held that:

> It is settled law that Community legislation must, so far as possible, be interpreted in a manner that is consistent with international law, in particular where its provisions are intended specifically to give effect to an international agreement concluded by the Community.[104]

The Court has also consistently held that Union external agreements have primacy over Union secondary legislation. In addition, the Court has held that the primacy of Union external agreements over provisions of Union secondary legislation means that such provisions must, so far as possible, be interpreted in a manner that is consistent with those agreements.[105] This limits the possibilities for incompatibilities between EU law and the ECT, and the Member States would arguably not have to give effect to Union secondary legislation that is incompatible with the obligations of the Union vis-à-vis third countries. In addition, the Court can examine the validity of Union secondary legislation in the light of a Union external agreement in a case pleaded before a national court 'where the nature and the broad logic of the latter do not preclude this and, in addition, the

---

[102] Ibid para 42. See also Opinion of AG Sharpston of 10 September 2009 in ibid para 26: 'to my mind the issue is not whether (as indeed it does) Community law forms part of national law. Rather, the crux of the matter is whether Finland's potential ability to rely on the phrase "within the limits authorised by its own laws and decrees" against the third countries with which it has concluded those agreements constitutes a *sufficient guarantee* that restrictions to capital movements and to payments involving third countries, as provided for in Articles 57(2), 59 and 60(1) TEC, could be applied' (emphasis added).

[103] C-286/90 *Poulsen* [1992] ECR I-6019, para 9.

[104] C-341/95 *Safety Hi-Tech v S & T Srl* [1998] ECR I-4355, para 20.

[105] C-61/94 *Commission v Germany* [1996] ECR I-3989, para 52.

treaty's provisions appear, as regards their content, to be unconditional and sufficiently precise'.[106]

In sum, pursuant to Article 351(1) TFEU, the principle of primacy is suspended in relation to pre-accession agreements of the Member States with third countries. At the same time, the Member States need to take all appropriate measures to eliminate any incompatibilities with EU law under Article 351(2) TFEU, which is an obligation of result. So far as the nature of such incompatibilities is concerned, not only do they need to be sufficiently clearly established, but it has also been argued that the Court did not apply a general 'hypothetical incompatibility' test in the 'BITs' judgments. This limits the scope for incompatibilities between EU law and Member State BITs. Yet, the Court did not accept a role for international law principles in reducing the scope for incompatibilities between the transfer clauses in pre-accession BITs and the TFEU provisions under which the Council can take restrictive measures with regard to capital transfers to and from third countries. Moreover, similar capital transfer clauses can be found in other pre-accession (as well as post-accession) BITs. For this reason, the 'BITs' cases have been criticised for selectively challenging the transfer clauses in BITs of only a few Member States.[107] In view of the possibilities for interaction between Member State BITs and EU law that were identified in the previous section, Article 351 TFEU may be applicable in the context of other provisions in pre-accession BITs with third countries too. The application of Article 351 TFEU to the obligations of some of the Member States under the ECT is more complicated in view of the fact that the Union is a contracting party to the ECT.

B. EU Law and Post-accession BITs

Unlike Article 351 TFEU, which lays down the EU legal framework that governs the relationship between EU law and pre-accession agreements of Member States with third countries, there is no specific provision in the EU Treaties dealing with issues of compatibility between EU law and post-accession agreements of the Member States. So far as concerns the Member States' practice of concluding BITs, these agreements were concluded at a time when the Union did not yet have an exclusive external FDI competence. While, in principle, only an exclusive Union competence precludes the Member States from acting unless such action is authorised by the Union,[108] the Member States are nevertheless constrained by the need to act consistently with EU law and by the need to observe the principle of sincere cooperation.[109] These duties of compliance and of sincere cooperation

---

[106] C-308/06 *Intertanko* [2008] ECR I-4057, para 45.

[107] Denza, 'Bilateral Investment Treaties and EU Rules on Free Transfer' (above n 30) 263.

[108] See the text at III and accompanying notes.

[109] Pursuant to Art 4(3) TEU, 'the Union and the Member States shall, in full mutual respect, assist each other in carrying out the tasks which flow from the Treaties'. In addition, the Member States 'shall take any appropriate measure, general or particular, to ensure fulfilment of the obligations arising out

serve mainly to *prevent* inconsistencies between Member State agreements with third countries and their obligations under EU law. Incompatibilities could nevertheless arise, for example, as a result of the subsequent adoption of Union secondary legislation. Unlike in the case of pre-accession agreements, the EU Treaties do not explicitly provide for the suspension of the principle of primacy in relation to post-accession agreements. Yet, similar to the context of pre-accession agreements, the Member States are under an obligation to eliminate such incompatibilities. These interrelated points will be discussed in turn.

The competence of the Member States to conclude agreements with third countries must be exercised consistently with their obligations under EU law.[110] Importantly, the duty of compliance, which is based on Article 4(3) TEU,[111] reaches beyond the limits of Union competence, since it concerns the whole scope of application of EU law.[112] Furthermore, the duty of compliance arguably sets the same standard of compatibility as was at issue in the 'BITs' judgments in relation to Article 351 TFEU. In other words, the same type of compatibility test will be applied to pre-accession and post-accession BITs of the Member States with third countries. However, there is no *ex ante* control mechanism under EU primary law for the compatibility with EU law of envisaged Member State agreements with third countries. First, there does not exist any general type of authorisation mechanism under EU primary law for the conclusion of Member State agreements with third countries. This can be contrasted with Article 103 of the Euratom Treaty, which provides for a detailed procedure in this respect.[113] Secondly, Article 218(11) TFEU, under which an opinion may be obtained from the CJEU on whether an envisaged agreement is compatible with the EU Treaties, is part of the

---

of the Treaties or resulting from action taken by the institutions of the Union'. They shall moreover 'facilitate the achievement of the Union's tasks and refrain from any measure which could jeopardise the attainment of the Union's objectives'. The obligations flowing from the principle of sincere cooperation are arguably equivalent to those under the duty of loyal cooperation, which is based on Art 4(3) TEU. See C Hillion, 'Mixity and Coherence in EU External Relations: The Significance of the "Duty of Cooperation"' in C Hillion and P Koutrakos (eds), *Mixed Agreements Revisited: The European Union and the Member States in the World* (Oxford, Hart Publishing, 2010).

[110] See, eg C-307/97 *Saint-Gobain* [1999] ECR I-6161, paras 57–58; C-124/95 *Centro-Com* [1997] ECR I-81, paras 25 and 27.

[111] M Cremona, 'Defending the Community Interest: the Duties of Cooperation and Compliance' in M Cremona and B de Witte, *EU Foreign Relations Law: Constitutional Fundamentals* (Oxford, Hart Publishing, 2008) 126.

[112] AA Dashwood, 'The Limits of European Community Powers' (1996) 2 *EL Rev* 113.

[113] Consolidated version of the Treaty establishing the European Atomic Energy Community [2010] OJ C84/1, Art 103: 'Member States shall communicate to the Commission draft agreements or contracts with a third state, an international organization or a national of a third State to the extent that such agreements or contracts concern matters within the purview of this Treaty. If a draft agreement or contract contains clauses which impede the application of this Treaty, the Commission shall, within one month of receipt of such communication, make its comments known to the State concerned. The State shall not conclude the proposed agreement or contract until it has satisfied the objections of the Commission or complied with a ruling by the Court of Justice, adjudicating urgently upon an application from the State, on the compatibility of the proposed clauses with the provisions of this Treaty. An application may be made to the Court of Justice at any time after the State has received the comments of the Commission.'

provisions that lay down the procedure for the conclusion of external agreements by the Union.

So far as the duty of compliance is concerned, it was feared by a number of (intervening) Member States in the 'BITs' cases that a finding of incompatibility by the CJEU would be open to challenge from the perspective of the distribution of powers between the Community and the Member States, since it would risk turning a shared competence into an exclusive Union competence.[114] In fact, as was discussed above, the Council had not yet adopted any restrictive measures that were liable to be affected by the transfer clauses in the investment agreements at issue. The Member States argued not only that the question of the compatibility of the agreements at issue with a provision of the EC Treaty did not arise in the absence of restrictions on capital transfers decided upon by the Council, but also that their freedom to act under shared competences in relations with third countries would be severely curtailed upon a finding of incompatibility by the Court. A similar competence-based analysis was prevalent in the Opinion of AG Maduro, who also noted the risk of turning empowering provisions into 'supposedly limited exclusive competences'.[115] He adopted the formulation used by the Court in *Inter-Environnement Wallonie*[116] regarding the transposition of Directives into national law, referring to the duty of loyal cooperation enshrined in Article 4(3) TEU, with the result that Member States would be obliged to 'refrain from any measures liable seriously to compromise the exercise of Community competence' and to 'take all appropriate steps to prevent their pre-existing international obligations from jeopardising the exercise of Community competence'.[117]

While the CJEU did not adopt the specific wording that was used by AG Maduro, the Court did accommodate the concerns addressed by the Member States with regard to the division of powers between the Community and the Member States by carefully situating the incompatibilities at issue in the specific context of the precise measures to be taken by the Council under the EC Treaty provisions in question. Without displaying the same type of competence-based analysis or referring to Article 4(3) TEU, the Court approached the question of compatibility from the perspective of the practical effectiveness of the restrictive measures to be taken by the Council. As was noted above, the empowering provisions in question expressly conferred on the Council a very specific power to take a certain type of urgent measures. The Court's reasoning in the 'BITs' cases therefore arguably limits the degree to which these judgments impinge upon the exercise of remaining competences of the Member States to assume investment-related commitments in relations with third countries, including in the post-Lisbon era.

---

[114] *Commission v Sweden* (above n 28) para 19.

[115] Opinion of AG Maduro of 10 July 2008 in *Commission v Austria* and *Commission v Sweden* (above n 28) para 31.

[116] C-129/96 *Inter-Environnement Wallonie* [1997] ECR I-7435.

[117] Opinion of AG Maduro of 10 July 2008 in *Commission v Austria* and *Commission v Sweden* (above n 28) paras 36–42.

While Article 351(1) TFEU suspends the application of the principle of primacy to international agreements that pre-date accession, it can also be observed that the Member States in principle cannot invoke agreements concluded after accession as against EU law.[118] In the eyes of EU law, such international agreements are equivalent to unilateral acts of the Member State with the status of national legislation.[119] It has been suggested by Van Panhuys that the principle of primacy should be suspended for post-accession agreements between Member States and third countries that were concluded prior to the adoption of conflicting (now) Union secondary legislation, provided that the international agreement is compatible with EU primary law at the moment of its conclusion.[120] Yet the Court seems to have confirmed the supremacy of EU law not only where an agreement is concluded after the adoption of Union secondary legislation,[121] but also where a Member State has concluded an agreement prior to the adoption of conflicting Union secondary legislation. This follows from *Procureur Général v Arbelaiz-Emazabel*.[122] In this case, a Spanish national was caught fishing in French waters in 1977, before the accession of Spain, without the licence required by (then) Community secondary legislation. The Court affirmed a duty for national courts to give priority to such Community secondary legislation over the conflicting and earlier international obligations of France with Spain, such as a 1967 French-Spanish exchange of notes that was based on the 1964 London Fisheries Convention, to which both France and Spain were contracting parties.[123] At the same time, the Court noted that the London Fisheries Convention in fact recognised the possibility of supervening Community secondary legislation.[124]

Since EU law precludes a Member State from justifying a breach of EU law by invoking a post-accession international agreement with a third country, the application of the principle of primacy will in such situations trigger the international responsibility of the Member State concerned. As a result of the application of the principle of primacy to post-accession international agreements of the Member States, they effectively need to choose between incurring liability under EU law and bearing international responsibility for a breach of the international agreement in question in the event of incompatible obligations. In that light, it has

---

[118] See Opinion of AG Kokott of 20 November 2007 in C-308/06 *Intertanko* [2008] ECR I-4057, para 77: 'This applies at least where the relevant Community powers already existed at the time the agreement was concluded.'

[119] R Schütze, 'EC Law and International Agreements of the Member States: An Ambivalent Relationship?' (2006–2007) *Cambridge Yearbook of European Legal Studies* 387, 432.

[120] HF van Panhuys, 'Conflicts between the Law of the European Communities and Other Rules of International Law' (1966) *CML Rev* 420, 434.

[121] See Joined Cases C-176 and 177/97 *Commission v Belgium and Luxembourg* [1998] ECR I-3557, in which the Court assessed the compatibility of a post-accession agreement concluded by the BLEU states with Malaysia on maritime transport with previously adopted EU secondary legislation on maritime transport services.

[122] 181/80 *Arbelaiz-Emazabel* [1981] ECR 2961.

[123] Ibid para 31. But see the Opinion of AG Kokott of 13 March 2008 in C-188/07 *Commune de Mesquer v Total* [2008] ECR I-4501, paras 94–96.

[124] Ibid paras 12–13. See generally RR Churchill and NG Foster, 'European Community Law and Prior Treaty Obligations of the Member States: The Spanish Fishermen's Cases' (1987) 3 *ICLQ* 504.

been observed that Article 351(2) TFEU, which by its wording only applies to pre-accession agreements, can be understood as a specific expression of Article 4(3) TEU.[125] The obligation to eliminate incompatibilities between Member State agreements with third countries and EU law therefore arguably extends to agreements which, as in the case of many Member State BITs, post-date accession to the Union of the Member State concerned.[126] It can, moreover, similarly be assumed that the obligation to eliminate such incompatibilities by taking all appropriate measures is an obligation of result, as in the context of pre-accession agreements. By consequence, the Member States will have to enter into negotiations with third countries in order to agree on the elimination of any incompatibilities, which may result in the need to terminate such agreements.

In exercising their competences, the Member States are also under the obligation to comply with the principle of sincere cooperation.[127] Under this principle, which was originally developed in the context of mixed agreements,[128] the Member States are not only required to abstain from action that may jeopardise the Union's objectives, but also have the positive obligation to take any appropriate measure, general or particular, to ensure fulfilment of the obligations arising out of the EU Treaties or resulting from action taken by the institutions of the Union, as well as to facilitate the achievement of the Union's tasks. A number of specific obligations have been recognised by the CJEU to flow from the principle of sincere cooperation, both in the context of Member State bilateral agreements and mixed agreements.

So far as the conclusion of bilateral agreements by the Member States is concerned, the Court has held in *Commission v Luxembourg* that Luxembourg had breached the principle of sincere cooperation by negotiating, concluding and ratifying a bilateral agreement without cooperating or consulting with the Commission, after the Council had decided to authorise the Commission to negotiate an agreement on behalf of the Union on the same subject matter.[129] In the view of the Court, the adoption of a decision authorising the Commission to

---

[125] Opinion of AG Maduro of 10 July 2008 in *Commission v Austria* and *Commission v Sweden* (above n 28) para 33; P Koutrakos, *EU International Relations Law* (Oxford, Hart Publishing, 2006) 304. See also Neframi, 'The Duty of Loyalty' (above n 75) 344, who takes the view that a pre-accession agreement may not conflict with EU law at the time of accession, but if EU law and policy develop subsequently to the point that an incompatibility arises, Art 351(2) TFEU applies.

[126] As was noted above at II.A, the ECT has the additional complication that it was concluded by both the Union and the Member States. Some Member States concluded the ECT as a post-accession agreement.

[127] Neframi, 'The Duty of Loyalty' (above n 75) 323 ff; C Hillion, 'A Look Back at the Open Skies' in M Bulterman, L Hancher, A McDonnell and HG Sevenster (eds), *Views of European Law from the Mountain* (Alphen a/d Rijn, Kluwer Law International, 2009); PJ Kuijper, 'Re-reading External Relations Cases in the Field of Transport: The Function of Community Loyalty' in M Bulterman, L Hancher, A McDonnell and HG Sevenster (eds), *Views of European Law from the Mountain* (Alphen aan den Rijn, Kluwer Law International, 2009).

[128] See, eg *Opinion 1/94* [1994] ECR I-5267, para 108, where the Court emphasised the importance of the duty of loyal cooperation incumbent on both the Member States and the Community in the exercise of their respective competences under the WTO Agreement.

[129] C-266/03 *Commission v Luxembourg* [2005] ECR I-4805, para 66.

negotiate such an agreement 'marks the start of a concerted [Union] action at international level', which requires, if not a duty of abstention on the part of the Member States, at the very least a duty of close cooperation between the latter and the Community institutions in order to facilitate the achievement of the Union's tasks and to ensure the coherence and consistency of the action and its international representation.[130] Similarly, in *Commission v Germany*, the Court held that Germany had breached the principle of sincere cooperation by ratifying and implementing agreements with Poland, Romania and Ukraine, after the Council had decided to authorise the Commission to negotiate a multilateral agreement on behalf of the Union. The Court held that the principle of sincere cooperation had not been complied with even if the German government would denounce the bilateral agreements upon the conclusion of the multilateral agreement by the Union. In the view of the Court, such a denunciation would not have facilitated the multilateral negotiations conducted by the Commission, since it would take place only after the negotiation and conclusion of the agreement.[131] A similar duty to abstain from concluding a specific agreement where the Council has already decided to authorise the Commission to negotiate an external agreement with provisions in the same field would seem to apply in relation to the exercise by the Member States of their remaining investment-related competences. This has specific relevance in the post-Lisbon era, as will be discussed in the next section in the context of the transitional arrangements.

Member State action under the ECT may also be constrained as a result of the application of the principle of sincere cooperation.[132] Similarly, the principle of sincere cooperation will be relevant under future Union investment agreements.[133] With regard to dispute settlement under the terms of a mixed agreement (the United Nations Convention on the Laws of the Sea, UNCLOS), the CJEU held that a Member State (Ireland), pursuant to the principle of sincere cooperation, has a duty to inform and consult the Union institutions prior to engaging in individual action by instituting dispute settlement proceedings against another Member State (United Kingdom).[134] A similar duty of information and consultation arguably applies in the context of claims by either EU or non-EU investors against a host Member State under the ECT, as well as under future Union investment agreements. In addition, in the context of the Stockholm Convention on Persistent Organic Pollutants, of which both the Union and the Member States

---

[130] Ibid para 60. With reference to 804/79 *Commission v United Kingdom* [1981] ECR I-1045.

[131] C-433/03 *Commission v Germany* [2005] ECR I-6985, para 72.

[132] For an elaborate analysis of the implications of the principle of sincere cooperation in the context of the negotiation, conclusion and implementation of mixed agreements, see J Heliskoski, *Mixed Agreements as Technique for Organizing the International Relations of the European Community and its Member States* (The Hague, Kluwer Law International, 2001). See also Hillion, 'Mixity and Coherence in EU External Relations' (above n 109).

[133] See the text at chapter 3, II.B(ii) for an analysis of the provisions on cooperation between the Commission and the Member States under the proposed Regulation on financial responsibility. See the text at III.B for an analysis of the provisions on cooperation between the Commission and the Member States under Regulation 1219/2012.

[134] C-459/03 *Commission v Ireland* [2006] ECR I-4635, para 179.

are contracting parties, the Court ruled that Sweden had breached Article 4(3) TEU by listing a chemical substance (PFOS) in an Annex to that Convention, while this issue was being discussed and there was an intention to act within the Council.[135] The Court said that Sweden had 'dissociated itself from a concerted common strategy within the Council'.[136] Such a situation was 'likely to compromise the principle of unity in the international representation of the Union and its Member States and weaken their negotiating power with regard to the other parties to the Convention concerned'.[137] Similarly, the Member States have to abide by the principle of unity of external representation in relation to their action under the ECT, as well as under future Union investment agreements, such as in the context of the conduct of disputes.

To sum up the findings of this section, the EU legal framework governing the interplay between EU law and Member State agreements with third countries has a number of potential implications for existing external BITs. While for pre-accession agreements the principle of primacy is suspended under Article 351(1) TFEU, this is not the case for post-accession agreements. EU law thus mandates that the Member States set aside incompatible obligations in relations with third countries that post-date accession in order to comply with their obligations under EU law. So far as the Member States' investment-related competences are concerned, these ought to be exercised consistently with their obligations under EU law. The Member States must, moreover, observe the principle of sincere cooperation in doing so, under which they need to facilitate the achievement of the Union's tasks. Moreover, also in the context of post-accession agreements, there is a duty for the Member States to take all appropriate measures to eliminate incompatibilities with EU law, which is an obligation of result. This leaves the issue of the possible effect of supervening exclusive external competence of the Union in the field of FDI under the TFEU provisions on the CCP and the exercise of the Union's post-Lisbon FDI competence for existing and future BITs, which will be analysed in the next section as part of the discussion of Regulation 1219/2012 establishing transitional arrangements for Member State BITs with third countries.

III. POST-LISBON DEVELOPMENTS WITH REGARD TO THE MEMBER STATES' PRACTICE OF CONCLUDING BITS WITH THIRD COUNTRIES

Pursuant to the entry into force of the Treaty of Lisbon, the Union has acquired exclusive external competence in the field of FDI. As was discussed in chapter 3, the Union is currently developing a common international investment policy with regard to both the liberalisation and protection of investment. This section addresses the implications of the Lisbon transfer of competence in the field of FDI to the Union, as well as its exercise, for both existing and possible future Member

---

[135] C-246/07 *Commission v Sweden* [2010] ECR I-3317, para 87.
[136] Ibid para 91.
[137] Ibid para 104.

State BITs with third countries. With a view to this transfer of competence, Regulation 1219/2012 establishing transitional arrangements for bilateral investment agreements between Member States and third countries has entered into force on 9 January 2013.[138] To be analysed first is the replacement mechanism enshrined in Regulation 1219/2012 for existing bilateral investment agreements in view of the legal principles governing supervening exclusivity, as well as its implications for existing Member State external BITs. The second part discusses the arrangements for the amendment of existing Member State BITs and the conclusion of new BITs, both of which now have to be authorised by the Union.

A. The Replacement Mechanism under Regulation 1219/2012 for Existing Member State BITs with Third Countries

The Lisbon transfer of exclusive FDI competence to the Union gives rise to the question what implications the existence and exercise by the Union of this exclusive competence will have for existing Member State BITs. Regulation 1219/2012 addresses the status of existing Member State investment agreements with third countries from the perspective of the Union's post-Lisbon FDI competence. Explicitly drawing inspiration from the transitional arrangement for Member State commercial agreements following the introduction of the common commercial policy in the 1960s, Regulation 1219/2012 is intended to facilitate the development of the common international investment policy. For existing Member State BITs with third countries, Regulation 1219/2012 establishes a requirement of notification and a replacement mechanism, which will be discussed in this part. In addition, Regulation 1219/2012 contains an authorisation mechanism for the amendment of existing BITs and for the conclusion of new BITs, which will be discussed in the next part.

So far as existing Member State BITs with third countries are concerned, Regulation 1219/2012 in the first instance maintains the status quo by catering for their continued existence. Even if Regulation 1219/2012 recognises that existing BITs continue to be binding on the Member States under international law, the stated objective of confirming their continued existence by means of a legal instrument is to provide legal certainty and thereby to prevent the potential erosion of the rights and benefits available to investors under existing BITs.[139] Under the transitional arrangements, existing Member State BITs are allowed to be maintained in force (as a matter of EU law) pursuant to the act of notifying an agreement to the Commission. To this end, Article 2 of Regulation 1219/2012 provides that the Member States shall notify to the Commission all bilateral investment agreements with third countries signed before 1 December 2009 or

---

[138] Regulation 1219/2012 of the European Parliament and of the Council of 12 December 2012 establishing transitional arrangements for bilateral investment agreements between Member States and third countries [2012] OJ L351/40.

[139] Ibid Preamble paras 5 and 6.

before the date of their accession, that they either wish to maintain in force or permit to enter into force. In other words, the notification requirement applies both to bilateral investment agreements that a Member State wishes to maintain in force, and to agreements which have been signed before 1 December 2009 but have not yet entered into force upon the entry into force of the transitional arrangements. Such notification was to occur by 8 February 2013 and, for acceding Member States, needs to occur within 30 days of the date of their accession to the Union. Pursuant to Article 4 of Regulation 1219/2012, the Commission has published in the *Official Journal of the European Union* a list of bilateral investment agreements notified under the transitional arrangements.[140]

As regards the scope of this notification requirement and consequently of the transitional arrangements as a whole, Article 1(2) stipulates that for the purpose of the Regulation the term 'bilateral investment agreement' means 'any agreement with a third country that contains provisions on investment protection'. In view of the fact that the legal basis of Regulation 1219/2012 is Article 207(2) TFEU, it can be asked whether the scope of the Regulation is therefore restricted to the provisions on investment protection in bilateral investment agreements insofar as they relate to FDI. If this is indeed the case, the transitional arrangements would not apply to the investment protection provisions in bilateral investment agreements insofar as they relate to foreign portfolio investment. Yet the Preamble to Regulation 1219/2012 also refers to the TFEU provisions on free movement of capital as being relevant for the purpose of the transitional arrangements.[141] The choice of legal basis therefore seems to rely on the presumption of the ancillary nature of the TFEU provisions on free movement of capital with regard to the TFEU provisions on the CCP in relation to the issue of investment protection.[142] The scope of the transitional arrangements is thus intended to be broader than FDI so as to reflect the scope of application of Member State BITs to both foreign direct investment and foreign portfolio investment.

In view of the fact that Article 1(2) refers to *any* agreement that contains provisions on investment protection, it seems possible to argue that the scope of the transitional arrangements in Regulation 1219/2012 extends beyond Member State BITs and includes all Member State agreements with third countries that contain provisions on investment protection. Provisions on investment protection can, for example, arguably be found in some friendship, commerce and navigation treaties, as well as in trade agreements and agreements on economic and technical cooperation.[143] At the same time, it is specified in Article 1(2) that the Regulation

---

[140] List of the bilateral investment agreements referred to in Art 4(1) of Regulation 1219/2012 of the European Parliament and of the Council establishing transitional arrangements for bilateral investment agreements between Member States and third countries [2013] OJ C131/2.

[141] Regulation 1219/2012, Preamble para 2.

[142] See the text at chapter 3, I.C and accompanying notes for an analysis of the scope of Union competence to conclude international investment agreements pursuant to the Lisbon reform of the CCP.

[143] The list of notified bilateral investment agreements ([2013] OJ C131/2) shows that Belgium, Estonia, Greece, Italy, the Netherlands, Poland and Sweden have notified one or more of such type of agreements.

'covers *only* those provisions of bilateral investment agreements dealing with investment protection' (emphasis added).

That the Member States are only allowed, under the transitional arrangements, to maintain in force bilateral investment agreements that have been notified in accordance with Article 2 of Regulation 1219/2012 follows from Article 3, which provides that:

> Without prejudice to other obligations of the Member States under Union law, bilateral investment agreements notified pursuant to Article 2 of this Regulation may be maintained in force, or enter into force, in accordance with the TFEU and this Regulation, until a bilateral investment agreement between the Union and the same third country enters into force.

Consequently, Regulation 1219/2012 serves to maintain the status quo in the treaty relations of the Member States with a specific third country in the field of investment protection until the Union has developed and implemented the common international investment policy with the result of concluding a Union investment agreement with that same third country. To some extent, a replacement mechanism in Union secondary legislation for managing the interplay between the development and implementation of a new external policy of the Union, on the one hand, and existing Member State agreements with third countries in the same field, is reminiscent of the transitional arrangement in the field of trade in the early years of the common commercial policy, as will be discussed below.

Notification of bilateral investment agreements by a Member State does not automatically lead to being permitted, under the transitional arrangements, to maintain in force the agreements in question. First, the transitional arrangements explicitly make the possibility of being allowed to maintain in force or to enter into force Member State bilateral investment agreements subject to the requirement for this to be 'without prejudice to other obligations of the Member States under Union law'. This provision would seem to cover, for instance, the situation with regard to the pre-accession BITs of Sweden, Austria and Finland, the capital transfer provisions of which have been ruled by the CJEU to be incompatible with the TFEU provisions under which the Council can take restrictive measures with regard to capital transfers to and from the Union. These Member States are under the obligation under Article 351(2) TFEU to eliminate the incompatibilities at issue – a type of obligation which is explicitly left untouched by the transitional arrangements pursuant to the phraseology of Article 3. Along the same lines of the duty of compliance, Article 3 of Regulation 1219/2012 specifies that bilateral investment agreements notified under Article 2 may be maintained in force or may enter into force 'in accordance with the TFEU and this Regulation'.

Secondly, Article 5 of Regulation 1219/2012 provides for the possibility for the Commission to assess the bilateral investment agreements notified pursuant to Article 2, 'by evaluating whether one or more of their provisions constitute a serious obstacle to the negotiation or conclusion by the Union of bilateral investment agreements with third countries' with a view to their progressive replacement. In other words, in addition to an explicit requirement of compatibility of Member State bilateral investment agreements with EU law, Regulation 1219/2012 provides for an assessment by the Commission of Member State bilateral investment agreements against the yardstick of a 'serious obstacle' test. This test seems to have been inspired by the former transitional arrangements for Member State commercial agreements with third countries in the early years of the common commercial policy. Both the 1961 Decision on the standardisation of the duration of trade agreements with third countries[144] and Council Decision 69/494 on the progressive standardisation of agreements concerning commercial relations between Member States and third countries and on the negotiation of Community agreements[145] made provision for the examination of Member State commercial agreements through consultation between the Commission and the Member States for the purpose of ensuring that they did not form an obstacle to the development of the common commercial policy, in particular by reason of divergences between the policies of the Member States.[146]

The application of this 'serious obstacle' test with regard to the negotiation or conclusion by the Union of investment agreements with third countries could lead to difficulties in practice. For the purpose of ascertaining what types of interaction between existing Member State BITs and the negotiation and conclusion by the Union of investment agreements with third countries are envisaged by the Commission to potentially give rise to problems in the development of the common international investment policy, it may be instructive to look at the Commission's original proposal for the transitional arrangements for Member State bilateral investment agreements.[147] Article 6(1) of the original proposal for the transitional arrangements referred to four criteria for not being allowed to maintain in force existing BITs or being allowed to enter into force BITs concluded before 1 December 2009, namely, in the cases where:

(a) an agreement conflicts with the law of the Union other than the incompatibilities arising from the allocation of competence between the Union and its Member States; or

(b) an agreement overlaps, in part or in full, with an agreement of the Union in force with that third country and this specific overlap is not addressed in the latter agreement; or

(c) an agreement constitutes an obstacle to the development and the implementation of the Union's policies relating to investment, including in particular the common commercial policy; or

---

[144] Council Decision of 9 October 1961 on the standardisation of the duration of trade agreements with third countries [1961] OJ 71/1274.

[145] Council Decision 69/494 of 16 December 1969 on the progressive standardisation of agreements concerning commercial relations between Member States and third countries and on the negotiation of Community agreements [1969] OJ L326/39.

[146] See the analysis below.

[147] Commission Proposal for a Regulation of the European Parliament and of the Council establishing transitional arrangements for bilateral investment agreements between Member States and third countries, COM(2010)344 final, 7 July 2010, Brussels.

(d) the Council has not taken a decision on the authorisation to open negotiations on an agreement which overlaps, in part or in full, with an agreement notified under Article 2, within one year of the submission of a recommendation by the Commission pursuant to Article 218(3) of the Treaty.

The first criterion enshrined in this provision in the original proposal is reflected in Regulation 1219/2012 in the duty of compliance enshrined in Article 3. As regards the second criterion, it is unlikely that any overlap (rather than conflict) between a Member State BIT and a Union external agreement constitutes a serious obstacle to the negotiation and conclusion of a Union investment agreement. In addition, as was shown above (I), such overlap already existed for a number of provisions in BITs with respect to the Community's pre-Lisbon external practice in the field of FDI, such as the provisions on investment treatment and capital transfers. This criterion in the original proposal therefore added an additional element, namely, that the overlap is not addressed in the Union agreement in force.

The third criterion in the original proposal for the transitional arrangements is currently (with the addition of the adjective 'serious') reflected in the ground for assessment of Member State BITs by the Commission in view of the negotiation and conclusion of Union investment agreements, while it was originally proposed as a ground for a withdrawal of authorisation in view of the development and the implementation of the common international investment policy. The fourth criterion envisages the specific situation in which a mere overlap between an existing Member State bilateral investment agreement and a possible Union investment agreement with the same third country may turn out to be an obstacle to the negotiation and conclusion of the latter agreement. However, in the case of the fourth criterion in the original proposal the Commission has not been authorised to open negotiations and the issue of overlap with the negotiation and conclusion of a Union investment agreement for that very reason does not seem to occur. Arguably, the qualification of a mere overlap between a Member State BIT and a possible future Union investment agreement as an obstacle to the implementation of the common international investment policy would fly against the purpose of a replacement mechanism, which presupposes that Member State BITs continue to be in force until a Union investment agreement (necessarily on the same subject matter) enters into force.

So far as concerns the more precise scope of the 'serious obstacle' test in the transitional arrangements, little inspiration could arguably be drawn from the 'BITs' judgments. In those cases, the CJEU assessed the compatibility of the capital transfer provisions in a number of Member State BITs with the (now) TFEU provisions on free movement of capital from the perspective of the latter's practical effectiveness and in view of their specialised purpose. Although it cannot be excluded that the situation that gave rise to these infringement proceedings could – in the post-Lisbon era – give rise to a serious obstacle to the negotiation and conclusion of a Union investment agreement, the agreements in question were challenged by the Commission in view of their incompatibility with EU primary law, not in view of being a serious obstacle to the negotiation and conclusion of a Union investment agreement with a third country. Arguably, for obstacles in the sense of Article 5 of Regulation 1219/2012 to be sufficiently serious for the purpose of the assessment by the Commission, such obstacles need to actually arise in practice, and not be merely potential; and they need to constitute an impediment serious enough for the negotiation and conclusion of a Union investment agreement with a third country to founder. In that light, it may be possible to argue that the failure of a Member State to comply with its obligations under EU law by not being able to remedy an incompatibility between a specific bilateral investment agreement and EU law could potentially give rise to a serious obstacle under the common international investment policy if and when it becomes implicated negatively in the negotiation and conclusion of a Union investment agreement with the same third country.

The transitional arrangements are careful to avoid couching the issue of the continued existence of Member State BITs pursuant to the Lisbon reform of the CCP as an issue of authorisation under Article 2(1) TFEU[148].[149] While Article 2(1) TFEU codifies the principle that exclusive Union competence precludes Member State action in that field unless a Member State is authorised by the Union to do so, or if Member State action is necessary for the implementation of acts of the Union,[150] this is a provision about taking action and it is thus silent on the effect of supervening exclusivity on existing legally binding acts, such as Member State agreements with third countries. The more appropriate term for the legal effect (under EU law) of the transitional arrangements on existing Member State bilateral investment agreements with third countries, therefore, is arguably that of (temporary) confirmation of their continued validity and application, rather than authorisation.

There are two reasons for drawing a distinction between the act of authorising and that of confirming the (at least initial) continued existence of Member State BITs with third countries. In the first place, it helps to clarify the consequences of not notifying a bilateral investment agreement to the Commission under Article 2 of the transitional arrangements, which a Member State would like to maintain in force. In the second place, it serves to clarify the possible implications for a Member State bilateral investment agreement of not meeting the 'serious obstacle' test in Article 5 of Regulation 1219/2012. Before tackling these two issues, it is

---

[148] Article 2(1) TFEU: 'Where the Treaties confer on the Union exclusive competence in a specific area, only the Union may legislate and adopt legally binding acts, the Member States being able to do so themselves only if so empowered by the Union or for the implementation of acts of the Union.'

[149] But see Art 3 of the original proposal (above n 147). It can be observed that a transitional mechanism for existing Member State BITs has also been referred to in the academic literature as being tantamount to a 'grandfathering' of existing Member State external BITs – a term that is used, for example, in the context of Art 64(1) TFEU, which shields certain national measures from the application of the TFEU free movement of capital. See R Leal-Arcas, 'The European Union's Trade and Investment Policy after the Treaty of Lisbon' (2010) 4 *Journal of World Investment and Trade* 463, 489.

[150] See 41/76 *Donckerwolcke* [1976] ECR 1921, para 32: 'As full responsibility in the matter of commercial policy was transferred to the Community by means of Article 113(1) measures of commercial policy of a national character are only permissible after the end of the transitional period by virtue of specific authorisation by the Community.'

appropriate to address briefly the implications under EU law of the Union's post-Lisbon exclusive FDI competence for the validity and continued application of Member State BITs with third countries.

There is little case law to support any view with particular certainty as regards the precise legal implications of the Union's post-Lisbon exclusive FDI competence for the validity and continued application of existing Member State BITs with third countries. [151] The issue of the effect of supervening exclusivity on existing Member State agreements with third countries came up in the 'Open Skies' cases, where AG Tizzano considered that:

> supervening external competence of the Community in matters previously regulated by agreements of the Member States does not suffice in itself to render those agreements incompatible with the rules and principles governing the division of powers.[152]

Along the same lines, it can be argued that the issue of the post-Lisbon status of existing Member State BITs with third countries is arguably one of compatibility, rather than of competence, because the agreements in question had already been concluded before the Lisbon reform of the TFEU provisions on the CCP.[153] Given that the continued validity and application of Member State bilateral investment agreements is arguably not subject to legal challenge in view of the Union's post-Lisbon exclusive FDI competence, there is also no need for authorisation of Member State bilateral investment agreements with third countries in the sense of Article 2(1) TFEU.

---

[151] On this issue, see in particular F Hoffmeister and G Ünüvar, 'From BITs and Pieces towards European Investment Agreements' in M Bungenberg, A Reinisch and C Tietje (eds), *EU and Investment Agreements: Open Questions and Remaining Challenges* (Baden-Baden, Nomos, 2013) 80 ff; R Vidal Puig, 'The Scope of the New Exclusive Competence of the European Union with regard to Foreign Direct Investment' (2013) 2 *Legal Issues of European Integration* 133, 147 n; F Ortino and P Eeckhout, 'Towards an EU Policy on Foreign Direct Investment' in A Biondi, P Eeckhout and S Ripley, *EU Law After Lisbon* (Oxford, Oxford University Press, 2012) 320; JA Bischoff, 'Just a Little *Bit* of "Mixity"? The EU's Role in the Field of International Investment Protection Law' (2011) 5 *CML Rev* 1527, 1546 ff; PJ Kuijper, 'Foreign Direct Investment: The First Test of the Lisbon Improvements in the Domain of Trade Policy' (2010) 4 *Legal Issues of European Integration* 261, 262 ff; T Eilmansberger, 'Bilateral Investment Treaties and EU Law' (2009) 2 *CML Rev* 383, 397 ff.

[152] See Joined Opinion of AG Tizzano of 31 January 2002 in the 'Open Skies' cases (above n 57) para 113. The Court did not rule on this point, however, since it held that the air transport agreements at issue had been concluded after the Community had exercised its competence in the field covered by the agreements, which was thus already exclusive. For an analysis of the status of Member State commercial agreements under the transitional arrangement following the conclusion of the Treaty of Rome, see below.

[153] The question arises whether a distinction may need to be drawn between an *a priori* exclusive external competence of the Union and exclusive external competence as a result of the adoption of common rules, which are capable of being affected by Member State agreements with third countries (*AETR* exclusivity). Such a distinction does not find support in the Court's case law. As will be argued below, the reference to a transfer of 'full responsibility' to the (then) Community in matters of commercial policy upon the entry into force of the Treaty of Rome, as a result of which measures of commercial policy of a national character were only permissible after the end of the transitional period by virtue of specific authorisation by the Community, should arguably be understood in the context of the substantive requirement of the progressive move during the transitional period towards the required uniformity in shaping the external dimension of the customs union, such as the single external tariff. See 41/76 *Donckerwolcke* [1976] ECR 1921, para 32.

Against this backdrop, non-notification of a bilateral investment agreement by a Member State, while keeping the agreements in force or making them enter into force, does not constitute an infringement of the Union's exclusive FDI competence, but of the procedural requirement for being allowed to maintain in force or being permitted to enter into force a bilateral investment agreement under the transitional arrangements. Consequently, a Member State would no longer (as a matter of EU law) be allowed to keep the bilateral investment agreement in force or be permitted to have such an agreement enter into force under the transitional arrangements. The appropriate means of eliminating an incompatibility with the transitional arrangements flowing from an infringement of the procedural requirement of notification under Article 2 of Regulation 1219/2012 would seem to be for a Member State to terminate the bilateral investment agreement in question. In view of the scope of the transitional arrangements, this obligation extends only to the provisions on investment protection in such agreements. Importantly, Regulation 1219/2012 therefore does not provide for the automatic termination of Member State bilateral investment agreements that have not been notified in accordance with Article 2.

For an assessment of the legal implications for a Member State bilateral investment agreement in the event that it constitutes a serious obstacle to the negotiation and conclusion of a Union investment agreement with a third country, it is instructive to look at Article 6 of Regulation 1219/2012. This provision refers to the duty of cooperation incumbent on the Commission and the Member States in the management of the replacement mechanism with regard to Member State bilateral investment agreements with third countries. Under Article 6(1), the Member States shall:

> take all appropriate measures to ensure that the provisions of the bilateral investment agreements notified pursuant to Article 2 do not constitute a serious obstacle to the negotiation or conclusion by the Union of bilateral investment agreements with third countries, with a view to the progressive replacement of the bilateral investment agreements notified pursuant to Article 2.

The wording of this provision resembles the phraseology of Article 351(2) TFEU, under which the Member States are under an obligation to take all appropriate measures to eliminate incompatibilities between prior agreements with third countries and the EU Treaties. Both Article 351(2) TFEU and Article 6(1) of Regulation 1219/2012 are a specific application of the duty of cooperation enshrined in Article 4(3) TEU. Even though Article 6(1) of Regulation 1219/2012 establishes a different substantive test than Article 351(2) TFEU, both provisions refer to the obligation to take all appropriate means to remove any serious obstacle to the negotiation and conclusion of a Union investment agreement (in the case of the transitional arrangements) or incompatibilities with EU law (in the case of Article 351(2) TFEU). It therefore seems possible to draw inspiration from the case law in the context of Article 351(2) TFEU for an assessment of the legal consequences of failing to remove any serious obstacles to the negotiation and conclusion of Union investment agreements under the transitional arrangements.[154]

It therefore cannot be excluded that the obligation for a Member State to take all appropriate measures to ensure that the provisions of a bilateral investment agreement with a third country do not constitute a serious obstacle to the negotiation or conclusion by the Union of investment agreements with third countries may give rise in practice to the need to amend or even to terminate such an agreement. Importantly, however, as in the situation where a Member State fails to notify a bilateral investment agreement that it subsequently maintains in force, Regulation 1219/2012 does not presuppose the automatic termination of existing BITs with third countries pursuant to a finding that a Member State investment agreement with a third country constitutes a serious obstacle to the negotiation or conclusion of a Union investment agreement with a third country. Such a finding that a Member State bilateral investment agreement constitutes a serious obstacle to the negotiation or conclusion by the Union of an investment agreement with a third country, failure to resolve which matter gives rise to an incompatibility with the transitional arrangements, would constitute a *res inter alios acta* that could not affect the continued validity of existing BITs under international law.

Before any such legal consequences might arise, Article 6(2) of the transitional arrangements stipulates that consultation is to take place between the Commission and the Member States pursuant to an assessment by the Commission that one or more provisions of a Member State bilateral investment agreement constitute a serious obstacle to the negotiation or conclusion by the Union of an investment agreement with a third country. In the event that appropriate actions to resolve the matter have not been identified through consultation within 90 days, Article 6(3) of the transitional arrangements provides that the Commission shall indicate, within 60 days of the end of the consultations, the appropriate measures to be taken by a Member State concerned in order to remove the obstacles in question. While Article 6(3) does not provide for the Commission to take a decision on this matter, the Commission could start infringement proceedings against a Member State, which in the assessment of the Commission has not taken all appropriate measures to remove a serious obstacle to the negotiation and conclusion of a Union investment agreement with a third country.

For an analysis of the replacement mechanism in Regulation 1219/2012, it is also instructive to compare it with the transitional arrangement for Member State commercial arrangements in the early years of the CCP. Regulation 1219/2012 explicitly takes its cue from the transitional arrangement for the CCP, which was introduced in the 1960s.[155] Unlike the Treaty of Lisbon provisions on the CCP, the Treaty of Rome did not merely provide for Community competence in the field of external trade, but also explicitly provided for a transitional period, which was originally set to lapse on 31 December 1969, by the end of which the gradual

---

[154] See the text at II.
[155] See COM(2010)344 (above n 147) 2.

convergence of the Member States' commercial policy was to be achieved. To this effect, Article 111(1) EEC provided that the:

> Member States shall coordinate their trade relations with third countries so as to bring about, by the end of the transitional period, the conditions needed for implementing a common policy in the field of external trade.

Moreover, Article 113(1) EEC provided that:

> After the transitional period has ended, the common commercial policy shall be based on uniform principles, particularly in regard to changes in tariff rates, the conclusion of tariff and trade agreements, the achievement of uniformity in measures of liberalisation, export policy and measures to protect trade such as those to be taken in case of dumping or subsidies.

This transitional phase was linked, inter alia, to the establishment of the common customs tariff, which was facilitated by progressively moving towards the required uniformity and which was introduced on 1 July 1968.[156] In order to foster the convergence of commercial relations between Member States and third countries, it was moreover considered necessary to address the status of existing Member State commercial agreements and those to be concluded during the transitional period.

In November 1961, the Council adopted a Decision on the standardisation of the duration of trade agreements with third countries.[157] The Decision first addressed the issue of the conclusion of commercial agreements with third countries by the Member States after the adoption of the Decision, for which Article 1 provided that they would not extend beyond the end of the transitional period in the EEC Treaty. Pursuant to Article 2, agreements containing neither an 'EEC clause', whereby amendments to such agreement made necessary by obligations of the Member States under the Treaty of Rome might be negotiated without delay, nor a clause providing for annual notice of termination, would not be valid for more than one year, subject to the limit posed by the end of the transitional period of the EEC Treaty and to any exceptions authorised by the Council. For the purpose of ensuring that existing Member State commercial agreements would not constitute an obstacle to the development of the common commercial policy as provided for in the Treaty, Article 3 provided that:

> As soon as possible, and in any event not later than 1 January 1966, the Commission shall examine with Member States all existing agreements concerning commercial relations and all trade and navigation treaties concluded by Member States.

---

[156] See Art 111(4) EEC, which provided that the 'Member States shall, in consultation with the Commission, take all necessary measures, particularly those designed to bring about an adjustment of tariff agreements in force with third countries, in order that the entry into force of the common customs tariff shall not be delayed'. See also Art 112(1) EEC, under which the Member States would progressively harmonise their national systems for export aid before the end of the transitional period.

[157] Council Decision of 9 October 1961 on the standardisation of the duration of trade agreements with third countries [1961] OJ 71/1274.

Under Article 4, the Member States, acting in consultation with the Commission, would moreover 'arrange that the terminal dates of their bilateral trade agreements with third countries shall coincide'.

Unlike Regulation 1219/2012, it can be observed that the 1961 Decision did not contain a replacement mechanism for existing Member State commercial agreements. The Member States agreed to standardise (and thereby limit) the duration of commercial agreements in view of the transitional period enshrined in the EEC Treaty, by the end of which the conditions for implementing a common policy in the field of external trade had to have been brought about. To this effect, the 1961 Decision contained an obligation of coordination of termination of the relevant agreements.

The 1961 Decision was followed by Council Decision 69/494 on the progressive standardisation of agreements concerning commercial relations between Member States and third countries and on the negotiation of Community agreements.[158] This 1969 Decision established a procedure for the progressive replacement of Member State commercial agreements by Community agreements, without, however, providing for a replacement mechanism in the sense of Regulation 1219/2012. Article 1 of Decision 69/494 provided for a notification requirement for Member State commercial agreements, the application of which a Member State wanted to extend beyond the transitional period. The continued existence of Member State commercial agreements beyond the transitional period was possible under Article 3, provided that their extension did not hinder the implementation of the common commercial policy. If certain provisions in Member State commercial agreements did not constitute an obstacle to the implementation of the common commercial policy, even if they fell within its scope, Article 3 provided that:

> the Commission may propose to the Council that the Member State or States concerned be authorised, by way of derogation from Article 1 of Council Decision of 9 October 1961 on standardisation of the duration of trade agreements with third countries, to extend, expressly or tacitly, for a period to be specified, the provisions in question of the instruments which were the subject of the consultation.

It can be observed that authorisation under Article 3 of the 1969 Decision constituted an explicit derogation from the 1961 Decision, under which the duration of future agreements was limited in accordance with the transitional period enshrined in EU primary law. Arguably, the explicit source of the legal obligation to terminate those agreements was therefore the 1961 Decision itself, rather than the issue of supervening exclusivity pursuant to the entry into force of the Treaty of Rome. Even if such exclusivity was effectively suspended pending the expiry of the transitional period pursuant to Article 1 of the 1961 Decision because the Member States could continue to conclude commercial agreements, the continued existence of Member State agreements simply did not present an issue of

---

[158] Decision 69/494 of 16 December 1969 [1969] OJ L326/39.

competence, precisely because it related to pre-existing commercial agreements of the Member States. It is, moreover, conceivable that a failure to terminate such commercial agreements could give rise to an issue of substantive incompatibility with the transitional period enshrined in the EEC Treaty, which laid down the obligation to create the conditions needed for implementing a common commercial policy in the field of external trade, provided that the continued existence of Member State commercial agreements indeed constituted an obstacle in this respect.

Unlike the Treaty of Rome, the TFEU provisions on the CCP do not stipulate a transitional period in the field of FDI pursuant to the Lisbon reform of these provisions. As a result, it is arguably not necessary to standardise the duration of investment agreements as part of a progressive move towards uniformity in the way that happened with Member State commercial agreements in the 1960s. The absence of such a transitional period also arguably makes it unnecessary to authorise the continued existence of Member State investment agreements beyond such a transitional phase. Instead, Regulation 1219/2012 lays down a replacement mechanism for existing Member State BITs, under which existing Member State investment agreements are allowed to remain in force (upon the procedural requirement of their notification) until they are replaced by Union agreements. In addition, existing Member State BITs ought not to form a serious obstacle to the negotiation and conclusion of Union investment agreements, which it is up to the Commission to assess. So far as concerns Member State commercial agreements, the Council authorised the continued existence of numerous agreements and continued to do so for some agreements until 30 April 2005.[159] So far, no Member State investment agreement has been replaced by a Union investment agreement.[160]

Regulation 1219/2012 seems to provide for a practical and workable transitional arrangement for existing Member State BITs with third countries and constitutes an important post-Lisbon development with regard to these agreements. The maintenance of the status quo of existing BITs confirms the legal certainty of investors that will continue to invoke such agreements, which is certainly to be welcomed. Some existing Member State investment agreements with third coun-

---

[159] Decision 2001/855 of 15 November 2001 [2001] OJ L320/13 last authorised the automatic renewal or continuation in force of provisions governing matters covered by the common commercial policy contained in the friendship, trade and navigation treaties and trade agreements concluded between Member States and third countries.

[160] An example of a Union agreement with a third country suspending or superseding existing Member State bilateral agreements is the Agreement on civil aviation safety between the European Community and Canada [2009] OJ L153/11. Article 26(2) of the Agreement provides: 'During the period of provisional application pursuant to paragraph 2 of Article 23 (Entry into Force and Provisional Application) of the Agreement, the bilateral agreements listed in Annex 3 to this Agreement shall be suspended except to the extent provided in Annex 2 of this Agreement. Upon entry into force pursuant to paragraph 1 of Article 23 of this Agreement, this Agreement shall supersede the relevant provisions of the bilateral agreements listed in Annex 3 to this Agreement except to the extent provided in Annex 2 to this Agreement'. Annex 3 provides a list of agreements between Member States and Canada to be suspended or superseded by the Agreement.

tries could be phased out in the short term, although this depends on the speed with which they are replaced by Union investment agreements. The Lisbon reform of the CCP has not introduced a transitional period with regard to the shaping of the common international investment policy and it cannot be assumed that all Member State BITs will eventually be replaced. There may not be a Union interest in concluding an investment agreement with every third country, as con-tradistinguished from the specific investment relations of some Member States with particular third countries.[161] In view of the priorities set by the Commission in the 2010 Communication on the common international investment policy and the negotiations that are currently ongoing with a number of third countries, it seems that Member State BITs with some of the larger foreign markets are likely to be replaced sooner than others.[162]

B. Issues Pertaining to the Need for Authorisation to Amend Existing BITs or to Conclude New BITs

It has been shown above (II.B) that the Member States are in principle free to assume international commitments in the field of investment under shared com-petences, subject to the duty of compliance and the principle of sincere coopera-tion. An important aspect of the EU legal framework governing the interaction between EU law and Member State BITs with third countries, which have been concluded either before accession or after accession, is the duty for the Member States to take all appropriate measures to eliminate any incompatibility with EU law, notwithstanding the specific division of competence between the Union and the Member States. That obligation has not been affected by the Lisbon transfer of exclusive external competence in the field of FDI to the Union. The Union's exclusive FDI competence gives rise to the need for authorisation to amend exist-ing BITs, however, where the subject matter of such amendments falls under the scope of the Union's FDI competence. The same need for authorisation arises where a Member State wants to conclude a new bilateral investment agreement with a third country. The transitional arrangements therefore establish joint pro-visions for the amendment of existing agreements and the conclusion of new agreements.

The amendment of existing Member State BITs with third countries is needed so far as concerns the capital transfer clauses in many BITs in view of the 'BITs' judgments. The amendment of existing BITs could, moreover, be at issue for other areas of interaction between Member State investment agreements and EU law that have been identified above (I.B). Since the transitional arrangements are intended to extend to all investment protection provisions in Member State BITs, any incompatibility with EU law is, upon that presumption, arguably subsumed under the authorisation mechanism that it lays down. For example, while the

---

[161] See the text at chapter 1, I.
[162] COM(2010)343 (above n 1). For analysis, see the text at chapter 3, II.B.

incompatibilities at issue in the 'BITs' judgments arguably related to an area of shared competence,[163] the amendment of the relevant provisions would have to be authorised under Regulation 1219/2012. In addition, the implementation of the common international investment policy does not mean that the Member States would no longer want to conclude new BITs. In fact, some Member States have concluded new BITs with third countries after the entry into force of the Treaty of Lisbon. For instance, a new Germany-Pakistan BIT was concluded on 1 December 2009 and Latvia and India concluded a BIT on 18 February 2010.[164]

The issue of Union authorisation to amend existing BITs and to conclude new BITs can be distinguished from a number of other legal categories of Member State action under Union exclusive competence, both of which, however, would not be suitable for the development and implementation of the Union's international investment policy. First, the CJEU has accepted reasons of political expediency for Member State action under Union exclusive competence without specific authorisation in *AETR*.[165] In that case, the Member States were engaged in ongoing negotiations, the subject matter of which had later become subject to (then) Community exclusivity.[166] The Court held that the Member States, while acting in the manner decided on by the Council, acted in the interest and on behalf of the Community in accordance with their obligations under (now) Article 4(3) TEU.[167] This can be distinguished from the second category of Member State action without specific authorisation in fields where the Union holds exclusive competence, namely, where this is expressly allowed under EU primary law. This was the case under Article 115 EEC in the context of the CCP, where the Member States could act in case of urgency during the transitional period, after having notified the Commission, in the event of Union inactivity. A third, and more radical, kind of Member State action under Union exclusive competence is a transfer of competence from the Union back to the Member States. In two early cases, however, the Court was sceptical of the possibility for the Community to discharge itself of any responsibilities by restoring tasks to the authority of the Member States.[168] To restore to the Member States the power and freedom to act unilaterally in fields of exclusive competence in the case of Union inactivity also appears to be legally unacceptable.[169] The remaining option is therefore the authorisation by the Union of Member State action in the sense of Article 2(1) TFEU, which needs to be specific but has earlier been given a wide interpretation by the CJEU in *Bulk Oil* in the context of the CCP.[170]

The transitional arrangements contain a mechanism under which the Member States can be empowered to make specific amendments to existing BITs with third

---

[163] See the text at chapter 3, I.B.
[164] UNCTAD, *Investment Policy Monitor*, No 2, 20 April 2010, 7.
[165] 22/70 *Commission v Council (AETR)* [1971] ECR 263.
[166] Ibid para 86.
[167] Ibid para 90.
[168] 23/75 *Rey Soda* [1975] ECR 1279, para 25; 7/71 *Euratom* [1971] ECR 1003, para 20.
[169] 804/79 *Commission v United Kingdom* [1981] ECR 1045, para 20.
[170] 174/84 *Bulk Oil* [1986] ECR 559, paras 32–33.

countries or to enter into new investment agreements.[171] This authorisation mechanism could have been modelled after the mechanism that was established in the field of air transport services. As in the field of investment, aviation relations with third countries were traditionally governed by means of bilateral air transport agreements of the Member States. Moreover, as in the 'BITs' judgments, the CJEU took the view in the 'Open Skies' cases[172] that these agreements were incompatible with (then) EC law. In the same judgments, the Court held that the Union was exclusively competent to conclude some aspects of these air transport agreements, which the Member States had infringed by concluding the agreements in question. Pending the negotiation of Community agreements, the Member States were under the obligation to bring existing agreements into line with EC law, while they might also want to conclude new air transport agreements until the time that the Community had concluded an agreement with a specific third country.

For that purpose, the Air Transport Regulation[173] was adopted. The authorisation mechanism enshrined in Article 1 of that Regulation is quasi-automatic, subject to the requirement to comply with a cooperation procedure. Under this procedure, any relevant standard clauses need to be included in the agreement and the Commission, as well as the other Member States, need to be notified where a Member State wishes to amend an existing agreement or conclude a new agreement. The Commission is also invited to participate as an observer in any negotiations and must inform the Member State in question if it takes the view that negotiations are likely to constitute an obstacle to Union policy in the field of international aviation relations.[174] The Member States are moreover required to notify the Commission of the outcome of the negotiations, but are automatically allowed to conclude the agreement if it contains the relevant standard clauses.[175]

The transitional arrangements for Member States' bilateral investment agreements do not follow the model of a cooperation procedure, under which Union authorisation is quasi-automatic. Instead, the authorisation mechanism for the modification of existing agreements and the conclusion of new agreements draws inspiration from the procedural framework that has been established in two Regulations in the field of judicial cooperation in civil matters.[176] This policy area

---

[171] Pursuant to Art 12 of Regulation 1219/2012, this authorisation mechanism also applies to agreements signed by the Member States between 1 December 2009 and 9 January 2013.

[172] Above n 57.

[173] Regulation 847/2004 of the European Parliament and of the Council of 29 April 2004 on the negotiation and implementation of air service agreements between Member States and third countries [2004] OJ L157/7.

[174] Ibid Art 1(1).

[175] Ibid Art 4(1)–(2).

[176] Regulation 662/2009 of the European Parliament and of the Council of 13 July 2009 establishing a procedure for the negotiation and conclusion of agreements between Member States and third countries on particular matters concerning the law applicable to contractual and non-contractual obligations [2009] OJ L200/25; Council Regulation 664/2009 of 7 July 2009 establishing a procedure for the negotiation and conclusion of agreements between Member States and third countries concerning jurisdiction, recognition and enforcement of judgments and decisions in matrimonial matters, matters of parental responsibility and matters relating to maintenance obligations, and the law applicable to matters relating to maintenance obligations [2009] OJ L200/46.

was also traditionally dealt with by Member State agreements with third countries. Moreover, the CJEU held in *Opinion 1/03*[177] that the Community had exclusive external competence in the field in question with regard to those matters affecting the rules laid down in (then) EC secondary legislation.[178] Both Regulations, which were subsequently adopted, contain an authorisation and supervision mechanism for the amendment of existing agreements and the conclusion of new agreements in the relevant fields. The Member States need to notify the Commission in case they want to amend an existing agreement or to negotiate and conclude a new agreement with a third country.[179] In addition, the Commission needs to authorise the Member States to open formal negotiations and to conclude the agreement.[180] The Regulations also contain a supervision mechanism, under which the Commission may participate as an observer in the negotiations between the Member State and the third country in question so far as concerns the matters falling within the scope of the Regulations.[181]

So far as the grounds for a refusal to authorise the conclusion of an agreement are concerned, under the two Regulations the Commission should first check, upon a request for permission to open formal negotiations, whether any relevant negotiating mandate with a view to concluding a Community agreement with the third country concerned is specifically envisaged within the next 24 months after the notification.[182] If this is not the case, the Commission needs to assess whether:

(a) the Member State concerned has provided information showing that it has a specific interest in concluding the agreement due to economic, geographic, cultural, historical, social or political ties between the Member State and the third country concerned;
(b) on the basis of the information provided by the Member State, the envisaged agreement appears not to render Community law ineffective and not to undermine the proper functioning of the system established by that law; and
(c) the envisaged agreement would not undermine the object and purpose of the Community's external relations policy as decided by the Community.[183]

In other words, where a Member State can show that it has a specific interest in concluding a particular agreement which does not undermine the application of EU law or encroach upon the Union's external relations policy in this field, the Member State will be authorised under both Regulations to conclude the agreement concerned. Moreover, Article 5(2) of the two Regulations stipulates that the envisaged agreement shall contain a clause providing for either (a) full or partial denunciation of the agreement; or (b) direct replacement of the relevant provisions of the agreement in the event of the conclusion of a subsequent agreement

---

[177] *Opinion 1/03* [2006] ECR I-1145.
[178] Council Regulation 44/2001 of 22 December 2000 on jurisdiction and the recognition and enforcement of judgments in civil and commercial matters [2001] OJ L12/1.
[179] Regulations 662/2009, Art 3; Regulation 664/2009, Art 3.
[180] Regulation 662/2009, Arts 5 and 8; Regulation 664/2009, Arts 5 and 8.
[181] Regulation 662/2009, Art 7; Regulations 664/2009, Art 7.
[182] Regulation 662/2009 Art 4(2); Regulation 664/2009, Art 4(2).
[183] Ibid.

between the Community or the Community and its Member States, on the one hand, and the same third country, on the other hand.

The authorisation mechanism in Regulation 1219/2012 is similar in a number of respects. Article 7 of Regulation 1219/2012 lays down an obligation to notify the Commission where a Member State wishes to enter into negotiations with a third country in order to amend an investment agreement or conclude a new agreement. Pursuant to Article 9(1), the opening of formal negotiations will be authorised unless the Commission concludes that the opening of such negotiations would:

(a) be in conflict with Union law other than the incompatibilities arising from the allocation of competence between the Union and its Member States;
(b) be superfluous, because the Commission has submitted or has decided to submit a recommendation to open negotiations with the third country concerned pursuant to Article 218(3) TFEU;
(c) be inconsistent with the Union's principles and objectives for external action as elaborated in accordance with the general provisions laid down in Chapter 1 of Title V of the Treaty on European Union; or
(d) constitute a serious obstacle to the negotiation or conclusion of bilateral investment agreements with third countries by the Union.

These grounds for a refusal of authorisation resemble those in the two Regulations in the field of judicial cooperation in civil matters. In addition, Article 9(2) of Regulation 1219/2012 provides that the Commission may require the Member State to include or remove in such negotiations any clauses where necessary to ensure consistency with the Union's investment policy or compatibility with EU law. While Regulation 1219/2012 does not specify any clauses that must feature in the new agreements, the explanatory memorandum to the original proposal specifies that such clauses may contain the right to terminate an agreement in the event of the conclusion of a subsequent agreement by the Union, as well as specific capital transfer clauses and the inclusion of Article 49 TFEU clauses with a view to ensuring equal treatment under the agreement of all EU investors in the relevant third country.[184] The Commission is, moreover, to be kept informed of the progress of the negotiations and may request to participate in the negotiations under Article 10.

The outcome of the negotiations is to be notified to the Commission under Article 11(1). Authorisation to sign and conclude the agreement is granted by the Commission pursuant to Article 11(4) if the negotiated agreement does not meet any of the grounds for refusal in Article 9(1) and (2). Article 11(4) specifies that Articles 3, 5 and 6 of Regulation 1219/2012 apply to such agreements, as if they had been notified under Article 2 of the Regulation. In other words, Member State BITs which have been authorised to be amended or concluded under the transitional arrangements continue to fall under the replacement mechanism under Chapter 2 of the Regulation, including the obligation under Article 6(1) to take any

---

[184] COM(2010)344 (above n 147) 5.

appropriate measures to ensure that the provisions of a BIT do not constitute a serious obstacle to the negotiation or conclusion of Union investment agreements with third countries. Both the decision to authorise the negotiation and the conclusion of a Member State BIT are subject to the advisory procedure referred to in Article 16(2) of the Regulation.[185] In addition, Article 16(1) provides that the Commission shall be assisted by the Committee for Investment Agreements[186] and Article 16(2) refers to the advisory procedure in Article 4 of Regulation 182/2011.[187]

So far as the authorisation mechanism for the amendment of existing BITs and the conclusion of new BITs is concerned, it reflects the exclusive nature of the Union's post-Lisbon FDI competence. It can be observed that the Member States act as trustees of the common interest under the authorisation mechanism enshrined in Regulation 1219/2012.[188] In general terms, both the replacement mechanism with regard to existing Member State BITs and the authorisation mechanism for the amendment of existing BITs and the conclusion of new BITs constitute a specific application of the principle of sincere cooperation. It is recalled that Article 4(3) TEU requires the Member States to facilitate the achievement of the Union's tasks and to abstain from any measure which could jeopardise the attainment of the objectives of the Treaties, as well as that this duty is of general application and does not depend on whether the Union's competence is exclusive. It can be observed that Regulation 1219/2012 gives effect to the principle of sincere cooperation in a substantive sense through the mandatory inclusion of any clauses in existing and future Member State BITs, which are necessary to ensure compatibility with EU law and consistency with the common international investment policy. Regulation 1219/2012 also gives effect to the principle of sincere cooperation in a procedural sense through the requirement of notification for the maintenance in force of existing BITs and for the purpose of authorisation by the Commission of the amendment of existing and conclusion of new BITs.[189]

In the spirit of the principle of sincere cooperation, Article 13 of the transitional arrangements moreover stipulates specific obligations for the conduct of the Member States where a bilateral investment agreement falls within the scope of Regulation 1219/2012. First, it stipulates that the Member States have an obligation to inform the Commission without undue delay of all meetings which take

---

[185] Regulation 1219/2012, Arts 9(3) and 11(5).

[186] Summaries of meetings of the Committee for Investment Agreements, as well as voting records on Commission implementing decisions authorising specific Member States to maintain in force or permit to enter into force under EU law specific bilateral investment agreements with third countries, can be found in the comitology register (see http://ec.europa.eu/transparency/regcomitology/index.cfm).

[187] Regulation 182/2011 of the European Parliament and of the Council of 16 February 2011 laying down the rules and general principles concerning mechanisms for control by Member States of the Commission's exercise of implementing powers [2011] OJ L55/13.

[188] Article 206 TFEU stipulates that 'the Union shall contribute, *in the common interest*, to . . . the progressive abolition of restrictions on foreign direct investment' (emphasis added). For analysis, see M Cremona, *Member States as Trustees of the Community Interest: Participating in International Agreements on Behalf of the European Community*, EUI Working Paper Law 2009/17.

[189] Similarly, with regard to Regulation 847/2004: Neframi, 'The Duty of Loyalty' (above n 75) 343.

place under the provisions of the agreement. Secondly, a Member States must inform the Commission without undue delay of any representations made to it that a particular measure is inconsistent with the agreement and must inform the Commission of any request for dispute settlement lodged under the auspices of the BIT. In the event of such a dispute, the Member State and the Commission are required to cooperate fully and take all necessary measures to ensure an effective defence, including the participation by the Commission in the procedure, if appropriate. Thirdly, the Member State must seek the agreement of the Commission before activating any mechanism for dispute settlement against a third country under a BIT and must, where requested by the Commission, activate such mechanism. The Member State and the Commission are required to cooperate fully in the conduct of such procedures.

To sum up the findings of this section, the Lisbon transfer of competence in the field of the FDI to the Union, as well as its exercise, has a number of implications for both existing and any future Member State BITs with third countries. The continued existence of Member State BITs has been confirmed under the transitional arrangements upon the act of notification of numerous such agreements by the Member States. The Commission's assessment with regard to the question whether Member State BITs constitute a serious obstacle to the negotiation and conclusion of Union investment agreements will be undertaken on a case-by-case basis. So far as the amendment of existing investment agreements and the conclusion of new agreements are concerned, the application of the grounds for a refusal by the Commission to authorise a Member State to do so remains to be seen in practice. The Member States will arguably have to include specific clauses in their BITs. All in all, the adoption of Regulation 1219/2012 is an important step in the shaping of the external dimension of the Single European Market in the field of FDI and it reflects the Union's ambition in developing the common international investment policy. There is no necessary reason why these transitional arrangements will affect the level of protection currently offered to investors under Member States' BITs with third countries. At the same time, the precise implications of the transitional arrangements will depend on the Union's success in the implementation of the common international investment policy, a subject that has been discussed in the previous chapter.

IV. CONCLUSION

This chapter has examined the interplay between EU law and Member State BITs with third countries. It has been demonstrated that there are various ways in which Member State BITs substantively interact with EU law. This is not only evidenced by the 'BITs' judgments, but also by the MoU that was signed with the United States, which identified numerous areas of interaction and the need to protect the *acquis*. This interaction is with the internal market mechanism (as evidenced by the need to include an Article 49 TFEU clause in external BITs), with Union secondary legislation and with the Union's external practice in the field of FDI. The EU legal framework governing the interaction between EU law and Member State agreements consists of the duty of compliance and the principle of sincere cooperation. A distinction needs to be drawn between pre- and post-accession agreements, since in relation to the former the principle of primacy is suspended, but not in relation to the latter. The issue of substantive compatibility of external BITs with EU law is arguably not the subject of a general 'hypothetical incompatibility' test, but governed by the principle that such BITs may not affect the application of EU law. This, in turn, is itself a wide understanding of the scope for incompatibilities between EU law and such agreements, which reflects the fact that international law prevents Member States from setting aside international agreements with third countries upon a finding of incompatibility with EU law.

So far as concerns the implications of the Union's post-Lisbon exclusive FDI competence for existing and any future Member State BITs with third countries, the adoption of Regulation 1219/2012 constitutes an important step in the shaping of the external dimension of the Single European Market in the field of FDI. Regulation 1219/2012 establishes both a replacement mechanism for existing Member State BITs and an authorisation mechanism for the amendment of existing Member State BITs and for the conclusion of new BITs. It confirms the status quo of existing investment agreements and thereby leaves unaffected the level of protection currently offered to investors under Member States' BITs with third countries. The precise implications of the application of the 'serious obstacle' test in respect of the negotiation or conclusion by the Union of investment agreements with third countries remains to be seen in practice. The successful implementation of the Union's international investment policy will result in the gradual replacement of at least some Member State BITs by Union investment agreements. For this purpose, Regulation 1219/2012 constitutes a practical and workable arrangement.

5

The Interplay between EU Law and intra-EU Bilateral Investment Agreements

There appears to be no need for agreements of this kind in the single market and their legal character after accession is not entirely clear. It would appear that most of their content is superseded by [Union] law upon accession of the respective Member State ... In order to avoid such legal uncertainties and unnecessary risks for Member States, it is strongly recommended that Member States exchange notes to the effect that such BITs are no longer applicable, and also formally rescind such agreements.[1]

THE INTERPLAY BETWEEN EU law and Member State bilateral investment treaties (BITs) is not limited to the agreements that are currently in force between the Member States and third countries. Some of these agreements, which were initially concluded by Member States with third countries, have, as a consequence of enlargement, been imported into the Union as international legal commitments of the Member States *inter se*. After accession of Croatia, more than 200 BITs can be estimated to be in force between Member States.[2] The interplay between EU law and intra-EU BITs gives rise to a number of controversial issues in view of the fact that both of the contracting parties of these agreements are currently Member States of the European Union. Arbitral tribunals have already dealt with the question what implications accession to the Union of these formerly third countries has had for the validity of the investment agreements concerned, as well as with questions of compatibility between EU law and the investment treatment standards enshrined in intra-EU BITs.[3] The European Commission, moreover, considers that these agreements should be terminated, while the Member States have been reported to be divided on this matter.[4]

[1] November 2006 note by DG Internal Market and Services to the Economic and Financial Committee, quoted in: *Eastern Sugar v Czech Republic*, Partial Award of 27 March 2007, SCC no 088/2004, para 126, available at http://italaw.com/sites/default/files/case-documents/ita0259_0.pdf.
[2] About 190 intra-EU BITs were reported to be in force after accession of Bulgaria and Romania. See Annex to *2008 Annual EFC Report to the Commission and the Council on the Movement of Capital and Freedom of Payments*, No 17363/08, 17 December 2008, Brussels, para 16.
[3] For the argument, as part of the jurisdictional objections, that the Czech Republic-Netherlands BIT had terminated upon accession of the Czech Republic to the EU, see *Eastern Sugar v Czech Republic* (above n 1) Partial Award. For issues of substantive compatibility between intra-EU BITs and EU law that have come up in investment treaty arbitration, see, eg *Telenor v Hungary*, ICSID Case no ARB/04/15, Award of 13 September 2006; *ADC v Hungary*, ICSID Case no ARB/03/16, Award of 2 October 2006.
[4] See Annex to *2008 Annual EFC Report* (above n 2) para 17: 'a clear majority of Member States preferred to maintain the existing agreements'.

This chapter first sketches the historical background to the phenomenon of intra-EU BITs. The chapter proceeds by considering the argument that intra-EU BITs would be redundant with a view to the investment protection standards enshrined in the EU legal order. The chapter subsequently analyses a number of constitutional aspects of the phenomenon of intra-EU BITs, such as the way in which EU law has been claimed to impinge upon the validity of these agreements and the operation of the principle of primacy as a substantive conflict rule between EU law and intra-EU BITs. The chapter then analyses two ways in which intra-EU BITs have been argued to infringe the EU principle of equal treatment, namely, with regard to the principle of most favoured nation (MFN) treatment and the principle of national treatment (NT). The chapter then looks at the interplay between investor-state arbitration under intra-EU BITs and the autonomy of the EU legal order. The chapter argues that accession has not directly posed a challenge to the continued validity of the BITs that have consequently acquired intra-EU status. In addition, insofar as these agreements raise issues of compatibility with EU law, this does not automatically call into question their continued existence.

I. HISTORICAL BACKGROUND TO THE PHENOMENON OF INTRA-EU BITS

The controversy as regards the interplay between EU law and intra-EU BITs was effectively born in 2004 with the accession of a number of Central and Eastern European countries to the European Union. In view of the specific international context in which BITs have been concluded from the late 1950s onwards,[5] the problem of investment security had never been associated to the same extent with investments in other Member States. Because the Member States never perceived the need to conclude investment agreements with each other, all intra-EU BITs that are presently in force were originally concluded with third countries. Until the early 1990s, only two intra-EU investment agreements existed.[6] Both the Germany-Greece BIT and the Germany-Portugal BIT had gone relatively unnoticed, however. It was in the aftermath of the collapse of the Soviet Union, which created many opportunities for foreign investors in Central and Eastern Europe, that a large number of BITs has been concluded with the newly independent Central and Eastern European countries. The accession rounds of 2004 and 2007 have imported the vast majority of current intra-EU investment agreements into the Single Market. It has, furthermore, only been in this recent context of enlargement, and mostly posterior to the accession of the countries concerned, that questions have arisen as regards the interplay between EU law and these agreements.

In view of the current controversy over both the continued validity of intra-EU BITs and their compatibility with EU law, it is worth noting that the Central and Eastern European countries were in fact encouraged to enter into BITs with EU

---

[5]   See the text at chapter 4, I.A and accompanying notes.

[6]   Germany-Greece BIT (signed 27 March 1961, entered into force 15 July 1963); Germany-Portugal BIT (signed 16 September 1980, entered into force 23 April 1982).

Member States during the accession process. Europe Agreements (EAs) were concluded by the (then) Community and the Member States with these countries, which were designed to provide an appropriate framework for the gradual integration of these countries into the Community *acquis*.[7] Importantly, the EAs contained provisions on the conclusion of BITs by these countries with the Member States. For example, Article 73(2) of the EA with Poland,[8] which dealt with 'Investment promotion and protection', stipulated that one of the particular aims of cooperation would be:

> for Poland to establish a legal framework which favours investment; this could be achieved where appropriate by the Member States and Poland extending agreements for the promotion and protection of investment.

The reason for the inclusion of this type of provision may have been that the state of transition towards a market economy and stable political and legal institutions of these countries at the time was considered to pose investment security risks, notwithstanding the prospect of membership, which could be mitigated by the conclusion of BITs.

It may therefore seem that the conclusion of BITs between EU Member States and the Central and Eastern European countries concerned was in some way complementary to the accession process. At the same time, the inclusion of investment promotion provisions in Union external agreements with the effect of encouraging the Member States and the third country concerned to conclude BITs was not in any way specific to the context of accession. As was discussed in chapter 3, these provisions are, in fact, part of a more general practice of Union external relations and can also be found in external agreements that do not envisage accession of the third country concerned.[9] Moreover, there is very little evidence of discussions on the imminent intra-EU status of the BITs in issue during the accession process of the Central and Eastern European countries concerned. Insofar as the interplay between EU law and Member State BITs was discussed, such discussions seem to have taken place as part of the external relations aspects of accession.[10] For example, in a 2002 Report of the European Commission on the progress towards accession by the (then) candidate countries, the interplay between EU law and BITs was tackled exclusively as an external relations *problématique*.[11] It can be observed that a screening report for Croatia also contained

---

[7] EAs were concluded with Hungary, Poland, the Czech Republic, Slovakia, Romania, Bulgaria, Estonia, Latvia, Lithuania and Slovenia.

[8] [1993] OJ L348/2. See also Art 74(2) of the EA with the Czech Republic [1994] OJ L360/2.

[9] See, eg Art 58(2) of the PCA with Russia [1997] OJ L327/3, under which one of the aims of cooperation in order to establish a favourable climate for investment was 'the conclusion, where appropriate, between the Member States and Russia of agreements for the promotion and protection of investment'.

[10] See *Eastern Sugar v Czech Republic* (above n 1) Partial Award, para 119.

[11] *Towards the Enlarged Union*, Strategy Paper and Report of the European Commission on the progress towards accession by each of the candidate countries, COM(2002)700 final, 9 October 2002, Brussels, 20. See also Communication from the Commission, 'Monitoring report on the state of preparedness for EU membership of Bulgaria and Romania', COM(2006)549 final, 26 September 2006, Brussels, where the question of compatibility between EU law and BITs is not addressed.

merely general language with regard to potential incompatibilities of its BITs with EU law, and seems to focus rather on BITs with third countries.[12] Furthermore, the Accession Treaties did not directly deal with the subject. It thus seems that there have been few specific concerns over the imminent intra-EU status of the agreements concerned.

That some of the legal issues potentially arising from the future intra-EU status of these BITs were not foreseen is underscored by the conclusion of the Energy Charter Treaty (ECT) at around the same time that the Member States had started to conclude BITs with the Central and Eastern European countries concerned. The ECT was concluded as a mixed agreement, which as a matter of international law has legal effect between the Member States.[13] Moreover, the Community and the Member States did not have recourse to a disconnection clause. Such a clause would have excluded the applicability of provisions of the ECT in purely intra-EU situations when there is an EU rule that covers the same subject matter, and would have ensured the application of EU law in such intra-EU situations without potentially affecting the obligations of the Union and the Member States vis-à-vis third parties to the agreement.[14] While the Community issued a statement[15] upon the conclusion of the ECT, which specifies, inter alia, the modalities of participation of the Community in the ECT dispute settlement system, this statement does not address the *inter se* effect of the ECT.[16] The ECT thus establishes a compre-

---

[12] *Screening Report for Croatia, Chapter 4 – Free Movement of Capital*, 4 July 2006, 4, available at http://ec.europa.eu/enlargement/pdf/croatia/screening_reports/screening_report_04_hr_internet_en.pdf. It is also mentioned that 'Croatia should confirm its readiness to bring its bilateral investment agreements into compliance with the *acquis* if incompatible, or to renounce them' (8).

[13] PJ Kuijper, 'The Conclusion and Implementation of the Uruguay Rounds Results by the European Community' (1995) 2 *EJIL* 222, 223 ff: 'It is clear as a matter of international law that a mixed Community agreement, concluded simultaneously between the Community, its Member States and third States, is in principle capable of creating rights and obligations between all the parties and hence also between the Member States inter se.'

[14] See M Cremona, 'Disconnection Clauses in EU Law and Practice' in C Hillion and P Koutrakos (eds), *Mixed Agreements Revisited* (Oxford, Hart Publishing, 2010) 182, who explains that disconnection clauses go further than a rule of priority that governs instances of conflict between EU law and the agreement; they are a choice of law rule under which EU law applies between the Member States whether or not there is a conflict.

[15] Statement submitted by the European Communities to the Secretariat of the Energy Charter pursuant to Art 26(3)(b)(ii) of the Energy Charter Treaty [1998] OJ L69/115.

[16] But see M Burgstaller, 'European Law and Investment Treaties' (2009) 2 *Journal of International Arbitration* 181, 209, who takes the view that Art 26(3)(b)(ii) ECT and this statement 'may well be regarded as to effectively make use of a disconnection clause and thus prohibit EU nationals to submit disputes against other Member States to international arbitration'. Yet, the statement only explicitly enables the Union to withhold consent from referring a dispute to arbitration that has already been seized by the Union courts. In this, some of the Member States do allow investors to resubmit the same dispute to international arbitration, since they are not listed in Annex ID, which in conjunction with Art 26(3)(a) serves as a so-called fork-in-the-road provision. The 'partial' disconnection clause that could *in limine* be read in the statement concerns the question whether the Union or the Member States are the proper responding party to a dispute, so that the Union did not give unconditional consent to the submission to arbitration of disputes, which are inappropriately addressed to either the Union or the Member States.

hensive legally-binding effect between the EU Member States.[17] As a result, under the dispute settlement provisions of the ECT, investors from one Member State can bring claims against another Member State even if the dispute is also governed by EU law.[18] There is thus the possibility of disputes under the ECT, in which the state of origin of the claimant and the respondent state are both Member States of the Union. Unlike inter-Member State BITs, however, the ECT has not 'acquired' its intra-EU status. The ECT was actually concluded as such.

A number of Central and Eastern European countries have in the meantime been faced with claims by investors under BITs with other Member States. In this context, different arguments have been advanced with regard to the continued existence and applicability of these agreements. Some Member States have argued that their intra-EU BITs have ceased to be in force upon accession to the EU.[19] For instance, in *Eastern Sugar*, the Czech Republic submitted that the BIT would have been 'superseded by the intra-EU regime'.[20] At the same time, this argument has not been advanced by the Czech Republic in other arbitration proceedings.[21] Similarly, other investment disputes under intra-EU BITs have not given rise to jurisdictional objections on the basis that the BIT would have automatically terminated or ceased to apply upon accession of the responding Member State to the Union. For example, in *ADC*, Hungary invoked the need to comply with EU law in defence to a claim under an intra-EU BIT, without thereby claiming that the BIT would have ceased to be applicable upon its accession to the Union.[22] In general terms, capital exporting Member States, such as the United Kingdom, the Netherlands and Germany, are likely to be more favourably disposed towards the continued existence and applicability of these agreements.

There have been a number of disputes in which arbitral tribunals have been asked to rule on whether an acceding Member State violated the standards of treatment in an intra-EU BIT when it was bringing its legislation in line with the EU *acquis*. In some of these disputes, a Member State invoked the need to comply with EU law in defence to a claim under the BIT.[23] In other disputes, the respondent Member State was alleged not to have complied with its obligations under EU law and was claimed therefore to have violated the investment treatment standards in the BIT.[24] Arbitral tribunals have so far not been very assertive in interpreting the EU legal

---

[17] C Tietje, The Applicability of the Energy Charter Treaty in ICSID Arbitration of EU Nationals vs EU Member States' (2008) 78 *Beiträge zum Transationalen Wirtschaftrecht* 8.

[18] See *AES v Hungary*, ICSID Case no ARB/07/22, Award of 23 September 2010; *Electrabel v Hungary*, ICSID Case no ARB/07/19, Decision on Jurisdiction, Applicable Law and Liability of 30 November 2012.

[19] *Eastern Sugar v Czech Republic* (above n 1) Partial Award; *Eureko v Slovakia*, Permanent Court of Arbitration Case no 2008-13, Award on Jurisdiction, Arbitrability and Suspension of 26 October 2010, IIC 463 (2010).

[20] *Eastern Sugar v Czech Republic* (above n 1) Partial Award, para 104.

[21] See, eg *Saluka v Czech Republic*, Partial Award of 17 March 2006, available at http://italaw.com/sites/default/files/case-documents/ita0740.pdf.

[22] *ADC v Hungary* (above n 3) Award.

[23] Ibid; *Eastern Sugar v Czech Republic* (above n 1) Partial Award.

[24] *Telenor v Hungary* (above n 3) Award; *Saluka v Czech Republic* (above n 21) Partial Award.

obligations of a responding Member State. In some arbitral proceedings this was in part due to the fact that the legal nexus with EU law was created prior to accession of the Member States concerned, such as in *Eastern Sugar*. Other arbitral tribunals, such as in *Eureko*,[25] are not able to put aside questions about the substantive interaction between EU law and intra-EU BITs for that reason when dealing with the merits of an investment claim. In view of the problem of potentially conflicting legal obligations of the Member States under EU law and an intra-EU BIT, questions on the interplay between EU law and intra-EU BITs could in future be referred to the CJEU for a preliminary ruling under Article 267 TFEU by a national court of a Member State in the context of a challenge to an arbitration award.[26]

The Commission takes the view that the agreements in question are incompatible with EU law and has presented observations in a number of arbitration proceedings.[27] The Commission not only considers that there is no need for intra-EU BITs, since the Single Market allegedly provides for common internal investment protection rules, but also that 'most of their content [was] superseded by Community law' upon accession of the respective Member States.[28] In *Eureko*, the Commission moreover submitted that intra-EU BITs are incompatible with the EU principle of equal treatment.[29] In addition, the Commission has a number of procedural concerns, one of which is that investors could practice forum-shopping by submitting claims to arbitration instead of to national or the Union courts. The Commission could institute infringement proceedings under Article 258 TFEU against a Member State that refuses to terminate its intra-EU BITs. In 2008, the Czech Republic initiated the process of the termination of 23 BITs that were then in force with other Member States.[30] Some Member States (eg Denmark and Italy) have terminated their BIT with the Czech Republic, with other (but certainly not all) Member States reportedly to follow.[31]

---

[25] The final award in *Eureko v Slovakia*, Permanent Court of Arbitration Case no 2008-13, is not available to the public, however.

[26] Eg in *Eureko*, Slovakia has challenged the jurisdiction of the arbitral tribunal in annulment proceedings and has appealed against a ruling from the Frankfurt Court of Appeal before the German Supreme Court (Bundesgerichtshof). See S Balthasar, Kluwer Arbitration Blog, 28 August 2012, available at http://kluwerarbitrationblog.com/blog/2012/08/28/investment-arbitration-under-intra-eu-bits-recent-developments-in-eureko-v-slovakia/; L Peterson, Kluwer Arbitration Blog, 6 March 2009, available at http://kluwerarbitrationblog.com/blog/2009/03/06/will-ecj-look-at-intra-eu-bilateral-investment-treaties-next/.

[27] *Eureko v Slovakia* (above n 19) Award on Jurisdiction, Arbitrability and Suspension. The Commission was also granted leave to appear as *amicus curiae* in *Electrabel v Hungary* (above n 18), and *AES v Hungary* (above n 18). In both arbitrations under the ECT, the Commission was not allowed to give its opinion on issues of jurisdiction, as this was undisputed by the parties to the disputes, but only to address issues of substance, such as the compatibility of the PPA with EU competition law and the relevance of EU law to the dispute. See 1(16) *IAReporter*, 11 December 2008. The Commission is reportedly also intervening in *Micula v Romania*, ICSID Case no ARB/05/20, under the Sweden-Romania BIT; 2(8) *IAReporter*, 11 May 2009.

[28] European Commission (DG Markt) Note to the Economic and Financial Committee of November 2006, quoted in *Eastern Sugar v Czech Republic* (above n 1) Partial Award, para 126.

[29] *Eureko v Slovakia* (above n 19) Award on Jurisdiction, Arbitrability and Suspension, para 175 ff.

[30] *UNCTAD World Investment Report* (2009) 32.

[31] See also 2(13) *IAReporter*, 6 August 2009.

II. THE EU LEGAL ORDER AND INVESTMENT PROTECTION

Problems of investment security for a long time had not been associated with investments in other Member States to the degree to which it has more recently been the case. Against this backdrop, it has been argued that an additional layer of investment protection within the Single Market would in fact be superfluous in view of the framework of investment protection enshrined in the EU legal order. For example, in *Eastern Sugar*, the arbitral tribunal quoted from a note of the Czech Ministry of Finance to the Czech Government, in which it was stated that:

> With the exception of the possibility to file a complaint against the host country in an international arbitration proceeding, the protection of investments within the EU is on a comparative level with the protection that is provided to investors according to bilateral treaties for the protection of investments.[32]

Moreover, Slovakia argued in *Eureko* that, by acceding to the European Union, it became part of a specific system of law which creates a much more complex, wide-reaching and elaborate framework of investment protection than that provided by the Netherlands-Slovakia BIT.[33] Similarly, the Commission has argued that intra-EU BITs would be obsolete in view of the investment protection standards enshrined in the EU legal order.[34] According to some, the EU legal regime is even more favourable towards foreign investors than bilateral investment protection agreements.[35] At the other extreme, it has been argued that EU law does not deal with cross-border investment and consequently has no bearing on the issue of investment protection whatsoever.[36]

While clearly considerations of investment protection are not absent from EU law, investors seemingly do invoke intra-EU BITs because they consider that their claims can be more successfully pursued under these legal instruments. An important dimension of the investment protection regime in Member State BITs is that investors have access to international arbitration. At the same time, in the event of a claim that has a nexus with EU law, the EU legal order provides for investors to seek damages for a breach of EU law by a Member State for which it is responsible,[37] albeit only in the courts of the Member States and only in the case of a 'sufficiently serious' breach of directly effective provisions of EU law, where there is a direct causal link between the breach and the sustained injury.[38] The 'decisive test' for the imposition of state liability is whether a Member State has 'manifestly and

---

[32] *Eastern Sugar v Czech Republic* (above n 1) Partial Award, para 127.

[33] *Eureko v Slovakia* (above n 19) Award on Jurisdiction, Arbitrability and Suspension, para 58.

[34] *Eastern Sugar v Czech Republic* (above n 1) Partial Award, para 126.

[35] B Poulain, 'Quelques interrogations sur le status des traités bilatéraux de promotion et de protection des investissements au sein de l'Union européenne' (2007) 4 *Revue Générale de Droit International Public* 803, 809 ff.

[36] C Söderlund, 'Intra-EU Investment Protection and the EC Treaty' (2007) 5 *Journal of International Arbitration* 455.

[37] Joined Cases C-6/90 and C-9/90 *Francovich* [1991] ECR I-5357, para 41.

[38] Joined Cases C-46/93 and C-48/93 *Brasserie du Pêcheur* [1996] ECR I-1029, para 51.

gravely disregarded the limits of its discretion under EU law'.[39] Whether a breach of EU law by a Member State is 'sufficiently serious' is assessed, inter alia, in relation to the level of clarity of the rule breached; the measure of discretion left by that rule to public authorities; whether the infringement and the damage caused was intentional or involuntary by the state; and whether the adoption or retention of national measures or practices was contrary to EU law.[40] Moreover, damages under EU law are in principle predicated on domestic rules of liability in the Member State that is responsible for the breach, subject to minimum requirements of effectiveness and non-discrimination.[41]

As will be shown, however, investors arguably do not only challenge host Member State measures under BITs in view of the procedural rights enshrined in these investment agreements, but also because of the substantive rights that they grant to investors. In this regard, it is important that EU law focuses primarily on issues of investment mobility, while investment agreements focus on the issue of investment security.[42] Without purporting to provide a systematic comparison of the investment protection regime of BITs and the investment protection rights enshrined in the EU legal order,[43] this section investigates the investment protection rights that can be derived from the TFEU freedoms, the EU fundamental right to property and the protection of legitimate expectations in the EU legal order. These are set off against a number of aspects of the investment protection regime in BITs.

A. The TFEU Freedoms and Investment Protection

The TFEU freedoms are constitutive of a liberal international economic order between the Member States. At the same time, EU law reserves the right of the Member States to regulate national systems of property rights. Article 345 TFEU provides that 'This Treaty shall in no way prejudice the rules in Member States governing the system of property ownership'.

It follows from the wording of Article 345 TFEU that the Member States have not given up their sovereign right to regulate their national systems of property ownership so that they may privatise public assets and nationalise private assets.[44] Indeed, notwithstanding the predominantly shared liberal economic purpose of the Member States' economic policies, nationalisations have occurred in recent

---

[39]   Ibid para 55.
[40]   Ibid para 56.
[41]   *Francovich* (above n 37) para 42.
[42]   See the text at chapter 4, I.A.
[43]   See also L Azoulai and W Ben Hamida, 'La protection des investissements par le droit primaire – droit conventionnel des investissements et droit primaire communautaire: étude comparé des régimes et des approches' in C Kessedjian and C Leben (eds), *Le droit européen et l'investissement* (Paris, Éditions Panthéon-Assas, 2009).
[44]   For analysis, see V Akkermans and E Ramaekers, 'Article 345 TFEU (ex Article 295 EC), Its Meanings and Interpretations' (2010) *ELJ* 292.

European economic history. The 1980s have seen a number of takings by France in the banking and telecommunications sector. Much more recently, the financial crisis has precipitated the nationalisation of private financial institutions, such as Northern Rock in the United Kingdom and Fortis in the Netherlands.

Although the TFEU does not call into question the Member States' right to establish their national systems of property ownership, Article 345 TFEU does not have the effect of exempting measures establishing such a system from the fundamental rules of the TFEU, including the rules on the freedom of establishment and free movement of capital.[45] Insofar as nationalisations constitute restrictions or obstacles for investors from other Member States within the meaning of the TFEU freedoms, they need to be justified and be proportionate to the aim that is pursued. Case law on Article 345 TFEU and the interaction with the TFEU freedoms predominantly deals with the issue of limited privatisation by means of golden shares, and does not deal with the reversion of private property to public ownership. In the first 'Golden Shares' cases, AG Colomer took the view that since a state can retain full control over companies through public ownership, *a fortiori* it can retain more limited control in privatised undertakings through certain special rights.[46] The Court, however, held that the Member States could not:

> plead their own systems of property ownership, referred to in Article [345 TFEU], by way of justification for obstacles, resulting from privileges attaching to their position as shareholder in a privatised undertaking, to the exercise of the freedoms provided for by the [TFEU].[47]

It can be surmised that for a national measure to fall under Article 345 TFEU does not in itself qualify as a justification for posing an obstacle to free movement.

The extent to which the obligation to comply with the TFEU freedoms may limit the potential scope of Member State action in the context of reversion measures was addressed in the EFTA hydroelectric case, which could provide guidance as to how such questions may be dealt with in the EU legal order.[48] The EFTA Surveillance Authority challenged a Norwegian measure granting to private undertakings and all undertakings from other contracting parties to the EEA Agreement, a time-limited concession for the acquisition of waterfalls for energy production, with an obligation to surrender all installations to the Norwegian state without compensation at the expiry of the concession period, whereas Norwegian public undertakings benefitted from concessions for an unlimited period, on the basis that this would be discriminatory. In defence, Norway argued that the measure fell under Article 125 EEA, which corresponds to Article 345

---

[45] C-452/01 *Ospelt* [2003] ECR I-9743, para 24; C-302/97 *Konle* [1999] ECR I-3099, para 38 and 182/83 *Fearon* [1984] ECR 3677, para 7.

[46] Opinion of AG Colomer of 3 July 2001 in Joined Cases C-367/98 *Commission v Portugal* [2002] ECR I-4731, C-483/99 *Commission v France* [2002] ECR I-4781 and C-503/99 *Commission v Belgium* [2002] ECR I-4809, para 66.

[47] C-483/99 *Commission v France* [2002] ECR I-4781, para 44.

[48] E-2/06 *EFTA Surveillance Authority v Kingdom of Norway,* judgment of 26 June 2007 [2007] OJ C301/18.

TFEU, and would therefore fall outside of the scope of the EEA Agreement. The European Commission intervened in the case, and submitted that:

> The Commission interprets Article 125 EEA to the effect that States have the sovereign right to choose whether to privatise undertakings, nationalise or maintain such a status. Accordingly, the Defendant is in principle fully entitled to pursue the aim of public ownership, provided that it does so in a manner conforming with the fundamental rules of the EEA Agreement.[49]

The EFTA Court took the view that 'There are no specific circumstances in the case at hand which would warrant an interpretation of Article 125 EEA different from the interpretation of (now) Article 345 TFEU'.[50] It then held that the measures constituted a restriction on freedom of establishment and free movement of capital, because they stipulated that Norwegian public entities must own at least two-thirds of the shares of the undertaking in order for them to obtain a concession for an indefinite period.[51]

As to whether this restriction was justified, the EFTA Court, with reference to Article 125 EEA, held that 'Norway may legitimately pursue the objective of establishing a system of public ownership over these properties, provided that the objective is pursued in a non-discriminatory and proportionate way'.[52] The Norwegian system, however, was considered by the EFTA Court to constitute temporary public ownership, rather than establishing a 'system of property ownership', since the regime did not 'aim at attaining a situation where, as a matter of principle, the assets at issue are owned by public entities'.[53] The EFTA Court continued:

> A regime which merely brings or keeps this class of assets predominantly under public ownership, while at the same time leaving it to the discretion of the relevant authorities whether private ownership of the assets should be re-established, cannot be said to aim at establishing a system of property ownership under Article 125 EEA. Rather, such a regime aims at achieving a certain level of public control of the relevant sector of the economy – by means of securing public ownership of most of the relevant assets.[54]

The EFTA Court, moreover, took the view that acquiring public control as such does not qualify as a mandatory requirement, although it could be a means of attaining other goals which may qualify as legitimate aims, such as ensuring energy supply and the protection of the environment.[55] Yet, Norway failed to demonstrate that ownership control is necessary in order to meet the aims of security of energy supply or environmental protection.[56] In particular, Norway

---

[49] Ibid para 52.
[50] Ibid para 61.
[51] Ibid para 66.
[52] Ibid para 72.
[53] Ibid para 73.
[54] Ibid para 73.
[55] Ibid para 78.
[56] Ibid para 84.

had not demonstrated that 'other forms of control, even if administratively more burdensome, may not achieve the relevant public interest objectives in an equally effective way'.[57]

This suggests that EU law does not call into question the right of Member States to nationalise private property. Member State measures that interfere with private property must, however, comply with the TFEU freedoms. Such interferences must, in particular, be non-discriminatory and proportionate to the aim that is sought to be achieved. The fact that a measure falls under Article 345 TFEU cannot be pleaded as a justification for obstacles to investors from other Member States. While this poses limits to Member State action, investors only seem to derive limited rights from the need for Member States to comply with the TFEU freedoms. Similarly, the contracting Member States to BITs that have acquired intra-EU status may in principle also nationalise foreign property, subject to the condition that the measure serves a public purpose and is not arbitrary or discriminatory.[58] Importantly, BITs contain an obligation of prompt, adequate and effective compensation. It can be observed that the lack of any compensation was not considered as part of the proportionality test in the EFTA hydroelectric case. The issue of compensation for investors pursuant to interferences with property rights under EU law will be dealt with in more detail below.

B. The EU Fundamental Right to Property

Another source of investment protection rights in the EU legal order is the EU system of fundamental rights protection. Article 17(1) of the Charter of Fundamental Rights of the European Union provides that:

> Everyone has the right to own, use, dispose of and bequeath his or her lawfully acquired possessions. No one may be deprived of his or her possessions, except in the public interest and in the cases and under the conditions provided for by law, subject to fair compensation being paid in good time for their loss. The use of property may be regulated by law in so far as is necessary for the general interest.[59]

The fundamental rights guaranteed by the Charter need to be respected by the Union institutions and by the Member States when they act within the scope of

---

[57] Ibid para 88.

[58] R Dolzer and C Schreuer, *Principles of International Investment Law* (Oxford, Oxford University Press, 2008) 89 ff. See, eg Art 5(1) of the United Kingdom-Poland BIT: 'Investments of investors of either Contracting Party shall not be nationalized, expropriated or subjected to measures having effect equivalent to nationalization or expropriation (hereinafter referred to as "expropriation") in the territory of the other Contracting Party except for a public purpose which is not discriminatory and against prompt, adequate and effective compensation'.

[59] Article 6(1) TEU: 'The Union recognises the rights, freedoms and principles set out in the Charter of Fundamental Rights of the European Union of 7 December 2000, as adapted at Strasbourg, on 12 December 2007, which shall have the same legal value as the Treaties.' See Charter of Fundamental Rights of the European Union [2010] OJ C83/02.

EU law.[60] In other words, the Charter applies to all situations governed by EU law, but not outside such situations. In addition, the CJEU has ruled that where an EU legal act calls for national implementing measures, national authorities and courts remain free to apply national standards of protection of fundamental rights, provided that the level of protection provided for by the Charter, as interpreted by the Court, and the primacy, unity and effectiveness of EU law are not thereby compromised.[61]

The Court has held that in order to assess the scope of the fundamental right to respect for property 'account is to be taken of, in particular, Article 1 of the First Additional Protocol to the [European Convention for the Protection of Human Rights and Fundamental Freedoms (ECHR)], which enshrines that right'.[62] Article 1 of the First Additional Protocol refers to both natural and legal persons. The fundamental right to property is one of the general principles of EU law.[63] The Court has taken the view that it has no power to examine the compatibility with the ECHR of national rules which do not fall within the scope of EU law.[64] When the Member States act outside the scope of EU law, they must respect the right to property in conformity with the ECHR. The EU fundamental right to property and the investment protection rights under Article 1 of the First Additional Protocol will therefore be analysed in tandem.[65]

---

[60] Article 51 of the Charter provides that 'The provisions of this Charter are addressed to the institutions, bodies, offices and agencies of the Union with due regard for the principle of subsidiarity and to the Member States only when they are implementing Union law'. See C-617/10 *Aklagaren v Hans Akerberg Fransson* (nyr, 2013) paras 17–22.

[61] Article 53 of the Charter provides that 'Nothing in this Charter shall be interpreted as restricting or adversely affecting human rights and fundamental freedoms as recognised, in their respective fields of application, by Union law and international law and by international agreements to which the Union or all the Member States are party, including the European Convention for the Protection of Human Rights and Fundamental Freedoms, and by the Member States' constitutions'. See C-399/11 *Stefano Melloni v Ministerio Fiscal* (nyr, 2013), para 60.

[62] Joined Cases C-402/05 P and C-415/05 P *Kadi and Al Barakaat v Council and Commission* [2008] ECR I-6351, para 356. Article 1 of the First Additional Protocol provides that: 'Every natural or legal person is entitled to the peaceful enjoyment of his possessions. No one shall be deprived of his possessions except in the public interest and subject to the conditions provided for by law and by the general principles of international law. The preceding provisions shall not, however, in any way impair the right of a State to enforce such laws as it deems necessary to control the use of property in accordance with the general interest or to secure the payment of taxes or other contributions or penalties.'

[63] Article 6(3) TEU: 'Fundamental rights, as guaranteed by the European Convention for the Protection of Human Rights and Fundamental Freedoms and as they result from the constitutional traditions common to the Member States, shall constitute general principles of the Union's law.' As a general principle of EU law, it binds not only the Union institutions, but also the Member States when they act within the scope of EU law. See 5/88 *Wachauf* [1989] ECR 2609, para 19. The Court has also held that where a Member State seeks to derogate from the TFEU freedoms, its justifications for doing so must be compatible with the general principles of EU law. See C-260/89 *ERT* [1991] ECR I-2925, para 43.

[64] C-12/86 *Demirel* [1987] ECR 3719, para 28.

[65] As to the relationship between the EU legal order and the ECHR as regards the protection of property rights, see *Bosphorus Hava Yollari Turizm ve Ticaret Anonim irketi (Bosphorus Airways) v Ireland* (2005) 42 EHRR 1. In this case, the question arose 'whether, and if so to what extent, the important general interest of compliance with [EU] obligations can justify the impugned interference by the State with the applicant's property rights' (para 151). The European Court of Human Rights (ECtHR) considered that equivalent property right protection is provided by the Union, so that the presumption

The CJEU has consistently held that the right to property is not absolute, but 'must be viewed in relation to its function in society'.[66] The Union legislator can in principle restrict the exercise of the right to property for the purpose of a structural policy, but it cannot '[impair] the very substance of the right so guaranteed'.[67] The Court has shown a degree of deference in its scrutiny of the extent to which a measure may serve a public interest. For example, in *SMW Winzersekt*,[68] as regards the alleged interference with the peaceful enjoyment of property rights (the protection of indications of the geographical origin of wines) the Court held that in matters concerning the common agricultural policy the Union legislature has a broad discretion, so that:

> the lawfulness of a measure adopted in that sphere can be affected only if the measure is manifestly inappropriate, having regard to the objective which the competent institution is seeking to pursue.[69]

Instead, the Court's scrutiny focuses on the proportionality of the challenged measure. In this respect, the Court assesses whether there is 'a reasonable relationship of proportionality between the means employed and the aim sought to be realized' and whether 'a fair balance has been struck between the demands of the public interest and the interest of the individuals concerned'.[70]

The European Court of Human Rights (ECtHR) has similarly shown a degree of deference in its scrutiny of the policy objectives of interferences with property rights.[71] In *Lithgow*, which dealt with the nationalisation of a number of British undertakings in the aircraft and shipbuilding industries, the ECtHR held that:

> A decision to enact nationalisation legislation will commonly involve consideration of various issues on which opinions within a democratic society may reasonably differ widely. Because of their direct knowledge of their society and its needs and resources, the national authorities are in principle better placed than the international judge to appreciate what measures are appropriate in this area and consequently the margin of appreciation available to them should be a wide one.[72]

---

will be that a Member State has not departed from the obligations under the ECHR when it does no more than implement legal obligations flowing from its EU membership. The ECtHR added, 'However, any such presumption can be rebutted if, in the circumstances of a particular case, it is considered that the protection of Convention rights was manifestly deficient' (para 156). For a comparison between the investment protection rights under the ECHR and international investment law, see U Kriebaum, 'Is the European Court of Human Rights an Alternative to Investor-State Arbitration?' in PM Dupuy, F Francioni and EU Petersmann (eds), *Human Rights and International Investment Law and Arbitration* (Oxford, Oxford University Press, 2009).

[66] *Kadi and Al Barakaat* (above n 62) para 355.
[67] 44/9 *Hauer* [1979] ECR 3727, para 23.
[68] C-306/93 *SMW Winzersekt* [1994] ECR I-5555.
[69] Ibid para 22.
[70] *Kadi and Al Barakaat* (above n 62) para 360.
[71] See CB Schutte, *The European Fundamental Right to Property: Article 1 of Protocol No 1 of the European Convention on Human Rights: Its Origins, Working and Its Impact on National Legal Orders* (Deventer, Kluwer, 2004) 55 ff.
[72] *Lithgow v United Kingdom* Series A no 102 (1986) 8 EHRR 329, para 122.

In the context of measures affecting the use of property, the ECtHR has confirmed in *Mellacher*, which dealt with the interference by the Austrian authorities with the rental income of property owners, that:

> The Court will respect the legislature's judgment as to what is in the general interest unless that judgment be manifestly without reasonable foundation.[73]

The scrutiny of the ECtHR also focuses rather on the proportionality of the measure. It has held that measures interfering with the peaceful enjoyment of a person's possessions must strike a fair balance between the demands of the general interest of the community and the requirements of the protection of the individual's fundamental rights.[74] In so doing, the ECtHR recognises that the legislature enjoys a wide margin of appreciation, with regard both to choosing the means of enforcement and to ascertaining whether the consequences of enforcement are justified in the public interest for the purpose of achieving the object of the law in question.[75] Yet the ECtHR has also pointed out that the ECHR is intended to safeguard rights that are 'practical and effective', which involves looking behind appearances of the situation complained of, as well as the existence of procedural safeguards in order to ensure that the impact on property rights is neither arbitrary nor unforeseeable.[76]

The issue of compensation has been recognised by both the CJEU and the ECtHR as a dimension of the protection of the right to property, and is considered as part of the proportionality test. Unlike Article 1 of the First Additional Protocol, Article 17(1) of the Charter explicitly provides for the need for 'fair compensation being paid in good time'.[77] Neither court, however, propounds the need for full compensation in every circumstance. It has been observed by AG Mischo in *Booker Aquaculture* that the CJEU has so far never stated that any interference with property rights must necessarily be accompanied by compensation.[78] Some cases seem to evidence a relatively restrictive approach to compensation as a dimension of the EU fundamental right to property. For instance, *Booker Aquaculture*[79] involved claims for compensation on the basis of the fundamental right to property by Irish farmers in the context of the government-ordered destruction of diseased fish stock. The Court held that, while the Union legislature may consider, in the context of its broad discretion in the field of agricultural

---

[73]   *Mellacher v Austria* Series A no 169 (1989) 12 EHRR 391, para 45.

[74]   *Sporrong and Lönnroth v Sweden* Series A no 52 (1982) 5 EHRR 35, para 69.

[75]   *JA Pye (Oxford) Ltd v United Kingdom* (2007) 46 EHRR 1083, paras 50 and 70.

[76]   *Broniowski v Poland* (2005) 40 EHRR 495, para 151.

[77]   The drafting committee (the Praesidium of the Convention) added to this that 'the meaning and scope of the right are the same as those of the right guaranteed by the ECHR and the limitations may not exceed those provided for there'. See Art 41 of the ECHR: 'If the Court finds that there has been a violation of the Convention or the Protocols thereto, and if the internal law of the High Contracting Party concerned allows only partial reparation to be made, the Court shall, if necessary, afford just satisfaction to the injured party'. See also Art 340(2) TFEU: 'In the case of non-contractual liability, the Union shall, in accordance with the general principles common to the laws of the Member States, make good any damage caused by its institutions or by its servants in the performance of their duties'.

[78]   Opinion of AG Mischo, 20 September 2001, in Joined Cases C-20/00 and C-64/00 *Booker Aquaculture* [2003] ECR I-7411, para 80.

[79]   Joined Cases C-20/00 and C-64/00 *Booker Aquaculture* [2003] ECR I-7411.

policy, that full or partial compensation is appropriate in such circumstances, 'nonetheless, the existence, in [Union] law, of a general principle requiring compensation to be paid in all circumstances cannot be inferred from that fact'.[80] The Court, moreover, took a relatively restrictive approach to the issue of compensation in *ERSA*.[81] In relation to the prohibition of the use of certain terminology for the description and presentation of a number of Italian quality wines, it ruled that:

> the lack of any compensation for the dispossessed wine producers of Friuli . . . does not in itself constitute a circumstance demonstrating incompatibility between the prohibition at issue in the main proceedings and the right to property.[82]

It can be assumed that the EU fundamental right to property does not include a general right to full compensation.

Under Article 1 of the First Additional Protocol, the terms of compensation under the relevant legislation are also material to the assessment whether the contested measure imposes a disproportionate burden on the proprietor.[83] Similarly, however, the ECtHR has held that there is not always the need for full compensation in relation to interferences with property rights. A distinction is drawn between expropriations leading to a transfer of ownership, which fall within the first paragraph of Article 1 of the First Additional Protocol, and measures impairing the use of property, which fall under the second paragraph of Article 1 of the First Additional Protocol. With regard to the former, the ECtHR has held that:

> the taking of property without payment of an amount reasonably related to its value would normally constitute a disproportionate interference which could not be considered justifiable under Article 1 [of the First Additional Protocol].[84]

A total lack of compensation can be justifiable under the first paragraph of Article 1 of the First Additional Protocol only in exceptional circumstances.[85] The ECtHR has also held that Article 1 of the First Additional Protocol does not, however, guarantee a right to full compensation in all circumstances.[86] While in many cases of lawful expropriation, such as the expropriation of land with a view to building a road, only full compensation can be regarded as reasonably related to the value of the property, that rule is not without exceptions.[87] The ECtHR has held that:

---

[80] Ibid para 85.
[81] C-347/03 *ERSA* [2005] ECR I-3785.
[82] Ibid para 123.
[83] *Papachelas v Greece* (1999) 30 EHRR 923, para 48.
[84] *James v United Kingdom* Series A no 98 (1986) 8 EHRR 123, para 54.
[85] See *Jahn v Germany* (2005) 42 EHRR 1084, paras 91–93, where the 'exceptional circumstances' test was met as regards a land reform Act in the context of German reunification, and expropriation without compensation was considered justified in view of the uncertain legal position of the owners of land prior to reunification.
[86] *James* (above n 84) para 54.
[87] *Former King of Greece v Greece* (2000) 33 EHRR 516, para 78; *Scordino v Italy (No 1)* (2006) 45 EHRR 207, para 96.

Legitimate objectives of "public interest", such as pursued in measures of economic reform or measures designed to achieve greater social justice, may call for less than reimbursement of the full market value.[88]

Furthermore, the ECtHR has held that its power of review is limited to ascertaining whether the choice of compensation terms fall outside the state's wide margin of appreciation in this domain.[89]

The reference to the 'general principles of international law' in the first paragraph of Article 1 of the First Additional Protocol is potentially a source of the right to compensation for foreign investors that goes beyond what has just been outlined. This reference was originally included precisely because an express reference to a right to compensation in preparatory drafts of Article 1 of the First Additional Protocol was excluded.[90] It was the subject of several statements to the effect that it protects only foreign investors, as opposed to domestic investors.[91] In *James*, the ECtHR added to this that:

> although a taking of property must always be effected in the public interest, different considerations may apply to nationals and non-nationals and there may well be legitimate reason for requiring nationals to bear a greater burden in the public interest than non-nationals.[92]

Even though the reference to 'the general principles of international law' can be understood to entail the obligation to pay compensation to non-nationals in cases of expropriation, the level of compensation has so far been left unaddressed by the ECtHR.[93]

Foreign investors are less assured of adequate compensation as part of the proportionality test in relation to interferences with property rights falling under the second paragraph of Article 1 of the First Additional Protocol. That provision refers specifically to 'the right of a State to enforce such laws as it deems necessary to control the use of property in accordance with the general interest'. In *Pye (Oxford)*, the ECtHR observed that:

> in the cases in which a situation was analysed as a control of use, even though the applicant had lost possessions . . . no mention was made of a right to compensation.[94]

---

[88] *James* (above n 84) para 54. See also *Pye* (above n 75) para 54.

[89] *James* (above n 84) para 54. See also *Holy Monasteries v Greece* Series A no 301-A (1994) 20 EHRR 1, para 71. See also Art 41 of the ECHR: 'If the Court finds that there has been a violation of the Convention or the Protocols thereto, and if the internal law of the High Contracting Party concerned allows only partial reparation to be made, the Court shall, if necessary, afford just satisfaction to the injured party'.

[90] *James* (above n 84) para 64.

[91] See also Schutte, *European Fundamental Right to Property* (above n 71) 21.

[92] *James* (above n 84) para 64.

[93] In *James*, the applicant claimed that the international law requirement is that of 'prompt, adequate and effective compensation' (para 58), but the ECtHR did not deal with the issue. See in particular U Kriebaum, 'Nationality and the Protection of Property Rights under the European Convention on Human Rights' in I Buffard, J Crawford, A Pellet and S Wittich (eds), *International Law between Universalism and Fragmentation, Festschrift in Honour of Gerhard Hafner* (Leiden, Nijhoff, 2008).

[94] *Pye* (above n 75) para 79.

In relation to the forfeiture of coins under the procedure for the control of the use of gold coins in the United Kingdom, the ECtHR in *AGOSI*[95] did not refer to the need for compensation as part of the proportionality test.[96] In *Air Canada*,[97] in the context of the seizure of an Air Canada aircraft and subsequent payment required for the return of the aircraft as part of a policy of seeking to prevent carriers from bringing prohibited drugs into the United Kingdom, the ECtHR also did not refer to the need for compensation under the proportionality test in relation to measures interfering with the use of property.[98]

In short, the criteria for the legality of takings are fairly permissive in the EU legal order as well as under the ECHR. While both the CJEU and the ECtHR have shown deference in relation to the assessment of whether a public interest is at stake, the legitimacy of interferences is ultimately based on a balancing act between the public interest concerned and the property rights of the individual. The type of interference and the public interest concerned influence the weighing exercise to be made with respect to the need for compensation. Although in cases of deprivation of property there is a need for compensation, the level of compensation is not always that of full compensation. For interferences with the use of property, adequate compensation is less likely. Against this backdrop, it has been suggested that the approach to the issue of compensation in EU law and under the ECHR can be characterised as stemming from a public law and administrative law perspective, which is relatively restrictive of investor's rights in the light of the concern not to immobilise governmental action.[99]

Member State BITs in principle also respect the right of the Member States to interfere with property rights, subject to the condition that such measures (a) are taken in the public interest and under due process of law; (b) are not discriminatory; and (c) are accompanied by provision for the payment of just compensation.[100] In this regard, it has been observed by the tribunal in *Eureko* that there are overlaps with the right to property as secured by Article 17 of the Charter and Article 1 of the First Additional Protocol to the ECHR. However, the considerable body of jurisprudence on indirect takings that has emerged in the context of BITs and the fact that BITs protect 'assets' and 'investments' rather than the arguably narrower concepts of 'possessions' and 'property', seem to give rise to wider protection under intra-EU BITs.[101] Compensation for lawful expropriation under

---

[95] *AGOSI v United Kingdom* Series A no 108 (1986) 9 EHRR 1.

[96] *Ibid* paras 52–62.

[97] *Air Canada v United Kingdom* Series A no 316-A (1995) 20 EHRR 150.

[98] Ibid para 36 ff.

[99] TW Wälde and B Sabahi, 'Compensation, Damages, and Valuation' in P Muchlinski, F Ortino and C Schreuer (eds), *The Oxford Handbook of International Investment Law* (Oxford, Oxford University Press, 2008) 1055; G van Harten, *Investment Treaty Arbitration and Public Law* (Oxford, Oxford University Press, 2007) 101 ff.

[100] See, eg Art 5 of the Netherlands-Czech Republic BIT.

[101] *Eureko v Slovakia* (above n 19) Award on Jurisdiction, Arbitrability and Suspension, para 261. But see Kriebaum, 'Is the European Court of Human Rights an Alternative to Investor-State Arbitration?' (above n 65), who points out, inter alia, that property rights under the ECHR are protected independently from a specific economic usage. See also U Kriebaum and C Schreuer, 'The Concept of Property

most, if not all, investment agreements follows the principle of compensation awarded against the fair market value and is an objective standard that consists of what a willing buyer would have paid to a willing seller in a free transaction. For instance, Article 5(1) of the United Kingdom-Czech Republic BIT provides for 'prompt, adequate and effective compensation' in case of expropriation or measures having equivalent effect to nationalisation or expropriation. It is added that such compensation shall amount to:

> the real value of the investment expropriated immediately before the expropriation or before the impending expropriation became public knowledge, whichever is the earlier, and shall be paid within three months of the expropriation, be effectively realizable and be freely transferable.[102]

Reparation for an unlawful expropriation must even, insofar as possible, restore the situation that would have existed had the illegal act not been committed.[103] Damages in investment arbitration will consist mostly of monetary compensation in the case of unlawful expropriation too and may include lost profit where there is a deprivation of income. It thus seems possible to conclude that investors are more likely to receive appropriate compensation for interferences with their property rights under intra-EU BITs than under the investment protection rights that they enjoy pursuant to the fundamental right to property under EU law and the ECHR.

C. The Protection of 'Legitimate Expectations' in the EU Legal Order

In addition to the level of compensation in respect of a successful claim for direct or indirect expropriation under a BIT, foreign investors have the advantage of being able to turn to the standard of fair and equitable treatment (FET) in investment arbitration where a claim of direct or indirect expropriation cannot be substantiated. It has been observed that the key issue in assessing whether a host state has breached the FET standard is 'whether the host state has adversely affected the investment by substantially altering the legal and/or economic framework of the investment against the legitimate expectations of the investor'.[104] An example of

in Human Rights Law and International Investment Law' in S Breitmoser (ed), *Human Rights, Democracy and the Rule of Law* (Baden-Baden, Nomos, 2007).

[102] Article IV(3) of the World Bank Guidelines on the Treatment of Foreign Direct Investment, available at http://ita.law.uvic.ca/documents/WorldBank.pdf, stipulates that compensation will be deemed 'adequate' 'if it is based on the fair market value of the taken asset as such value is determined immediately before the time at which the taking occurred or the decision to take the asset became publicly known'. For the argument that 'adequate' compensation is not the same as 'full' compensation, see I Marboe, 'Compensation and Damages in International Law, the Limits of "Fair Market Value"' (2006) 5 *Journal of World Investment and Trade* 723, 731.

[103] See *Amco v Indonesia*, ICSID Case no ARB/81/1, Resubmitted Case, Award of 5 June 1990, (1990) 1 ICSID Rep 569, paras 163–284.

[104] L Paradell, 'The BIT Experience of the Fair and Equitable Treatment Standard' in F Ortino (ed), *Nationality and Investment Treaty Claims. Fair and Equitable Treatment in Investment Treaty Law, Current Issues II* (London, British Institute of International and Comparative Law, 2007) 131. More

an arbitration in which the tribunal first examined the claim for expropriation, which was unsuccessful, and then turned to the notion of legitimate expectations under the FET standard, is *CMS v Argentine*.[105] CMS claimed that the Argentinean government had suspended a tariff adjustment formula for gas transportation, in reliance on which CMS had invested in an Argentinean enterprise. From this award it seems to emerge that the threshold for a breach of the FET standard is in fact lower than that of a claim for direct or indirect expropriation, so that the former provides an additional layer of investment protection rights. Whereas the concept of legitimate expectations also exists in EU law, the tribunal in *Eureko* did not consider that a principle of FET, 'independent of concepts of non-discrimination, proportionality, legitimate expectation and of procedural fairness, is yet established in EU law'.[106] To be determined in this part is whether the principle of legitimate expectations under EU law provides for investment protection rights that are equivalent to those under the FET standard in Member State BITs.

The EU principle of legitimate expectations is a general principle of EU law and a specific expression of the principle of legal certainty.[107] The right to rely on the principle of legitimate expectations extends to any person in a situation where a Union authority has caused him to entertain expectations which are justified.[108] The Union itself must therefore have created a situation by means of specific assurances which can give rise to a legitimate expectation.[109] Such assurances may arise out of Union secondary legislation[110] or out of the conduct of the Union authorities that have led the investor to entertain reasonable expectations.[111] At the same time, if a prudent and alert economic operator could have foreseen the adoption of a Union measure likely to affect his interests, he cannot plead that principle when the measure is adopted.[112] The CJEU has also repeatedly held that a practice of a Member State which does not conform to Union rules may never give rise to a legitimate expectation on the part of an economic operator who has benefitted from the situation thus created.[113] The Court has moreover confirmed

generally, see M Potestà, 'Legitimate Expectations in Investment Treaty Law: Understanding the Roots and Limits of a Controversial Concept' (2013) 1 *ICSID Review* 88; I Tudor, *The Fair and Equitable Treatment Standard in the International Law of Foreign Investment* (Oxford, Oxford University Press, 2008); C Schreuer, 'Fair and Equitable Treatment in Arbitral Practice' (2005) 3 *Journal of World Investment and Trade* 357.

[105] *CMS v Argentine*, ICSID Case no ARB/01/08, Award of 12 May 2005, (2005) 44 ILM 1205.

[106] *Eureko v Slovakia* (above n 19) Award on Jurisdiction, Arbitrability and Suspension, para 250.

[107] T Tridimas, *The General Principles of EC Law* (Oxford, Oxford University Press, 2006) 242–97.

[108] Joined Cases C-182/03 and C-217/03 *Kingdom of Belgium and Forum 187 ASBL v Commission* [2006] ECR I-5479, paras 147–49.

[109] C-506/03 *Germany v Commission* (nyr, 2005) para 58. See also C-177/90 *Kühn* [1992] ECR I-35, para 14.

[110] 74/74 *CNTA v Commission* [1975] ECR 533, para 44.

[111] 289/81 *Mavridis v European Parliament* [1983] ECR 1731, para 21. See also C-630/11 P to C-633/11 P *HGA Srl and others v European Commission* (nyr, 2013) para 132: 'Precise, unconditional and consistent information, in whatever form it is given, constitutes such an assurance'.

[112] 265/85 *Van den Bergh and others v Commission* [1987] ECR 1155, para 44.

[113] C-568/11 *Agroferm A/S v Ministeriet for Fødevarer, Landbrug og Fiskeri* (nyr, 2013) para 52.

that the protection of legitimate expectations must be observed all the more strictly in the case of rules liable to have financial consequences.[114] Since the kind of legitimate expectations protected under EU law arise in relation to measures taken by or conduct of the Union institutions or national authorities, such legitimate expectations arise predominantly in regulated environments, such as the common market for agriculture.[115]

In the sphere of the common organisation of the markets within the Union, whose purpose involves constant adjustments to meet changes in the economic situation, the Court has taken the view that economic agents cannot legitimately expect that they will not be subject to restrictions arising out of future market rules or a structural policy.[116] It has been observed that one must establish a situation which 'crosses the line between what is merely "hard business luck" and what is unreasonable treatment' in order to rely on the principle of legitimate expectations.[117] In other words, a legitimate expectation is not created in a situation which can be altered by a Union institution exercising its discretionary powers.[118] As the Court held in *Faust*:

> Since [Union] institutions enjoy a margin of discretion in the choice of the means needed to achieve their policies, traders are unable to claim that they have a legitimate expectation that an existing situation which is capable of being altered by decisions taken by those institutions within the limit of their discretionary power will be maintained.[119]

In every case there will be a weighing exercise between the interests of the person in having his or her legitimate interest protected against the public interest that is in issue.[120] An example of a successful claim for damages in the context of a breach of the principle of legitimate expectations is *CNTA v Commission*.[121] In that case, the Commission had violated the legitimate expectations of a trader by failing to allow for a transitional period before abolishing a system for compensatory amounts applicable to rape and colza seeds. Compensation was limited to the positive damage suffered as a result of the expectation, but did not extend to any loss of profit which resulted from the disappointment of the expectation. This can be contrasted with the case of *Mulder*,[122] where the Court showed a willingness to compensate for lost profits.[123] However, the Court held that any income from replacement activities should be deducted from the sum of lost profits and that an 'injured party must show reasonable diligence in limiting the extent of his loss or

---

[114] Ibid para 47.

[115] E Sharpston, 'Legitimate Expectations and Economic Reality' (1990) *EL Rev* 103, 104.

[116] C-177/90 *Kühn* [1992] ECR I-35, para 13.

[117] Opinion of AG Slynn of 13 January 1988 in 120/86 *Mulder* [1988] ECR 2321, 2341.

[118] G Barrett, 'Protecting Legitimate Expectations in European Community Law and in Irish Domestic Law' (2001) *Yearbook on European Law* 191, 206.

[119] 52/81 *Faust* [1982] ECR 3745, para 27.

[120] Barrett, 'Protecting Legitimate Expectations' (above n 118) 213.

[121] 74/74 *CNTA v Commission* [1975] ECR 533.

[122] Joined Cases C-104/89 and C-37-90 *Mulder and others v Council and Commission* [1992] ECR I-3061.

[123] Ibid para 26 ff.

risk having to bear the damage himself'.[124] At the same time, it has been observed that challenges to Union or national measures on the basis of the principle of legitimate expectations in the EU legal order are usually not successful.[125]

Under investment agreements, the 'dominant element' of the FET standard is the notion of legitimate expectations.[126] That notion also focuses on the conduct of public authorities and relates to a situation, created by the public authorities, which can give rise to a legitimate expectation. To this effect, the arbitral tribunal in *LG&E* has stated that:

> the fair and equitable standard consists of the host State's consistent and transparent behaviour, free of ambiguity that involves the obligation to grant and maintain a stable and predictable legal framework necessary to fulfil the justified expectations of the foreign investor.[127]

The FET standard consists of the obligation of the contracting parties to provide a stable business environment for investors, consisting of a predictable legal framework. In particular, it is not acceptable for public authorities to renege on commitments on which the investor based its decision to invest.[128] Other specific rights related to the notion of legitimate expectations are 'the observation by the host State of such well-established fundamental standards as good faith, due process, and non-discrimination'.[129]

At the same time, it may seem that the notion of legitimate expectations under investment agreements has been interpreted by some arbitral tribunals as a source of investment protection rights that (at least in part and in certain circumstances) is capable of restricting the regulatory space of public authorities to a greater extent than EU law does. This seems to be evidenced by the approach taken by the arbitral tribunal in *Tecmed*, which stated that:

> The foreign investor expects the host State to act in a consistent manner, free from ambiguity and totally transparent in its relations with the foreign investor, so that it may know beforehand any and all rules and regulations that will govern its investments, as well as the goals of the relevant policies and administrative practices or directives, to be able to plan its investment and comply with such regulations.[130]

---

[124] Ibid para 33. The Court added that 'Any operating losses incurred by the applicants in carrying out such a replacement activity cannot be attributed to the Community, since the origin of such losses does not lie in the effects of the Community rules'.

[125] Barrett, 'Protecting Legitimate Expectations' (above n 118) 202; Sharpston, 'Legitimate Expectations' (above n 115) 132.

[126] *Saluka v Czech Republic* (above n 21) Partial Award, paras 301–02.

[127] *LG&E Energy v Argentina*, ICSID Case no ARB/02/1, Decision on Liability of 3 October 2006, (2007) 46 ILM 36, para 131.

[128] This is also illustrated by *CME v Czech Republic*, Partial Award of 13 September 2001, (2001) 9 ICSID Rep 121, para 611: 'The Media Council breached its obligation of fair and equitable treatment by evisceration of the arrangements in reliance upon which the foreign investment was induced to invest'.

[129] *Saluka v Czech Republic* (above n 21) Partial Award, para 306.

[130] *Tecmed v Mexico*, ICSID Case no ARB(AF)/00/2, Award of 29 May 2003, (2004) 43 ILM 133, para 154.

By stating that an investor has the right to know beforehand 'any and all rules and regulations' to which its investment will be subject, the FET standard would curtail the discretionary power of the state to implement structural policies that are designed to regulate certain sectors. It suggests that public authorities may have a duty to compensate investors in case of loss incurred as a result of any change of the regulatory environment that existed at the time of the investment. Similarly, the arbitral tribunal in *LG&E* stated that:

> the investor's fair expectations . . . are based on the conditions offered by the host State at the time of the investment; they may not be established unilaterally by one of the parties; they must exist and be enforceable by law; in the event of infringement by the host State, a duty to compensate the investor for damages arises except for those caused in the event of state of necessity; however, the investor's fair expectations cannot fail to consider parameters such as business risk or industry's regular patterns.[131]

While the arbitral tribunal points out that public authorities are not liable for any loss incurred by the investor in a state of necessity or resulting from ordinary business risks, it does not refer to the discretion of the state in exercising its regulatory authority.

Other arbitral tribunals have given more guidance as to the potential limits to the scope of the notion of legitimate expectations under investment agreements, with the effect that the FET standard was not interpreted so as to contain an obligation of stability or predictability.[132] For example, in *Saluka* the tribunal indicated that it did not consider it reasonable or legitimate for the investor to expect that the circumstances prevailing at the time that the investment is made remain totally unchanged.[133] Instead, the arbitral tribunal referred to 'the host state's legitimate right to regulate domestic matters' without, however, specifying the scope of the host state's regulatory authority.[134] Similarly, in *CMS*, the arbitral tribunal held that 'It is not a question of whether the legal framework might need to be frozen as it can always evolve and be adapted to changing circumstances.'[135] It was thus recognised that an investor cannot legitimately expect that the regulatory framework remains completely unchanged. In the light of the fact that investors have a legitimate interest in a stable and predictable regulatory framework, whereas public authorities may perceive a need to regulate certain domestic matters, the tribunal in *Saluka* pointed out that the notion of legitimate expectations ultimately 'requires a weighing of the Claimant's legitimate and reasonable expectations on the one hand and the Respondent's legitimate regulatory interests on the other'.[136] Yet, while there is thus a need for arbitral tribunals to weigh the interests of investors against legitimate public interests, the FET standard

---

[131] *LG&E* (above n 127) Decision on Liability, para 130.
[132] A Newcombe and L Paradell, *Law and Practice of Investment Treaties* (Alphen aan den Rijn, Kluwer Law International, 2009) 285 ff.
[133] *Saluka v Czech Republic* (above n 21) Partial Award, para 305.
[134] Ibid.
[135] Award in *CMS* (above n 105) para 277.
[136] *Saluka v Czech Republic* (above n 21) Partial Award, para 306.

arguably has to be interpreted in light of the objective of the promotion and protection of foreign investment.[137] The goal of encouraging business confidence has therefore been analysed as having taken precedence in some arbitrations over other concerns of public interest, such as the environment (*Metalclad*[138]) and public health (*Azurix*[139]).[140] As such, the approach favoured by some tribunals has been characterised as being predicated on the protection of the rights of investors while discarding the need to accommodate the exercise of official authority.[141]

The FET standard under Member State BITs has been interpreted by some arbitral tribunals with a predominant focus on the provision of a stable and predictable investment environment, but to a lesser extent by other tribunals. The principle of legitimate expectations under EU law seems to be inherently focused on the regulatory purpose of the measures concerned in conjunction with the legitimate intention of the legislator, pursuant to which the regulatory powers of public authorities might be respected to a larger extent. Given that differences in the scrutiny of certain Member State measures by Union or Member State courts, on the one hand, and by arbitral tribunals under BITs, on the other, are not inconceivable, it cannot be excluded that actions by investors under the FET standard succeed in investment treaty arbitration, whereas they would be unsuccessful in Union or Member State courts. In addition to a different weighing exercise that could be made by an arbitral tribunal in respect of the legitimate expectations of the investor and the state's discretionary power to regulate domestic matters, investors will not be entitled to full compensation in all circumstances of interferences with property rights under EU law, in particular when there is a public interest that mandates the interference. While compensation for breaches of the FET standard depends on the seriousness of the breach, there have been instances where these may have surpassed the level of compensation that would be appropriate under EU law. For instance, in *CMS*,[142] the tribunal followed the standard of compensation for expropriation by awarding the fair market value of the investment since a wrongful act led to total deprivation of property rights. Compensation for a breach of legitimate expectations under EU law normally amounts to the reasonable costs incurred by the claimant in reliance on governmental assurances rather than its interest in future performance.[143]

---

[137] Newcombe and Paradell, *Law and Practice of Investment Treaties* (above n 132) 268.

[138] *Metalclad Corporation v Mexico*, ICSID Case no ARB(AF)/97/1, Award of 30 August 2000, (2002) 5 ICSID Rep 212.

[139] *Azurix v Argentine Republic*, ICSID Case no ARB/01/12, Award of 14 July 2006.

[140] A Dimopoulos, 'Shifting the Emphasis from Investment Protection to Liberalization and Development: The EU as a New Global Factor in the Field of Foreign Investment' (2010) 1 *JWI* 5, 7.

[141] Van Harten, *Investment Treaty Arbitration and Practice* (above n 99) 143. But see C Schreuer and U Kriebaum, 'From Individual to Community Interest in International Investment Law' in U Fastenrath and B Simma (eds), *From Bilateralism to Community Interest: Essays in Honour of Judge Bruno Simma* (Oxford, Oxford University Press, 2011) 1079–96; M Waibel et al (eds), *The Backlash Against Investment: Perceptions and Reality* (Alphen aan den Rijn, Kluwer Law International, 2010).

[142] Award in *CMS* (above n 105).

[143] Wälde and Sabahi, 'Compensation, Damages, and Valuation' (above n 99) 1089.

It therefore seems possible to conclude that intra-EU investment agreements can be regarded as a useful complement for investors to the investment protection rights held in the EU legal order, including in relation to matters that fall under the scope of EU law. Even insofar as there is a degree of overlap in the investment protection rights enshrined in the EU legal order and in investment agreements, these rights are not always entirely equivalent.[144] This, moreover, is not solely due to the fact that investors have access to international arbitration under BITs. That Member States never perceived the need to conclude intra-EU BITs can thus only be partly explained with reference to the investment protection rights held by investors under EU law. It is therefore also no surprise that disputes, of which the legal nexus with EU law postdates accession of the Member State against which the claim is directed, have been brought under intra-EU BITs and will continue to be so as long as these agreements remain in force.

III. EU LAW AND INTRA-EU BITS: CONSTITUTIONAL ASPECTS

In this section a number of constitutional aspects of the interplay between EU law and intra-EU BITs will be discussed in view of the latter's acquired intra-EU status. First to be scrutinised is the claim that EU law has directly impinged on the validity of the BITs concerned upon accession of the Central and Eastern European Member States concerned. The section then probes the operation of the principle of primacy in relation to the agreements in issue. The section argues that the EU legal framework governing the interplay between EU law and intra-EU BITs does not affect the validity of these agreements. At the same time, it would be ill-conceived to be too dismissive of the EU legal aspects of investment disputes between an EU investor and a host Member State in view of the operation of the principle of primacy.

A. The Validity of Intra-EU BITs is Not in Issue

Both the Czech Republic and Slovakia have argued in recent investment arbitrations that their BITs with the Netherlands had automatically terminated upon accession to the EU.[145] In *Eastern Sugar*, even if the BIT in issue had not been expressly terminated, the Czech Republic claimed that it had been implicitly terminated because the agreement and EU law are 'competing legal frameworks addressing the same subject-matter' in the light of Article 59 of the Vienna Convention on the Law of Treaties (VCLT). It has also been suggested that these

---

[144] See also the analysis of the tribunal in *Eureko v Slovakia* (above n 19) Award on Jurisdiction, Arbitrability and Suspension, paras 250–62.

[145] *Eastern Sugar v Czech Republic* (above n 1) Partial Award, para 97 ff; *Eureko v Slovakia* (above n 19) Award on Jurisdiction, Arbitrability and Suspension, para 63 ff.

agreements were naturally going to be extinct upon accession of the Central and Eastern European countries concerned.[146] In the view of Poulain, these agreements only had 'valeur conjoncturelle' in the context of the 'rattrapage économique' of these countries.[147] Drawing a parallel between the BITs in issue and the EAs that were concluded with these countries at about the same time, Poulain contends that nobody was seriously going to argue that the EAs had remained in force after accession.[148] Upon this view, the Accession Treaties substituted for both the EAs and the BITs in issue. Yet, the view that these agreements would have automatically terminated upon accession of the countries concerned cannot be accepted for a number of reasons.

In the first place, it is prima facie implausible that accession would *ipso facto* have brought an end to these agreements. There is no mention in the BITs that they would apply only until accession, nor do any of the EAs or the Accession Treaties give any explicit indication as to the presumed temporary application of these agreements. As was explained above (I), the Central and Eastern European countries were encouraged to conclude BITs with Member States under the investment promotion provisions in the EAs. While these instruments were supposed to prepare these countries for accession, there is no explicit provision in the EAs with regard to the automatic termination of these agreements. The same point is evidenced by Article 6(12) of the 2003 Act of Accession, under which the new Member States were to:

> take appropriate measures, where necessary, to adjust their position in relation to . . . international agreements to which the Community or to which other Member States are also parties, to the rights and obligations arising from their accession to the Union.[149]

It thus seems that there was no presumption of the contracting parties to these agreements as to their alleged termination upon accession. Similarly, under the ECT, the (then) Community did not issue any declaration with regard to the intra-EU applicability of the agreement, nor with regard to the effect of accession of the Central and Eastern European countries concerned on the intra-EU status of the agreement. It is thus difficult to argue that there was any intention of the contracting parties of the BITs in issue to the effect that these agreements would automatically cease to be in force upon accession.

---

[146] B Poulain, 'Quelques interrogations sur le status des traités bilatéraux de promotion et de protection des investissements au sein de l'Union européenne' (2007) 4 *Revue Générale de Droit International Public* 803, 809.

[147] Ibid 809.

[148] Ibid 815.

[149] Concerning the conditions of accession of the Czech Republic, the Republic of Estonia, the Republic of Cyprus, the Republic of Latvia, the Republic of Lithuania, the Republic of Hungary, the Republic of Malta, the Republic of Poland, the Republic of Slovenia and the Slovak Republic [2003] OJ L236/33.

Under international law,[150] the appropriate starting point of an analysis of whether accession has impinged on the validity of these BITs is Article 59(1) VCLT,[151] which sets two conditions on the implicit termination of an agreement as a result of the conclusion of a later agreement as between the same contracting parties. First, the later agreement must have the same subject matter as the earlier agreement. Secondly, the parties must, in addition, either have intended the later agreements to substitute for the earlier agreement or the two agreements must be widely incompatible. As to the first condition, for two treaties to deal with the 'same subject matter' does not mean that they need to cover exactly the same issues.[152] In this respect, arbitral tribunals in both *Eastern Sugar* and *Eureko* have taken the view that EU law, without prejudice to the wide array of issues that EU law deals with, is not specifically devoted to investment protection. Yet it has been argued above (II) that considerations of investment protection are certainly not absent from EU law, so that the subject matter of BITs and that of EU law are clearly related. At the same time, EU law does not seem to set entirely the same standards of investment protection as bilateral investment agreements. EU law also does not provide for the same kind of legal remedies as investment agreements, which are to be considered as part and parcel of the investment protection regime established by intra-EU BITs.

As to the second condition, the point has already been made that it is difficult to argue that the parties intended the agreements to be substituted by EU law upon accession of the countries concerned. Yet, as will be discussed below (IV, V), it has been argued that issues of substantive compatibility between intra-EU BITs and EU law arise. The question whether these issues of compatibility are such as to make intra-EU BITs sufficiently widely incompatible with EU law under the terms of Article 59(1)(b) VCLT is more appropriately addressed in that section. For the present purpose, it can, however, be pointed out that even if issues of substantive or procedural compatibility exist between intra-EU BITs and EU law, the Union regime on treaty conflicts is not such as to directly affect the validity of the BITs in issue. Whereas the EU Treaties do not contain any provision that specifically addresses the post-accession status of pre-accession agreements with former third countries, the case law of the CJEU does not directly support any

---

[150] For analysis of the extent to which the courts of the Union consider the VCLT as applicable only to treaties concluded by the Union or also to the EU Treaties, see PJ Kuijper, 'The Court and the Tribunal of the EC and the Vienna Convention on the Law of Treaties 1969' (1998) 1 *Legal Issues of European Integration* 1. Article 59 is not considered, however.

[151] Article 59 VCLT: '1. A treaty shall be considered as terminated if all the parties to it conclude a later treaty relating to the same subject-matter and (a) it appears from the later treaty or is otherwise established that the parties intended that the matter should be governed by that treaty; or (b) the provisions of the later treaty are so far incompatible with those of the earlier one that the two treaties are not capable of being applied at the same time.'

[152] Report of the Study Group of the International Law Commission, 'Fragmentation of International Law: Difficulties Arising from the Diversification and Expansion of International Law', finalised by M Koskenniemi, UN doc A/CN.4/L.682, 13 April 2006, para 254: 'the test of whether two treaties deal with the "same subject matter" is resolved through the assessment of whether the fulfillment of the obligation under one treaty affects the fulfillment of the obligation of another'.

purported effect of EU law on the validity of such agreements. Rather, the effect of EU law on Member State agreements, which have acquired intra-EU status, is arguably not to invalidate these agreements, but merely to render them inapplicable insofar as they are incompatible with EU law.[153]

This is evidenced by the case of *Matteucci*,[154] which concerned the implementation of a cultural agreement between Belgium and Germany of 1956. In view of the fact that the agreement strictly reserved scholarships to nationals of the two Member States that are parties to the agreement, which was ruled to be incompatible with the principle of non-discrimination, the Court held that 'the application of [Union] law cannot be precluded on the ground that it would affect the implementation of a cultural agreement between two Member States'.[155]

In *Matteucci*, the Court thus approached the interplay between the intra-EU agreement and EU law from the angle of the application of the agreement concerned, and not from that of its validity. In *Exportur*,[156] which dealt with the effect of accession of Spain on a pre-existing agreement with France, notwithstanding issues of compatibility, the Court also did not question the validity of the agreement concerned. In this case, the Court ruled that:

> the provisions of a convention concluded after 1 January 1958 by a Member State with another State could not, from the accession of the latter State to the Community, apply in the relations between those States if they were found to be contrary to the rules of the Treaty.[157]

In other words, even if a pre-existing agreement of an acceding Member State with another Member State gives rise to issues of compatibility with EU law, EU law does not directly purport to impinge on the validity of the pre-existing agreement.

Since the two Member States that are parties to an intra-EU BIT have subscribed to the *acquis*, which even in the case of incompatibilities with EU law does not purport to directly affect the validity of these agreements, it is implausible that they would have been implicitly terminated in the light of Article 59(1) VCLT.[158] Given that the purported effect of EU law on the BITs in issue has not been to terminate automatically these agreements pursuant to the new legal obligations assumed by the acceding Member States, significant doubt is cast on the proposition that the validity of these agreements would have been directly affected under international law pursuant to accession of the Central and Eastern European Member States concerned. It seems difficult to argue that the agreements would

---

[153] See R Schütze, 'EC Law and International Agreements of the Member States: An Ambivalent Relationship?' (2006–2007) *Cambridge Yearbook of European Legal Studies* 387, 408. But see J Klabbers, *Treaty Conflict and the European Union* (Cambridge, Cambridge University Press, 2009) 126; A Dimopoulos, 'The Validity and Applicability of International Investment Agreements between EU Member States under EU and International Law' (2011) 1 *CML Rev* 63, 71.

[154] 235/87 *Matteucci* [1988] ECR 5589.

[155] Ibid para 14.

[156] C-3/91 *Exportur* [1992] ECR I-5529.

[157] Ibid para 8.

[158] But see Dimopoulos, 'The Validity and Applicability of International Investment Agreements' (above n 153) 73.

be sufficiently widely incompatible with EU law for that very reason, since intra-EU BITs can in principle co-exist with EU law in the eyes of the *acquis*.

The validity argument has, moreover, been rejected from an international law point of view by the arbitral tribunals in *Eastern Sugar* and *Eureko*.[159] An important reason for rejecting the validity argument from an international law point of view is that the operation of Article 59 VCLT is subject to the provisions of Article 65 VCLT, which deals with the procedure to be followed with respect to invalidity, termination, withdrawal from or suspension of the operation of a treaty. Article 65(1) VCLT provides that:

> A party which, under the provisions of the present Convention, invokes either a defect in its consent to be bound by a treaty or a ground for impeaching the validity of a treaty, terminating it, withdrawing from it or suspending its operation, must notify the other parties of its claim. The notification shall indicate the measure proposed to be taken with respect to the treaty and the reasons therefor.

The tribunal in *Eureko* did not accept that a notification for the purposes of Article 65 VCLT had been issued.[160] In addition, while Article 65(5) VCLT provides the possibility for a state, which has not previously made the notification as prescribed in Article 65(1) VCLT, to make such a notification in answer to another party claiming performance of the treaty or alleging its violation, the tribunal in *Eureko* countered this argument by pointing out that the investor claimant was not a contracting party to the BIT and that the other conditions for the application of Article 59 VCLT were in any case not met.[161]

B. The Operation of the Principle of Primacy in relation to Intra-EU BITs

The argument has been advanced that EU law does not impinge on the validity of intra-EU BITs, but also that 'the intra-EU effects of BITs have not been affected or amended by a state's membership in the EU'.[162] A number of arbitral tribunals have taken a similarly dismissive view of the legal effect of EU law on the continued application of intra-EU BITs. For example, in *ADC*, the need to comply with EU law was not accepted as a line of defence of a Member State against an alleged breach of the investment treatment standards under an intra-EU BIT.[163] For the purpose of addressing those claims, arbitral tribunals have resorted to Article 59(2) VCLT, which provides that:

> The earlier treaty shall be considered as only suspended in operation if it appears from the later treaty or is otherwise established that such was the intention of the parties.

[159] See also T Eilmansberger, 'Bilateral Investment Treaties and EU Law' (2009) 2 *CML Rev* 383, 400 ff.
[160] *Eureko v Slovakia* (above n 19) Award on Jurisdiction, Arbitrability and Suspension, para 236.
[161] Ibid para 238.
[162] C Söderlund, 'Intra-EU Investment Protection and the EC Treaty' (2007) 5 *Journal of International Arbitration* 455, 457.
[163] *ADC v Hungary* (above n 3) Award para 272.

Moreover, Article 30(3) VCLT provides:

> When all the parties to the earlier treaty are parties also to the later treaty, but the earlier treaty is not terminated or suspended in operation under article 59, the earlier treaty applies only to the extent that its provisions are compatible with those of the later treaty.

Importantly, while Article 59 is concerned with the termination of the entire treaty, Article 30 deals with the primacy between certain provisions of the earlier and later treaty in relation to the same subject matter. As a result, it has been observed that Article 59 requires a broader incompatibility between the two treaties.[164]

Without prejudice to these rules of treaty conflict under international law, the substantive conflict rule under EU law that governs the relation between the obligations of Member States under EU law and those under international agreements *inter se,* is the principle of primacy. Under EU law, the application of intra-EU BITs can potentially be affected as a result of the operation of the principle of primacy, since EU law precludes that intra-EU BITs impinge on the EU legal obligations of the Member States. The principle of primacy determines that EU law prevails over conflicting *inter se* agreements.[165] To be determined is the precise operation of the principle of primacy in relation to intra-EU BITs, the extent to which it deviates from the ordinary treaty conflict rules under international law, and what potential effect it has on dispute settlement under intra-EU BITs.

The early case of *Commission v Italy,*[166] which involved pre-existing obligations of the Member States in their relations *inter se* under the GATT, confirmed that (now) Article 351(1) TFEU, which protects the rights of third countries under pre-accession agreements, does not apply to agreements that have subsequently been imported into the Union as international legal commitments of the Member States *inter se.*[167] The CJEU held that Article 351(1) TFEU cannot be relied on to enforce obligations against other Member States, since:

> by virtue of the principles of international law, by assuming a new obligation which is incompatible with rights held under a prior treaty a State *ipso facto* gives up the exercise of these rights to the extent necessary for the performance of its new obligations.[168]

The principle that the obligations of a Member State under EU law take precedence over the obligations under a pre-existing agreement with another Member State reflects the rule of Article 30(3) VCLT that a later treaty prevails among the

---

[164] See also *Eureko v Slovakia* (above n 19) Award on Jurisdiction, Arbitrability and Suspension, paras 240–41, with reference to the ILC Commentary on the draft Article 59 (then numbered Article 56), 253, para 4, available at http://untreaty.un.org/ilc/texts/instruments/english/commentaries/1_1_1966.pdf.

[165] B de Witte, 'Old-fashioned Flexibility: International Agreements between the Member States of the European Union' in G de Búrca and J Scott (eds), *Constitutional Change in the EU: From Uniformity to Flexibility* (Oxford, Hart Publishing, 2000).

[166] 10/61 *Commission v Italy* [1962] ECR 1.

[167] Ibid 10: 'the terms "rights and obligations" in [Art 351(1) TFEU] refer, as regards the "rights", to the rights of third countries and, as regards the "obligations", to the obligations of Member States'.

[168] Ibid.

states parties to both treaties. While the principle of primacy is suspended under Article 351(1) TFEU in relation to pre-existing agreements with third countries, the Court took the view that:

> in matters governed by the EU Treaties, [those Treaties take] precedence over agreements concluded between Member States before its entry into force, including agreements made within the framework of GATT.[169]

In other words, since the Member States have subscribed to EU law upon accession to the Union, they cannot plead the need to comply with obligations under prior agreements *inter se* if, by doing so, they would act in violation of their obligations under EU law.

In *Matteucci*, the Court confirmed that the (then) EEC Treaty took precedence over agreements concluded between Member States before its entry into force.[170] The application of the intra-EU agreement was held to be incompatible with Article 7(2) of Regulation 1612/68.[171] The case of *Matteucci* confirms that the principle of primacy operates not only so far as incompatibilities between *inter se* agreements and the Treaties are concerned, but also in relation to incompatibilities between *inter se* agreements and Union secondary legislation. The case of *Exportur* is an example of a situation in which a national court had accepted that an international agreement had to be set aside after accession of a third country to the Union. In this case, the Court observed that the referring French court had rightly considered that:

> the provisions of a convention concluded after 1 January 1958 by a Member State with another State could not, from the accession of the latter State to the [Union], apply in the relations between those States if they were found to be contrary to the rules of the [Treaties].[172]

The Court has thus specified that the effect of EU law taking precedence over international legal obligations of the Member States *inter se* is that the agreement, which has acquired intra-EU status as a result of accession of a former third country to the Union, has to be set aside by national courts.[173] In other words, the operation of the principle of primacy in relation to international agreements of the Member States *inter se* is that such agreements need to be disapplied insofar as they are incompatible with EU law.[174]

---

[169] Ibid.

[170] 235/87 *Matteucci* [1988] ECR 5589, para 22.

[171] Council Regulation 1612/68 of 15 October 1968 on freedom of movement for workers within the Community [1968] OJ L257/2.

[172] C-3/91 *Exportur* [1992] ECR I-5529, para 8.

[173] So far as concerns an international agreement that applies between Member States *inter se* but that also has non-Member States as contracting parties, which is of relevance to the ECT, the Court has taken the view that pre-accession obligations vis-à-vis non-Member States need to be honoured under Art 351(1) TFEU, but that the Member States cannot exercise rights under such agreements in intra-EU relations in defiance of EU law. See 34/79 *Henn and Darby* [1979] ECR 3795, para 26; C-147/03 *Commission v Austria* [2005] ECR I-563, para 58.

[174] Similarly, national courts do not need to invalidate or annul, but merely disapply, provisions of domestic law that are in conflict with EU law. See 106/77 *Simmenthal* [1978] ECR 629, para 21; Joined Cases C-10 to C-22/97 *IN.CO.GE'90* [1998] ECR I-6307, para 21.

With respect to the post-accession status of intra-EU BITs, the Commission has drawn the conclusion from this line of case law that 'For facts occurring after accession, the BIT is not applicable to matters falling under [Union] competence'.[175] This is arguably an incorrect approach to the operation of the principle of primacy in relation to intra-EU BITs. The main issue as regards the interplay between EU law and intra-EU BITs is not that of competence, but compatibility. The principle of primacy has the effect that intra-EU agreements, in the eyes of EU law, are inapplicable insofar as they are incompatible with matters falling under the scope of application of EU law. The use of the term 'competence' suggests that intra-EU BITs are inapplicable insofar as they merely overlap with existing Union secondary legislation, or even with a mere legislative competence of the Union. Under EU law, intra-EU BITs are in fact only inapplicable if there is an actual conflict (in the sense of a substantive incompatibility) with EU primary law or existing secondary legislation.[176] The operation of the principle of primacy in relation to intra-EU BITs is thus not to limit their applicability to issues outside the scope of EU law: it prescribes that Member States may not renege on their obligations under EU law in order to comply with agreements with other Member States. Insofar as intra-EU BITs are compatible with EU law, they remain applicable.

The principle of primacy entails specific obligations for the Member States in their relations with other Member States. They are not only precluded from pleading the need to comply with intra-EU BITs in order to justify their acting in derogation from EU law. In *Matteucci*, the Court observed that the obligation under (now) Article 351(2) TFEU to modify, or even to denounce, international agreements that are incompatible with EU law does not extend to international agreements between the Member States *inter se*.[177] However, as the Court observed, (now) Article 4(3) TEU provides that the Member States must take all appropriate measures to ensure fulfilment of their EU legal obligations. The Court considered that:

> If, therefore, the application of a provision of [Union] law is liable to be impeded by a measure adopted pursuant to the implementation of a bilateral agreement . . . every Member State is under a duty to facilitate the application of the provision and, to that end, to assist every other Member State which is under an obligation under [Union] law.[178]

The Court held in particular that a Member State may not prevent another Member State from fulfilling the obligations imposed on it by EU law where this

---

[175] *Eastern Sugar v Czech Republic* (above n 1) Partial Award, para 119.

[176] But see Dimopoulos, 'The Validity and Applicability of International Investment Agreements' (above n 153) 78, who extends the notion of 'incompatibilities' to 'potential incompatibilities'.

[177] 235/87 *Matteucci* [1988] ECR 5589, paras 21–22. But see B de Witte, 'Internationale verdragen tussen lidstaten van de Europese Unie' in RA Wessel and B de Witte, *De plaats van de Europese Unie in het veranderende bestel van de volkenrechtelijke organisatie, Mededelingen van de Nederlandse Vereniging voor Internationaal Recht* (The Hague, TMC Asser Press, 2001) 79, 116.

[178] Ibid para 19.

is mandated by a bilateral agreement between those two Member States.[179] In other words, whenever the principle of primacy requires a Member State to yield to its EU legal obligations in derogation from its obligations under an international agreement with another Member State, the latter should not oppose the intra-EU agreement to the Member State that would consequently have to act in defiance of EU law.

The operation of the principle of primacy in relation to BITs which have acquired intra-EU status does not depart from the ordinary conflict rules of international law. In fact, it accords with the principle that later treaties prevail over earlier treaties amongst the same contracting parties. However, it seems possible to argue that EU law departs from the ordinary conflict rules of international law insofar as the principle of primacy precludes *inter se* modifications of the commitments assumed by the Member States under EU law.[180] Under international law, *inter se* modifications are a way of revising multilateral agreements without affecting the application of the earlier multilateral agreement with other contracting parties.[181] *Inter se* modifications thus give rise to two types of legal relations: there are the 'general' relations that apply between all the parties to the original treaty and the 'special' relations that apply between the states parties to the later *inter se* agreement.[182] Yet, the Member States can under no circumstance 'contract out' of their EU legal obligations pursuant to the principle of primacy.[183] At the same time, the impossibility of *inter se* modifications under EU law could arguably be mandated by Article 41(b) VCLT, under which two or more of the parties to a multilateral treaty may conclude an agreement to modify the treaty as between themselves alone if 'the modification in question is not prohibited by the treaty and (i) does not affect the enjoyment by the other parties of their rights under the treaty or the performance of their obligations; (ii) does not relate to a provision, derogation from which is incompatible with the effective execution of the object and purpose of the treaty as a whole'.

Since the Member States have never perceived the need to conclude intra-EU investment agreements, for an arbitral tribunal to be asked to consider the effect of EU law on the applicability of an intra-EU BIT in the light of the fact that the BIT was concluded posterior to when the two contracting parties assumed their obligations under EU law, is a situation that is unlikely to arise in future. If two Member States did envisage concluding an intra-EU BIT, this would not, however, affect their obligations under EU law. This can be further illustrated with

---

[179] See also de Witte, 'Old-fashioned Flexibility' (above n 165) 51; M Cremona, 'Defending the Community Interest: The Duties of Cooperation and Compliance' in M Cremona and B de Witte, *EU Foreign Relations Law: Constitutional Fundamentals* (Oxford, Hart Publishing, 2008) 125, 134 ff.

[180] See de Witte, 'Old-fashioned Flexibility' (above n 165) 47.

[181] Report of the Study Group of the International Law Commission, *Fragmentation of International Law: Difficulties Arising from the Diversification and Expansion of International Law*, finalised by M Koskenniemi, UN doc A/CN.4/L.682, 13 April 2006, paras 295–96.

[182] Ibid para 301.

[183] Cf HF van Panhuys, 'Conflicts between the Law of the European Communities and other Rules of International Law' (1966) *CML Rev* 420, 438 ff, who argues that EU law does not necessarily preclude such *inter se* modifications.

reference to the ECT, which was concluded as a mixed agreement with a number of third countries. Since the ECT does not contain a disconnection clause, it was also concluded as having legal effect between the Member States *inter se*. In the eyes of international law, the ECT could possibly be characterised as a modification of the commitments of these Member States under EU law, as the ECT was concluded by some of the present Member States after they had assumed their obligations under EU law. Importantly, however, the principle of primacy precludes such modifications of the *acquis*. In the eyes of EU law, the ECT cannot affect the Member States' commitments under EU law insofar as intra-EU situations are concerned, and a Member State would act in violation of EU law if it would give priority to such conflicting legal obligations under the ECT.

It can, moreover, be observed that the Union is a contracting party to the ECT. It is thus binding on the Union and it has become part of the EU legal order. This raises the issue that the obligations of the Union under the ECT have for that reason (as a matter of EU law) primacy over Union secondary legislation.[184] Under the ECT, the issue of the application of Article 351 TFEU can moreover potentially come into play as regards the obligations of the newly acceded Member States vis-à-vis third countries under the ECT that pre-date accession.[185] These obligations are to be distinguished from those of the same Member States, which acceded to the Union after assuming their obligations under the ECT, vis-à-vis other Member States. This qualifies neither as an *inter se* modification of the obligations of the Member States under EU law, nor as a situation that primarily involves the obligations of the Union vis-à-vis a third country. It is similar to the problem of the continued validity and application of intra-EU BITs.[186]

Inter se agreements of the Member States trigger the principle of primacy only insofar as they give rise to issues of substantive incompatibility with EU law. The principle of primacy is not a choice of law rule, so that *inter se* agreements of the Member States continue to apply insofar as these agreements merely overlap with EU law. The circumstances in which intra-EU BITs reveal an incompatibility with EU law are arguably less broadly defined than those in which extra-EU BITs do. It has been shown in chapter 4 that a logic of affectation is at work in the context of Member State agreements with third countries, while intra-EU agreements only give rise to an incompatibility with EU law insofar as there is an actual conflict. As a result, the type of incompatibilities found in the 'BITs' judgments could be of limited relevance to issues of compatibility between EU law and intra-EU BITs.[187] In those cases, the CJEU was concerned with the *effet utile* of provisions empowering

---

[184] See C-61/94 *Commission v Germany* [1996] ECR I-3989, para 52. See also the text at chapter 4, II.A and accompanying notes.

[185] See the text at chapter 4, II.A.

[186] It can be observed that the tribunal in *Electrabel* took the view that EU law prevails over the ECT in intra-EU situations. See *Electrabel v Hungary*, ICSID Case no ARB/07/19, Decision on Jurisdiction, Applicable Law and Liability of 30 November 2012, para 4.178 ff. For more analysis, see the text at V and accompanying notes.

[187] But see F Benyon, *Direct Investment, National Champions and the EU Treaty Freedoms* (Oxford, Hart Publishing, 2010) 111.

the Council to take restrictive measures in relation to capital transfers to and from third countries. The Court explicitly referred to the incompatibilities in question as pertaining to the 'risk of conflict'.[188] A need to preclude a mere *risk* of conflict, it can be argued, is more appropriate in the context of Member State agreements with third countries, since the *pacta tertiis* rule prevents the obligations of the Member States vis-à-vis the latter from being affected by EU law and an agreement with a third country for that reason cannot be disapplied. It is therefore also quite clear that it is even more difficult to make a case for the appropriateness of a general 'hypothetical incompatibility' test in the context of intra-EU BITs than it is in the context of extra-EU BITs.

Unlike Member State agreements with third countries, an intra-EU agreement can in principle be set aside when both contracting states are Member States of the European Union in view of their EU law obligations. Nevertheless, the technique of disapplying incompatible provisions of intra-EU agreements is arguably circumscribed by the need to safeguard the principle of legal certainty. This is illustrated in *Commission v Belgium*,[189] where the Court took the view that:

> Even if, in practice, the authorities of a Member State do not apply a national provision which is at variance with Community law, the principle of legal certainty nevertheless requires that that provision be amended.[190]

In other words, maintaining a provision of national law in force that is incompatible with EU law, even if it is not applied, may nevertheless amount to a failure by the Member State in question to comply with its EU law obligations. It seems possible to argue that the principle of legal certainty circumscribes the technique of disapplying incompatible provisions of intra-EU agreements in the same way as regards incompatible provisions of national law. What this could mean in the specific context of intra-EU BITs, remains to be seen, however.

As a result of the operation of the principle of primacy, a Member State cannot plead the need to comply with the standards of treatment enshrined in an intra-EU BIT as a justification for non-compliance with its obligations under EU law. There is not much of a problem where a Member State is found to have infringed BIT standards of treatment when it had discretion in giving effect to its obligations under EU law. This may be different where a Member State acted more specifically in order to comply with its obligations under EU law. As to the implications of the principle of primacy for the application of intra-EU BITs, the Commission has taken the view that, 'where the [EU Treaties] or secondary legislation are in conflict with some of these BITs' provisions – or should the EU adopt such rules in the future – [Union] law will automatically prevail over the non-conforming BIT provisions'.[191] But what does it mean for EU law to '*automatically* prevail' over conflicting provisions of an intra-EU BIT, especially in the light of the procedural

[188]   C-205/06 *Commission v Austria* [2009] ECR I-1301, para 42.
[189]   C-522/04 *Commission v Belgium* [2007] ECR I-5701.
[190]   Ibid para 70.
[191]   *Eastern Sugar v Czech Republic* (above n 1) Partial Award, para 119.

characteristics of investor-state dispute settlement? Recently, arbitral tribunals have been faced with the question as to what extent Member State treatment was incompatible with the relevant standards of investment treatment when a Member State was implementing EU law.[192] Such an award could potentially fly in the face of the legal obligations of a Member State under EU law.

In this respect, a distinction is to be drawn between compliance with an international investment agreement and the procedural issues arising in the context of the review and recognition of arbitral awards. In the context of a challenge to an arbitral award, a national court could well be asked to rule on the compatibility of an award with EU law, be it in a court of a Member State or outside the Union. Non-ICSID arbitral awards may be subject to review in accordance with the local arbitration rules in the country where the award is rendered. The conditions for the recognition and enforcement of such awards in other countries are governed by the 1958 New York Convention on the Recognition and Enforcement of Foreign Arbitral Awards ('New York Convention'). Article V of the New York Convention sets limited grounds for a refusal to recognise and enforce arbitral awards. As far as Member State court review and recognition of arbitral awards in the light of EU law is concerned,[193] the CJEU held in *Eco Swiss*[194] that:

> it is in the interest of efficient arbitration proceedings that review of arbitration awards should be limited in scope and that annulment of or refusal to recognise an award should be possible only in exceptional circumstances.[195]

The national rules of procedure in issue provided that the annulment of an arbitral award could only be ordered on a limited number of grounds, which included the ground that the award was contrary to public policy.[196] The Hoge Raad had stated that, under Dutch law, the mere fact that, because of the terms of enforcement of an arbitration award, a prohibition laid down in competition law is not applied, is not generally regarded as being contrary to public policy.[197] The CJEU held that, in the eyes of EU law, the prohibition laid down in (now) Article 101 TFEU is a fundamental rule that has the same status as national rules of public policy.[198]

Provisions of EU law can thus constitute public policy requirements within the meaning of national rules of procedure of the Member States. To this, the Court added:

> That conclusion is not affected by the fact that the New York Convention of 10 June 1958 on the Recognition and Enforcement of Foreign Arbitral Awards, which has been

---

[192] See the text at V and accompanying notes.

[193] See P Landolt, 'Limits on Court Review of International Arbitration Awards Assessed in the Light of States' Interests and in particular in Light of EU Law Requirements' (2007) 1 *Arbitration International* 63.

[194] C-126/97 *Eco Swiss* [1999] ECR I-3055.

[195] Ibid para 35.

[196] Ibid para 7.

[197] Ibid para 24.

[198] Ibid para 37.

ratified by all the Member States, provides that recognition and enforcement of an arbitration award may be refused only on certain specific grounds, namely where the award does not fall within the terms of the submission to arbitration or goes beyond its scope, where the award is not binding on the parties or where recognition or enforcement of the award would be contrary to the public policy of the country where such recognition and enforcement are sought (Articles V(1)(c) and (e) and II(b) of the New York Convention).[199]

The Court ruled that Member State courts must treat a failure to comply with EU competition law, in this case the prohibition laid down in (now) Article 101(1) TFEU, as a violation of public policy within the meaning of the New York Convention.[200] EU consumer protection law has also been recognised as a matter of public policy by the Court.[201] *Centro Móvil* goes even further than *Eco Swiss* in that the Court ruled that EU consumer protection law is explicitly characterised as 'mandatory' so that issues of compatibility ought to be raised *ex proprio motu* by the reviewing Member State court, irrespective of the applicable law and specific pleadings of the parties.[202] At the same time, neither *Eco Swiss*, nor *Centro Móvil*, place arbitral tribunals under an obligation to apply EU law of their own motion, although in practice, if arbitrators fail to apply it (correctly), the enforcement of non-ICSID awards can be barred in case of a challenge in a Member State court.[203]

Although every Member State legal system recognises public policy grounds for review of arbitral awards, and for refusing to enforce an award, it is clear, however, that the possibility for review and refusal to enforce an award in view of Member State obligations under EU law in Member State courts does not arise in the context of awards rendered under the ICSID Convention.[204] Unlike awards rendered in ad hoc arbitrations, review of ICSID awards can only take place by ICSID ad hoc tribunals, which derive their authority to annul awards from the limited grounds for review provided by Article 52(3) of the ICSID Convention.[205] Moreover, the enforcement of ICSID awards is automatic.[206] Since ICSID arbitra-

---

[199] Ibid para 38.

[200] Confirmed, with reference to both Arts 101 and 102 TFEU, in Joined Cases C-295/04 and C-298/04 *Manfredi* [2006] ECR I-6619, para 31.

[201] C-168/05 *Centro Móvil* [2006] ECR I-10412.

[202] Ibid paras 38–39.

[203] For an overview of views on the issue of the mandatory application of EU competition law in arbitration proceedings, irrespective of the will of the parties, see P Landolt, *Modernised EC Competition Law in International Arbitration* (The Hague, Kluwer Law International, 2006) 134–39.

[204] See G Sacerdoti, 'Investment Arbitration under ICSID and UNCITRAL Rules: Prerequisites, Applicable Law, Review of Awards' (2005) 1 *ICSID Review* 1. By contrast, awards rendered under the ICSID Additional Facility Rules are subject to the New York Convention.

[205] Article 52(1) of the ICSID Convention provides for the following exhaustive grounds for annulment: (a) that the tribunal was not properly constituted; (b) that the tribunal has manifestly exceeded its powers; (c) that there was corruption of the part of the tribunal; (d) that there has been a serious departure from a fundamental rule of procedure; (e) that the award has failed to state the reasons on which it is based.

[206] Under Art 54(1) ICSID awards are recognised as binding and to be enforced like final domestic judgments in all states parties to the Convention.

tion proceedings are completely detached from the EU legal order, the obligation for Member States to comply with ICSID awards does not give rise to issues pertaining to the interplay between EU law and Member State procedural law. Non-compliance with an award rendered by an arbitral tribunal under ICSID rules means that a Member State acts in direct contravention of the ICSID Convention. It is in this context that the principle of primacy comes back into play. Insofar as non-compliance with an ICSID award constitutes a breach of the ICSID Convention, which unlike intra-EU BITs was concluded by the Member States with a number of third countries, this may also give rise to the set of problems discussed in chapter 4.

In sum, as a result of the operation of the principle of primacy, the Member States cannot invoke an intra-EU BIT to justify acting in derogation from their obligations under EU law. Even if the validity of intra-EU BITs is not at issue pursuant to their acquired intra-EU status, it is not possible to dismiss the EU legal aspects of investment disputes between an EU investor and another Member State. The situation is complicated by the fact that compliance with intra-EU BITs also gives rise to various procedural issues in relation to the review and enforcement of arbitral awards. It goes too far to claim that intra-EU BITs have ceased to be applicable in matters which merely overlap with EU primary law and secondary legislation or fall under the scope of application of EU law. At the same time, EU law mandates the deferral by Member States to their obligations under EU law in the settlement of investment claims in case of conflicting obligations under intra-EU investment agreements.

IV. INTRA-EU BITS AND THE EU PRINCIPLE OF EQUAL TREATMENT

Investors in the Union do not have access to investor-state arbitration under EU law. While investment protection rights are granted to investors under EU law, as well as under the ECHR, the enforcement of these rights against Member States requires investors in the first instance to challenge Member State measures in Member State courts. Intra-EU BITs do provide for the possibility to refer disputes to arbitration. Concerns have arisen with regard to the fact that access to BIT dispute settlement is restricted to investors from the other contracting Member State to an intra-EU BIT. Such discriminatory access to intra-EU investment treaty arbitration has been argued to be at odds with the EU principle of equal treatment by the Commission[207] and by some scholars.[208] The issue underlying such concerns is

---

[207] *Eastern Sugar v Czech Republic* (above n 1) Partial Award, para 119.

[208] See C Leben, 'Introduction' in C Kessedjian and C Leben (eds), *Le droit européen et l'investissement* (Paris, Éditions Panthéon-Assas, 2009) 19. See also Eilmansberger, 'Bilateral Investment Treaties and EU Law' (above n 159) 383, 402 ff, who argues that EU investors are entitled to MFN treatment under EU law with regard to the dispute settlement provisions in intra-EU BITs, even if not under the MFN clauses in the BITs themselves. But see H Wehland, 'Intra-EU Investment Agreements and Arbitration: Is European Community Law an Obstacle?' (2009) 2 *ICLQ* 297, 315 ff, who argues that EU investors are not entitled to MFN treatment under EU law with regard to the procedural provisions in intra-EU BITs.

the fundamental tension that exists between the EU principle of equal treatment and the scope of manoeuvre for the Member States to engage in closer cooperation outside the framework of EU law.

It has been observed that *inter se* agreements between the Member States can legitimately bring some Member States closer to each other without necessarily breaching the principle of non-discrimination.[209] Examples of such closer cooperation are the Benelux Agreement as well as various other types of bilateral agreements, such as Double Taxation Conventions (DTCs) and agreements on social security. Against this backdrop, the first part of this section analyses the plausibility of a breach of the EU principle of equal treatment by the host Member State of an investment, in which case the argument would concern a breach of the principle of most favoured nation (MFN) treatment. The second part analyses a possible breach of the EU principle of equal treatment by the Member State through which an investment is channelled to the host Member State from a third Member State, in which case the argument would concern a breach of the principle of national treatment (NT).

A. Dispute Settlement under Intra-EU BITs and MFN Treatment

The consequence of an incomplete network of intra-EU BITs is that investors from one Member State, but not from another, have access to investor-state arbitration under such an agreement. If certain investment protection rights are granted by a host Member State to investors from one Member State under an intra-EU BIT, shouldn't they also be granted to investors from other Member States? The extension of the scope of application of MFN clauses in BITs to the procedural provisions in other BITs is controversial, and in any case would not apply to situations in which there is no BIT in force between the country of origin of an EU investor and the host Member State.[210] Various commentators have defended the view that the EU principle of equal treatment, as enshrined in Article

---

[209] R Schütze, 'EC Law and International Agreements of the Member States: An Ambivalent Relationship?' (2006–2007) *Cambridge Yearbook of European Legal Studies* 387, 424. On *inter se* agreements in relation to the EU principle of equal treatment, see also B de Witte, 'Internationale verdragen tussen lidstaten van de Europese Unie' in RA Wessel and B de Witte, *De plaats van de Europese Unie in het veranderende bestel van de volkenrechtelijke organisatie, Mededelingen van de Nederlandse Vereniging voor Internationaal Recht* (The Hague, TMC Asser Press, 2001) 107–16; B de Witte, 'Chameleonic Member States: Differentiation by Means of Partial and Parallel International Agreements' in B de Witte, D Hanf and E Vos (eds), *The Many Faces of Differentiation in EU Law* (Antwerp, Intersentia, 2001); de Witte, 'Old-fashioned Flexibility' (above n 165) 48 ff.

[210] Z Douglas, 'The MFN Clause in Investment Arbitration: Treaty Interpretation Off the Rails' (2011) 2 *Journal of International Dispute Settlement* 97; R Teitelbaum, 'Who's Afraid of *Maffezini*? Recent Developments in the Interpretation of Most Favored Nation Clauses' (2005) 3 *Journal of International Arbitration* 225. See also A Faya Rodriguez, 'The Most-Favored-Nation Clause in International Investment Agreements: A Tool for Treaty Shopping?' in (2008) 1 *Journal of International Arbitration* 89, who observes that there is inconsistency in the jurisprudence on the applicability of MFN clauses in investment agreements in relation to the importation of dispute settlement provisions from other BITs.

18 TFEU, is constitutive of a right to MFN treatment for EU nationals.[211] MFN treatment can here be understood as the right to equal treatment with the EU investor that receives the most favourable treatment with respect to all other EU investors. Yet it can be observed that the CJEU's case law seems to suggest that the EU principle of equal treatment does not imply such a right to MFN treatment in respect of every aspect of each agreement that is in force between Member States *inter se*.

An important limit set by EU law to differential treatment between EU nationals under *inter se* agreements is that the granting of EU rights cannot be made conditional upon reciprocal treatment. In *Avoir fiscal*,[212] French tax law provided for a tax credit to shareholders, who received dividends from companies paying corporation tax in France. For non-French companies, whether or not corporation tax had to be paid in France depended on the DTC concluded with the Member State of origin. The measures had the effect that incorporated entities received different tax treatment from unincorporated entities, such as branches or agencies. This was argued by the Commission to constitute indirect discrimination of foreign undertakings, which are usually unincorporated and whose shareholders would thus not receive a tax credit. The Court held that the difference in treatment was not due to the DTCs, but were the result of French tax law, which laid down the conditions for the granting of the tax credits.[213] France could thus not invoke the DTC as a justification for the differential treatment in issue. The Court also clarified that the fundamental freedoms are unconditional and that a Member State cannot make respect for them subject to the contents of an agreement concluded with another Member State. (Now) Article 49 TFEU, in particular, cannot 'permit those rights to be made subject to conditions of reciprocity imposed for the purpose of obtaining corresponding advantages in other Member States'.[214]

In *Avoir fiscal*, the Court took the view that the refusal to grant EU rights (in this case the right to equal treatment between resident and non-resident entities) could not be justified with reference to a DTC. Yet, the Court did not hold that the granting of rights under a DTC could not be made subject to conditions of reciprocity. In other words, the Court did not say that differential treatment as a result of a bilateral agreement, such as a DTC, is at all times incompatible with the EU principle of equal treatment. Case law on the Benelux agreement confirms not only that certain rights under intra-EU agreements may be subject to the condition of

---

[211] C Tietje, 'Die Meistbegünstigungsverpflichtung im Gemeinschaftsrecht' (1995) 4 *Europarecht* 398; KE Sørensen, 'The Most-Favoured-Nation Principle in the EU' (2007) 4 *Legal Issues of European Integration* 315; S Hindelang, *The Free Movement of Capital and Foreign Direct Investment: The Scope of Protection under EU Law* (Oxford, Oxford University Press, 2009) 129–35.

[212] 270/83 *Commission v France (avoir fiscal)* [1986] ECR 273.

[213] Ibid para 26.

[214] Ibid. This is confirmed in *Athinaiki*, in which the Court ruled that rights conferred under Union legislation, in this case Art 5(1) of Council Directive 90/435 of 23 July 1990 on the common system of taxation applicable in the case of parent companies and subsidiaries of different Member States [1990] OJ L225/6, 'are unconditional and a Member State cannot make their observance subject to an agreement concluded with another Member State'. See C-294/99 *Athinaiki* [2001] ECR I-6797, para 32.

reciprocity, but also that Member State cooperation may go beyond the framework of cooperation constituted by EU law. In *Pakvries*,[215] the Court ruled that the Benelux transit rules took precedence over the (then) EC transit rules. The Court held that Article 306 EC (now Article 350 TFEU):

> enables the three Member States concerned to apply, in derogation from the [Union] rules, the rules in force within their union in so far as it is further advanced than the common market.[216]

That differential treatment as a result of a DTC is not at all times incompatible with the EU principle of equal treatment was confirmed in *Gilly*,[217] where the Court held with respect to the Germany-France DTC that:

> the fact that in allocating powers of taxation between them the contracting parties have chosen various connecting factors, in particular nationality . . . cannot in itself constitute discrimination prohibited by [Union] law.[218]

Although issues of compatibility of DTCs with EU law do arise, as subsequent case law has shown, DTCs serve the important goal of allocating powers of taxation in the absence of EU harmonising measures. That their underlying objective is in principle compatible with EU law was moreover recognised in Article 293 EC,[219] which was repealed by the Treaty of Lisbon.

The question whether DTCs violate the principle of equal treatment between EU nationals from different Member States came before the CJEU in *D*.[220] At issue in *D* was a situation in which a non-resident was treated differently from another non-resident, which received special benefits in the form of a tax allowance under a DTC. Mr D, a German national, claimed that he was treated differently by the Netherlands from a hypothetical person residing in Belgium and also having only 10 per cent of its wealth in the Netherlands, as a result of a tax advantage granted under the Netherlands-Belgium DTC but not under the Netherlands-Germany DTC. Mr D claimed that this was incompatible with (now) Articles 18 and 63 TFEU. Advocate General (AG) Colomer took the view that in this case it was not the allocation of taxation powers that was at stake, but 'a mere privilege for which no consideration is given and for which there is no reciprocal basis'.[221] In the view of the AG,

---

[215]   105/83 *Pakvries* [1984] ECR 2101.

[216]   Ibid para 11. See also Joined Cases C-367 to C-377/93 *Roders* [1995] ECR I-2229, para 18: 'Under Article [350 TFEU], the provisions of [Union] law are not to preclude the existence or completion of the union between Belgium, Luxembourg and the Netherlands, to the extent that the objectives of that union are not attained by application of the [Treaties]'. The Court held that the non-extension of tax benefits to traders from Member States other than the Benelux countries was not incompatible with the principle of equal treatment, but the Benelux countries were not allowed to accord preferential treatment that 'cannot be regarded as necessary for the functioning of the Benelux system' (para 25).

[217]   336/96 *Gilly* [1996] ECR I-2793.

[218]   Ibid para 53.

[219]   'The Member States shall, so far as is necessary, enter into negotiations with each other with a view to securing for the benefit of their nationals: . . . the abolition of double taxation within the Community.'

[220]   C-376/03 *D* [2005] ECR I-5821.

[221]   Opinion of AG Colomer of 26 October 2004 in C-376/03 *D* [2005] ECR I-5821, para 82.

the provision under analysis was 'completely unrelated to the specific substance of the arrangements intended to abolish international double taxation'.[222] A negative ruling in this case would therefore not call into question the system of concluding DTCs for the allocation of taxation powers, which in the view of the AG suggested that a more rigorous test of compatibility was appropriate in the situation at hand.[223] Specifying that he did not consider that MFN treatment was at stake, but rather discrimination on grounds of nationality, he concluded that Mr D ought to have access to the benefits of the Netherlands-Belgium DTC.[224] With regard to the argument of some of the Member States that the balance of the agreement at issue was the result of complex negotiations, the AG took the view that 'those difficulties must not become obstacles to the establishment of the single market'.[225]

The CJEU observed that there are situations where the benefits under a bilateral agreement may have to be extended to a resident of a Member State which does not have the status of party to that agreement.[226] This was the case in *Saint Gobain*,[227] in which the Court held that the NT principle requires the Member State which is a party to a convention with a third country to grant to permanent establishments of non-resident companies the benefits provided for by that convention on the same conditions as those which apply to resident companies.[228] Crucial in such a case is that the non-resident taxable person having a permanent establishment in a Member State can be regarded as being in a situation equivalent to that of a taxable person resident in that state.[229] This was not held by the Court to be the case in the situation of D. Rather, the Court held that:

> The fact that those reciprocal rights and obligations apply only to persons resident in one of the two contracting Member States is an inherent consequence of bilateral double taxation conventions. It follows that a taxable person resident in Belgium is not in the same situation as a taxable person resident outside Belgium so far as concerns wealth tax on real property situated in the Netherlands.[230]

In other words, the Court ruled that the situations of two non-resident taxpayers were not comparable precisely because a DTC had been concluded. The Court did not share the view of the AG that the benefit granted under the DTC was not strictly related to the allocation of tax powers. The Court held that such a benefit is 'an integral part thereof and contributes to its overall balance'.[231] The Court thus took a permissive stance with regard to the fact that DTCs may grant benefits to nationals from one Member State, but not from other Member States.

---

[222] Ibid.
[223] Ibid.
[224] Ibid paras 96 and 103.
[225] Ibid para 101.
[226] Ibid para 55.
[227] C-307/97 *Saint-Gobain* [1999] ECR I-6161.
[228] C-376/03 *D* [2005] ECR I-5821, para 56, with reference to *Saint Gobain* (above n 227) para 59.
[229] Ibid para 57.
[230] Ibid para 61.
[231] Ibid para 62.

A similarly permissive approach can be found in the case of *ACT,*[232] in which the UK law on advance corporation tax (ACT) was in issue. A company that was resident in the United Kingdom and that paid dividends to its shareholders was liable to pay ACT. Shareholders resident in the United Kingdom received a tax credit, whereas non-resident shareholders could only receive such a tax credit under the provisions of a DTC. The Court examined whether different non-resident entities were in objectively comparable situations. It took the view that this was not the case, because the difference in treatment was due to the existence of a DTC providing for such a credit, which reflected the characteristics of the different national tax regimes. Since there was a direct link between the granting of a tax credit and the tax rate laid down in a DTC, the Court held that the granting of a tax credit could not be regarded as a benefit separable from the remainder of those DTCs, but is an integral part of them and contributes to their overall balance.[233] There was no violation of the EU principle of equal treatment, since:

> The fact that those reciprocal rights and obligations apply only to persons resident in one of the two contracting Member States is an inherent consequence of bilateral double taxation conventions.[234]

In other words, the Court held that EU law does not preclude a situation in which the entitlement to a tax credit laid down in a DTC concluded by a Member State with another Member State for shareholders resident in the second state who receive dividends from a company resident in the first state, does not extend to shareholders resident in a third Member State with which the first state has concluded a DTC which does not provide for such an entitlement.[235]

The CJEU has thus shown a relatively permissive approach to the restriction of rights by the host Member State of an investment to investors from the contracting Member States to a DTC. In this, the Court has neither explicitly confirmed nor rejected a general principle of MFN treatment.[236] The Court's scrutiny focuses on equal treatment of like situations, in which the question whether an EU national is entitled to benefits under a DTC has been considered as part of the factual situation of the investor for the purpose of determining whether two investors are in like situations. In both *D* and *ACT* the non-resident investors concerned were found not to be in objectively comparable situations, because the DTCs differed, as a result of which they were treated differently. These differences, in turn, were due to the

---

[232] C-374/04 *ACT Group Litigation* [2006] ECR I-11673.

[233] Ibid para 88.

[234] Ibid para 91.

[235] Ibid para 92.

[236] But see KE Sørensen, 'The Most-Favoured-Nation Principle in the EU' (2007) 4 *Legal Issues of European Integration* 315, 319, who claims that EU law does not explicitly provide for a principle of MFN treatment, but that it can be implied from the TFEU provisions on free movement, from the general principle of equal treatment enshrined in Art 18 TFEU and from the principle of sincere cooperation under (now) Art 4(3) TEU. See also Hindelang, *The Free Movement of Capital and Foreign Direct Investment* (above n 111) 133, who claims that, although the Court in *D* denied a violation of Art 63 TFEU, 'it did not do so on the basis of the argument that the MFN treatment standard is completely alien to [EU] law in general or free movement of capital in particular'.

particular characteristics of the tax regimes and what the Member States could agree on when they negotiated the conventions at issue.

Even if intra-EU BITs were originally concluded with third countries, after accession of the latter they are a source of investment protection rights that are not granted under EU law. In that sense, they do not make the granting of EU rights conditional on whether or not the Member State of origin of an investor is a contracting party to a bilateral agreement with the host Member State. In the light of the case law on DTCs, investors from different Member States could seem not to be in like situations as a result of the possibility for one, but not another, investor to invoke in investor-state arbitration the standards of treatment enshrined in an intra-EU BIT. To a degree this can be seen as an inherent consequence of intra-EU BITs. On the other hand, in the case of DTCs it is the allocation of fiscal jurisdiction (a legitimate purpose that used to be mandated explicitly under Article 293 EC) that necessitates recourse to connecting factors such as nationality.

A crucial issue thus seems to be whether the investment protection rights enshrined in intra-EU BITs are of equal importance for inter-Member State relations outside the framework of EU law to the allocation of fiscal jurisdiction so as to justify a similarly permissive test as to whether the restricted access of EU investors to the benefits under these agreements is compatible with the EU principle of equal treatment. Whereas the Court has so far not been very assertive in relation to alleged violations by international agreements of the Member States *inter se* of an obligation of MFN treatment, for the purpose of advancing Single Market integration it would arguably be best to harmonise the investment protection regime in the internal market under current intra-EU BITs, including access to investor-state arbitration.

B. Dispute Settlement under Intra-EU BITs and NT

There is also the question whether the 'home' Member State of an investment infringes the EU principle of equal treatment where it is a contracting party to an intra-EU BIT that does not grant protection to investments which are channelled through that Member State to the 'host' Member State from a 'third' Member State. Such a situation would come under the scope of application of EU law where an investor from a third Member State has exercised its free movement rights by becoming economically active in the home Member State, such as through a subsidiary, through which an investment in the host Member State is structured. At issue in those circumstances would be a denial of NT, since the home Member State treats other EU investors differently from its own nationals by restricting access to investor-state arbitration when investing in the host Member State. This section shows that the CJEU has been more assertive in its case law on the issue of NT in relation to a restriction of rights under bilateral agreements of the Member States, both *inter se* and with third countries.

In *Matteucci*,[237] in relation to a Belgo-German cultural agreement under which scholarships were reserved for candidates of Belgian nationality, the Court was asked to rule on whether an EU worker who is residing and pursuing an activity as an employed person in Belgium should be eligible for such a scholarship. Mrs Matteucci, an Italian national, argued that for her not to be eligible would be incompatible with Regulation 1612/68 relating to equality of treatment between national workers and workers who are nationals of another Member State.[238] The Court observed that the right to equal treatment may be relied on by an EU worker in connection with the award of scholarships pursuant to a bilateral agreement between two Member States such as the one in issue. The Court did not accept the argument that the eligibility of Mrs Matteucci would not be called into question by the application of Regulation 1612/68 because the benefits of such scholarships would not be enjoyed in Belgium, but in Germany.[239] Nor did the Court accept the argument that Belgium did not infringe the EU principle of equal treatment because the scholarships in question were granted by Germany, since Belgium was responsible for drawing up the list of candidates. The Court ruled that the Belgian authority's decision not to include EU nationals who resided and worked on Belgian territory violated the EU principle of equal treatment.[240]

The operation of the EU principle of equal treatment in relation to a restriction of rights under a bilateral agreement with respect to legal persons has been confirmed in *Saint Gobain*.[241] With regard to restricted benefits relating to liability to tax on dividend receipts in Germany from shares in foreign subsidiaries under DTCs of Germany with Switzerland and the United States, the Court held that Germany as the home country had to grant NT to Saint Gobain ZN, a branch which was registered as a permanent establishment of Saint Gobain SA. The latter, in turn, was incorporated in France. The Court considered that resident companies and permanent establishments of non-resident companies are in objectively comparable situations for the purpose of taxation on dividends received from foreign companies.[242] In the case of a DTC concluded between a Member State and a non-member country, the EU principle of equal treatment therefore requires the Member State which is a party to the agreement to grant to permanent establishments of non-resident EU companies the advantages provided for by that agreement on the same conditions as those which apply to resident EU companies.[243] In response to the argument that the agreements concerned were concluded with third countries, and that the extension of the benefits in issue would affect the balance and reciprocity of these agreements, the

[237] 235/87 *Matteucci* [1988] ECR 5589.
[238] Regulation 1612/68.
[239] *Matteucci* (above n 237) para 16.
[240] Ibid para 23.
[241] C-307/97 *Saint-Gobain* [1999] ECR I-6161.
[242] Ibid para 47.
[243] Ibid para 58.

Court pointed out that the obligations which EU law imposes on Germany would not affect in any way those resulting from its agreements with Switzerland and the United States. On the contrary:

> The balance and reciprocity of the treaties concluded by [Germany] with those two countries would not be called into question by a unilateral extension, on the part of [Germany], of the category of recipients in Germany of the tax advantage provided for by those treaties, in this case corporation tax relief for international groups, since such an extension would not in any way affect the rights of the non-member countries which are parties to the treaties and would not impose any new obligation on them.[244]

In other words, the unequal treatment in issue was thus not an inherent consequence of the DTC. Since Germany would grant the concessions in issue, which would not in any way affect its obligations vis-à-vis the other contracting parties, Germany discriminated between resident companies and permanent establishments of non-resident companies.

In *Gottardo*,[245] the Court ruled that Italy had to extend the benefit of the aggregation principle under an Italian-Swiss social security convention to an application for a pension scheme in Italy by a French national, Mrs Gottardo, who had worked both in Switzerland and in Italy. The Court held that:

> when a Member State concludes a bilateral international convention on social security with a non-member country which provides for account to be taken of periods of insurance completed in that non-member country for acquisition of entitlements to old-age benefits, the fundamental principle of equal treatment requires that that Member State grants the same advantages as those which its own nationals enjoy under that convention unless it can provide objective justification for refusing to do so.[246]

In other words, a Member State is in principle under the obligation to extend the benefits that it grants to its own nationals under bilateral agreements, even those with third countries, to nationals of other Member States. As in *Saint Gobain*, the Court subsequently recognised that:

> Disturbing the balance and reciprocity of a bilateral international convention concluded between a Member State and a non-member country may, it is true, constitute an objective justification for the refusal by a Member State party to that convention to extend to nationals of other Member States the advantages which its own nationals derive from that convention.[247]

The Court observed, however, that the unilateral extension of social security benefits by Italy to nationals from other Member States would in no way compromise the rights that Switzerland derived from the bilateral agreement, and the agreement would not impose any new obligations on that country.[248]

---

[244] Ibid para 59.
[245] C-55/00 *Gottardo* [2002] ECR I-413.
[246] Ibid para 34.
[247] Ibid para 36.
[248] Ibid para 37.

In the 'Open Skies' cases,[249] the Commission successfully challenged a number of bilateral agreements in the field of air transport concluded by some of the Member States with the United States, inter alia, because the clauses on ownership and control of airlines in these agreements were contrary to Article 49 TFEU. The effect of these clauses was that they permitted the United States to refuse or withdraw licences or authorisations in respect of an airline designated by the Member State in question, but of which a substantial part of the ownership and effective control was not vested in that Member State or in nationals of that Member State or the United States.[250] By consequence, these Member States did not accord to nationals of other Member States, and in particular to airlines and undertakings established in the territory of the contracting Member State to the agreement, but which are controlled by nationals or legal persons from these other Member States, the treatment reserved for its own nationals. This was found by the CJEU to be in violation of the EU principle of equal treatment.

In response to the argument that, unlike the situation in *Saint Gobain*, it was the third country, *in casu* the United States, that would ultimately deny the advantage in issue (ie refuse or withdraw such licences or authorisations) to undertakings, which are not controlled by nationals from the other contracting Member State, the Court observed that:

> the direct source of that discrimination is not the possible conduct of the [United States] but the clause on the ownership and control of airlines, which specifically acknowledges the right of the [United States] to act in that way.[251]

In other words, the Court did not find it important that the benefits in question in the agreements concerned were granted by the United States, since the contracting Member States could not shift their responsibility under Article 49 TFEU to the United States.[252] In addition, in the 'Open Skies' cases, the Court did not consider the argument that such extension of benefits could potentially affect the balance and reciprocity of these agreements. The clauses on ownership and control were simply ruled to be incompatible with the obligation under EU law for the Member States to grant equal treatment to airlines which are established in their territory, even when they are controlled by nationals from other Member States.

In relation to an Agreement between Germany and Poland on the posting of workers, the Court held that the competent German authorities were not allowed to interpret the term 'undertaking from the other side' in Article 1(1) of that agreement as referring only to German undertakings or German subsidiaries of

---

[249] Joined Cases C-466/98 *Commission v United Kingdom* [2002] ECR I-9427; C-467/98 *Commission v Denmark* [2002] ECR I-9519; C-468/98 *Commission v Sweden* [2002] ECR I-9575; C-469/98 *Commission v Finland* [2002] ECR I-9797; C-471/98 *Commission v Belgium* [2002] ECR I-9681; C-472/98 *Commission v Luxembourg* [2002] ECR I-9741; C-475/98 *Commission v Austria* [2002] ECR I-9797; C-476/98 *Commission v Germany* [2002] ECR I-9855.

[250] C-467/98 *Commission v Denmark* [2002] ECR I-9519, para 128.

[251] Ibid para 132.

[252] Ibid para 115.

companies from other Member States.[253] As a result of that practice, undertakings from Member States other than Germany supplying services in that Member State were prevented from concluding works contracts with Polish undertakings. This was ruled to constitute an instance of direct discrimination contravening (now) Article 56 TFEU.[254] The Court did not accept the argument of Germany that the disputed practice was justified by the fact that the provision was contained in a bilateral agreement, since the Member States are under an obligation to comply with EU law unless such an agreement is subject to (now) Article 351 TFEU.[255] The Court also did not find merit in the argument that the balance and reciprocity of an intra-EU agreement may be disturbed by extending certain benefits to other EU nationals, the relevance of which the Court explicitly circumscribed to the context of Member State agreements with third countries.[256]

The case of *ACT* provides an interesting comparator to the cases discussed so far in connection with the application of the principle of NT to the restriction of rights under an international agreement between two Member States, or between a Member State and a third country. In *ACT*, the CJEU was faced with the question whether it is permissible for a Member State to apply a so-called 'limitation of benefits' clause in a DTC between two Member States, pursuant to which a tax credit under the DTC is not granted to a company resident in the other contracting Member State if that company is controlled by a company resident in a third Member State with which a DTC is concluded that makes no provision for a tax credit.[257] The Court took the view that the restriction of rights under a limitation of benefits clause contributes to the overall balance of such agreements and is an integral part thereof.[258] The Court in this case therefore rejected the need to extend benefits under a DTC to companies that are resident in the other contracting Member State of a DTC but controlled by a company that is resident in a third Member State.

Even if the differential treatment between resident and non-resident companies was accorded by the Member State, *in casu* the United Kingdom, that granted the tax credit (ie the 'host' Member State of the investment), the Court did not give any indication that the Member State in which the company receiving the tax credit is resident could be acting in violation of the EU principle of equal treatment if such benefits were not extended to companies resident in that Member State but controlled by a company resident in a third Member State. At the same time, while the Court ruled that such a limitation of benefits clause is in principle compatible with the EU principle of equal treatment, various commentators have pointed to the fact that the limitation of benefits clause at issue in *ACT* differed from the clause on ownership and control in the 'Open Skies' cases because the

[253] C-546/07 *Commission v Germany* [2010] ECR I-439.
[254] Ibid para 40.
[255] Ibid para 42.
[256] Ibid para 43.
[257] C-374/04 *ACT Group Litigation* [2006] ECR I-11673, para 76.
[258] Ibid para 90.

former referred to residence as distinguishing criterion and not to nationality, which was at issue in the air transport agreements.[259]

Whether an issue of compatibility with the principle of NT arises in relation to a restriction of rights under intra-EU BITs in a particular situation may depend on the scope of application *ratione personae* of the BIT in issue. In investment agreements, the investor's nationality is the connecting factor with the legal order of the home state, not the origin of the capital.[260] Usually, only investors holding the nationality of the home state can invoke the BIT standards of investment treatment and have access to international arbitration.[261] Corporate nationality in most cases presupposes legal personality, so that unincorporated entities usually do not enjoy legal protection.[262] An example of a BIT that refers to incorporation for the purpose of the definition of 'investor' is the Czech Republic-Netherlands BIT, Article 1(b)(ii) of which refers to 'legal persons constituted under the law of one of the Contracting Parties'.

BITs that define the nationality of a company with reference to incorporation do not look at the nationality of the company's owners. This is evidenced by *Saluka*, in which the arbitral tribunal rejected the Czech Republic's argument that Saluka was merely a shell company in the Netherlands, which was owned by a Japanese investor, and should therefore not be able to invoke the BIT. The tribunal held that the agreed definition of 'investor' only required that the claimant should be constituted under the laws of the Netherlands.[263]

Other intra-EU BITs refer to the entity's principal seat of business, or combine a reference to the seat of a company with a reference to incorporation.[264] An example of the former is the Italy-Bulgaria BIT, Article 1(b) of which provides that the term 'investor' for Italian investors comprises:

> le persone giuridiche, società commerciali od altre società con o senza personalità giuridica con sede nel territorio della Repubblica Italiana, legalmente riconosciute, indipendentemente dal fatto che la loro responsabilità sia limitata o meno.[265]

---

[259] T O'Shea, 'Limitation on Benefits (LoB) Clauses and the EU: Part II' (2008) 11 *International Tax Report* 1. But see P Pistone, 'Test Claimants in Class IV of the ACT Group Litigation: Limitation-of-Benefits Clauses are Clearly Different from Most-Favoured-Nation-Clauses' (2007) 4 *BTR* 363.

[260] Some investment agreements extend the status of foreign investor to permanent residents: Art 1(7)(a)(i) ECT.

[261] See Dolzer and Schreuer, *Principles of International Investment Law* (above n 58) 46–56.

[262] *Impregilo v Pakistan*, ICSID Case no ARB/3/03, Decision on Jurisdiction of 22 April 2005, (2005) 12 ICSID Rep 245, paras 131–39. With reference to C Schreuer, *The ICSID Convention: A Commentary*, 1st edn (Cambridge, Cambridge University Press, 2001) 276–77.

[263] *Saluka v Czech Republic* (above n 21) Partial Award, para 241. See also *Tokios Tokelès v Ukraine*, ICSID Case no ARB/02/18, Decision on Jurisdiction of 29 April 2004, (2004) 11 ICSID Rep 313, paras 27–41.

[264] R Wisner and R Gallus, 'Nationality Requirements in Investor-State Arbitration' (2004) 6 *Journal of World Investment and Trade* 927.

[265] Translation: 'legal persons, trading companies or other companies with or without legal personality with their seat in the territory of the Italian Republic, legally recognised, regardless of whether their liability is limited or otherwise'.

An example of an intra-EU BIT that combines seat with incorporation is the Czech Republic-France BIT, Article 1(2)(b) of which provides that the term 'investor' comprises:

> toute personne morale constituée sur le territoire de l'une des Parties contractantes, conformément à la legislation de celle-ci et y possédant son siège social.[266]

Yet other intra-EU BITs go beyond the requirements of seat or incorporation, and require effective control over the entity by nationals of that state.[267] An example of this is Article 1(3) of the France-Estonia BIT, under which the term 'investor' comprises:

> Le terme de 'sociétés' désigne toute personne morale constituée sur le territoire de l'une des Parties contractantes, conformément à la legislation de celle-ci et y possédant son siège social, ou contrôlée, directement ou indirectement, par des nationaux de l'une des Parties contractantes, ou par des personnes morales possédant leur siège social sur le territoire de l'une des Parties contractantes et constituées conformément à la legislation de celle-ci.[268]

Other BITs explicitly require an economic bond between the entity and the home state by means of a denial of benefits clause, which reserves the right to deny the benefits of the treaty to a company that does not have an economic connection to the state on whose nationality it relies. For instance, Article 1(c) of the Sweden-Bulgaria BIT provides that:

> Each Contracting Party reserves the right to deny to any legal person the advantages of this Agreement if nationals of any third State control such legal person and the said legal person is established on the territory of one of the Contracting Parties with the only or predominant purpose to invest in the territory of the other Contracting Party.[269]

---

[266] Translation: 'every legal person constituted on the territory of one of the contracting Parties, in conformity with its laws and having its seat in that country'.

[267] Acconci observes that: 'As for the definition of control, so differently used to determine the scope of application of the substantive treaty rules concerning foreign investments, treaties tend to refer more to the direct or indirect power to make decisions rather than to the mere ownership of the majority percentage of a company's capital stock, even if some of these treaties do not provide a specific definition for it'. P Acconci, 'Determining the Internationally Relevant Link between a State and a Corporate Investor: Recent Trends concerning the Application of the "Genuine Link" Test' (2004) 1 *Journal of World Investment and Trade* 139, 154.

[268] Translation: 'the term "companies" means every legal person constituted on the territory of one of the contracting Parties, in conformity with its laws and having its seat there, or controlled, directly or indirectly, by nationals of one of the contracting Parties, or by legal persons having their seat on the territory of one of the contracting Parties and constituted in conformity with its laws'.

[269] Another example is Art 17(1) ECT, under which each contracting party reserves the right to deny the advantages of the relevant part of the ECT to 'a legal entity if citizens or nationals of a third state own or control such entity and if that entity has no substantial business activities in the Area of the Contracting Party in which it is organized'. In *Plama v Bulgaria*, Bulgaria invoked the ECT's denial of benefit clause and argued that Plama had no substantial business activities in Cyprus. See *Plama v Bulgaria*, ICSID Case no ARB/03/24, Decision on Jurisdiction of 8 February 2005, (2005) 44 ILM 721, paras 152–78. For analysis, see AC Sinclair, 'The Substance of Nationality Requirements in Investment Treaty Arbitration' (2005) 2 *ICSID Review* 357. See also *Generation Ukraine v Ukraine*, ICSID Case no ARB/00/9, Award of 16 September 2003, (2005) 44 ILM 404.

There is thus a wide variety of definitions of 'investor' in intra-EU BITs, which evidences different practices in relation to the issue of corporate nationality.

In short, *inter se* agreements between the Member States can legitimately bring some Member States closer to each other without necessarily breaching the EU principle of equal treatment. However, the CJEU has been more assertive in cases relating to the alleged infringement of the principle of NT than with regard to an alleged breach of a principle of MFN treatment in relation to the restriction of rights under bilateral agreements between two Member States. Unlike a general principle of MFN treatment, which the Court has so far neither explicitly rejected nor confirmed with respect to inter-Member State agreements, the principle of NT has been confirmed in that context to be part and parcel of Single Market integration. In the view of the Court, a Member State in principle violates the EU principle of equal treatment if other EU investors are excluded from the benefits enshrined in an agreement with another Member State, or with a third country, who are in like situations to its own nationals, unless such difference in treatment can be justified. In principle, a problem of compatibility with EU law seems to arise when an entity that is incorporated in the 'home' Member State is excluded from investment protection in the 'host' Member State under the BIT in force between those two Member States, because the entity is controlled by a national or legal person from a 'third' Member State.[270] In this regard, some intra-EU BITs seem to be more likely to give rise to an incompatibility with EU law in particular situations than others.

Whereas some intra-EU BITs seem to be more susceptible of giving rise to an incompatibility with the principle of equal treatment under EU law than others, the question arises whether these issues of compatibility are capable of rendering intra-EU BITs sufficiently widely incompatible with EU law under the terms of Article 59(1)(b) VCLT. It seems possible to argue that intra-EU BITs, which restrictively define the scope of application *ratione personae* of the investment treatment standards enshrined in these agreements, such as by means of a denial of benefits clause, reveal an incompatibility with the principle of NT insofar as this difference of treatment cannot be justified. It follows from the Court's case law on the operation of the principle of primacy to intra-EU agreements that this does not necessarily seem to give rise to the need under EU law to terminate these agreements. Instead, their scope of application needs to be extended to such investors from a 'third' Member State. In addition, the 'host' Member State has a duty to assist the 'home' Member State in complying with this requirement pursuant to the principle of sincere cooperation enshrined in Article 4(3) TEU. As several arbitral tribunals have also found, this casts doubt on the argument that intra-EU BITs are capable of being sufficiently widely incompatible with EU law so as to trigger the application of Article 59(1)(b) VCLT. It could moreover be further explored how to harmonise the investment protection rights under intra-EU BITs to the top, rather than to the bottom, in order to guarantee compliance with the EU principle of equal treatment.

[270] But see H Wehland, 'Intra-EU Investment Agreements and Arbitration: Is European Community Law an Obstacle?' (2009) 2 *ICLQ* 297, 312 ff.

V. INVESTOR-STATE ARBITRATION UNDER INTRA-EU BITS
AND THE AUTONOMY OF THE EU LEGAL ORDER

The Commission has expressed a number of concerns in relation to investor-state arbitration under intra-EU BITs.[271] It has referred, in particular, to 'the risk . . . that arbitration instances, possibly located outside the EU, proceed with investor-to-state dispute settlement procedures without taking into account that most of the provisions of such BITs have been replaced by provisions of Community law'.[272] It has also noted that investors could engage in forum-shopping, by submitting claims to arbitration instead of (or in addition to) national courts.[273] In the Commission's view, this could lead to arbitration taking place without relevant question of EU law being litigated before national or the Union courts. The legal issue underlying these concerns is the question of whether EU law permits disputes involving issues of EU law between an investor from one Member State, on the one hand, and another Member State, on the other, to be decided not in one of the courts of the Member States or in Luxembourg, but by an arbitral tribunal under an intra-EU BIT.

This section explores the interplay between investor-state arbitration under intra-EU BITs and the autonomy of the EU legal order.[274] It first examines some of the main features of the autonomy of the EU legal order, as evidenced in the case law of the CJEU. It then turns to the way in which EU law may feature in investor-state arbitration under intra-EU BITs and how this seems to tally with some of the constitutive features of the EU legal order. This section highlights that the way in which arbitral tribunals handle issues of EU law may foster the synergy between investor-state arbitration under intra-EU BITs and EU law.

A. Autonomy of the EU Legal Order

As a preliminary note, it seems difficult to square the concerns identified by the Commission with regard to the interplay between investor-state arbitration under

---

[271] Annex to *2009 Annual EFC Report to the Commission and the Council on the Movement of Capital and Freedom of Payments*, no 17446/09, 10 December 2009, Brussels, para 17.

[272] Note by the European Commission, DG Markt, of November 2006 on free movement of capital, quoted in *Eastern Sugar v Czech Republic* (above n 1) Partial Award, para 126.

[273] Ibid.

[274] This section draws on PFJS Strik, 'From Washington with Love: Investor-State Arbitration and the Jurisdictional Monopoly of the Court of Justice of the European Union' (2009–2010) *Cambridge Yearbook of European Legal Studies* 425. See also S Hindelang, 'Circumventing Primacy of EU Law and the CJEU's Judicial Monopoly by Resorting to Dispute Resolution Mechanisms Provided for in Inter-Se Treaties? The Case of Intra-EU Investment Arbitration' in (2012) 2 *Legal Issues of European Integration* 179; Dimopoulos, 'The Validity and Applicability of International Investment Agreements' (above n 153); Eilmansberger, 'Bilateral Investment Treaties and EU Law' (above n 159) 383; M Burgstaller, 'European Law and Investment Treaties' (2009) 2 *Journal of International Arbitration* 181; H Wehland, 'Intra-EU Investment Agreements and Arbitration: Is European Community Law an Obstacle?' (2009) 2 *ICLQ* 297.

intra-EU BITs and EU law, legitimate as they may be, with the fact that the Union is itself, together with the Member States, a contracting party to the ECT. As was discussed above (I), the ECT is a mixed agreement and does not contain a disconnection clause, which would have precluded the intra-EU applicability of the agreement. The ECT also provides for the possibility of investor-state arbitration, so that investors from one EU Member State can bring a claim against another EU Member State. This is exemplified by *Electrabel*, in which a claim was brought by a Belgian investor against Hungary under the ECT pursuant to Hungary's decision to terminate a power purchase agreement.[275] Hungary's measure followed a Decision by the Commission that this agreement constituted illegal state aid. The Commission acted as *amicus curiae* and made jurisdictional objections based on EU law, arguing, inter alia, that decisions of the Commission are binding on the Member States and that compliance with such decisions cannot constitute a violation of the ECT in view of the equivalent protection of the rights of investors under EU law.[276] The Commission submitted that a harmonious interpretation of the ECT and EU law is, moreover, required in intra-EU situations and that, in case of contradiction, EU law prevails over the ECT.[277] It can be observed that the Commission's submission in *Electrabel* reflects some of the concerns that it has expressed in the context of investor-state dispute settlement under intra-EU BITs.

The interplay between investor-state arbitration under intra-EU BITs and the autonomy of the EU legal order needs to be examined in light of some of the constitutive features of EU law, as laid down by the CJEU in the classical authorities.[278] In general terms, the Union's founding treaties have established a new legal order, possessing its own institutions, for the benefit of which the Member States have limited their sovereign rights.[279] One of the essential characteristics of the EU legal order is its primacy over the laws of the Member States and the direct effect of a considerable number of provisions which are applicable to the Member States and to its nationals.[280] The CJEU and the courts and tribunals of the Member States are the guardians of that legal order pursuant to Article 19(1) TEU and it is for the CJEU to ensure respect for the autonomous nature of the EU legal order by ensuring that 'in the interpretation and application of the Treaties the law is observed'.[281] The judicial system of the Union is, moreover, a complete system of legal remedies and procedures designed to ensure review of the legality of acts of the institutions and such review has been entrusted to the CJEU.[282] Under Article 344 TFEU, moreover:

[275] *Electrabel v Hungary* (above n 186) Decision on Jurisdiction, Applicable Law and Liability. See also *AES v Hungary* (above n 18) Award.
[276] *Electrabel v Hungary* (above n 186) Decision on Jurisdiction, Applicable Law and Liability, paras 4.89–4.110.
[277] Ibid.
[278] See the overview in *Opinion 1/09* [2011] ECR I-1137, paras 65–70.
[279] 26/62 *NV Algemene Transporten Expeditie Onderneming van Gend & Loos v Netherlands Inland Revenue Authority* [1963] ECR 1; 6/64 *Flaminio Costa vs ENEL* [1964] ECR 585.
[280] *Opinion 1/91* [1991] ECR I-6079, para 35.
[281] Ibid.
[282] C-50/00 P *Unión de Pequeños Agricultores v Council* [2002] ECR I-6677, para 40.

Member States undertake not to submit a dispute concerning the interpretation or application of the Treaties to any method of settlement other than those provided for therein.

This provision has been identified as a potential stumbling block for the compatibility between investor-state arbitration under intra-EU BITs and the autonomy of the EU legal order.[283]

Article 344 TFEU reflects the fact that the EU judiciary is itself an international dispute settlement system, with a very special status and function in the Union's institutional architecture. This provision has been applied by the CJEU to alternative systems of international dispute settlement in two cases. First, in *Mox Plant*,[284] the Commission challenged Ireland for having commenced arbitration proceedings against the United Kingdom under the United Nations Convention on the Law of the Sea (UNCLOS) in relation to radioactive discharges from the Mox Plant in Sellafield, England. Ireland was claimed, inter alia, to have violated Article 344 TFEU (ex Article 292 EC) by referring to the arbitral tribunal a dispute which required for its resolution the interpretation and application of measures of (then) EC law.[285] Moreover, the arbitral tribunal was invited by Ireland to give an interpretation of the United Kingdom's obligations under EC law, which Ireland claimed that the United Kingdom had breached.[286] The Court ruled that, by thus invoking provisions of EC law for the purpose of obtaining a declaration that another Member State had breached its obligations under EC law, Ireland had not respected the exclusive jurisdiction of the CJEU to resolve disputes on the interpretation and application of provisions of EU law.[287] In the view of the Court, the arbitration proceedings ran the manifest risk that 'the autonomy of the Community's legal system may be adversely affected'.[288]

Secondly, the CJEU was asked in *Opinion 1/09*[289] to rule on the compatibility of the draft agreement establishing a European and Community patents court with the EU Treaties. The draft agreement was to be concluded between the Union, the Member States and a number of third countries. The draft agreement would establish a new court structure outside the institutional and judicial structure of the Union that was to be called upon to interpret and apply not only the provisions of that agreement but also future regulation on the Union patent and other instruments of EU law, such as Regulations and Directives, as well the TFEU rules on the internal market and competition law.[290] The patents court to be created under the draft agreement would rule on disputes between individuals in the field

---

[283] See generally the references above n 272.

[284] C-459/03 *Commission v Ireland* [2006] ECR I-4635.

[285] Ibid para 59.

[286] In particular, Council Directive 85/337 of 27 June 1985 on the assessment of the effects of certain public and private projects on the environment [1985] OJ L175/40.

[287] *Commission v Ireland* (above n 284) para 152.

[288] Ibid para 154. Although Art 344 TFEU refers exclusively to 'the Treaties', it can thus be inferred that this obligation extends to secondary legislation.

[289] *Opinion 1/09*, above n 278.

[290] Ibid para 78.

of patents and was to be granted the possibility of referring questions for a preliminary ruling to the CJEU on the interpretation and application of EU law. In *Opinion 1/09*, the Court ruled that the creation of the patents court could not be in conflict with Article 344 TFEU 'given that that article merely prohibits *Member States* from submitting a dispute concerning the interpretation or application of the Treaties to any method of settlement other than those provided for in the Treaties' (emphasis added).[291] The Court thus confirmed that Article 344 TFEU does not apply to disputes between two private parties.

Yet both *Mox Plant* and *Opinion 1/09* seem to provide insufficient authority for the proposition that investor-state dispute settlement would be incompatible with Article 344 TFEU. In particular, while Article 344 TFEU refers only to disputes brought by Member States, under intra-EU BITs claims are brought against a Member State by an investor. In *Mox Plant*, a dispute was brought to arbitration on issues of EU law between two Member States and was therefore caught by Article 344 TFEU. In *Opinion 1/09*, no Member State would be directly implicated in a dispute before the patents court and the situation therefore fell outside the scope of Article 344 TFEU. It can moreover be observed that the question of whether Article 4(3) TEU (ex Article 10 EC) amounts to a general duty of abstention for a Member State from settling disputes concerning issues of EU law by arbitration, even if these are brought by a private party, does not find explicit confirmation in *Mox Plant* or *Opinion 1/09*. Furthermore, disputes between Member States concerning the interpretation or the application of EU law are covered by one of the methods of dispute settlement under EU law. In particular, Article 259 TFEU provides that:

> A Member State which considers that another Member State has failed to fulfil an obligation under the Treaties may bring the matter before the Court of Justice of the European Union.[292]

At the same time, private applicants may also challenge the legality under EU law of acts adopted by the Union before the CJEU pursuant to Article 263(4) TFEU.[293] Moreover, as was discussed above (II), the EU legal order provides for investors to seek damages for a breach of EU law by a Member State for which it is responsible in the courts of that Member State.[294]

---

[291] Ibid para 63.

[292] *Opinion 1/09* (above n 278) para 89.

[293] Article 263(4) TFEU provides that 'Any natural or legal person may, under the conditions laid down in the first and second paragraphs, institute proceedings against an act addressed to that person or which is of direct and individual concern to them, and against a regulatory act which is of direct concern to them and does not entail implementing measures'. On the standing of non-privileged applicants, see 25/62 *Plaumann & Co v Commission* [1963] ECR 95: 'Persons other than those to whom a decision is addressed may only claim to be individually concerned if that decision affects them by reason of certain attributes which are peculiar to them or by reason of circumstances in which they are differentiated from all other persons and by virtue of these factors distinguishes them individually just as in the case of the person addressed'. See also *Unión de Pequeños Agricultores v Council* (above n 282); T-177/01 *Jégo-Quéré et Cie SA v Commission* [2002] ECR II-2365.

[294] Joined Cases C-6/90 and C-9/90 *Francovich* [1991] ECR I-5357, para 41.

The EU legal order and investor-state dispute settlement under intra-EU BITs can to a large extent be conceived of as two parallel systems of legal remedies. This is in part a consequence of the absence of a rule of exhaustion of local remedies under intra-EU BITs. These agreements generally contain a standing offer of consent by the host state to the investor of the other contracting party to resolve disputes by means of arbitration and do not require local remedies to have been exhausted before such international proceedings can be instituted.[295] Moreover, it seems that arbitral tribunals in investor-state disputes under intra-EU BITs cannot refer questions to the CJEU under Article 267 TFEU.[296] In *Nordsee*, the Court took the view that the link between an arbitral tribunal in the context of a contractual dispute submitted for arbitration with the system of legal remedies in the Member State in question was not sufficiently close for the arbitral tribunal to qualify as a 'Court or tribunal of a Member State' in the sense of Article 267 TFEU (ex Article 234 EC).[297] In *Eco Swiss*, the Court confirmed its ruling in *Nordsee* in respect of commercial arbitration by taking the view that 'Arbitrators, unlike national courts and tribunals, are not in a position to request this Court to give a preliminary ruling on questions of interpretation of Community law'.[298] Moreover, in *Miles* the Court took the view that a Complaints Board, which dealt exclusively with disputes between the staff and the administration of the European Schools, was not a 'court of a Member State' but 'a body of an international organisation which, despite functional links which it has with the Union, remains formally distinct from it and from the Member States'.[299] It can also be observed that the arbitral tribunal in *Eastern Sugar* took the view that a referral to the CJEU is not a route open to an arbitral tribunal in investor-state dispute settlement under intra-EU BITs even if the arbitration has its seat in an EU Member State.[300]

Opinion 1/09 sheds further light on the constitutional importance of Article 267 TFEU in the context of alternative systems of international dispute settlement. The CJEU took the view that the draft agreement on the creation of a

---

[295] See J Paulsson, 'Arbitration Without Privity' (1995) 10 *ICSID Review* 232, 239. Critical of this view is M Sornarajah, *The International Law on Foreign Investment*, 3rd edn (Cambridge, Cambridge University Press, 2010) 254.

[296] Article 267 TFEU provides that 'The Court of Justice of the European Union shall have jurisdiction to give preliminary rulings concerning: (a) the interpretation of the Treaties; (b) the validity and interpretation of acts of the institutions, bodies, offices or agencies of the Union; Where such a question is raised before any court or tribunal of a Member State, that court or tribunal may, if it considers that a decision on the question is necessary to enable it to give judgment, request the Court to give a ruling thereon. Where any such question is raised in a case pending before a court or tribunal of a Member State against whose decisions there is no judicial remedy under national law, that court or tribunal shall bring the matter before the Court'. On the scope of the obligation to refer questions to the Court for a preliminary ruling, see C-283/81 *Srl CILFIT and Lanificio di Gavardo SpA v Ministry of Health* [1982] ECR I-3415.

[297] 102/81 *Nordsee v Reederei Mond* [1982] ECR 1095, para 13. But see also para 9: 'the jurisdiction of the Court to rule on questions referred to it depends on the nature of the arbitration in question'.

[298] C-126/97 *Eco Swiss v Benetton* [1999] ECR I-3055, para 34.

[299] C-196/09 *Paul Miles and Others v Écoles européennes* [2011] ECR I-5105, para 42.

[300] *Eastern Sugar v Czech Republic* (above n 1) Partial Award, para 131. But see Hindelang, 'Circumventing Primacy of EU Law' (above n 274) 201 ff.

patents court, whilst not violating Article 344 TFEU, would in fact take the place of national courts by being the only court allowed to examine and refer questions to the CJEU for a preliminary ruling concerning the interpretation and application of EU law.[301] The Court observed that the patents court could be called to determine a dispute pending before it in the light of the fundamental rights and general principles of EU law or even to examine the validity of an act of the Union.[302] In addition, the patents court would become, in its field of exclusive jurisdiction, the sole court to refer questions to the Court for a preliminary ruling concerning the interpretation and application of EU law. The patents court would therefore deprive national courts and tribunals of their task as 'ordinary' courts within the EU legal order to implement EU law and of their power, or obligation, to refer questions for a preliminary ruling in the field concerned as provided for in Article 267 TFEU.[303] The Court therefore ruled that the draft agreement establishing the patents court 'would alter the essential character of the powers which the Treaties confer on the institutions of the European Union and the Member States and which are indispensible to the preservation of the very nature of European Union law'.[304]

It has been argued that arbitral tribunals should be allowed to refer questions for a preliminary ruling to the CJEU so that Article 267 TFEU would not be circumvented as a result of bypassing national courts of the Member States by submitting a dispute to arbitration.[305] In light of the constitutional significance of the preliminary reference procedure provided for in Article 267 TFEU, there is certainly something to be said for an arbitral tribunal being able to refer questions to the CJEU, particularly in view of the need to safeguard the uniform application of EU law.[306] It follows from the Court's ruling in *Opinion 1/09* that questions for a preliminary ruling by arbitral tribunals in intra-EU investor-state disputes could not in any event deprive national courts or tribunals of their task of referring questions for a preliminary ruling to the CJEU. This could be an issue where an arbitration is conducted entirely outside the control of Member State courts, in the review as well as in the recognition and enforcement stage. At the same time, it seems difficult to conceive how arbitral tribunals in intra-EU investor-state disputes can qualify as a 'court of tribunal of a Member State' within the meaning of Article 267 TFEU and refer a question to the CJEU for a preliminary ruling. Even if they would qualify as a tribunal able to refer questions for a preliminary ruling, these would be admissible only if the Court's ruling would be considered as binding by the referring arbitral tribunal.[307]

---

[301] *Opinion 1/09* (above n 278) para 79.

[302] Ibid.

[303] Ibid para 80.

[304] Ibid para 89.

[305] Hindelang, 'Circumventing Primacy of EU Law' (above n 274) 197.

[306] *Eco Swiss* (above n 298) para 40: 'it is manifestly in the interest of the Community legal order that, in order to forestall differences of interpretation, every Community provision should be given a uniform interpretation, irrespective of the circumstances in which it is to be applied'.

[307] See *Opinion 1/92* [1992] ECR I-2821, para 33.

So far as the review and enforcement of investor-state arbitral awards is concerned, it can be observed that investor-state arbitration is mostly designed so as to limit the degree of court interference. Under the ICSID Convention, awards are not subject to review by domestic courts, but by ICSID ad hoc tribunals. In addition, under Article 54(1) of the ICISD Convention, awards are recognised as binding and are to be enforced like final domestic judgments in all parties to the Convention. So far as the review of non-ICSID awards is concerned, it can be observed that the seat of an arbitration can be outside the Union and so it is detached from the EU legal order. Moreover, Article V of the New York Convention lays down strict criteria for denying the recognition and enforcement of arbitral awards, such as the improper composition of the tribunal, the invalidity of the arbitration agreement and conflict with the public policy of the state in which enforcement is sought. As regards the interplay between EU law and the review and enforcement of arbitral awards, the Court took the view in *Eco Swiss* that 'it is in the interest of efficient arbitration proceedings that review of arbitration awards should be limited in scope and that annulment or refusal to recognise an award should be possible only in exceptional circumstances'.[308] At the same time, the Court ruled that Member State courts must treat a failure to comply with EU competition law (in that case the prohibition laid down in Article 101(1) TFEU (ex Article 81(1) EC)) as a violation of public policy within the meaning of the New York Convention.[309] While *Eco Swiss* does not place an arbitral tribunal under an intra-EU BIT under an obligation to apply EU competition law of its own motion, the enforcement of an arbitral award is potentially barred in case of a challenge in a Member State court if arbitrators fail to apply EU competition law correctly.[310]

In sum, an examination of the compatibility between investor-state arbitration under intra-EU BITs and the autonomy of the EU legal order touches on some of the constitutive features of the EU legal order. The autonomous nature of the EU legal order of which the CJEU and the courts and tribunals of the Member States are the guardians is reflected in the finely balanced judicial architecture designed so as to safeguard the uniform application of EU law. In particular, the EU judiciary is itself an international dispute settlement system with a very special status and function in the Union's institutional architecture, which may not be undermined. In this respect, it can be observed that under intra-EU BITs claims are brought against a Member State by an investor, whereas Article 344 TFEU refers only to disputes brought by Member States. Moreover, while there is certainly something to be said for an arbitral tribunal being able to refer questions to the CJEU, this does not seem to be a route open for arbitral tribunals in investor-state disputes under intra-EU BITs. The main issue with regard to the autonomy of the EU legal order seems to be that investor-state arbitration is mostly designed so as to limit the degree of court interference. This raises the question of how EU law is

---

[308] *Eco Swiss* (above n 298) para 35.
[309] Ibid para 37.
[310] EU consumer protection law was recognised as a matter of public policy by the Court in C-168/05 *Mostaza Claro v Centro Movil* [2006] ECR I-10412.

actually handled by arbitral tribunals in investor-state disputes under intra-EU BITs.

B. EU Law in Investor-State Arbitration under Intra-EU BITs

Arbitral tribunals have in the past years been faced with claims in which EU law is invoked by either the investor claimant or the responding Member State. In some arbitration proceedings, the investor has used EU law as a sword by claiming that a Member State had not complied with its obligations under EU law – be it primary law, secondary legislation or an external agreement – which was, in turn, allegedly constitutive of a violation of BIT standards of treatment.[311] For example, in *Saluka*, a claim was brought under the Netherlands-Czech Republic BIT in relation to financial assistance given by the Czech Republic to a number of banks (but not to Saluka) to overcome the systemic problem of bad loans in the Czech banking system. In relation to facts predating accession of the Czech Republic to the Union, Saluka claimed, inter alia, that these state aid measures contravened the Czech Republic's obligations as a third country under the Europe Agreement,[312] and were therefore in breach of the standard of fair and equitable treatment.[313] The Czech Republic submitted that compliance of the Czech Republic with its obligations under the BIT could not be assessed in the light of its performance under the Europe Agreement, as the rules on state aid in this agreement were not directly effective. The tribunal ruled that it was not for it to assess the legality of the state aid measures under the Europe Agreement but only under the terms of the BIT, and it did not rule on the alleged failure of the Czech Republic to comply with its obligations under the Europe Agreement.[314]

In other arbitrations, Member States have used EU law as a shield by pleading the need to comply with EU law as a defence to a claim for a breach of an investment agreement.[315] For example, in *ADC* the exploitation of airport facilities in Hungary had been reorganised in order to implement EU law within the aviation sector in preparation for Hungary's accession to the Union in 2004. ADC had been awarded contracts with a view to the reconstruction and operation of (new) facilities at the airport of Budapest. These projects were subsequently taken over by Decree by another company. The investor claimant argued that the specific measures were intended to exclude foreign investors from the operation of the airport, while Hungary relied on the need to comply with EU law against the claim of unlawful expropriation under the Cyprus–Hungary BIT. The tribunal did 'not accept that compliance with EU law mandated the steps actually taken by

---

[311]   See, eg *Telenor v Hungary* (above n 3) Award; *Saluka v Czech Republic* (above n 21) Partial Award.
[312]   [1994] OJ L360/2.
[313]   *Saluka v Czech Republic* (above n 21) Partial Award, para 438.
[314]   Ibid paras 440–44.
[315]   See, eg *ADC v Hungary* (above n 3) Award; *Eastern Sugar v Czech Republic* (above n 1) Partial Award.

the Respondent, the subject matter of this arbitration'.[316] Doubt was therefore cast over the specific link between the measures and Hungary's obligations under EU law. Yet the tribunal did not explicitly contest that an assessment of the compatibility of the Hungarian measures at issue with the BIT could have involved a test of whether the measures actually taken were in line with Hungary's EU law obligations.

Although the precise wording of applicable law clauses in BITs differs, investment agreements generally refer to both domestic and international law. Generally, in investor-state arbitration a distinction can be drawn between the law applicable to the ascertainment of property rights and the law applicable to the claim for interference with such rights.[317] Domestic law plays an important role for the identification of rights *in rem*. By violating provisions of its domestic law, a host state may commit a breach of an investment agreement. International law (the investment agreement interpreted in the light of general principles of international law) serves to identify the minimum protection that is to be accorded to these rights. Arbitral tribunals can be faced with directly effective provisions of EU law that are argued by the investor claimant to confer rights which are constitutive of the investment that is to be protected under the investment agreement. In the case that an arbitral tribunal would take a position on the rights held by an investor under EU law, it would therefore apply EU law as a preliminary step in finding a breach of the BIT.

The breach of an investment agreement is a matter of international law. A Member State could argue that the investment protection rights enshrined in an intra-EU BIT should be interpreted in light of the EU law obligations of that Member State in accordance with Article 31(3)(c) VCLT, which requires for the interpretation of an international agreement the taking into account of 'any relevant rules of international law applicable in the relations between the parties'.[318] For example, a Member State could argue that the investment protection standards in an intra-EU BIT should be interpreted in the light of specific obligations of that Member State under EU law, as well as the requirement to comply with the EU general principle of legal certainty and the protection of legitimate expectations. It seems possible for EU law to play such a role in investor-state dispute settlement under intra-EU BITs. The tribunal would in such a scenario seem to be applying primarily the investment agreement itself rather than EU law, however. An arbitral tribunal will therefore most likely grapple with issues of EU law as a preliminary step or as an interpretative tool in finding a breach of an intra-EU BIT, rather than purporting to give an authoritative ruling on a Member State's performance under EU law that is binding on that Member State or the Union.

---

[316] *ADC v Hungary* (above n 3) Award, para 272.

[317] Z Douglas, *The International Law of Investment Claims* (Cambridge, Cambridge University Press, 2009) 40 ff. See also Dolzer and Schreuer, *Principles of International Investment Law* (above n 58) 270; G Sacerdoti, 'Investment Arbitration Under ICSID and UNCITRAL Rules: Prerequisites, Applicable Law, Review of Awards' (2005) 1 *ICSID Review* 1, 23 ff.

[318] C McLachlan, 'The Principle of Systemic Integration and Article 31(3)(c) of the Vienna Convention' (2005) 2 *ICLQ* 279.

Arbitral tribunals have recently taken a more explicit stance on the way in which EU law may feature in investor-state arbitration under intra-EU BITs. The tribunal in *Eureko* distinguished between a number of ways in which EU law may be implicated in investor-state arbitration under an intra-EU BIT. The tribunal took the view that EU law may affect the capacity of a state to consent to an international treaty, may affect the performance of obligations under the treaty, or may be part of the law applicable to determine the scope of obligations under the treaty, or may affect the manner in which disputes arising under the treaty must be settled and the jurisdiction of tribunals established outside the EU legal order.[319] The tribunal moreover took the view that 'Far from being precluded from considering and applying EU law the Tribunal is bound to apply it to the extent that it is part of the applicable law(s), whether under [the BIT], German law or otherwise'.[320] The tribunal did not accept that the CJEU has an interpretative monopoly on the application of EU law, since courts and arbitration tribunals throughout the EU interpret and apply EU law.[321] The tribunal concluded that it could consider and apply EU law, if required, both as a matter of international law and of German law.[322] The tribunal considered that 'in principle the EU legal doctrines, including those of supremacy, precedence, direct effect, direct applicability, are part of the body of EU law that might fall to be applied by the Tribunal in this case under Article 8(6) of the BIT [on applicable law]'.'[323] To this the tribunal added, however, that 'its jurisdiction is confined to ruling upon alleged breaches of the BIT. The Tribunal does not have jurisdiction to rule on alleged breaches of EU law as such'.[324]

Under the ECT, the tribunal in *Electrabel* also took the view that EU law is applied as international law and as national law in arbitration proceedings under the ECT in an intra-EU situation.[325] While EU law is based on international treaties and should therefore, according to the tribunal, be treated like other rules and principles of international law in the proceedings, they are introduced in the national legal order of the Member States and are therefore to be treated as 'facts'.[326] As regards concerns with regard to the autonomy of the EU legal order, the tribunal pointed to the fact that the *acte clair* doctrine leaves a degree of discretion to national courts to refer questions to the CJEU, that courts and tribunals of non-EU states may be seized with questions on the interpretation of EU law that they cannot refer to the CJEU, and took the view that Article 344 TFEU only refers to disputes between two Member States.[327] In respect of ICSID awards,

---

[319] *Eureko v Slovakia* (above n 19) Award on Jurisdiction, Arbitrability and Suspension, para 229.
[320] Ibid para 281.
[321] Ibid para 282.
[322] Ibid para 283.
[323] Ibid para 289.
[324] Ibid para 290.
[325] *Electrabel v Hungary* (above n 186) Decision on Jurisdiction, Applicable Law and Liability, para 4.195.
[326] Ibid para 4.127.
[327] Ibid para 4.146 ff.

where there cannot be ultimate control by the courts of the Member States, the tribunal referred to the possibility for the Commission to initiate infringement proceedings under Article 258 TFEU where the award gives rise to an inconsistency with EU law.[328] The Commission's jurisdictional objections were rejected by the tribunal in *Electrabel*, inter alia, because the investor did not challenge the validity of the Commission's Decision and did not claim that the Decision had been breached by Hungary.[329]

More specifically as regards the interplay between EU law and the ECT, the tribunal stated that 'the ECT's historical genesis and its text are such that the ECT should be interpreted, if possible, in harmony with EU law.'[330] Against this backdrop, the tribunal took the view that EU law prevails over the ECT in intra-EU situations.[331] The tribunal noted on the basis of an *a contrario* reading of Article 351 TFEU that, while this provision safeguards earlier agreements between a Member State and a non-Member State from the application of EU law, this means that EU law must prevail over earlier agreements between two Member States.[332] The tribunal added to this that the same result would have followed under Article 30 VCLT, albeit under the hypothesis that the two treaties relate to the same subject matter.[333] As a result, EU law would prevail over the ECT in the event of any material inconsistency.[334] In this case, however, the tribunal was not asked to adjudicate on the validity of the Commission's decision under EU law, nor on compliance by Hungary with its obligation under EU law. The main role to be played by EU law in investor-state arbitration under the ECT is thus analogous to that in the context of intra-EU BITs, so that EU law may be applied for the identification of rights *in rem* and as a tool for the interpretation of the investment agreement.

Arbitral tribunals have so far not been very assertive in interpreting the rights held by investors under EU law. Importantly, arbitral tribunals have emphasised that their jurisdiction is limited to alleged breaches of an intra-EU BIT and does not extend to alleged breaches of EU law. In this regard, it is possible to draw a

---

[328] Ibid para 4.160.

[329] Ibid para 5.34.

[330] Ibid para 4.130 ff. The tribunal referred to T Wälde, 'Arbitration in the Oil, Gas and Energy Field: Emerging Energy Charter Treaty Practice' (2004) 2 *Transnational Dispute Management* 1, 4: 'The ECT is largely a product of EU external political, economic and energy policy. It is meant to integrate the formerly Communist countries, provides an ante-chamber and preparation area for EU accession for many of them; it is intended to promote EU investment in these countries and energy flows from these countries to the EU. It is therefore linked more closely to EU integration, accession to the EU and EU external relations law than the "run-of the mill" BIT'.

[331] Ibid para 4.178 ff.

[332] Ibid para 4.183.

[333] Ibid para 4.190, with reference to Art 30(4) VCLT: 'When the parties to the later treaty do not include all the parties to the earlier one: (a) as between States parties to both treaties the same rule applies as in paragraph 3; (b) as between a State party to both treaties and a State party to only one of the treaties, the treaty to which both States are parties governs their mutual rights and obligations.' For an analysis of the incidence of Art 30(3) VCLT on the application of intra-EU BITs, see the text at III and accompanying notes.

[334] Ibid para 4.191.

parallel with the way in which Andean Community law has been implicated in investor-state arbitration. In *EnCana*,[335] the investor claimed that it had wrongfully been denied a refund of VAT under Ecuadorian law. It also claimed that the Ecuadorian measure at issue was contrary to Andean Community law. The tribunal held that:

> From the tribunal's perspective, unless and until action is successfully taken to . . . bring [Ecuadorian tax law] into line with what are said to be the obligations of Ecuador within the Andean Community, that [l]aw must be taken to define the extent to which oil companies are entitled to VAT refunds in respect of the acquisition of goods and services.[336]

The tribunal was thus not going to assess whether Ecuador had violated its obligations under Andean Community law, which was considered an issue more appropriately dealt with by Ecuadorian courts. In addition, on the broader issue of determining whether the rights of the investor claimant existed, the tribunal took the view that not taking a definite position on this matter was not tantamount to a requirement of exhaustion of local remedies, because the question was not whether the claim was inadmissible but whether the relevant rights existed and whether there had been an interference with these rights.[337]

Similarly, arbitral tribunals in investor-state arbitration under intra-EU BITs may show restraint in taking a position on the EU law obligations of the Member States, in particular as to whether a Member State has violated its obligations under EU law. Investors should more appropriately challenge Member State measures for reason of an alleged breach of EU law in Member State courts. Member State measures are consequently tested in investor-state arbitration under an intra-EU BIT exclusively against the standards of treatment of the BIT, even if these measures also fall within the scope of EU law. As a result, in many if not all situations an intra-EU BIT will at most prevent a Member State from enjoying its freedom under EU law to legislate in a certain way.[338] In other words, the intra-EU BIT primarily requires a Member State to act in a certain way within the discretion offered by EU law. In such situations an intra-EU BIT will not require a Member State to act inconsistently with EU law. In the case that a directly enforceable arbitral award does give rise to problems of contradictory legal obligations

---

[335] *EnCana v Ecuador*, LCIA Case no UN 3481, Award of 3 February 2006, (2006) 12 ICSID Rep 427, paras 187–200.

[336] Ibid para 187.

[337] Ibid para 200n. But see also *Occidental v Ecuador*, LCIA Case no UN 3467, Award of 1 July 2004, (2004) 12 ICSID Rep 59, where the tribunal took position on the rights of an investor under specific Andean Community Decisions in relation to a claim for a right to a VAT refund. The tribunal took the view that such a right existed both under Ecuadorian law and Andean Community law. As regards the binding nature of Andean Community Decisions, the tribunal moreover observed that 'If such obligations [under Andean Community law] are not carried out by a member country, aside from incurring international responsibility, it will not be able to invoke this omission to the disadvantage of a citizen or investor that has relied on the rules' (para 150).

[338] See also *Eureko v Slovakia* (above n 19) Award on Jurisdiction, Arbitrability and Suspension, paras 251–54.

for a Member State, the principle of primacy prevents a Member State from invoking the need to comply with an intra-EU BIT in order to justify acting in derogation from its obligations under EU law, as has been discussed above (III). The principle of primacy can ultimately be safeguarded by way of infringement proceedings under Article 258 TFEU.[339]

This section has found that the CJEU's case law provides only limited authority for considering the issues that arise in the context of the interplay between investor-state arbitration under intra-EU BITs and the autonomy of the EU legal order. The main issue with regard to the autonomy of the EU legal order seems to be that investor-state arbitration is mostly designed so as to limit the degree of court interference. Arbitral tribunals will most likely grapple with issues of EU law as a preliminary step in finding a breach of an intra-EU BIT by identifying the rights *in rem* of the investor claimant, or as a tool for the interpretation of the intra-EU BIT in light of the EU law obligations of a Member State. Importantly, arbitral tribunals have emphasised that their jurisdiction is limited to ruling on alleged breaches of an intra-EU BIT and does not extend to breaches of EU law. As a result, they do not purport to give an authoritative ruling on a Member State's performance under EU law or to take a position on the interpretation of EU law that is binding on that Member State or the Union. Arbitral tribunals have, moreover, so far not been very assertive in interpreting the rights held by investors under EU law. It is submitted that in many if not all situations an intra-EU BIT will at most prevent a Member State from enjoying its freedom under EU law to legislate in a certain way.

VI. CONCLUSION

The two rounds of accession of Central and Eastern European countries have raised a series of questions in relation to the interplay between EU law and the current network of intra-EU BITs. It has been shown that intra-EU investment agreements can be regarded as a useful complement for investors to the investment protection rights held in the EU legal order, even in relation to matters that fall under the scope of EU law. Not only do investors have access to investor-state arbitration under intra-EU BITs, the substantive rights of protection are also arguably not entirely equivalent. This is because EU law focuses primarily on issues of investment mobility, while investment agreements focus more explicitly on issues of investment security. The investment protection regime established by intra-EU BITs seems to go beyond that enshrined in EU law. This chapter has shown that the discriminatory access to dispute settlement under intra-EU BITs may raise issues of compatibility with EU law, though arguably more clearly so for some BITs than for others. At the same time, it has been argued that accession did not directly pose a challenge to the continued validity of these agreements.

---

[339] See also Eilmansberger, 'Bilateral Investment Treaties and EU Law' (above n 159) 406.

As a result of the operation of the principle of primacy, the Member States cannot invoke an intra-EU BIT in order to justify acting in derogation from their obligations under EU law. It has been argued that intra-EU agreements only reveal an incompatibility with EU law insofar as there are instances of actual conflict, while a logic of affectation is at work in the context of Member State agreements with third countries. Insofar as these agreements raise issues of compatibility with EU law, such as in relation to the EU principle of equal treatment, the effect of EU law is arguably in the first instance that the personal scope of application of these agreements should be extended to investors from Member States that are not contracting parties to a BIT. As regards the interplay between investor-state arbitration under intra-EU BITs and the autonomy of the EU legal order, the main problem seems to be that investor-state arbitration is mostly designed so as to limit the degree of court interference. Yet arbitral tribunals have not purported to give an authoritative ruling on a Member State's performance under EU law or to take a position on the interpretation of EU law that is binding on that Member State or the Union. Unlike in the context of Member State agreements with third countries, there is no explicit obligation to modify or terminate intra-EU agreements, although Member States may not oppose the intra-EU agreement to a Member State that would consequently have to act in defiance of EU law.

6

Conclusion

[By pooling sovereignty in the field of the production and distribution of coal and steel], there will be realised simply and speedily that fusion of interest which is indispensable to the establishment of a common economic system; it may be the leaven from which may grow a wider and deeper community between countries long opposed to one another by sanguinary divisions.[1]

T HIS STUDY HAS examined a number of aspects of EU legal integration in the field of foreign direct investment (FDI). The Union's post-Lisbon FDI competence and the first steps in the development of the common international investment policy have been the onset for a close analysis not only of the implications of the Lisbon reform of the (now) TFEU provisions on the common commercial policy (CCP) for the Union's competence and practice in the field of FDI, but also of the operation of the internal market mechanism in relation to direct investment and the interaction between EU law and Member State BITs. The process of EU legal integration in the field of FDI has been appreciated particularly in the light of a gradual opening up to direct investment and the remaining possibilities for restrictions, not only within the Single Market but also in relations with third countries. In addition, this study has probed the EU legal organisation insofar as concerns investment protection.

While the precise contours of a number of facets of EU legal integration in the field of direct investment are still in the process of being worked out, this concluding chapter brings together the various interrelated strands of analysis of this study pertaining to the shaping of the Single European Market in the field of FDI. Close jurisprudential analysis and a thorough examination of the context, purpose and evolution of different facets of EU legal integration in the field of FDI have revealed that there are certainly indications of a progressive move towards a level playing field for both EU and non-EU direct investors in the Single Market. This conclusion highlights the finding in this study that EU legal integration in the field of FDI is still some way from constituting a truly *single* European Market in this field.

---

[1] Schuman Declaration of 9 May 1951.

I. THE UNION'S POST-LISBON FDI COMPETENCE AND ITS EXERCISE

The shaping of the external dimension of the Single Market in the field of direct investment lags behind the more elaborate EU legal framework for the liberalisation of direct investment within the Single Market. The increased prominence of the liberalisation of foreign direct investment on the multilateral trade agenda from the late 1980s created a demand for reform of the legal basis for the Union's commercial policy. While the Community's limited external competence in the field of FDI under the EC Treaty provisions on the CCP could not satisfactorily be supplemented by having recourse to additional legal bases, the Lisbon reform of the TFEU provisions on the CCP has extended the Union's external competence to the field of FDI. While the Union's FDI competence under Article 207 TFEU is exclusive pursuant to Article 3(e) TFEU, its scope is more contentious. The Union's FDI competence seems to cover both the admission and treatment of FDI. It also seems possible to argue that the Union's FDI competence extends to the protection of FDI. By contrast, portfolio investment is excluded from the Union's FDI competence and it seems more difficult to ground the exclusivity of Union competence with regard to capital transfers on the TFEU provisions on free movement of capital. It can be expected that litigation before the CJEU will eventually clarify the various contentious issues pertaining to the scope of the Union's FDI competence. Nonetheless, it seems likely that the Union and the Member States will jointly conclude investment agreements under the common international investment policy. This could resemble the situation under the ECT, which contains investor-state dispute settlement provisions and to which both the Union and the Member States are contracting parties.

It has been shown that for Union external agreements to contain comprehensive investment provisions, including a standard of FET treatment and investor-state dispute settlement provisions, would constitute both a deepening and a widening of the Union's external action. The common international investment policy needs to be embedded in the overarching framework of EU external relations as part of the TFEU provisions on the CCP. Moreover, a common international investment policy along the lines suggested by the European Commission would further reinforce the autonomous character of the CCP in relation to the Union's internal legal organisation in the field of direct investment. This is because EU investors do not hold investment rights under EU law tantamount to standards of treatment such as FET treatment that can be invoked in investment arbitration against another Member State. The Lisbon reform of the CCP may contribute to the extent to which the Single Market constitutes a single investment area for non-EU investors. Existing Member State legislation dealing with FDI in principle remains unaffected, subject to the obligation of compliance with instruments adopted under the common international investment policy, whereas there is now a need for authorisation for the adoption of new measures and for the amendment of existing measures that fall under the scope of the Union's FDI competence. In addition, the admission and treatment of FDI in the Single Market may be increasingly subject to Union measures, which could further contribute to the shaping of the external dimension of the Single Market in the field of direct investment.

In addition to possible disputes over the scope of the Union's FDI competence, the implementation of the common international investment policy is likely to give rise to a number of further challenges. While there is agreement between the Commission, the Council and the European Parliament (EP) on the need for an ambitious policy on both the liberalisation and protection of investment, there are a number of issues on which agreement will need to be found. The broadening of the Union's investment policy to the issue of investment protection precipitates the need for a balancing act of the Commission between the views of the different institutions. In particular, the requirement of high standards of investment protection, including access to investor-state dispute settlement, on the one hand, and the recognition of the importance of the right for public authorities to regulate in the public interest, on the other hand, is a controversial issue in the implementation of the common international investment policy. The EP also takes the view that changes need to be made to the practice of investor-state dispute settlement with the result that Union investment agreements should contain an obligation to exhaust local judicial remedies where they are reliable enough to guarantee due process, allow for greater transparency, the opportunity for parties to appeal, the possibility to use *amicus curiae* briefs and an obligation to select one single place of investor-state arbitration.

The conclusion of Union investment agreements will also need to be supplemented with an internal arrangement with a view to shaping the modalities for the Union and the Member States' participation in investor-state dispute settlement under Union investment agreements. In view of the financial stakes involved in litigating over alleged breaches of future Union investment agreements, the Commission has proposed procedural arrangements in order to clarify the responsibility for a breach of the agreement between the Union and the Member States and who is the appropriate responding party in a dispute under such agreements. Negotiations on the proposed Regulation on financial responsibility are currently still ongoing.[2] This instrument needs to be in place before the conclusion of the first Union investment agreement under the common international investment policy.

The common international investment policy should enable the Union to remain a major player in international economic relations, on terms of equality with countries such as the United States, China, India, Brazil and Russia. While Germany may be able to continue to play at the highest level for a longer period of time, it seems more difficult to imagine that other Member States will continue to

---

[2] Proposal for a Regulation of the European Parliament and of the Council establishing a framework for managing financial responsibility linked to investor-state dispute settlement tribunals established by international agreements to which the European Union is a party, COM(2012)335 final, 21 June 2012, Brussels.

be able to take on this task on their own. A truly common international investment policy has the potential to equip the Union to deal with the growing economic clout of a considerable number of third countries. Against this backdrop, it will be important to assess the substance of the investment agreements that the Union envisages to conclude with countries such as China and India. The common international investment policy also raises the question what effect the ambition of concluding agreements with developed countries like the United States and Canada will have on the substance of future Union investment agreements as compared to the practice of some of the Member States. The investment treaty practice of these countries is based on a model investment treaty with features such as investor-state dispute settlement applying to the pre-entry phase of an investment. For a comparison it is necessary to await the conclusion of the first series of Union investment agreements.

The early history of the politicised clash between the Member States and capital-importing third countries has gradually transformed into a reality of international investment relations in which many (emerging) third countries increasingly export (state-owned) capital to the Single Market. The implementation of the common international investment policy will therefore take shape as part of an altered dynamic of international investment relations. One aspect of this changed environment of international investment relations concerns the issue of how to deal with investments in the Single Market, such as by sovereign wealth funds. In this respect, a proposal was reportedly floated by Commissioners Tajani and Barnier in 2011 to introduce an EU screening mechanism on grounds of national security by a centralised vetting committee for non-EU FDI inflows in the Single Market.[3] Countries such as the United States, Canada, Australia, Japan and China already have FDI screening mechanisms in place. The common international investment policy will have to be implemented whilst also taking into account that dimension of a changed reality of international investment relations.

II. THE INTERNAL MARKET FREEDOMS AND INWARD FDI

While a common international investment policy is likely to create opportunities for EU investors in third countries in the form of market access, investment treatment and protection rights, the issue of inward FDI raises questions with regard to the interplay of this policy with the law of the internal market. Unlike the Union's post-Lisbon FDI competence, no single provision in the EU Treaties has been dedicated to direct investment within the Single Market. At the hard core of European integration, the freedom of establishment and the free movement of capital have, from the early years of the Community, served to eliminate restrictions on intra-EU direct investment. The free movement of capital, but not the freedom of establishment, can be invoked by third-country investors when seeking access to the

---

[3] 'Analysis: rising foreign investment fuels EU vetting debate', Reuters, 8 March 2011, available at http://uk.reuters.com/article/2011/03/08/uk-eu-industry-investment-idUKTRE7272C720110308.

Single Market. It has been argued that the guiding principle for dealing with the area of overlap between these TFEU freedoms is that national measures are not tested against the free movement of capital when they primarily affect the freedom of establishment, even if they also affect transfers of capital in relation to direct investment, as well as vice versa. As a result of this centre of gravity approach, the Union has not unilaterally opened up to third-country direct investment under the internal market mechanism insofar as specific transactions primarily constitute establishment. At the same time, recent case law shows that the free movement of capital may be primarily affected where a national measure has a restrictive effect on a controlling holding, depending on the purpose of the measure.

An important task in studying EU legal integration in the field of FDI has been to dissect the notion of investment 'treatment' under EU law. In this regard, a distinction has been drawn between issues relating to the primary and secondary rights of mobility for third-country direct investors. So far as concerns the post-establishment treatment of FDI in the Single Market, the Union's external FDI competence seems to cover the treatment granted in connection with the primary establishment of third-country direct investors. For the purpose of the operation of the internal market mechanism in relation to FDI, this aspect of the post-establishment treatment of FDI has been characterised as the participation of third-country direct investors in the internal economy of a Member State. While there is EU secondary legislation containing provisions on the primary and secondary rights of mobility of third-country direct investment, existing Member State investment codes and the various commitments of the Member States in the schedules of commitments under the GATS evidence the lack of uniform conditions for the admission and treatment of FDI flowing into different Member States from outside the Single Market. Notwithstanding the inward-looking character of the TFEU freedom of establishment, the admission of FDI may be more and more subject to both conventional and autonomous Union measures, and thus give rise to a more level playing field so far as concerns the post-establishment treatment of FDI in the Single Market.

In the field of trade in goods, there has always been a close link between the principle of free circulation within the Single Market of goods originating in third countries and the establishment of the CCP. The assimilation of goods in 'free circulation' to products originating within the Member States was even conditional upon the creation of a common commercial policy. A uniform regime for the importation of goods prevents goods from being imported into a Member State via another Member State so as to benefit from the latter's more advantageous import regime. By contrast, no such uniform admission regime has been created in the field of FDI and third-country direct investors can in principle circumvent a restrictive FDI admissions regime of a Member State by channelling their investment through a Member State with a more liberal admissions regime. After all, once a third-country investor has created a subsidiary in one of the Member States, it can invoke Article 54 TFEU and become economically active in another Member State. The Union's post-Lisbon FDI competence arguably does not seem to extend to the participation of third-country direct investors in those economic activities that are covered by the internal market mechanism. Yet both Member State and relevant Union practice shows that legal persons, which prima facie meet the requirements of Article 54 TFEU, have nevertheless not been granted secondary rights of mobility in the case that they are directly or indirectly controlled by third-country natural or legal persons. Such restrictions to or additional requirements for third-country direct investors could in practice be easier to justify under EU law than for EU investors. Moreover, such differential treatment by the Union could perhaps more easily be justified than differential treatment by the Member States in function of the development of a common international investment policy.

Dissecting the notion of investment 'treatment' under EU law also involves an interpretation of the scope of 'national' treatment (NT) commitments in Union investment agreements. Where a Regional Economic Integration Organisation (REIO) exception to most favoured nation (MFN) treatment is included in Union investment agreements, it has been argued that the NT commitments under such agreements, so far as concerns treatment of third-country direct investment by a Member State, should be interpreted so as to involve a comparison with the treatment by that specific Member State of investment of its own nationals and not of other EU nationals that are economically active in that Member State. Otherwise, the commitments carved out by the REIO exception to MFN treatment would be imported into the agreement via the provisions on NT and the REIO exception to the MFN clause would consequently be defunct. Moreover, it is arguably only by including both a REIO clause and the proposed interpretation of the commitments regarding NT that it is possible to encapsulate an approach to the issue of initial post-establishment treatment of FDI, which is consistent with the objectives of Single Market integration in the field of direct investment and with those of the CCP so far as concerns the shaping of the external dimension of the Single Market in that field. This study has therefore highlighted the importance of the intensity of commitments undertaken under the NT and MFN standards in Union investment agreements, as well as the interplay of such commitments with Article 54 TFEU.

The common international investment policy thus interacts with the law of the internal market. There seems to be a need to include internal market legal bases for some aspects of FDI flows into the Single Market in order to complement the Union's external FDI competence. It is therefore clear that there is a need for an integrated approach to the EU legal organisation in the field of FDI. At the same time, the common international investment policy seems to announce a move beyond parallelism between the internal and external dimension of the Single European Market in the field of FDI. While the Union's post-Lisbon FDI competence under the TFEU provisions on the CCP is exclusive, Union competence under the TFEU provisions on the internal market is in principle shared, unless it has been exercised. It is therefore important to delineate between Union competences under the TFEU provisions on the internal market and under Article 207 TFEU in relation to FDI. Moreover, it seems that the inclusion in Union investment agreements of a fair and equitable treatment (FET) standard that can be invoked in investor-state arbitration has no EU law equivalent within the Single Market. Under the common international investment policy, the Union will move into a territory that it had not previously charted, since it was hitherto covered exclusively by Member State BITs.

III. EU LAW AND MEMBER STATE BITS

The development of the common international investment policy raises questions with regard to the continued existence and application of Member State BITs. This study has emphasised that EU law, including Union external agreements, and Member State BITs have traditionally had a different regulatory emphasis. While BITs focus on issues of investment security so as to foster the profitability of foreign assets in the host state, EU law deals with investment primarily through economic integration by means of the liberalisation of direct investment and focuses predominantly on the free circulation of production factors so as to increase the efficiency of the Single Market. Even though the Union has acquired an exclusive competence in the field of FDI pursuant to the Lisbon reform of the (now) TFEU provisions on the CCP, the Member States are still contracting parties to numerous BITs with third countries, which have long co-existed with EU law. Regulation 1219/2012 establishes transitional arrangements for Member State investment agreements with third countries in view of the Union's post-Lisbon FDI competence and the implementation of the common international investment policy. It establishes a requirement of notification and a replacement mechanism for existing Member State BITs with third countries and contains an authorisation mechanism for the amendment of existing BITs and for the conclusion of new BITs.

It has been demonstrated that there are various ways in which Member State BITs with third countries interact with EU law. This is evidenced by the Memorandum of Understanding (MoU) that was signed with the United States in the context of accession of a number of Central and Eastern European Member States, as well as the 'BITs' judgments, which identified a number of areas of interaction and the need to protect the *acquis*. Such interaction is with both the internal market mechanism, EU secondary legislation and with the Union's external practice in the field of FDI. The EU legal framework that governs the interplay between EU law and these agreements focuses on issues of substantive compatibility and has potential implications for existing BITs. It is guided by the principle that such BITs may not affect the application of EU law, but is arguably not encapsulated by a general 'hypothetical incompatibility' test. This, in turn, is itself a wide understanding of the scope for incompatibility between EU law and such agreements, which reflects the fact that international law prevents Member States from setting aside international agreements with third countries in order to comply with their obligations under EU law when such obligations qualify as *res inter alios acta*. While the principle of primacy is suspended in relation to pre-accession agreements under Article 351(1) TFEU, it is not with regard to post-accession agreements. At the same time, for both categories of agreements there may ultimately be a duty to denounce them in the case that such incompatibilities cannot be eliminated by amending the agreements. In addition to the duty of compliance, the EU legal framework governing the interaction between EU law and Member State agreements with third countries consists of the principle of sincere cooperation.

The adoption of Regulation 1219/2012 is a significant development for Member State investment agreements with third countries. First and foremost, it confirms the status quo of existing Member State BITs with third countries and thereby leaves unaffected the level of protection currently offered to investors by these agreements. This is certainly to be welcomed. The Commission's assessment with regard to the question whether existing Member State BITs constitute a serious obstacle to the negotiation and conclusion of Union investment agreements will be undertaken on a case-by-case basis. Moreover, the application of the grounds for a refusal by the Commission to authorise a Member State to amend existing investment agreements and to conclude new agreements remains to be seen in practice. Overall, the adoption of Regulation 1219/2012 is an important step in the shaping of the external dimension of the Single Market in the field of FDI. Union investment agreements will not merely complement Member State BITs, but are envisaged to gradually replace at least some of them. Member State BITs with some of the large foreign markets might be replaced sooner than others, in view of the priorities set by the Commission for concluding Union investment agreements with third countries.

The fate of intra-EU BITs is uncertain. While intra-EU investment agreements can be regarded as a useful complement for investors to the investment protection rights held under EU law, the Commission considers that these agreements should be terminated. The Member States have been reported to be divided on the matter. One of the problems identified by the Commission is the discriminatory access of EU investors to dispute settlement under intra-EU BITs. This study has argued that the CJEU has so far neither explicitly rejected nor confirmed a general principle of MFN treatment in respect of every aspect of each inter-Member State agreement, which is of relevance to the host Member State of a direct investment within the Single Market. By contrast, the principle of NT has been confirmed to be part and parcel of Single Market integration, which is of relevance for the Member State through which an investment has been channelled. A Member State in principle violates the EU principle of equal treatment if EU investors, who are in like situations to its own nationals, are excluded from the benefits enshrined in an agreement with another Member State, unless this can be justified. In that light, some intra-EU BITs seem more susceptible of giving rise to an incompatibility with the EU law principle of equal treatment than others. Insofar as intra-EU BITs are incompatible with the principle of equal treatment, their scope of application has to be extended to other EU investors. Moreover, the other contracting Member State to an intra-EU BIT has a duty under Article 4(3) TEU to assist that Member State in complying with its obligations under EU law.

The question also arises whether EU law permits disputes involving issues of EU law between an investor from one Member State, on the one hand, and another Member State, on the other, to be decided not in one of the courts of the Member States or in Luxembourg, but by an arbitral tribunal under an intra-EU BIT. Arbitral tribunals will most likely grapple with issues of EU law as a preliminary step in finding a breach of an intra-EU BIT by identifying the rights *in rem* of the investor claimant, or for the interpretation of the intra-EU BIT in light of the EU law obligations of a Member State. It can be observed that arbitral tribunals have so far not been very assertive in interpreting the rights held by investors under EU law. Importantly, arbitral tribunals have emphasised on a number of occasions that their jurisdiction is limited to ruling on alleged breaches of an intra-EU BIT and does not extend to alleged breaches of EU law. Therefore, they do not purport to give an authoritative ruling on a Member State's performance under EU law or on the interpretation of EU law that is binding on that Member State or the Union. This significantly mitigates the extent to which investor-state dispute settlement under intra-EU BITs might encroach upon the autonomy of the EU legal order.

This study has argued that accession has not directly posed a challenge to the continued validity of these agreements. At the same time, the Member States cannot invoke an intra-EU BIT in order to justify acting in derogation from their obligations under EU law as a result of the operation of the principle of primacy. Unlike in the context of Member State agreements with third countries, there is no explicit obligation to modify or terminate intra-EU agreements that are incompatible with EU law. It has, moreover, been argued that intra-EU agreements only reveal an incompatibility with EU law insofar as there are instances of actual conflict, while a logic of affectation is at work in the context of Member State agreements with third countries. This seems to militate in favour of the continued existence of intra-EU BITs, even if EU law may at times affect their application. However, the operation of the principle of primacy is complicated by the fact that a Member State may need to give effect to an arbitral award, rather than to an intra-EU BIT as such. Non-compliance with an award rendered by an ICSID arbitral tribunal means that a Member State acts in direct contravention of the ICSID Convention. In addition, the technique of disapplying incompatible provisions of intra-EU agreements is arguably circumscribed by the need to safeguard the principle of legal certainty.

The implementation of the common international investment policy fosters the process of legal integration in the field of investment protection so far as concerns the external dimension of the Single Market. The Union is currently negotiating investment protection commitments with third countries, which will gradually replace existing Member State BITs with those third countries. However, legal integration in the field of investment protection within the Single Market seems to lag behind this process. While the EU legal order contains investment protection rights under the internal market freedoms, the Charter of Fundamental

Rights and the general principles of EU law, it has been argued that intra-EU BITs provide a useful complement for EU investors. For the purpose of advancing Single Market integration it would arguably be best to harmonise the investment protection regime in the internal market under current intra-EU BITs. In this respect, it would need to be further explored to what extent it would be legally possible and politically feasible to establish an intra-EU investment arbitration facility under EU secondary legislation or in the form of enhanced cooperation with less than all Member States, but which continues to be open for other Member States under Article 331 TFEU. Such a facility could be complemented with procedural safeguards in respect of the autonomy of the EU legal order in response to the Commission's concerns.

IV. FUTURE DIRECTION OF EU LEGAL INTEGRATION IN THE FIELD OF FDI

More than 50 years after the conclusion of the Treaty of Rome, the precise contours of a number of facets of EU legal integration in the field of direct investment are still in the process of being worked out. While the freedom of establishment and the free movement of capital have, from the early years of the Community, served to eliminate restrictions on intra-EU direct investment, the internal market rights of third-country direct investors are still in the process of being crystallised. The issue of intra-EU BITs was effectively born in 2004 with the accession to the Union of a number of Central and Eastern European Member States. Pursuant to the Union's post-Lisbon FDI competence, the first steps in the implementation of a common international investment policy are currently being undertaken, which will contribute to the shaping of the external dimension of the Single Market in the field of FDI. The signing of an MoU with the United States as part of the process of accession of these Member States and, a few years later, the infringement proceedings brought against Austria, Sweden and Finland with regard to the capital transfer clauses in a number of their BITs has underlined the importance of the interaction between EU law and Member State investment agreements with third countries. Under the common international investment policy, the interplay between EU law and Member State BITs with third countries has now been addressed more systematically through the adoption of Regulation 1219/2012.

This study has examined a number of aspects of EU legal integration in the field of FDI. Each chapter has brought to light to what extent the Single European Market manifests itself as a *single* market in the field of FDI and may increasingly do so in future. The teleology of Single Market integration has been described by the CJEU as:

> [involving] the elimination of all obstacles to intra-[Union] trade in order to merge the national markets into a single market bringing about conditions as close as possible to those of a genuine internal market.[4]

---

[4] 15/81 *Gaston Schul* [1982] ECR 1309, para 33.

It seems accurate to characterise the process of Single Market integration in the field of direct investment as a process of elimination of obstacles, both as a result of negative and positive integration, rather than of moving towards strict uniformity. The Member States still have separate investment codes, investment promotion policies and extensive BIT networks with third countries, while about 200 BITs are also still in force between the Member States. Single Market integration in the field of direct investment, and particularly the automatic granting of rights of secondary mobility to third-country direct investors, gives rise to the need for a more coherent external policy in this field. The implementation of the common international investment policy may gradually lead to a more level playing field for third-country investors in the Single Market. The post-establishment treatment of FDI is likely to be increasingly subject to EU law, while also here the stated aim is the elimination of restrictions rather than the harmonisation of the conditions of establishment. Single Market integration in the field of FDI essentially constitutes a move towards a liberal international economic order. Such openness to FDI is now also more likely to be complemented with a more elaborate policy insofar as concerns the protection of FDI.

Underlying EU legal integration in the field of FDI is a specific configuration of interests of the Member States. While there certainly does not seem to have occurred a 'fusion of interests' of the Member States, as was envisaged by Schuman, this study has identified a number of modest indications of a purported move (at least, de jure) towards the defence of a common Union interest in the field of FDI. Under the Union's post-Lisbon FDI competence, the Union – instead of the Member States – is supposed to act in the common interest. It is this same common interest that the Member States are supposed to serve as trustees under Regulation 1219/2012 establishing transitional arrangements for Member State BITs with third countries, such as when they are authorised to amend existing BITs or to conclude new BITs. A similar gradual shift seems to be evidenced in the sectors of cultural and audiovisual services, educational services and social and human health services, where less provision has been made under the post-Lisbon TFEU provisions on the CCP to accommodate the special interests of the Member States in relation to FDI. Nevertheless, a truly Single European Market in the field of direct investment, characterised not only by the creation of a level playing field for EU and non-EU investors, but also by a recognition of collective responsibility by the Member States in dealing with the issue of direct investment within, to and from the Single Market, as opposed to a sense of exclusive responsibility for their national industries, seems to be some way from the current state of affairs.

Bibliography

BOOKS, ARTICLES ETC

Abdelal, R, *Capital Rules: The Construction of Global Finance* (Cambridge (MA), Harvard University Press, 2007)

Acconci, P, 'Determining the Internationally Relevant Link between a State and a Corporate Investor: Recent Trends concerning the Application of the "Genuine Link" Test' (2004) 1 *Journal of World Investment and Trade* 139

Akkermans, V and Ramaekers, E, 'Article 345 TFEU (ex Article 295 EC), Its Meanings and Interpretations' (2010) *European Law Journal* 292

Azoulai, L and Ben Hamida, W, 'La protection des investissements par le droit primaire: droit conventionnel des investissements et droit primaire communautaire: étude comparé des régimes et des approches' in C Kessedjian and C Leben (eds), *Le droit européen et l'investissement* (Paris, Éditions Panthéon-Assas, 2009) 69–88

Bakker, AFP, *The Full Liberalization of Capital Movements in Europe: The Monetary Committee and Financial Integration 1958–1994* (Dordrecht, Kluwer, 1995)

Balassa, B, *The Theory of Economic Integration* (London, Allen and Unwin, 1962)

Barnard, CS, 'Restricting Restrictions: Lessons for the EU from the US?' (2009) 3 *CLJ* 575

—— *The Substantive Law of the EU: The Four Freedoms*, 3rd edn (Oxford, Oxford University Press, 2010)

Barrett, G, 'Protecting Legitimate Expectations in European Community Law and in Irish Domestic Law' (2001) *Yearbook on European Law* 191

Benyon, F, 'Community Association Agreements: From the Sixties to the Nineties' in S Konstadinidis (ed), *The Legal Regulation of the European Community's External Relations after the Completion of the Internal Market* (Dartmouth, Aldershot, 1996) 51–59

—— *Direct Investment, National Champions and the EU Treaty Freedoms* (Oxford, Hart Publishing, 2010)

Bischoff, JA, 'Just a Little *Bit* of "Mixity"? The EU's Role in the Field of International Investment Protection Law' (2011) 5 *CML Rev* 1527

Bourgeois, JHJ, 'The EC in the WTO and Advisory Opinion 1/94: An Echternach Procession' (1995) 3 *CML Rev* 763

Brakeland, JF, 'Politique commerciale commune, coopération avec les pays tiers et aide humanitaire' in G Amato, H Bribosia and B de Witte (eds), *Genesis and Destiny of the European Constitution* (Brussels, Bruylant, 2007) 849–74

Brewer, TL and Young, S, *The Multilateral Investment System and Multinational Enterprises* (Oxford, Oxford University Press, 1998)

Brown, C and Naglis, I, 'Dispute Settlement in Future EU Investment Agreements' in M Bungenberg, A Reinisch and C Tietje (eds), *EU and Investment Agreements: Open Questions and Remaining Challenges* (Baden-Baden, Nomos, 2013) 17–35

Burgstaller, M, 'European Law and Investment Treaties' (2009) 2 *Journal of International Arbitration* 181

—— 'Investor-State Arbitration in EU International Investment Agreements with Third Countries' (2012) 2 *Legal Issues of European Integration* 207

Ceyssens, J, 'Towards a Common Foreign Investment Policy? Foreign Investment in the European Constitution' (2005) 3 *Legal Issues of European Integration* 259

Churchill, RR and Foster, NG, 'European Community Law and Prior Treaty Obligations of the Member States: The Spanish Fishermen's Cases' (1987) 3 *ICLQ* 504

Cremona, M, 'The Completion of the Internal Market and the Incomplete Commercial Policy of the European Community' (1990) 4 *EL Rev* 283

—— 'The External Dimension of the Single Market: Building (on) the Foundations' in CS Barnard and J Scott (eds), *The Law of the Single European Market: Unpacking the Premises* (Oxford, Hart Publishing, 2002) 351–93

—— 'The Draft Constitutional Treaty: External Relations and External Action' (2003) 6 *CML Rev* 1347

—— 'Defending the Community Interest: The Duties of Cooperation and Compliance' in M Cremona and B de Witte, *EU Foreign Relations Law: Constitutional Fundamentals* (Oxford, Hart Publishing, 2008) 125–69

—— *Member States as Trustees of the Community Interest: Participating in International Agreements on Behalf of the European Community*, EUI Working Paper Law 2009/17

—— 'The European Union and Regional Trade Agreements' in C Herrmann and JP Terhechte (eds), *European Yearbook of International Economic Law* (Heidelberg, Springer, 2010) 245–68

—— 'Disconnection Clauses in EU Law and Practice' in C Hillion and P Koutrakos (eds), *Mixed Agreements Revisited* (Oxford, Hart Publishing, 2010) 160–86

Dashwood, AA, 'The Limits of European Community Powers' (1996) 2 *EL Rev* 113

—— 'States in the European Union'(1998) 3 *EL Rev* 201

—— 'Implied External Competence of the EC' in M Koskenniemi (ed), *International Law Aspects of the European Union* (The Hague, Kluwer Law International, 1998) 113–23

—— 'Article 308 EC as the Outer Limit of Expressly Conferred Community Competence' in CS Barnard and O Odudu (eds), *The Outer Limits of European Union Law* (Oxford, Hart Publishing, 2009) 35–44

Dashwood, AA and Heliskoski, J, 'The Classic Authorities Revisited' in AA Dashwood and C Hillion (eds), *The General Law of EC External Relations* (London, Sweet and Maxwell, 2000) 3–19

De Búrca, G, 'The Tobacco Judgment: Political Will versus Constitutional Limits' in University of Cambridge Centre for European Legal Studies, *The ECJ's Tobacco Advertising Judgment*, Occasional Paper No 5 (July 2001), 5–18

Demaret, P (ed), *Relations extérieures de la Communauté européenne et marché intérieur: aspects juridiques et fonctionnels* (Brussels, Story-Scientia, 1988)

Denza, E, 'Bilateral Investment Treaties and EU Rules on Free Transfer: Comment on Commission v Austria, Commission v Sweden and Commission v Finland' (2010) 2 *EL Rev* 263–74

Dimopoulos, A, 'The Common Commercial Policy after Lisbon: Establishing Parallelism between Internal and External Economic Relations?' (2008) *Croatian Yearbook of European Law and Policy* 101

—— 'Shifting the Emphasis from Investment Protection to Liberalization and Development: The EU as a New Global Factor in the Field of Foreign Investment' (2010) 1 *JWI* 5

—— 'The Validity and Applicability of International Investment Agreements between EU Member States under EU and International Law' (2011) 1 *CML Rev* 63

—— 'The Compatibility of Future EU Investment Agreements with EU Law' (2012) 4 *Legal Issues of European Integration* 447

—— *EU Foreign Investment Law* (Oxford, Oxford University Press, 2012)

Dolzer, R, and Schreuer, C, *Principles of International Investment Law* (Oxford, Oxford University Press, 2008)

Douglas, Z, *The International Law of Investment Claims* (Cambridge, Cambridge University Press, 2009)

—— 'The MFN Clause in Investment Arbitration: Treaty Interpretation Off the Rails' (2011) 2 *Journal of International Dispute Settlement* 97

Dutheil de la Rochère, J, 'Le pouvoir des états membres de l'Union européenne de conclure des traités bilatéraux d'investissement' in C Kessedjian and C Leben (eds), *Le droit européen et l'investissement* (Paris, Éditions Panthéon-Assas, 2009) 27–39

Eeckhout, P, 'The External Dimension of the Internal Market and the Scope and Content of a Modern Commercial Policy' in M Maresceau (ed), *The European Community's Commercial Policy after 1992: The Legal Dimension* (Dordrecht, Martinus Nijhoff, 1993) 79–101

—— *The European Internal Market and International Trade: A Legal Analysis* (Oxford, Clarendon Press, 1994)

—— *External Relations of the European Union: Legal and Constitutional Foundations* (Oxford, Oxford University Press, 2005)

Eilmansberger, T, 'Bilateral Investment Treaties and EU Law' (2009) 2 *CML Rev* 383

Emch, A, 'News from Luxembourg: Is the New EU Investment Law Taking Shape?' (2008) 6 *Journal of World Investment and Trade* 497

Faya Rodriguez, A, 'The Most-Favored-Nation Clause in International Investment Agreements: A Tool for Treaty Shopping?' (2008) 1 *Journal of International Arbitration* 89

Fleischer, H, 'Case C-367/98 *Commission v Portugal*, Case C-483/99 *Commission v France* and Case C-503/99 *Commission v Belgium*' (2003) 2 *CML Rev* 493 (note)

Flynn, L, 'Coming of Age: The Free Movement of Capital Case Law 1993–2002' (2002) 4 *CML Rev* 773

Gaudissart, MA, 'Reflexions sur la nature et la portée du concept d'association à la lumière de sa mise en oeuvre' in MFC Tchakaloff (ed), *Le concept d'association dans les accords passés par la Communauté: essai de clarification* (Brussels, Bruylant, 1999) 3–36

Gilpin, R, *Global Political Economy: Understanding the International Economic Order* (Princeton (NJ), Princeton University Press, 2001)

Govaere, I, 'Beware of the Trojan Horse: Dispute Settlement in (Mixed) Agreements and the Autonomy of the EU Legal Order' in C Hillion and P Koutrakos (eds), *Mixed Agreements Revisited: The European Union and the Member States in the World* (Oxford, Hart Publishing, 2010) 187–207

Groeben, H von der, Thiessing, J and Ehlermann, CD, *Kommentar zum EWG-Vertrag*, 4th edn (Baden-Baden, Nomos, 1991) 1023–39

Guzman, AT, 'Why LDCs Sign Treaties that Hurt Them: Explaining the Popularity of Bilateral Investment Treaties' (1998) 4 *Virginia Journal of International Law* 639

Hanf, D and Dengler, P, 'Les accords d'association' in JV Louis and M Dony (eds), *Commentaire Mégret, Le droit de la CE et de l'Union européenne*, 2nd edn (Brussels, Édition de l'Université de Bruxelles, 2005) vol 12, 293–335

Harten, G van, *Investment Treaty Arbitration and Public Law* (Oxford, Oxford University Press, 2007)

Hedemann-Robinson, M, 'Third-Country Nationals, European Union Citizenship, and Free Movement of Persons: A Time for Bridges rather than Divisions' (1996) *Yearbook on European Law* 321

Heliskoski, J, 'The Nice Reform of Article 133 EC on the Common Commercial Policy' (2001) 1 *Journal of International Commercial Law* 1

—— *Mixed Agreements as Technique for Organizing the International Relations of the European Community and its Member States* (The Hague, Kluwer Law International, 2001)

Herrmann, C, 'Common Commercial Policy after Nice, Sisyphus Would have Done a Better Job' (2002) 1 *CML Rev* 7

Higgins, R, *The Taking of Foreign Property by the State: Recent Developments under International Law* (Collected Courses of The Hague Academy of International Law, 1982)

Hillion, C, '*Tous pour un, un pour tous!* Coherence in the External Relations of the European Union' in M Cremona (ed), *Developments in EU External Relations Law* (Oxford, Oxford University Press, 2008) 10–36

—— 'A Look Back at the Open Skies' in M Bulterman, L Hancher, A McDonnell and HG Sevenster (eds), *Views of European Law from the Mountain* (Alphen aan den Rijn, Kluwer Law International, 2009) 257–65

—— 'Mixity and Coherence in EU External Relations: The Significance of the "Duty of Cooperation"' in C Hillion and P Koutrakos (eds), *Mixed Agreements Revisited: The European Union and the Member States in the World* (Oxford, Hart Publishing, 2010) 87–115

Hindelang, S, 'The EC Treaty's Freedom of Capital Movement as an Instrument of International Investment Law?' in A Reinisch and C Knahr (eds), *International Investment Law in Context* (Utrecht, Eleven International Publishing, 2008) 43–72

—— *The Free Movement of Capital and Foreign Direct Investment: The Scope of Protection under EU Law* (Oxford, Oxford University Press, 2009)

—— 'Circumventing Primacy of EU Law and the CJEU's Judicial Monopoly by Resorting to Dispute Resolution Mechanisms Provided for in Inter-Se Treaties? The Case of Intra-EU Investment Arbitration' (2012) 2 *Legal Issues of European Integration* 179

Hoffmeister, F, 'Litigating Against the European Union and its Member States: Who Responds under the ILC's Draft Articles on International Responsibility of International Organizations?' (2010) 3 *EJIL* 723

Hoffmeister, F and Ondrusek, P, 'The European Community in International Litigation' (2008) 1 *Revue Hellénique de Droit International* 205

Hoffmeister, F and Ünüvar, G, 'From BITs and Pieces towards European Investment Agreements' in M Bungenberg, A Reinisch and C Tietje (eds), *EU and Investment Agreements: Open Questions and Remaining Challenges* (Baden-Baden, Nomos, 2013) 57–85

Hoorn, V van, '"Unbundling", "Reciprocity" and the European Internal Energy Market: WTO Consistency and Broader Implications for Europe' (2009) 1 *European Energy and Environmental Law Review* 51

Jacobs, FG, 'Direct Effect and Interpretation of International Agreements in the Recent Case Law of the European Court of Justice' in AA Dashwood and M Maresceau (eds), *Law and Practice of EU External Relations: Salient Features of a Changing Landscape* (Cambridge, Cambridge University Press, 2008) 13–33

Jansen Calamita, N, 'The Making of Europe's International Investment Policy: Uncertain First Steps' (2012) 3 *Legal Issues of European Integration* 301

Jensen, NM, *Nation-States and the Multinational Corporation: A Political Economy of Foreign Direct Investment* (Princeton (NJ), Princeton University Press, 2006)

Juillard, P, *L'évolution des sources du droit des investissements* (Collected Courses of the Hague Academy of International Law, 1994)

—— 'MAI: A European View' (1998) 3 *Cornell International Law Journal* 477

—— 'Freedom of Establishment, Freedom of Capital and Freedom of Investment' (2001) 2 *ICSID Review* 322

Karl, J, 'Das Multilaterale Investitionsabkommen (MAI)' (1998) 6 *Recht der internationalen Wirtschaft* 432

—— 'The Competence for Foreign Direct Investment: New Powers for the European Union?' (2004) 3 *Journal of World Investment and Trade* 413

Kessedjian, C and Leben, C (eds), *Le droit européen et l'investissement* (Paris, Éditions Panthéon-Assas, 2009)

Kingston, S, 'A Light in the Darkness: Recent Developments in the ECJ's Direct Tax Jurisprudence' (2007) 5 *CML Rev* 1321

Klabbers, J, *Treaty Conflict and the European Union* (Cambridge, Cambridge University Press, 2009)

Kobrin, SJ, 'Sovereignty@Bay: Globalization, Multinational Enterprise, and the International Political System' in AM Rugman and TL Brewer (eds), *The Oxford Handbook of International Business* (Oxford, Oxford University Press, 2001) 181–205

Konstantinidis, SV, *The Legal Regulation of the European Community's External Relations after the Completion of the Internal Market* (Boston (MA), Dartmouth Publishing, 1996)

Koutrakos, P, *EU International Relations Law* (Oxford, Hart Publishing, 2006)

—— 'Legal Basis and Delimitation of Competence in EU External Relations' in M Cremona and B de Witte (eds), *EU Foreign Relations Law: Constitutional Fundamentals* (Oxford, Hart Publishing, 2008) 171–98

Krajewski, M, 'External Trade Law and Constitutional Treaty: Towards a Federal and More Democratic Common Commercial Policy?' (2005) 1 *CML Rev* 91

—— 'Of Modes and Sectors. External Relations, Internal Debates, and the Social Case of (Trade in) Services' in M Cremona (ed), *Developments in EU External Relations Law* (Oxford, Oxford University Press, 2008) 172–215

Kriebaum, U, 'Nationality and the Protection of Property Rights under the European Convention on Human Rights' in I Buffard, J Crawford, A Pellet, S Wittich (eds), *International Law Between Universalism and Fragmentation, Festschrift in Honour of Gerhard Hafner* (Leiden, Nijhoff, 2008) 649–66

—— 'Is the European Court of Human Rights an Alternative to Investor-State Arbitration?' in PM Dupuy, F Francioni and EU Petersmann (eds), *Human Rights and International Investment Law and Arbitration* (Oxford, Oxford University Press, 2009) 219–45

Kriebaum, U and Schreuer, C, 'The Concept of Property in Human Rights Law and International Investment Law' in S Breitmoser (ed), *Human Rights, Democracy and the Rule of Law* (Baden-Baden, Nomos, 2007) 743–62

Kuijper, PJ, 'The Conclusion and Implementation of the Uruguay Rounds Results by the European Community' (1995) 2 *EJIL* 222

—— 'The Court and the Tribunal of the EC and the Vienna Convention on the Law of Treaties 1969' (1998) 1 *Legal Issues of European Integration* 1

——'Re-reading External Relations Cases in the Field of Transport: The Function of Community Loyalty' in M Bulterman, L Hancher, A McDonnell and HG Sevenster (eds), *Views of European Law from the Mountain* (Alphen aan den Rijn, Kluwer Law International, 2009) 291–300

——'International Responsibility for EU Mixed Agreements' in C Hillion and P Koutrakos (eds), *Mixed Agreements Revisited: The EU and the Member States in the World* (Oxford, Hart Publishing, 2010) 208–27

Landolt, P, *Modernised EC Competition Law in International Arbitration* (The Hague, Kluwer Law International, 2006)

——'Limits on Court Review of International Arbitration Awards Assessed in the Light of States' Interests and in Particular in Light of EU Law Requirements' (2007) 1 *Arbitration International* 63

Lavranos, N, 'The Mox Plant and IJzeren Rijn Disputes: Which Court is the Supreme Arbiter?' (2006) 1 *Leiden Journal of International Law* 223

——'Protecting European Law from International Law' (2010) 2 *European Foreign Affairs Review* 265

——*Is an International Investor-to-State Arbitration System under the Auspices of the ECJ Possible?* (2011), available at http://papers.ssrn.com/sol3/papers.cfm?abstract_id=1973491

Leal-Arcas, R, 'The European Union's Trade and Investment Policy after the Treaty of Lisbon' (2010) 4 *Journal of World Investment and Trade* 463

Leben, C, 'Introduction' in C Kessedjian and C Leben (eds), *Le droit européen et l'investissement* (Paris, Éditions Panthéon-Assas, 2009)

Lévesque, C, 'The Challenges of "Marrying" Investment Liberalisation and Protection in the Canada-EU CETA' in M Bungenberg, A Reinisch and C Tietje (eds), *EU and Investment Agreements: Open Questions and Remaining Challenges* (Baden-Baden, Nomos, 2013) 121–44

Loussouarn, Y, 'Le droit d'établissement des sociétés' (1990) 2 *Revue trimestrielle de droit européen* 229

Lycourgos, C, *L'association avec union douanière: un mode de relations entre la CEE et des Etats tiers* (Paris, Presses universitaires de France, 1994)

Marboe, I, 'Compensation and Damages in International Law, the Limits of "Fair Market Value"' (2006) 5 *Journal of World Investment and Trade* 723

Maresceau, M, *The European Community's Commercial Policy after 1992: The Legal Dimension* (Dordrecht, Martinus Nijhoff, 1993)

——*Bilateral Agreements Concluded by the European Community* (Collected Courses of the Hague Academy of International Law, 2004) 125–451

Maydell, N, 'The European Community's Minimum Platform on Investment or the Trojan Horse of Investment Competence' in A Reinisch and C Knahr (eds), *International Investment Law in Context* (Utrecht, Eleven International Publishing, 2008) 73–92

Mayes, D and Kilponen, J, 'Factor Mobility' in AM El-Agraa, *The European Union: Economics and Policies*, 8th edn (Cambridge, Cambridge University Press, 2007) 144–64

McLachlan, C, 'The Principle of Systemic Integration and Article 31(3)(c) of the Vienna Convention' (2005) 2 *ICLQ* 279

Meester, B de, 'Europees- en internationaalrechtelijke aspecten van Sovereign Wealth Funds' (2008) 6 *Sociaal-Economische Wetgeving* 214

Molle, W, *The Economics of European Integration: Theory, Practice, Policy*, 5th edn (Aldershot, Ashgate, 2006)

Monar, J, 'Die Gemeinsame Handelspolitik der Europäischen Union im EU-Verfassungs-vertrag: Fortschritte mit einigen neuen Fragezeichen' (2005) 1 *Aussenwirtschaft* 99

Mortelmans, K, 'The Common Market, the Internal Market and the Single Market: What's in a Market?' (1998) 1 *CML Rev* 101

Müller-Ibold, T, 'Foreign Investment in Germany: Restrictions Based on Public Security Concerns and Their Compatibility with EU Law' in C Herrmann and JP Terhechte (eds), *European Yearbook of International Economic Law* (Heidelberg, Springer, 2010) 103–22

Neframi, E, 'La politique commerciale commune selon le Traité établissant une Constitution pour l'Europe' (2005) 2 *Revue trimestrielle de droit européen* 473

—— 'The Duty of Loyalty: Rethinking its Scope Through its Application in the Field of EU External Relations' (2010) 2 *CML Rev* 323

Newcombe, A, and Paradell, L, *Law and Practice of Investment Treaties* (Alphen aan den Rijn, Kluwer Law International, 2009)

Noirfalisse, C, 'The Community System of Fisheries Management and the *Factortame* Case' (1992) *Yearbook on European Law* 324

Nunnenkamp, P, 'European FDI Strategies in Mercosur Countries' (2001) 3 *JWI* 457

O'Brien, M, 'C-326/07 *Commission v Italy*' (2010) 1 *CML Rev* 245 (note)

Oliver, P, 'Non-Community Nationals and the Treaty of Rome' (1985) *Yearbook on European Law* 57

Ortino, F and Eeckhout, P, 'Towards an EU Policy on Foreign Direct Investment' in A Biondi, P Eeckhout and S Ripley, *EU Law After Lisbon* (Oxford, Oxford University Press, 2012) 312–27

O'Shea, T, 'Limitation on Benefits (LoB) Clauses and the EU: Part II' (2008) 11 *International Tax Report* 1

Ostry, S, *A New Regime for Foreign Direct Investment*, Occasional Paper 53 (Washington (DC), Group of Thirty, 1997)

Paasivirta, E, 'The European Union and the Energy Sector: The Case of the Energy Charter Treaty' in M Koskenniemi (ed), *International Law Aspects of the European Union* (The Hague, Kluwer Law International, 1998) 197–214

Panayi, CHJI, 'Corporate Mobility in Private International Law and European Community Law: Debunking Some Myths' (2009) *Yearbook on European Law* 123

Panhuys, HF van, 'Conflicts between the Law of the European Communities and Other Rules of International Law' (1966) *CML Rev* 420

Paradell, L, 'The BIT Experience of the Fair and Equitable Treatment Standard' in F Ortino (ed), *Nationality and Investment Treaty Claims: Fair and Equitable Treatment in Investment Treaty Law, Current Issues II* (London, British Institute of International and Comparative Law, 2007) 117–39

Paulsson, J, 'Arbitration Without Privity' (1995) 10 *ICSID Review* 232

Peers, S, 'EC Frameworks of International Relations: Co-operation, Partnership and Association' in AA Dashwood and C Hillion (eds), *EC External Relations Law* (London, Sweet & Maxwell, 2000) 160–76

Pistone, P, 'Test Claimants in Class IV of the ACT Group Litigation: Limitation-of-Benefits Clauses are Clearly Different from Most-Favoured-Nation Clauses' (2007) 4 *BTR* 363

Pollan, T, *Legal Framework for the Admission of FDI* (Utrecht, Eleven International Publishing, 2006)

Potestà, M, 'Legitimate Expectations in Investment Treaty Law: Understanding the Roots and Limits of a Controversial Concept' (2013) 1 *ICSID Review* 88

Poulain, B, 'Quelques interrogations sur le status des traités bilatéraux de promotion et de protection des investissements au sein de l'Union européenne' (2007) 4 *Revue Générale de Droit International Public* 803

Radu, A, 'Foreign Investors in the EU: Which "Best Treatment"? Interactions between Bilateral Investment Treaties and EU Law' (2008) 2 *European Law Journal* 237

Reinisch, A, 'The Future Shape of EU Investment Agreements' (2013) 1 *ICSID Review* 179

Sacerdoti, G, 'Investment Arbitration under ICSID and UNCITRAL Rules: Prerequisites, Applicable Law, Review of Awards' (2005) 1 *ICSID Review* 1

Sauvé, P, 'A First Look at Investment in the Final Act of the Uruguay Round' (1994) 5 *Journal of World Trade* 5

Schill, SW, 'Luxembourg Limits: Conditions for Investor-State Dispute Settlement under Future EU Investment Agreements' in M Bungenberg, A Reinisch and C Tietje (eds), *EU and Investment Agreements: Open Questions and Remaining Challenges* (Baden-Baden, Nomos, 2013) 37–54

Scholten, Y, 'Company Law in Europe' (1966–1967) *CML Rev* 377

Schreuer, C, *The ICSID Convention: A Commentary* (Cambridge, Cambridge University Press, 2001)

—— 'Fair and Equitable Treatment in Arbitral Practice' (2005) 3 *Journal of World Investment and Trade* 357

Schreuer, C and Kriebaum, U, 'From Individual to Community Interest in International Investment Law' in U Fastenrath and B Simma (eds), *From Bilateralism to Community Interest: Essays in Honour of Judge Bruno Simma* (Oxford, Oxford University Press, 2011) 1079–96

Schrijver, N, 'A Multilateral Investment Agreement from a North-South Perspective' in E Nieuwenhuys and MMTA Brus (eds), *Multilateral Regulation of Investment* (The Hague, Kluwer Law International, 2001) 17–33

Schroth, HJ, 'The Energy Charter Treaty (ECT) in the Context of the Treaties of the European Union' in T Wälde (ed), *The Energy Charter: An East-West Gateway for Investment & Trade* (London, Kluwer Law International, 1996) 240–48

Schutte, CB, *The European Fundamental Right to Property: Article 1 of Protocol No 1 of the European Convention on Human Rights: Its Origins, Working and Its Impact on National Legal Orders* (Deventer, Kluwer, 2004)

Schütze, R, 'Organised Change Towards an "Ever Closer Union": Article 308 EC and the Limits to the Community's Legislative Competence' (2003) *Yearbook on European Law* 79

—— 'EC Law and International Agreements of the Member States: An Ambivalent Relationship?' (2006–2007) *Cambridge Yearbook of European Legal Studies* 387

—— *From Dual to Cooperative Federalism: The Changing Structure of European Law* (Oxford, Oxford University Press, 2009)

Shan, W, 'Towards a Common European Community Policy on Investment Issues' (2001) 3 *Journal of World Investment and Trade* 604

—— *The Legal Framework of EU-China Investment Relations: A Critical Appraisal* (Oxford, Hart Publishing, 2005)

Shan, W and Zhang, S, 'The Potential EU-China BIT: Issues and Implications' in M Bungenberg, A Reinisch and C Tietje (eds), *EU and Investment Agreements: Open Questions and Remaining Challenges* (Baden-Baden, Nomos, 2013) 87–119

Sharpston, E, 'Legitimate Expectations and Economic Reality' (1990) *EL Rev* 103

Sinclair, AC, 'The Substance of Nationality Requirements in Investment Treaty Arbitration' (2005) 2 *ICSID Review* 357

Smit, DS, 'Capital Movements and Third Countries: The Significance of the Standstill-Clause ex-Article 57(1) of the EC Treaty in the Field of Direct Taxation' (2006) 4 *EC Tax Review* 203

Snell, J, 'Free Movement of Capital: Evolution as a Non-Linear Process' in P Craig and G de Búrca (eds), *The Evolution of EU Law*, 2nd edn (Oxford, Oxford University Press, 2010) 547

Söderlund, C, 'Intra-EU Investment Protection and the EC Treaty' (2007) 5 *Journal of International Arbitration* 455

Sørensen, KE, 'The Most-Favoured-Nation Principle in the EU' (2007) 4 *Legal Issues of European Integration* 315

Sornarajah, M, *The International Law on Foreign Investment*, 3rd edn (Cambridge, Cambridge University Press, 2010)

Spaventa, E, 'From Gebhard to Carpenter: Towards a (Non-)Economic European Constitution' (2004) 3 *CML Rev* 743

Ståhl, K, 'Free Movement of Capital between Member States and Third Countries' (2004) 2 *EC Tax Review* 47

Strik, PFJS, 'Transferclausules in bilaterale investeringsovereenkomsten in strijd met het EG-Verdrag' (2009) 6 *Nederlands Tijdschrift voor Europees Recht* 193

—— 'From Washington with Love: Investor-State Arbitration and the Jurisdictional Monopoly of the Court of Justice of the European Union' (2009–2010) *Cambridge Yearbook of European Legal Studies* 425

Swann, D, *The Economics of Europe: From Common Market to European Union*, 9th edn (London, Penguin, 2000)

Teitelbaum, R, 'Who's Afraid of *Maffezini*? Recent Developments in the Interpretation of Most Favored Nation Clauses' (2005) 3 *Journal of International Arbitration* 225

Tietje, C, 'Die Meistbegünstigungsverpflichtung im Gemeinschaftsrecht' (1995) 4 *Europarecht* 398

—— *Beschränkungen ausländischer Unternemensbeteiligungen zum Schutz vor 'Staatsfonds' – Rechtliche Grenzen eines neuen Investitionsprotektionismus*, Policy Papers on Transnational Economic Law (Transnational Economic Law Research Center, 2007)

—— 'The Applicability of the Energy Charter Treaty in ICSID Arbitration of EU Nationals vs. EU Member States' (Beiträge zum Transationalen Wirtschaftrecht, Heft 78, 2008)

Timmermans, CWA, 'Common Commercial Policy (Article 113 EEC) and International Trade in Services' in F Capotorti, CD Ehlermann et al (eds), *Du droit international au droit d'intégration: Liber Amicorum Pierre Pescatore* (Baden-Baden, Nomos, 1987) 675

Torrent, R, *Derecho y Práctica de las Relaciones Exteriores en la Unión Europea* (Barcelona, Cedecs, 1998)

—— 'Derecho comunitario e inversiones extranjeras directas: Libre circulación de los capitales vs. regulación no discriminatoria del establecimiento. De la *golden share* a los nuevos *open skies*' (2007) *Revista Española de Derecho Europeo* 283

—— 'The Contradictory Overlapping of National, EU, Bilateral, and the Multilateral Rules on Foreign Direct Investment: Who is Guilty of Such a Mess?' (2011) 5 *Fordham International Law Journal* 1377

Tridimas, T, *The General Principles of EC Law* (Oxford, Oxford University Press, 2006)

Tridimas, T and Eeckhout, P, 'The External Competence of the Community and the Case-Law of the Court of Justice: Principle versus Pragmatism' (1994) *Yearbook on European Law* 143

Tudor, I, *The Fair and Equitable Treatment Standard in the International Law of Foreign Investment* (Oxford, Oxford University Press, 2008)

Usher, JA, 'The Evolution of the Free Movement of Capital' (2007–2008) 5 *Fordham International Law Journal* 1533

Vandevelde, KJ, 'The Political Economy of a Bilateral Investment Treaty' (1998) 4 *AJIL* 621

——— *US International Investment Agreements* (Oxford, Oxford University Press, 2009)

Verwey, WD and Schrijver, NJ, 'The Taking of Foreign Property under International Law: A New Legal Perspective?' (1984) *Netherlands Yearbook of International Law* 3

Vidal Puig, R, 'The Scope of the New Exclusive Competence of the European Union with regard to Foreign Direct Investment' (2013) 2 *Legal Issues of European Integration* 133

Völker, ELM (ed), *Protectionism and the European Community* (Deventer, Kluwer Law and Taxation, 1983)

Volterra, R, 'Le point de vue des états tiers' in C Kessedjian and C Leben (eds), *Le droit européen et l'investissement* (Paris, Éditions Panthéon-Assas, 2009) 41–49

Voss, J, 'The Protection and Promotion of European Private Investment in Development Countries: An Approach Towards a Concept for a European Policy on Foreign Investment – A German Contribution' (1981) 3 *CML Rev* 363

——— 'The Protection and Promotion of Foreign Direct Investment in Developing Countries: Interests, Interdependencies, Intricacies' (1982) 4 *ICLQ* 686

Waibel, M (ed), *The Backlash Against Investment: Perceptions and Reality* (Alphen aan den Rijn, Kluwer Law International, 2010)

Wagau, K von and Rapp-Jung, B, 'The Case for a European System Monitoring Foreign Investment in Defence and Security' (2008) 1 *CML Rev* 47

Wälde, T, 'Arbitration in the Oil, Gas and Energy Field: Emerging Energy Charter Treaty Practice' in (2004) 2 *Transnational Dispute Management* 1

Wälde, TW and Sabahi, B, 'Compensation, Damages, and Valuation' in P Muchlinski, F Ortino and C Schreuer (eds), *The Oxford Handbook of International Investment Law* (Oxford, Oxford University Press, 2008) 1048

Wehland, H, 'Intra-EU Investment Agreements and Arbitration: Is European Community Law an Obstacle?' (2009) 2 *ICLQ* 297

Wisner, R and Gallus, R, 'Nationality Requirements in Investor-State Arbitration' (2004) 6 *Journal of World Investment and Trade* 927

Witte, B de, 'Old-fashioned Flexibility: International Agreements between the Member States of the European Union' in G de Búrca and J Scott (eds), *Constitutional Change in the EU: From Uniformity to Flexibility* (Oxford, Hart Publishing, 2000) 31–58

——— 'Internationale verdragen tussen lidstaten van de Europese Unie' in RA Wessel and B de Witte, *De plaats van de Europese Unie in het veranderende bestel van de volkenrechtelijke organisatie, Mededelingen van de Nederlandse Vereniging voor Internationaal Recht* (The Hague, TMC Asser Press, 2001) 79–131

——— 'Chameleonic Member States: Differentiation by Means of Partial and Parallel International Agreements' in B de Witte, D Hanf and E Vos (eds), *The Many Faces of Differentiation in EU Law* (Antwerp, Intersentia, 2001) 231–67

Wyatt, DA, 'Community Competence to Regulate the Internal Market' in M Dougan and S Curie (eds), *50 Years of the European Treaties: Looking Back and Thinking Forward* (Oxford, Hart Publishing, 2009) 93–136

——— 'Constitutional Significance of the Tobacco Advertising Judgment of the European Court of Justice' in University of Cambridge Centre for European Legal Studies, *The ECJ's Tobacco Advertising Judgment*, Occasional Paper No 5 (July 2001), 19–31

Young, S and Hood, N, 'Inward Investment Policy in the European Community in the 1990s' (1993) 2 *Transnational Corporations* 35

NEWSPAPER ARTICLES, ONLINE SOURCES ETC

Balthasar, S, Kluwer Arbitration Blog, 28 August 2012, available at http://kluwerarbitrationblog.com/blog/2012/08/28/investment-arbitration-under-intra-eu-bits-recent-developments-in-eureko-v-slovakia/
Peterson, L, Kluwer Arbitration Blog, 6 March 2009, available at http://kluwerarbitrationblog.com/blog/2009/03/06/will-ecj-look-at-intra-eu-bilateral-investment-treaties-next/
'Analysis: rising foreign investment fuels EU vetting debate', Reuters, 8 March 2011, available at http://uk.reuters.com/article/2011/03/08/uk-eu-industry-investment-idUK-TRE7272C720110308
'Do not panic over foreign wealth', *Financial Times*, 29 April 2008
'EADS bid to restrict foreign ownership', *Financial Times*, 7 March 2008
'EU reaches deal on foreign energy investors', *Financial Times*, 10 October 2008
'Germany opposes tighter investment rules', *Financial Times*, 6 October 2008
'Left in the cold: foreign bidders find themselves out of favour', *Financial Times*, 25 April 2008
'Small island for sale', *Economist*, 27 March 2010

EU AND OTHER DOCUMENTS

Communication from the Commission to the Council, 'Need for Community action to encourage European investment in developing countries and guidelines for such action', COM(78)23 final, 30 January 1978, Brussels
Communication from the Commission to the Council, the European Parliament, the Economic and Social Committee and the Committee of the Regions, 'The global challenge of international trade: a market access strategy for the European Union', COM(96)53 final, 14 February 1996, Brussels
Communication from the Commission, 'Certain legal aspects concerning intra-EU investment' [1997] OJ C220/15
Communication from the Commission and its Member States to the WTO Working Group on the Relationship between Trade and Investment, WT/WGTI/W/81, 20 September 1999
Communication from the European Community and its Member States to the WTO Working Group on the Relationship between Trade and Investment, WT/WGTI/W/115, 16 April 2002
Communication from the Commission to the Council, the European Parliament, the European Economic and Social Committee and the Committee of the Regions, 'European defence: industrial and market issues', COM(2003)113, 11 March 2003, Brussels
Communication from the Commission to the European Council, 'A citizen's agenda: delivering results for Europe', COM(2006)211 final, 10 May 2006, Brussels
Communication from the Commission, 'Monitoring report on the state of preparedness for EU membership of Bulgaria and Romania', COM(2006)549 final, 26 September 2006, Brussels

Communication from the Commission to the Council, the European Parliament, the European Economic and Social Committee and the Committee of the Regions, 'Global Europe: competing in the world: a contribution to the EU's growth and jobs strategy', COM(2006)567 final, 4 October 2006, Brussels

Communication from the Commission to the European Parliament, the Council, the European Economic and Social Committee and the Committee of the Regions, 'The European interest: succeeding in the age of globalisation', COM(2007)581 final, 3 October 2007, Brussels

Communication from the Commission to the European Parliament, the Council, the European Economic and Social Committee and the Committee of the Regions, 'A common European approach to Sovereign Wealth Funds', COM(2008)115 final, 26 February 2008, Brussels

Communication from the Commission to the European Parliament, the Council, the European Economic and Social Committee and the Committee of the Regions, 'On the external dimension of the Lisbon Strategy for Growth and Jobs: reporting on market access and setting the framework for more effective international regulatory cooperation', COM(2008)874 final, 16 December 2008, Brussels

Communication from the Commission, 'Europe 2020: a strategy for smart, sustainable and inclusive growth', COM(2010)2020, 3 March 2010, Brussels

Communication from the Commission to the Council, the European Parliament, the European Economic and Social Committee and the Committee of the Regions, 'Towards a comprehensive European international investment policy', COM(2010)343 final, 7 July 2010, Brussels

Communication from President Barroso in agreement with Vice-President Verheugen to the Spring European Council, 'Working together for growth and jobs: a new start for the Lisbon Strategy', COM(2005)24 final, 2 February 2005, Brussels

Conference of the Representatives of the Governments of the Member States, 'The European Union Today and Tomorrow. Adapting the European Union for the Benefit of its Peoples and Preparing it for the Future, Conference of the Representatives of the Governments of the Member States, Dublin II', CONF 2500/96, 5 December 1996

Council of the European Union, *Conclusions on a Comprehensive European International Investment Policy*, 25 October 2010, Luxembourg

Directorate General for Economic and Financial Affairs, Note of the Economic and Financial Committee, Bilateral Investment Treaties, Further Background Requested by Alternates, ECFIN/574/02- EN Rev 2, Brussels

Directorate-General for External Policies of the European Parliament, *Responsibility in Investor-State Arbitration in the EU: Managing Financial Responsibility Linked to Investor-State Dispute Settlement Tribunals Established by EU's International Investment Agreements* (2012), available at www.europarl.europa.eu/committees/en/inta/studiesdownload.html?languageDocument=EN&file=79450

EC Council, *Position communautaire sur les principes de protection des investissements dans les états acp*, ACP-EEC 2172/92, 3 November 1992, Brussels

Economic and Financial Committee, *Annual EFC Report to the Commission and the Council on the Movement of Capital and Freedom of Payments*, no 17363/08, 17 December 2008, Brussels

European Commission, *The Development of a European Capital Market, Report of a Group of Experts Appointed by the EEC Commission* (1966)

European Commission, *Report from the Commission to the Council, Investment Protection and Promotion Clauses in Agreements between the Community and Various Categories of Developing Countries: Achievements to Date and Guidelines for Future Action*, COM(80)204 final, 8 May 1980, Brussels

European Commission, *White Paper from the Commission to the European Council on 'Completing the Internal Market'*, COM(85)310 final, 14 June 1985, Brussels

European Commission, Opinion, 'Reinforcing Political Union and Preparing for Enlargement', COM(96)90 final, 28 February 1996

European Commission, Opinion in accordance with Article 48 of the Treaty on European Union on the Calling of a Conference of Representatives of the Governments of the Member States to Amend the Treaties, 'Adapting the Institutions to Make a Success of Enlargement', COM(2000)34, 26 January 2000, Brussels

European Commission, *Strategy Paper and Report of the European Commission on the Progress towards Accession by Each of the Candidate Countries, 'Towards the Enlarged Union'*, COM(2002)700 final, 9 October 2002, Brussels

Eurostat, *European Union Foreign Direct Investment Yearbook 2008*

Eurostat, *Eurostat Yearbook 2012: Europe in Figures*, available at http://epp.eurostat.ec.europa.eu/cache/ITY_OFFPUB/KS-CD-12-001/EN/KS-CD-12-001-EN.PDF

IMF, *Balance of Payment Manual* (1993), available at www.imf.org/external/pubs/ft/bopman/bopman.pdf

OECD, *Codes of Liberalisation of Capital Movements and Current Invisible Operations: 2003 Edition* (Paris, OECD Publications, 2003)

OECD, WTO and UNCTAD, *Report on G20 Trade and Investment Measures, September 2009 to February 2010*, 8-3-2010, available at www.oecd.org/dataoecd/22/16/44739159.pdf

Press release for the 3109th meeting of the General Affairs Council, doc no 13587/11, 12 September 2011

Press release for the 3136th meeting of the Foreign Affairs Council, doc no 18685/11, 14 December 2011

Press release for the 3203rd meeting of the Foreign Affairs Council, doc no 16943/12, 29 November 2012

Press release for the 3245th meeting of the Foreign Affairs Council, doc no 10862/13, 14 June 2013

Screening Report for Croatia, Chapter 4 – Free Movement of Capital, 4 July 2006, available at http://ec.europa.eu/enlargement/pdf/croatia/screening_reports/screening_report_04_hr_internet_en.pdf

Spaak Report, *Rapport des Chefs de Délégations aux Ministres des Affaires Etrangères, Secretariat of the International Conference* (Brussels, 21 April 1956)

Study Group of the International Law Commission, *Fragmentation of International Law: Difficulties Arising from the Diversification and Expansion of International Law*, finalised by M Koskenniemi, UN doc A/CN.4/L.682, 13 April 2006

UNCTAD, *Scope and Definition*, UNCTAD/ITE/IIT/11 (New York, United Nations Publication, 1999), vol II, available at http://unctad.org/en/docs/psiteiitd11v2.en.pdf

UNCTAD, *Bilateral Investment Treaties, 1959–1999*, UNCTAD/ITE/IIA/2 (New York, United Nations Publication, 2000), available at www.unctad.org/en/docs/poiteiiad2.en.pdf

UNCTAD, *International Investment Instruments: A Compendium* (New York, United Nations Publication, 2000) vol V, available at http://unctad.org/en/Docs/dite2vol5_en.pdf

UNCTAD, *World Investment Report 2009* (New York, United Nations Publication, 2009), available at http://unctad.org/en/docs/wir2009_en.pdf

Werner Report, *Report to the Council and the Commission on the Realization by Stages of Economic and Monetary Union in the Community*, Supplement to Bulletin II – 1970

WTO, Working Party of the Trade Committee, *The Investment Architecture of the WTO*, TD/TC/WP(2002)41/FINAL, 14 April 2003

Index

Lightning Source UK Ltd.
Milton Keynes UK
UKOW06f0809030916

282104UK00002B/93/P